*The Design, Development,
and Evaluation of
Instructional Software*

The Design, Development, and Evaluation of *Instructional Software*

MICHAEL J. HANNAFIN

THE PENNSYLVANIA STATE UNIVERSITY
UNIVERSITY PARK, PENNSYLVANIA

KYLE L. PECK

THE PENNSYLVANIA STATE UNIVERSITY
UNIVERSITY PARK, PENNSYLVANIA

MACMILLAN PUBLISHING COMPANY
NEW YORK
COLLIER MACMILLAN PUBLISHERS
LONDON

Copyright © 1988, Macmillan Publishing Company, a division of Macmillan, Inc.

PRINTED IN THE UNITED STATES OF AMERICA

Macmillan Publishing Company
866 Third Avenue, New York, New York 10022

Collier Macmillan Canada, Inc.

LIBRARY OF CONGRESS CATALOGING IN PUBLICATION DATA

Hannafin, Michael J.
    The design, development, and evaluation of instructional software.

    Bibliography: p.
    Includes indexes.
    1. Computer-assisted instruction—United States.
2. Education—United States—Curricula—Computer
programs—Authorship.   3. Instructional systems—United
States—Design.   I. Peck, Kyle L.   II. Title.
    LB1028.5.H317   1988   371.3'9445   86-32691
    ISBN 0-02-349990-7

Printing: 4 5 6 7 8   Year: 3 4 5 6 7

ISBN 0-02-349990-7

Preface

In the 1983–84 school year, two thirds of the schools in the United States used microcomputers (Ingersol and Smith, 1984). By 1986, there were more than a million microcomputers in elementary and secondary schools in the United States alone, and in the near future, it is estimated that the number will grow to approximately 2.8 million (National Task Force on Educational Technology, 1986). Computers in educational settings are diagnosing student needs, delivering instruction appropriate for each student, monitoring and reporting on student performance, evaluating the effectiveness of instructional units across many students, serving as tools with which students can analyze data and write reports, and more.

Although that sounds like a large number of computers and an impressive list of accomplishments, we have yet to see the profound effect that computers will have on education. More and more people are looking toward computer technology to play a key role in the transformation of the existing educational system, a role the technology is certainly capable of filling (Hannafin, Dalton, and Hooper, 1987).

The National Task Force on Educational Technology, established in late 1984 to investigate the potential large-scale contributions of technology applied to education, felt strongly that computerized teaching will play a critical role in the transformation of the existing educational system. The Task Force's report, issued in mid-1985, displayed its members' belief in the power and potential contribution of computers in education with statements like the following:

> To transform education, we must create a system in which an individual learning plan permits each learner to proceed at a rate and pace that is challenging but achievable, makes no unjust comparisons with the progress of others, prevents students from becoming passive, and assures positive reinforcement and steady progress. Such a plan will allow the most able to move to new realms without restriction and the least able to find their own unique achievement levels. [p. 23]
>
> The computer is a device uniquely suited for education. With related technology, it enables people to deal with vast amounts of information. It can be programmed to adapt learning to the needs of each student, providing corrective advice and allowing the student to proceed as rapidly or as slowly as he or she is able. [p. 15]

Although computers are capable of contributing to the educational process in many ways, the computer, *by itself*, is of little value. It is merely a tool. And, like other tools, the computer's contribution is directly related to its user's skill, knowledge, and commitment to quality. Many of the early computerized training products were ineffective, resembling training produced on other media. Such products were justifiably accused of being little more than "electronic page turners," and the cost-effectiveness of computerized training was questioned. We should have expected and avoided that. According to Foshay (1986), "the first plastics were made to resemble tortoise shell and amber. The first automobiles resembled horse-drawn carriages. The first instructional TV was merely a telecast lecture. And perhaps someday we will muse that the first CBI (computer-based instruction) resembled printed programmed instruction" (p. 29).

The quantity *and quality* of educational software must improve if computers are to have a meaningful, positive impact on education. The good news is that progress *is* being made. A meta-analysis combining the results of 42 controlled research studies in junior and senior high schools showed that computerized training lessons produced recently were more effective than their predecessors (Bangert-Drowns, Kulik, and Kulik, 1985). The authors of the study attribute the increased effectiveness to improvements in instructional technology, improvements in hardware and software, and teachers who are discovering more appropriate ways to use technology in teaching. Increasing numbers of educators are learning to employ principles of instructional design to develop creative, effective, involving, interactive educational experiences.

This book, and the exercises it contains, will prepare you to produce effective computer-assisted instruction (CAI). It has been designed for teachers and trainers seeking to add this powerful medium to the list of educational options available to them. The process of developing CAI is, for the most part, machine independent. Whether you will be producing programs to run on Apple, IBM, Commodore, Radio Shack, Zenith, other microcomputers, or minicomputer or mainframe systems, this book will enable you to produce effective instruction. When you have finished this book, you will be able to design CAI. Whether you intend to do the programming yourself or turn the lesson over to a programmer, the practices documented in this book will allow you to be confident that the results of your effects will be *effective* computer-based instruction. And you will find that you are able to transfer the skills and knowledge you gain to the production of instruction in other media as well.

The practices in this book are based on learning theory, research in educational psychology and CAI, the authors' experiences, and an analysis and synthesis of current publications on this topic. Some chapters provide you with important insights and orient you to larger fields of study; others develop demonstrable skills. Checklists and other tools are provided to help streamline the process of producing effective CAI.

CONTENT

The first section contains a brief overview of CAI and the instructional applications of microcomputers. Section II introduces relevant concepts from educational psychology and learning theory, as well as a "generic" instructional design model used throughout the text.

Section III provides methods for analyzing instructional tasks, determining whether CAI is appropriate for given instructional tasks, and writing behavioral objectives to assure that desired results are achieved. Section IV presents the options available to the designer of CAI, many of which are not available in more traditional forms of instruction.

Section V focuses on the differences between writing text to appear on paper and writing text for use in CAI. Computer-*managed* instruction (CMI), an option that evaluates and tracks student performance, is also explained in Section V. Section VI deals with the process of evaluating CAI and emphasizes the evaluation of CAI programs developed by others as well as products you develop. The final section discusses many of the emerging trends in the fields.

The indexes, glossary of computer and CAI terms, and comprehensive bibliography will help you to extend your studies in this field.

ORGANIZATION

Each of the text's seven sections and twenty-two chapters begins by prescribing important information and concepts to follow. Objectives are listed for each chapter and are divided into two categories: those dealing with *comprehension* of the information presented and those devoted to the *application* of what has been learned. Exercises *directly* related to these objectives follow each chapter. Two types of references are provided at the end of each chapter: a list of citations from the chapter and a list of recommended readings to supplement the material presented.

REFERENCES

BANGERT-DROWNS, R. L., J. A. KULIK, and C-L. KULIK (1985). Effectiveness of computer-based education in secondary schools. *Journal of Computer-Based Instruction, 12*(3), 59–68.

FOSHAY, R. (1986). CBI: The more things change. . . . *Performance & Instruction Journal, 25*(5), 29–30.

HANNAFIN, M., D. DALTON, and S. HOOPER (1987). Computers in education: Barriers and solutions. In E. MILLER and M. L. MOSLEY (Eds.), *Educational Media and Technology Year book*. Littleton, Co. Libraries Unlimited.

INGERSOLL, G. M., and C. B. SMITH (1984). Availability and growth of microcomputers in American schools. *Technological Horizons in Education, 12*(1), 84–87.

NATIONAL TASK FORCE ON EDUCATIONAL TECHNOLOGY (1986). Transforming American education: Reducing the risk to the nation. *Tech Trends, 31*(4), 12–24, 35.

ACKNOWLEDGMENTS

The authors wish to acknowledge the following for contributing to the many illustrations contained in this text: Brett Bixler for the frames related to reading music, Curtis Hughes for the model rocket lesson illustrated in various portions of the text; and Fred Grisham for the illustrations related to a lesson on Australia. The authors also gratefully acknowledge the assistance and support of NBI, Inc., in the preparation of many of the computer-generated illustrations contained in this text.

M. J. H.
K. L. P.

Contents

SECTION VI

SECTION VII

Overview of Computer-Assisted Instruction

This section presents background information, terminology, and perspectives essential to the development and production of effective CAI. In this section, you will learn what CAI is, how and why it is used in classrooms and training centers, the characteristics of effective CAI programs, and factors separating effective CAI programs from ineffective ones.

SECTION GOALS

After completing this section, you will

1. Understand how CAI is used today.
2. Begin to understand the potential of CAI.
3. Understand CAI's strengths and limitations.
4. Identify effective CAI lessons.

Introduction to CAI

The number of computers used in educational and industrial training environments is increasing consistently. What external factors and internal characteristics have contributed to this growth? Can the growth be expected to continue?

There are many strong advocates of computerized training, but few, if any, would say that computers are well suited to every instructional task. What types of instructional tasks generally lend themselves to a successful computerized solution? When should computerized solutions be avoided?

This chapter introduces and examines the instructional use of computers and the associated advantages and disadvantages. After you read this chapter, it is strongly recommended that you gain significant amounts of hands-on experience with both good and bad computerized instruction. The information you gain on techniques that you like and dislike from the student's perspective will be valuable to you as a designer of successful computerized training experiences.

OBJECTIVES

Comprehension

After completing this chapter, you will be able to

1. Define CAI.
2. Name at least three other acronyms used in reference to CAI.
3. List at least six significant advantages of CAI.
4. List at least six significant disadvantages of CAI.

Defining CAI

CAI is an acronym for "*Computer-Assisted Instruction.*" The computer assists by delivering an instructional program. Whether the instruction is delivered by a microcomputer costing hundreds of dollars or a mainframe system costing hundreds of thousands, if a computer delivers instruction, the process could be considered CAI.

There have been a number of other acronyms used to represent the use of computers to achieve educational or training objectives. Some additional acronyms and the titles they represent follow:

CAL = Computer-Assisted Learning
CaI = Computer-aided Instruction
CaL = Computer-aided Learning

Understanding CAI

Like teaching, CAI involves different types of activities, falling into four primary categories: (1) drill and practice sessions; (2) tutorial, or instructional, sessions; (3) games; and (4) simulation or modeling.

During *drill and practice* the computer provides practice and feedback on a *topic taught in another session, perhaps even by another medium.* For example, after a student has learned to multiply two-digit numbers, a CAI drill and practice program might present 50 problems using random two-digit numbers. The student's answers would be evaluated and remediation might occur, but the initial teaching of the concept is provided prior to the session. Practice is essential to learning many skills, but its importance is often overlooked. The computer's ability to manipulate numbers rapidly, to adapt to the needs of each individual student, to provide immediate feedback, and to continue to provide instruction when students find learning difficult (without experiencing the frustration human teachers often feel) makes it an excellent medium for drill and practice.

During CAI *tutorials* the computer actually teaches new information. The process resembles the interaction between the student and a tutor engaged in a one-to-one session. Concepts are presented, the student's understanding of each concept is checked, and subsequent instruction is provided based on the student's responses. For example, a tutorial CAI lesson might teach a student to separate words into syllables, to add decimals, or to read music.

Learning games have been used by educators for centuries. The computer's ability to manipulate numbers, to present attractive images on the screen and move them rapidly, and to captivate students makes it an ideal medium for many educational games. Although games may be used to teach new information or concepts, most educational games are used to reinforce concepts taught elsewhere. In addition to computerized versions of traditional learning games like "Hangman," CAI games have been developed to reinforce or teach such skills as coordinate geometry, using the game premise of searching for submarines. In addition, problem solving has been taught by asking students to assemble mechanical components to form machines capable of building particular products. The format and premise of instructional games are affected principally by the absence or presence of creativity of the game's designer.

Computers can also *simulate*, or *model*, complex concepts or events. The computer accepts inputs and then responds as if it were the system being simulated, allowing students to experience the results of good and bad decisions without risky or expensive consequences. For example, CAI simulations have modeled the effects of varying combinations of substances in chemistry classes as well as such topics as flight training for pilots. A popular example of computerized simulation used in elementary schools simulates the effects of business decisions such as advertising, quantity purchased, and changes in the recipe, as a hypothetical lemonade stand competes for local business.

A common misconception among CAI developers seems to be that simulation is the highest form of CAI and that other types of CAI are to be scoffed at. Little is to be gained by thinking of the modes of CAI as hierarchical. Each mode has been used successfully to meet educational objectives. Wise educators select the appropriate CAI mode based on the learning task, the learner profile, external constraints, and the specific objectives they are attempting to achieve.

What Is CAI?

As defined earlier, CAI is any instance in which instructional content or activities are delivered via computer. As such, *CAI is an educational medium with its own unique set of strengths and limitations*. CAI can be effective or ineffective, interesting or boring, good or bad. Consider the following scenarios.

A TYPICAL CAI SESSION

A student sits before a computer. The computer includes a keyboard, through which the student sends information to the computer, and a video monitor, through which the computer communicates with the student. Information is presented to the student in the form of text and graphics displayed attractively on the screen.

The pace of the presentation is generally controlled by the student. When he or she has finished reading the text and pictures on the computer's screen, the student indicates readiness to progress by pressing a key on the keyboard. At other times, the computer controls the time available to read the information by pausing an appropriate amount of time before automatically moving on.

After the information has been presented, a multiple-choice question appears on the screen, along with response options. The student selects an answer by pressing a key on the keyboard. The student's answer is correct, so the response is reinforced, and another question appears. The student responds again, but this time the answer is incorrect. Remedial instruction explains specifically why the answer was wrong. The concept is then retaught. After this remedial instruction, the question reappears, and the student tries again, answering correctly this time. The student is congratulated and the lesson advances.

AN UNUSUALLY ELABORATE CAI SESSION

A student sits before a computer. The computer system allows the student to send information to the computer several different ways: A keyboard may be used to send detailed typed responses, a touch-sensitive screen allows the student to communicate by simply touching areas on the screen, and a joystick similar to those used in video games allows the student to control the motion of objects on the screen. Information is presented to the student in several ways. A video monitor displays output either from the computer or a videodisc player controlled by the computer, or from both simultaneously. The student receives audio input through headphones carrying computer-generated sounds as well as words and music contained on the videodisc.

After a brief series of instructions on the use of the lesson, video-based instruction is presented. After a few moments, the student presses a key, and the video segment is replaced by a computerized *help message*, explaining the content of the video segment in more detail. At the bottom of the screen, prompts indicate that the student may repeat the video segment, may resume the video segment, may read a summary of the information contained in the video segment, may jump to the post-test for the lesson, or may leave the lesson. The student reads the screen, then presses a key and the video segment resumes, beginning with the first word of the sentence during which the student interrupted the lesson.

When the segment ends, the student touches a labeled location on the screen, and the entire video segment is repeated. After the segment has been repeated, the student touches a different location on the screen, and a multiple-choice question appears. By touching the correct answer, the student moves on to a second question. This time the student responds by using the keyboard to type an entire paragraph.

The computer evaluates the answer, finding four of the five major points. The moderator's voice informs the student of this as the four correct points are displayed. A subset of the videodisc segment containing the missing fifth point is replayed, after which the original question reappears. The student answers again, including all five of the critical items.

The student is then informed of the rules of a game that reinforces the learning that has just taken place. The student uses the joystick to control a computer-generated image superimposed over video images from the videodisc.

The game ends, and the next instructional unit begins.

AN UNUSUALLY BAD CAI SESSION

A student sits before a computer. The computer includes a keyboard, through which the student sends information to the computer, and a video monitor, through which the computer communicates with the student. Information is presented to the student in the form of page after page of text crammed on the screen.

The pace of the presentation is controlled either by the computer, in which case it is not unusual for information to be removed from the screen before the student has finished reading it, or by the student responding to a seemingly endless barrage of "PRESS RETURN TO CONTINUE" prompts.

After numerous pages of text have been presented, a fill-in-the-blank question appears on the screen. The student types in an answer. A cryptic response, indicating that the answer is incorrect, is displayed and the question is repeated. The student types another answer. The identical negative response is provided. The student tries repeatedly to answer the question without success. Because the student can neither progress nor indicate the need for assistance, the student becomes frustrated, then angry. The student reaches for the power switch, and the lesson ends.

The computer systems in the first and last scenarios were identical, but the quality of the sessions was vastly different. Ineffective CAI has been developed for the most expensive systems available, and superb instruction has been developed on a shoestring. Fiscal considerations are not nearly as important as the knowledge, skill, and dedication of the lesson's developers. The preceding scenarios also illustrate that CAI has weaknesses as well as strengths and that CAI will only be effective when it is designed to take advantage of strengths and minimize weaknesses.

RESEARCH ON THE EFFECTIVENESS OF CAI

Although some educators believe the computer has its own intrinsic characteristics that make it a superior medium for the delivery of instruction, little research exists to support such claims. When CAI is compared to traditional forms of instruction, the most common result is that there is no significant difference (Clark, 1984a; Dence, 1980; Leiblum, 1982). However, a meta-analysis, a statistical process that combines the results of similar studies, applied to 42 controlled research studies in junior and senior high schools showed that the CAI lessons were more effective than conventional training on the same topics and that recently developed CAI lessons were more effective than earlier lessons (Bangert-Drowns, Kulik, and Kulik, 1985). Other recent analyses support claims of CAI effectiveness (Atkinson, 1984).

Before we become eager to conclude that CAI is, in fact, a superior instructional medium, we would be wise to remember that in such comparison studies, the CAI lessons have often been prepared by skilled instructional designers and are compared to existing forms of instruction that did not benefit from the same careful development as their CAI counterparts (Bright, 1983; Clark, 1984a). When the CAI and traditional lessons are created by the same developer, the differences between computerized and traditional forms of instruction are considerably less apparent (Kulik, Kulik, and Cohen, 1980).

Although CAI has not proven to be an intrinsically superior educational medium, the following generalizations appear to be substantiated:

1. CAI may be an effective means of achieving educational objectives, both as the principal means of instruction and a supplement to other forms of instruction (Gleason, 1981; Splittgerber, 1979).
2. When CAI is compared to media that do not account for individual differences, it is likely that CAI (1) will produce more learning in a given amount of time, or (2) will produce a given amount of learning in a shorter period of time (Bright, 1983; Gleason, 1981; Splittgerber, 1979).
3. Retention following CAI lessons is at least as good as retention following more traditional methods of instruction (Dence, 1980).
4. Students favor well-designed CAI programs but reject poor programs (Gleason, 1981).

It is very tempting to view a new educational medium as a panacea for all problems. A case in point is instructional video. Some proponents felt that instructional use of videotape would eliminate the need for teachers and would significantly alter the course of education. Video is now acknowledged as *one* educational option, a tool appropriate for some tasks but not for others. Although many were excited by educational video in its early stages, the novelty has waned. Many students now struggle to remain attentive during programs that yesterday's audiences would have found spellbinding.

CAI is the carrier of instructional messages, much like a truck or railroad car carries commodities. Just as the type of cargo, the destination, and the required arrival time determine the most appropriate carrier for goods, the instructional message, the student population, and environmental constraints combine to influence the appropriateness of CAI as a medium for educational messages.

CAI CAN BE GOOD OR BAD

Although the potential of CAI as an educational medium has been established and many effective educational courseware programs have been developed, much of the courseware currently available is deplorable. General descriptions of the state of educational courseware include: "This form of instruction serves to re-create the very worst of what presently occurs in a traditional classroom ..." (Caldwell, 1980, p. 7) and "most are virtually devoid of any instructional value and in many cases are acting as deterrents to widespread acceptance ..." (Gleason, 1981, p. 12).

As with text, videotape, lecture, and other educational media, the medium is neither good nor bad. A given computerized lesson may succeed or fail, depending on the expertise of the developer and the care with which it is developed.

CAI's Strengths and Weaknesses

The successful designer of instruction capitalizes on the strengths of the selected medium and minimizes the impact of the medium's weaknesses. In the pages that follow, we will examine the advantages and disadvantages of CAI so that you will be able to do just that. As you read, remember that characteristics of the learning task, the learners, and the environments in which the instruction is to be delivered will influence the relative importance of each item.

ADVANTAGES OF CAI

CAI has significant advantages when compared to conventional educational media. Several of these are discussed here.

Increased Interaction   The attribute most often credited as contributing to the effectiveness of CAI sessions is interaction. Interaction refers to the active exchange of information between the computer and the student. The computer presents, and the student must respond. The computer then determines its course of action based on the student's response, and the process is repeated. In traditional forms of instruction, a student may daydream or consciously tune out as presented information misses its target. In CAI, progress through the lesson is usually tied directly to student responses. If the student's mind wanders, the computer waits patiently. If the student has not learned, additional instruction is provided. Effective CAI lessons encourage appropriate interaction in order to solicit and maintain student involvement (Bright, 1983; Caldwell, 1980).

Individualization   Interaction may be the primary contributor to the *effectiveness* of CAI, but individualization is largely responsible for its *efficiency*. This relationship is illustrated in Table 1.1. The one-to-one nature of CAI makes it

Table 1.1
The Role of Interaction and
Individualization in CAI

Interaction $\longrightarrow$ Effectiveness
Individualization $\longrightarrow$ Efficiency

possible to monitor student understanding constantly and to respond based on the needs of each individual student (Dence, 1980; Ross, 1984). In more extensive CAI lessons, it is theoretically possible that no two students will pass through exactly the same information in the same sequence.

Individualization may begin with a pretest. The pretest may be used to ascertain that the student has the prerequisite skills necessary to be successful in the session and to reduce the instruction to specific modules for which a need was demonstrated. Once the instruction on required topics has begun, student responses are used to indicate when mastery has occurred so that the lesson may proceed to the next topic. Remediation is provided when necessary.

Individualization may be used to make lessons more interesting, more relevant, and more efficient. For example, CAI programs designed to teach young students to read occasionally incorporate student-specific information into the story to be read. These inserts include information such as the student's name, the names of friends, favorite hobbies and foods, and other information obtained at the beginning of the session. CAI programs designed to train professionals often incorporate specific, job-related information in examples relevant to individual students.

Administrative Strengths and Cost Effectiveness   In many environments, the strongest reasons for using CAI are administrative (Clark, 1984a). Because CAI lessons may be used without the participation of a teacher, they can be employed during evenings and weekends in locations where teachers are normally unavailable. By not requiring a teacher, CAI makes it possible to have many students studying different topics simultaneously with little or no supervision. Where cost considerations make it impossible to justify the presence of a teacher for a small number of students, CAI may be considered a viable alternative.

CAI lessons are also inexpensive to reproduce and distribute. The process may be as simple as copying a program to a diskette, providing protective packaging, and sending the diskette through the mail. The total cost may be as little as three dollars.

Motivation   Many students find CAI appealing, although their reasons for liking CAI vary (Clement, 1981). Some students cite the low threat posed by learning from a machine as contrasted with a more critical human instructor (cf Brophy, 1981). Others like CAI due to an interest in computers and computer applications. Still others note the efficiency associated with computerized instruction (Bright, 1983) or the degree of student control of the instructional process (Hannafin, 1984). The novelty of CAI may also cause students to give it high marks (Bright, 1983; Clark, 1984b).

Immediate Feedback   The immediacy of the feedback provided by CAI is difficult if not impossible to replicate in other media. Most answers can be evaluated instantaneously. Other answers may take a few moments to analyze. In any case, the computer's ability to evaluate and respond surpasses by far the human instructor's ability to do so. This capability is a key factor in CAI's efficiency and effectiveness (Caldwell, 1980).

Ease of Record Keeping   A CAI lesson may be programmed to automate any or all aspects of record keeping (Splittgerber, 1979). A sequence of keystrokes known only to the teacher may be used to print a summary of the performance of individual students or groups. This information may be used to assign grades to students and to evaluate the quality of the lesson as well.

Lesson Integrity   With CAI, the designer may be confident that topics to be covered *are* covered and that irrelevant information does not undermine the lesson. When a teacher or professor delivers a lecture, it is never really the same twice. The computer, on the other hand, faithfully executes the prescribed sequence, never digressing to unrelated tangents.

   CAI may also be used to verify that instruction and/or learning actually took place. When a student is assigned to read a chapter or to view a videotape, the instructor never really knows whether the activity took place. It is also unclear whether or not learning has occurred. The quality of an instructional segment is of little consequence if the student never completes the lesson.

Learner Control   An alternative that is attractive to both students and CAI designers grants the student authority to make significant decisions during the instructional process to produce a more customized, personal lesson (Caldwell, 1980; Reigeluth, 1979). As examples of learner control, students may be allowed to determine the order in which units are administered, when to proceed to a post-test, how many practice exercises are required, when to review lesson segments, whether or not to seek additional instruction, whether or not hints are to be provided when responding to questions, whether or not computer-generated sounds are to be presented during the lesson, and the rate at which the computer displays information on the screen. In some cases, students may be best qualified to make instructional decisions; in others, however, they might make ineffective choices (Garhart and Hannafin, 1986). As might be predicted, the student is not always basing decisions on a genuine belief that educational objectives have been met. When in doubt as to whether to grant the student control of the course of a lesson, let the objectives of the lesson be the determining factor.

DISADVANTAGES OF CAI

Like any instructional delivery system, CAI has disadvantages. However, astute designers understand these limitations and routinely minimize their impact. Some potential limitations and suggested ways to compensate for them are discussed here.

Need for Specific, Expensive Hardware   Perhaps the major disadvantage of CAI is the requirement for specialized equipment. This equipment, known as *hardware*, may be expensive and not generally available. While a textbook may be used virtually any time or place, unless adequate access to equipment is provided, CAI may only be available in specific locations or during scheduled hours. Another equipment-related limitation is the lack of transportability from one computer system to another. CAI *software*, the computer programs that contain the commands and information the computer will execute and present to form the lesson, is written for a specific hardware environment (for example, an IBM PC with a certain amount of memory and two diskette drives). Software written to run on an IBM PC may require significant modifications before it will run on an Apple II and vice versa. Although there has been recent progress in this area, transportability from system to system remains a problem.

Difficulty in Reviewing Topics   Unlike text-based lessons, CAI lessons are often not easily accessed for subsequent study. For example, because hardware is not available, it may be impossible to review CAI lessons prior to a test or to use them as a reference tool while applying learned skills. Even if hardware and software are available, unless the CAI lesson is exceptionally well designed, it can be difficult to access specific topics for review.

There are, of course, many ways to avoid these potential problems. For example, by designing the lesson in modules and providing several levels of menus, it becomes possible for students to review topics within the CAI lesson easily. It may also be wise to print a set of notes for subsequent study or to provide each student with a written summary prior to the lesson as an orienting strategy.

Heavy Reliance on Reading and Visual Skills   Because the standard output device for CAI systems is the CRT (cathode ray tube), also known as the *video display* or *monitor*, a heavy demand is placed on the student's visual skills. Since the majority of the content is generally transmitted by text on the screen, the student's ability to read can be a major factor influencing the effectiveness of CAI lessons.

Peripheral devices such as videodisc and audiodisc players (discussed in Chapter 21) and the extensive use of graphics to convey information may be employed to minimize the demands on reading and visual skills.

Unrealistic Graphics   In many cases, computer-generated graphics bear little resemblance to the real-world objects they represent. Poor screen resolution, limitations in the colors and contrasts with which to work, and the time required to produce high-quality images are often deterrents to using graphics in CAI.

Some (usually more expensive) computer systems have extremely high-resolution screens capable of displaying many colors and textures. On such machines, graphic shapes and characters are easily produced and may be stored for use in other illustrations. However, increases in resolution tend to require greater computer memory and storage capacity. And, no matter how fine the resolution, there will always be applications for which these images cannot compete with those produced in other media. Imagine, for example, attempting to use computer graphics to develop an understanding of the diversity of lifestyles in foreign countries or the destruction caused by earthquakes, volcanoes, and tidal waves. destruction caused by earthquakes, volcanoes, and tidal waves.

There are good ways to include realistic images in CAI. Chapter 21, "Interactive Computer-Based Technologies," describes the combination of computers and devices such as videodisc players, audiodisc players, and slide projectors and the benefits associated with such combinations. By employing these technologies, it is possible to combine the realistic images provided by other media with the benefits provided by CAI.

Need for Additional Development Skills   The CAI designer must possess skills and knowledge beyond those required to produce instructional materials in most other media. The designer must understand the strengths and weaknesses of CAI and must know how to involve the learner in the instructional process: The CAI designer must learn to "think interactively" (Shaw, 1985). The designer must be able to selectively incorporate text in the presentation; must understand computer hardware in general; must have a working knowledge of the strengths and limitations of the computer system; and should have mastered at least one programming language, authoring system, or authoring language. Additionally, the CAI designer must understand how to thoroughly test CAI programs, how to manage and evaluate learner responses, and how to evaluate the success of the lesson itself.

Longer Development Time   Although the use of authoring systems or languages may reduce the programming time required during CAI development, the number of alternate paths through CAI lessons magnifies the programming and testing efforts. It is relatively easy to script and test a linear lesson such as one produced on videotape. By playing the tape from start to finish, it is possible to determine that all of the elements are present and working. The multitude of possible paths through a CAI lesson multiplies the programming effort required and complicates the testing process. In addition to evaluating CAI to determine the extent to which objectives have been met, a CAI lesson must also be tested extensively to ascertain that it executes all options as intended.

Every possible path a student may take must be investigated to verify that the program provides the appropriate response to anticipated and unanticipated student input. In fact, *every possible combination and sequence of paths must be tested* to ensure that the student will not end up in an endless loop from which there is no escape and that there are no unresolved branches leading the student to a program segment that does not exist.

Possibility of Limiting Incidental Learning   Well-designed instruction devoted to achieving specific objectives will usually produce the intended effect. However, although students receiving objective-based instruction may learn specified information, they may not learn other important information not specified in the objectives.

During live teaching an instructor may stray from the objectives of a session, presenting material not directly related to accomplishing the objectives. Although this type of information may detract from the efficiency of the lesson (when efficiency is defined as the rate at which objectives are achieved), the additional information may contribute to the overall education of the student.

Students learn more than content-related information from live instructors. They learn about relating to people, presenting topics to groups, and much more. This type of learning is not transmitted by CAI without conscious effort on the part of the designer.

Perception Only of Programmed Input   CAI only responds to the specific inputs defined by the program. A good teacher, on the other hand, adapts instruction based on additional cues. For example, a teacher may perceive when the student has had insufficient sleep, is emotionally distraught, or is preoccupied by

Table 1.2
The Advantages and Disadvantages of CAI

Advantages of CAI	Disadvantages of CAI
Increased interaction	Need for specific, expensive hardware
Individualization	Difficulty in reviewing topics
Administrative strengths and cost effectiveness	Heavy reliance on reading and visual skills
	Unrealistic graphics
Motivation	Need for additional development skills
Immediate feedback	Longer development time
Ease of record keeping	
Lesson integrity	Possibility of limiting incidental learning
Learner control	Perception only of programmed input

other matters. Unless otherwise designed, CAI only perceives whether the correct key or series of keys was pressed; it is blind to a great deal of information available to the human teacher.

Chapter Summary

CAI is a powerful tool for the professional educator. Like other tools, it is appropriate for some tasks but not for others. Although the advantages are significant, the disadvantages of CAI must also be considered. These advantages and disadvantages are summarized in Table 1.2.

The fact that eight advantages and eight disadvantages have been identified should not be misinterpreted as representative of a balance between CAI's advantages and disadvantages. An examination of the characteristics of the training task may identify a single advantage as sufficiently powerful to warrant the use of CAI or a single disadvantage as sufficiently detrimental to preclude its use.

In this chapter we have defined CAI and discussed how it is used. Information presented in this chapter will be combined with additional information and techniques presented in the remaining chapters. Careful consideration of the information and techniques presented will enable you to make wise decisions concerning the use of CAI.

References

ATKINSON, M. L. (1984). Computer-assisted instruction: Current state of the art. *Computers in the Schools*, **1**(1), 91–99.

BANGERT-DROWNS, R. L., J. A. KULIK, and C. C. KULIK (1985). Effectiveness of computer-based education in secondary schools. *Journal of Computer-Based Instruction*, **12**(3), 59–68.

BRIGHT, G. W. (1983). Explaining the efficiency of computer-assisted instruction. *AEDS Journal*, **16**(3), 144–153.

BROPHY, J. (1981). Teacher praise: Functional analysis. *Review of Educational Research*, **51**, 5–32.

CALDWELL, R. M. (1980). Guidelines for developing basic skills instructional materials for use with microcomputer technology. *Educational Technology*, **20**(11), 7–12.

CLARK, R. E. (April 1984a). Learning from computers: Theoretical problems. Paper presented at the annual meeting of the American Educational Research Association, New Orleans.

———. (1984b). Research on student thought processes during computer-based instruction. *Journal of Instructional Development*, **7**(3), 2–5.

CLEMENT, F. J. (1981). Affective considerations in computer-based education. *Educational Technology*, **21**(10), 28–32.

DENCE, M. (1980). Toward defining the role of CAI: A review. *Educational Technology*, **20**(11), 50–54.

GARHART, C. and M. J. HANNAFIN (1986). The accuracy of cognitive monitoring during computer-based instruction. *Journal of Computer-Based Instruction*, **13**(3), 88–93.

GLEASON, G. T. (1981). Microcomputers in education: The state of the art. *Educational Technology*, **21**(3), 7–18.

HANNAFIN, M. J. (1984). Guidelines for using locus of instructional control in the design of computer-assisted instruction. *Journal of Instructional Development*, **7**(3), 6–10.

KULIK, J. A., C. C. KULIK, and P. A. COHEN (1980). Effectiveness of computer-based college teaching: A meta-analysis of findings. *Review of Educational Research*, **50**(4), 525–544.

LEIBLUM, M. D. (1982). Factors sometimes overlooked and underestimated in the selection and success of CAL as an instructional medium. *AEDS Journal*, **15**(2), 67–79.

REIGELUTH, C. M. (1979). TICCIT to the future: Advances in instructional theory for CAI. *Journal of Computer-Based Instruction*, **6**(2), 40–46.

ROSS, S. M. (April 1984). Matching the lesson to the student: Alternative adaptive designs for individualized learning systems. *Journal of Computer-Based Instruction*, **11**, 42–48.

SHAW, M. (1985). Dancing with the disc: The latest step in training technology. *Data Training*, **4**(2), 26–27.

SPLITTGERBER, F. L. (1979). Computer-based instruction: A revolution in the making? *Educational Technology*, **19**(1), 20–26.

Related Reading

FUTRELL, M., and P. GEISERT (1984). *The Well-Trained Computer: Designing Systematic Instructional Materials for the Classroom Microcomputer*. Englewood Cliffs, NJ: Educational Technology Publications.

GRAYSON, L. P. (1984). An overview of computers in U.S. education. *Technological Horizons in Education*, **12**(1), 78–83.

Chapter Review Exercises

COMPREHENSION

1. Define CAI. (See pages 3–4.)
2. Name at least three other acronyms used in reference to CAI and the titles they represent. (See page 4.)
3. List at least six significant advantages of CAI. (See pages 8–10.)
4. List at least six significant disadvantages of CAI. (See pages 10–13.)

CHAPTER 2

Characteristics of Effective CAI

Before you can successfully build something, you must know what you are about to build. The goal of this book is to teach the building of effective computer-based instruction. Time spent understanding the characteristics of well-designed CAI is time well spent. Hours spent studying this chapter and evaluating CAI programs produced by others can save days, weeks, even months of revision. Adequate preparation can make the difference between instruction that works and instruction that does not.

OBJECTIVES

Comprehension

After completing this chapter you will be able to

1. Define *effective CAI*.
2. Name and discuss the twelve identified characteristics of well-designed CAI.
3. List the four pitfalls commonly associated with evaluating student performance.

Application

After completing this chapter you will be able to

Write a review of a given CAI program, mentioning the characteristics of good CAI present in the program as well as flaws in the program's design. Suggest three ways to make the program stronger.

What Is Effective CAI?

Arriving at a consensus on the best book ever written is next to impossible and is of little value. On the other hand, agreeing on a list of attributes that combine to make a good book, although difficult, is a simpler and more meaningful task. Aspects such as plot, character development, suspense, and romance are likely to be listed. Once the attributes have been identified, aspiring authors can use these attributes as guidelines.

The same could be said for CAI. Although it may not be possible to identify the "best" CAI ever produced, it is possible to identify the characteristics of successful CAI. Authors can improve the probability of producing successful CAI by ensuring that their lessons possess these characteristics. In this section, we will define *effective CAI* and then identify and describe characteristics that combine to produce it.

Effective CAI does what it was designed to do. That sounds much simpler than reality because CAI lessons are designed to do many things. For example, CAI lessons are designed to meet instructional objectives, to adapt to the needs of individual learners, to be easily implemented in a specified educational environment, to please learners and teachers, and to run flawlessly.

In an effort to define effective CAI, first consider the characteristics that describe *poor* CAI. Bork (1984) listed factors he believes have been associated with poor educational software. These factors included

> failure to use adequately the interactive capabilities of the computer, failure to use the individualizing capabilities of the computer, use of extremely weak forms of interaction such as multiple choice, heavily text-dependent presentations, heavily picture-dependent presentations where the pictures play no important role in the learning process, screens treated like the pages of a book, material that is entertaining or attractive, but with no, or vague, discernible educational objective, games which are nothing but games, long sets of "instructions" at the beginnings of programs, difficult to follow even by the teachers, and even more difficult to recall, dependence on auxiliary print material, small pieces of material lacking in context, and material which does not hold the student's attention. [p. 94]

By avoiding these pitfalls, an author can improve the quality of CAI substantially. However, there is a difference between eliminating weaknesses and creating strengths. In the remainder of this chapter, we will turn our attention to the characteristics associated with quality, many of which are the converses of shortcomings described by Bork.

Roblyer (1981) classified characteristics of effective CAI into three categories: essential characteristics, aesthetic characteristics, and differential characteristics. Roblyer's essential characteristics were viewed as critical and contained criteria appropriate for designing effective instruction in any educationl medium. These characteristics included statement of objectives, statement of entry skills (prerequisites), design of learning activities, design of tests, content integrity, and design of presentation.

Aesthetic characteristics, according to Roblyer, included spacing, format, and the use of color—in other words, how the lesson appeared on the computer screen. Apart from sporadic studies (e.g., Grabinger, 1984) there is very little research data on the importance of these factors, so they are often viewed as secondary.

Roblyer's differential characteristics are important but are not equally important across all types of, and applications for, courseware design. In the design or evaluation of a course for a specific purpose, these factors may be either very important or unimportant. Characteristics assigned to this category included the amount of learner control, the type and extent of feedback, the response formats, the amount of text on the screen, the use of peripherals, the use of graphics and animation, and the learning events to be included on-line.

Characteristics of Effective CAI

As the discussion of specific characteristics of effective CAI progresses, bear in mind that these characteristics vary in importance, depending on the circumstances for which the lesson is being evaluated.

1. *Effective CAI is based on instructional objectives.* There is consensus among instructional design professionals that the presence of appropriate, measurable objectives improves the probability of a lesson's success. Much has been written about instructional objectives during the last 25 years (for example, the comprehensive review by Hamilton in 1985). Although authors disagree on the components necessary, there is consensus that the utilization of objectives is important.

Objectives contribute to learning in several ways. Objectives help developers prescribe appropriate activities, focusing more on required topics than on tangential issues. Objectives help the learner by pointing out important topics. When the student knows what is important, attention may be focused more intensively on attainment of the specified behaviors. Objectives are also helpful in allowing teachers to determine whether or not a given lesson or course is appropriate for classroom use or for use with individual students. Finally, objectives provide the basis for evaluation of both the student and the lesson itself.

In order for objectives to improve the CAI lesson design process, they must be stated clearly so that designers, students, and teachers can read and understand them. Since objectives guide evaluation, they must also be measurable. It must be clear whether the student has, in fact, mastered the intended objectives.

Techniques for writing objectives for CAI and for modifying these objectives for student use are covered in detail in Chapter 8. Figure 2.1 illustrates a sample display informing the student of a lesson's objectives.

2. *Effective CAI matches learner characteristics.* CAI lessons are designed for specific subpopulations. For example, a CAI lesson may be designed for third-grade students, for students in Chemistry 101, or for graduate students preparing to become teachers. The instruction must be appropriate, given the characteristics of the learner for which it was developed.

The first step is to estimate the knowledge and skill levels of the target student population accurately. If students do not have required skills or knowledge or do not understand the terminology used in the lesson, the lesson is likely to fail. The reading level must also be appropriate for the target audience. If vocabulary or sentence structure is too difficult, learning may not take place. If, on the other hand, vocabulary and sentence structure are too simplistic for students, the lesson may be viewed as condescending.

The choice of input devices (keyboard, touch screen, mouse, and so on) should also reflect the skills present in the target population. For example, CAI designed for younger students should make use of touch screens, thereby minimizing the need to type extensive responses.

3. *Effective CAI maximizes interaction.* Perhaps the greatest advantage of computerized instruction over text-based instruction and other linear media is the potential for interaction during a lesson. Yet many designers make only minimal use of this potential. A common criticism of CAI programs is that the computer is used as an electronic page-turner, that the computer is merely an expensive way of

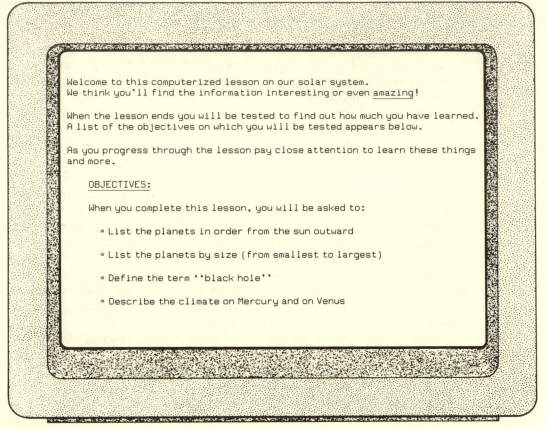

Welcome to this computerized lesson on our solar system.
We think you'll find the information interesting or even <u>amazing</u>!

When the lesson ends you will be tested to find out how much you have learned.
A list of the objectives on which you will be tested appears below.

As you progress through the lesson pay close attention to learn these things
and more.

   <u>OBJECTIVES:</u>

   When you complete this lesson, you will be asked to:

      ° List the planets in order from the sun outward

      ° List the planets by size (from smallest to largest)

      ° Define the term ''black hole''

      ° Describe the climate on Mercury and on Venus

Figure 2.1
Sample lesson objectives.

presenting information that could have been presented more economically on paper. In many instances, the criticism is valid.

At the other extreme, some CAI lessons require responses continuously. The result is that the questions appear contrived, rather than directly related to the accomplishment of lesson objectives. Or, in some cases, the questions are give-aways, which require more time to complete than is justified by their effectiveness. An example of a contrived response used simply to keep the student active is given in Figure 2.2.

To find the middle ground between these two extremes, the computer's potential to evaluate *meaningful* student responses should be used primarily for information related to the specific objectives of the lesson. Figure 2.3 illustrates meaningful interaction. Place a few consecutive text frames together if it is necessary or desirable in order to achieve lesson objectives. When it is sensible to involve the student, based on learning objectives, the lesson should require responses; when it is not sensible, the lesson should avoid unnecessary activities.

4. *Effective CAI is individualized.* The computer provides the potential to adapt an instructional sequence to individual learners. This potential can be used to teach

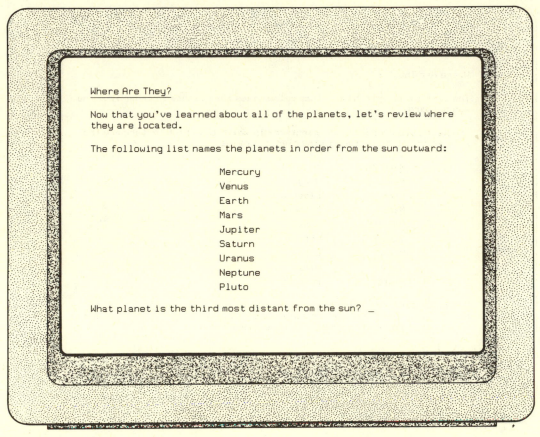

Figure 2.2
Example of contrived interaction.

only those topics the student requires and to provide remedial instruction as indicated.

It may also be useful to provide additional individualization. For example, some lessons gather the student's name, hobbies, names of friends, favorite foods, and other personal information for use during the lesson, perhaps by merging the information into a lesson reinforcing reading skills. For adults, the CAI lesson may determine an individual's occupation and provide job-related examples.

Some programs allow students to control lesson features such as the difficulty level, when to proceed to another topic, or when help is provided. Certain programs even allow the student to record comments that are subsequently reviewed by the lesson designer.

The issue of learner control is still a topic of much debate. Studies have shown that students do not always make the best decisions from a pedagogical point of view (Garhart and Hannafin, 1986; Hannafin, 1984; Tennyson, 1984). The objectives are the critical factor. In general, maximize interaction and student control, but not to the point that you jeopardize the achievement of objectives.

5. *Effective CAI maintains learner interest.* Do not assume that, simply because

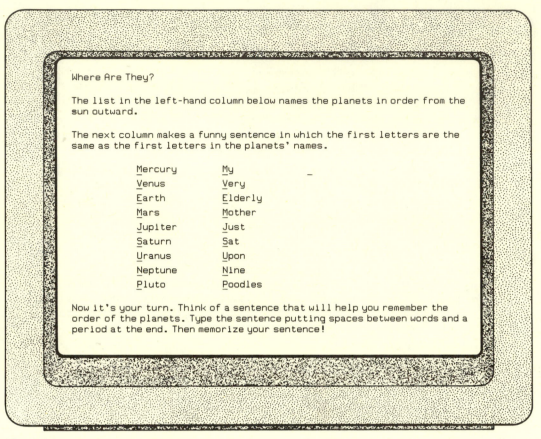

Figure 2.3
Example of meaningful interaction.

the computer is the vehicle for instruction, the lesson will be intrinsically motivating. Although some students might prefer computerized forms of instruction, this is likely to be a short-lived allegiance. When the novelty of the computer subsides, CAI lessons must survive on merit (cf. Clark, 1984). A lesson that does not *create and maintain* interest may not only fail instructionally, but also lessen student enthusiasm for subsequent lessons.

6. *Effective CAI approaches the learner positively.* The tone of an effective CAI lesson should approximate a conversation between a tutor and a student in a one-to-one session. Avoid punishing the student and using sarcasm with young students. One reason many students enjoy CAI is that they perceive it as a comfortable, nonthreatening medium. In contrast to live instructors, who are often perceived as threatening or critical, a competent designer makes the computer patient and forgiving without penalizing the student for errors. Mastery-based lessons, where the emphasis is on reaching specified performance levels without penalty for time taken, can do much to sustain the nonthreatening nature of CAI. In many cases, it is actually unnecessary to inform the student of the number of questions answered incorrectly.

7. *Effective CAI provides a variety of feedback.* Younger learners like, and

perhaps even need, positive feedback to indicate when they are doing well. Adult learners, on the contrary, often prefer to virtually eliminate positive feedback in favor of making the lesson more efficient. In either case, the designer should vary the form that positive feedback takes. While younger learners tolerate and even enjoy seeing the same animated graphic appear on the screen each time a correct answer is provided, adult learners soon tire of repetitious feedback.

Research indicates that error-free learning may be superior to learning riddled with errors (Terrace, 1963; Kay, 1955; Hilgard and Bower, 1966; Holding, 1970). Yet some CAI programs actually encourage learners to make incorrect responses. These programs may provide animated graphic displays, such as skiers crashing or boats sinking, in response to incorrect answers. In such cases, students may provide incorrect answers so that they may observe the consequences. Since the student knows that the responses are incorrect, it could be argued that little harm has been done (Kulhavy, Yekovich, and Dyer, 1976). It is difficult to deny, however, that lesson objectives would be achieved more efficiently if incorrect responses were not encouraged.

8. *Effective CAI fits the instructional environment.* Many of the CAI lessons developed for schools will be used by individual students in standard classroom environments while the teacher and other students are engaged in different activities. Therefore, the lesson must require minimal involvement on the part of the teacher. The student should be able to start the lesson and complete it without assistance. Data on student performance should be recorded by the CAI program so that the teacher may evaluate it when time to do so becomes available.

As the age of the student increases, so do the number and importance of other events scheduled during the day. CAI lessons must adapt easily to crowded and variable schedules. Lessons should be modular and should allow the student to resume the lesson with minimal redundancy following interruptions.

Although many schools place computers in labs where distractions are more tolerable than they might be in a typical classroom, CAI lessons should generally avoid extensive use of audible tones and music that will be distracting to the other students and teachers.

9. *Effective CAI evaluates performance appropriately.* The ability to adapt instruction to student needs is a major factor contributing to CAI's ability to teach. However, unless the right questions are asked, unless the student interprets questions correctly, and unless answers are evaluated appropriately, the ability to adapt based on need is lost. This is compounded by the fact that learning can be difficult to measure. Unless care is taken to write meaningful, measurable objectives, and unless the accomplishment of the objectives is accurately assessed, the validity of conclusions concerning the amount a student has learned and the quality of the lesson must be considered suspect. The following discussion highlights pitfalls to be avoided and techniques to apply in evaluating CAI.

a. *Ask the right questions.* The lesson's objectives delineate the learning to take place during the lesson. Questions should be directly related to the objectives and should measure the student's ability to respond in the specified manner. For example, if the objective is "The student will be able to name the planets in our solar system," a multiple-choice or true/false question would be inappropriate because the names of the planets are provided by the computer, not recalled by the student. Because multiple-choice and true/false questions are easily evaluated, they tend to be used inappropriately in CAI (as they are in other media). Objectives often call for test items requiring the student to provide more complex answers.

b.) *Avoid ambiguous or poorly worded questions.* Writing a test item that will be interpreted correctly by a variety of students is difficult. The test items should contain the same vocabulary as the presentation of the lesson, they should clearly specify the action the student is to take, and they should already have been proven valid by an examination of the responses provided by many previous students. By monitoring student performance, the designer may identify lesson problems, whether they are caused by faulty instruction or by a poorly worded question. Since it is often easier to change the question than to modify the instruction, and since the question is often the cause of inaccurate responses, it may be wise to evaluate and modify the question before assuming that the instruction is at fault.

c.) *Judge answers thoroughly.* Computers respond only as instructed. A teacher, on the other hand, even though he or she is expecting a particular answer, may also agree to accept a different, unanticipated but correct response. Computerized instruction, in order to minimize the impact of this problem, can look for three answer types: correct answers, incorrect answers, and unanticipated answers. When an unanticipated answer is received, the computer can inform the student that the answer had not been anticipated and can ask the student to revise the answer. Although this requires more work on the programmer's part and may extend the amount of time required to complete the lesson, it is certainly preferable to treating an unexpected form of the correct answer as if it were incorrect.

d. *Do not confuse inability to respond with ignorance of the correct answer.* Because CAI response generally involves the use of the computer's keyboard, it is common to confuse the student's inability to type or to spell with the inability to provide the correct answer. The problem often lies with the method of assessment. Consider the use of touch screens, light pens, and voice-recognition devices (discussed in detail in Chapter 20), or consider providing additional opportunities to respond for students who answer with near misses.

10. *Effective CAI uses the computer's resources wisely.* The computer screen can be a difficult medium for presenting text. The resolution is often poor compared to printed materials, making it more difficult to read. However, most computer systems used for CAI have other capabilities that may be employed to overcome this. Computer graphics, both static and animated, may be used to convey messages otherwise carried by text. Effective use of color, flashing, and sound as key words and phrases are presented will amplify ideas normally expanded on by additional words.

Even microcomputers are capable of incredible feats of "number crunching" and data management. Effective CAI simplifies the job of interpreting data gathered during the lesson. Use the computer's speed to calculate scores for sections as well as entire lessons and to prescribe additional instruction based on calculated results. Use the computer's ability to store and manipulate relatively large amounts of data, to simplify interpretation of student performance over time, and to compare performance among students and among groups.

The designer of effective CAI must understand the capabilities of the computer system for which the lesson is developed and must employ these capabilities to make the lesson more effective. The programmer or author must be aware of the machine's limitations in order to avoid introducing annoying or detrimental circumstances. Common examples of circumstances to be avoided include animated graphics that move too slowly, program segments too large to fit in available

Table 2.1
Characteristics of Effective CAI

Effective CAI
  Specifies instructional objectives
  Matches learner characteristics
  Maximizes interaction
  Adapts to the needs of individual students
  Maintains student interest
  Approaches the learner positively
  Provides a variety of feedback
  Fits the instructional environment
  Evaluates performance appropriately
  Uses the computer's resources wisely
  Is based on principles of instructional design
  Has been evaluated thoroughly

memory, and frustrating delays as the program repeatedly accesses the diskette or hard disk.

It is not critical that you capitalize on all of CAI's strengths. As mentioned earlier, a single characteristic may have proven powerful enough to justify the use of CAI in a given application. Periodically during development, recall the reasons CAI became the medium of choice for that particular educational message. Make a concerted effort to maximize the contribution of each characteristic that led to the selection of CAI. Recall and minimize the effects of significant disadvantages identified during the selection process.

11. *Effective CAI is based on principles of instructional design.* Like other educational media, a CAI lesson is composed of many phases, each of which may be critical. A well-designed lesson motivates the learner, informs the learner of the objectives of the lesson, reviews prerequisite skills required for the student to be successful in the lesson, presents well-organized instruction, evaluates progress frequently, provides adequate feedback, allows for adequate practice, and evaluates final performance of the student and of the lesson itself (Gagné and Briggs, 1979). Instructional design as applied to CAI is discussed in detail in Chapter 5.

12. *Effective CAI has been evaluated thoroughly.* CAI must be evaluated at several levels. Lessons must be evaluated for instructional quality, affective considerations, cosmetic appeal, and curricular relevance, as well as for the accuracy of the computer program. Instructionally sound CAI monitors both the achievement of objectives and the learners' attitudes toward the lesson. Although the identification and achievement of relevant objectives are paramount, student attitudes are especially important in cases where computerized training provides a major portion of the curriculum. If students do not like the computerized instruction they receive, they will be less likely to subsequently use and benefit from CAI lessons.

Evaluate the attractiveness of each display. Identify and eliminate such things as crowded text, offensive color combinations, and abuse of flashing or other means of highlighting information. In addition to evaluating computer program logic, the accuracy of branching destinations must be verified to determine that students receive necessary instruction and to ensure that all options are executed appropriately under specified conditions.

Chapter Summary

An effective CAI lesson enables students to attain performance objectives. This chapter focused on the characteristics of CAI lessons that consistently meet their objectives. These characteristics are summarized in Table 2.1.

References

BORK, A. (1984). Education and computers: The situation today and some possible futures. *Technological Horizons in Education*, **12**(3), 92–97.

CLARK, R. E. (1984). Research on student thought processes during computer-based instruction. *Journal of Instructional Development*, **7**(3), 2–5.

GAGNÉ, R. M., and L. J. BRIGGS (1979). *Principles of Instructional Design* (2nd ed.). New York: Holt, Rinehart and Winston.

GARHART, C., and M. J. HANNAFIN (1986). The accuracy of cognitive monitoring during computer-based instruction. *Journal of Computer-Based Instruction*, **13**(3), 88–93.

GRABINGER, R. S. (1984). CRT text design: Psychological attributes underlying the evaluation of models of CRT text displays. *Journal of Visual and Verbal Languaging*, **4**(1), 17–39.

HAMILTON, R. J. (1985). A framework for the evaluation of the effectiveness of adjunct questions and objectives. *Review of Educational Research*, **55**, 47–85.

HANNAFIN, M. J. (1984). Guidelines for determining locus of instructional control in the design of computer-assisted instruction. *Journal of Instructional Development*, **7**(3), 6–10.

HILGARD, E. R., and G. H. BOWER (1966). *Theories of Learning* (3rd ed.). New York: Meredith.

HOLDING, D. H. (1970). Repeated errors in motor learning. *Ergonomics*, **13**, 727–734.

KAY, H. (1955). Learning and retaining verbal material. *British Journal of Psychology*, **46**, 81–100.

KULHAVY, R. W., F. R. YEKOVICH, and J. W. DYER (1976). Feedback and response confidence. *Journal of Educational Psychology*, **68**, 522–528.

ROBLYER, M. D. (1981). When is it "good courseware"? Problems in developing standards for microcomputer courseware. *Educational Technology*, **21**(10), 47–54.

TENNYSON, R. (1984). Application of artificial intelligence methods to computer-based instructional design: The Minnesota Adaptive Instructional System. *Journal of Instructional Development*, **7**(3), 17–22.

TERRACE, H. S. (1963). Errorless transfer of a discrimination across two continua. *Journal of the Experimental Analysis of Behavior*, **6**, 233–232.

Related Reading

COHEN, V. B. (1983). Criteria for the evaluation of microcomputer courseware. *Educational Technology*, **23**(1), 9–14.

McPHERSON-TURNER, C. (1979). CAI readiness checklist: Formative author-evaluation of CAI lessons. *Journal of Computer-Based Instruction*, **6**(2), 47–49.

WADE, T. E., Jr. (1980). Evaluating computer instructional programs and other teaching units. *Educational Technology*, **20**(11), 32–35.

Chapter Review Exercises

COMPREHENSION

1. Define *effective CAI*. (See pages 15–16.)
2. Name and discuss the twelve identified characteristics of effective CAI. (See pages 17–23 and Table 2.1.)
3. List the four pitfalls commonly associated with evaluating student performance. (See pages 21–22.)

APPLICATION

1. Given a CAI program to evaluate, write a review of the program, mentioning the characteristics of good CAI present in the program as well as flaws in the program's design. Suggest three ways to make the program stronger.

CAI Design and Learning Theory

The goal of CAI is to facilitate learning. Although we can only speculate on how people learn, research in educational psychology has identified several ways in which we can improve the probability that learning will occur. The field of instructional design applies findings from educational psychology to produce efficient instructional systems. By identifying the most significant findings of educational psychology and by using an instructional design system, successful CAI programs can be developed.

Chapter 3 begins by presenting a discussion of the strengths of teachers and computers and describing ways of combining these strengths to produce powerful teaching systems. The extent to which computers are used in schools today and predictions for the immediate future are also discussed. Chapter 4 provides a summary of relevant findings from the field of educational psychology and the implications these findings have for the development of effective CAI.

Chapter 5 presents an instructional design model developed specifically for CAI. A comprehensive checklist is provided as a step-by-step process for designing and developing CAI lessons.

SECTION GOALS

After completing this section, you will

1. Understand the strengths and weaknesses of teachers and of computers in educational settings and how to bring teachers and computers together to form effective teaching systems.

2. Know the difference between the behavioral and cognitive learning theories and their implications for the development of CAI.
3. Understand the concept of congruence among objectives, instruction, and evaluation.
4. Understand the role of instructional design systems.
5. Understand the advantages and disadvantages of a team approach to CAI development.

CHAPTER 3

Teachers, Students, Schools, and Computers

A computer will never replace an effective teacher. On the other hand, a teacher will never replace an appropriately used computer. Each does certain things better than the other, and both can play important parts in the instructional process.

In this chapter, we will examine what teachers and computers do well and what they do poorly. Based on the strengths of each, we will describe how teachers and computers may team up to provide powerful instructional systems. Finally, we will examine the status of instructional computing and predict what can be expected in the near future.

OBJECTIVES

Comprehension

After completing this chapter you will be able to

1. Discuss the strengths and weaknesses of teachers and computers in educational settings.
2. Name and describe ways in which computers are often incorporated into educational environments.
3. Discuss the advantages and disadvantages of computer-lab approaches to placing micros in schools.
4. Discuss the advantages and disadvantages of placing microcomputers in classrooms.
5. Discuss the impact computers have had on education in the United States and why.
6. Discuss the extent to which microcomputers are currently available in high schools, junior high schools, and elementary schools in the United States.
7. Discuss trends in the availability of computers in schools and the impact these trends are likely to have on education in the United States.
8. Discuss the three critical obstacles to be removed if computers are to have a major impact on education in the United States.
9. Discuss how your state ranks on the availability of computers for instructional purposes.

The Role, Strengths, and Weaknesses of Teachers

THE TEACHER'S ROLE

In traditional classrooms, the teacher performs many functions. Teachers plan the course of study; evaluate and locate appropriate instructional materials; develop additional instructional materials as necessary; handle administrative details such as attendance and daily announcements; evaluate student progress; record indicators of student progress; inform students, parents, administrators, and other teachers of student progress; and, oh yes, teach. In addition to teaching, teachers also adapt the course of study for individual students for whom the standard course is inappropriate, evaluate the final performance of students and of the course itself, provide necessary discipline, serve as models of adult behavior and values, and provide a safe environment for students.

When a process continues with very little change for hundreds of years, the process generally has merit. Teachers have remained the primary delivery medium for instruction, not because other means were unavailable, but because teachers have strengths that make the process work. Table 3.1 and the brief discussion that follows summarize the teacher's strengths and weaknesses.

THE TEACHER'S STRENGTHS

The Ability to Plan   An effective teacher understands both students and curricular goals. Based on this understanding, the teacher plans and schedules a sequence of events to meet these goals. The plans include specific instructional events and special activities. In addition to creating the initial plan, the teacher is responsible for modifying the plan as necessary.

The Ability to Develop   Teachers have developed some outstanding instructional materials. Numerous instructional games, lessons, and simulations have

Table 3.1
Strengths and Weaknesses of Teachers

Strengths	Weaknesses
The ability to	*The inability to*
Plan courses of study	Spend adequate time with individuals
Develop instruction	Spend adequate time planning and developing
Bond with students	Grade and track student performance efficiently
Synthesize information	Evaluate student performance objectively
Respond to inquiries	
Model behaviors and values	*The ability to*
Empathize with students	
Work with large groups	Experience frustration
Motivate students to perform	Experience boredom
Adapt to changing demands	

been created by teachers, many spontaneously as the need arose in response to particular questions or difficulties. Although computers can *reproduce* instruction, they cannot presently *generate* it.

The Ability to Bond with Students   The bond between an effective teacher and a student is often significant. The student and the teacher accept each other as caring, worthwhile individuals. This relationship not only facilitates learning, but also helps students learn to relate to others.

The Ability to Synthesize   Effective teachers are able to identify and use information from several sources. For example, an effective teacher uses topics covered in social studies to initiate discussion for a creative writing project or reinforces mathematics concepts during a science lesson. The teacher's understanding of an entire curriculum makes synthesis possible. CAI programs written by different authors, on the other hand, cannot possibly capitalize on this type of synthesis. As a consequence, individual CAI authors are often incapable of relating particular lessons to other relevant curriculum material.

The Ability to Respond to Student Inquiries   Teachers often find themselves answering questions that are only marginally related to the topic at hand but that are certainly worthy of a response. In computerized instruction, there is generally little opportunity for such questions to be asked. Even if it were possible to ask such questions, it would probably be impossible for most computers to adequately decipher the question or to retrieve an appropriate answer.

The Ability to Model Behaviors and Values   A teacher is one of the most powerful role models in a student's life. The teacher is viewed as both an authority figure and an expert, factors which combine to make the student likely to accept and internalize the teacher's opinions and attitudes.

The Ability to Empathize   An effective teacher can empathize when a student experiences difficulty and can make necessary adjustments. Whether the problems are related to an inability to learn a new topic, strife at home, or peer pressure, the teacher can counsel the student. It is often possible to relay relevant personal experiences that reassure the student. A computer cannot compete with the teacher's warmth and empathy.

The Ability to Work with Large Groups   When viewed purely from an economic perspective, perhaps the greatest advantage of teachers is their ability to work with large groups. By working with groups, the cost per student hour is reduced. When the teacher's ability to work with several students concurrently is compared with the microcomputer's ability to work with one or two, an advantage becomes obvious.

The Ability to Motivate   Effective teachers find novel ways to motivate students. Whether by employing behavior management techniques, developing interesting topics, or presenting information in an interesting manner, the successful teacher is able to direct and maintain the students' interest. Although students may enjoy working with computers, this effect is likely to be short-lived.

Unless CAI is effectively designed, the computer may be unable to generate the kind of enthusiasm elicited by an outstanding teacher.

The Ability to Adapt to Changing Demands   An effective teacher is flexible. Rather than proceeding in lock-step through a lesson, the effective teacher identifies and capitalizes on opportunities to adjust lesson pace and is able to adapt to the inevitable events that interfere with anticipated progress. In addition, an effective teacher may determine that students do not have the necessary prerequisite skills and may choose to teach those skills before proceeding. CAI programs generally provide remedial instruction for anticipated problems, but unanticipated problems can seldom be reconciled within a lesson.

THE TEACHER'S WEAKNESSES

Teachers do many things well. However, there are also things that teachers do less effectively. A brief overview of the teacher's limitations is presented here.

Inability to Spend Adequate Time with Individual Students   Because one teacher generally works with a group of students, the amount of contact time per student is minimal. According to Spiller and Robertson (1984), the average student receives roughly 15 seconds of individualized teacher time per hour. This means that, although teachers are *capable* of individualizing instruction to meet the needs of students, in practice it is nearly impossible. Teachers enjoy working with individual students; most entered the field of education with a sincere desire to help students. Perhaps the principal reward for teachers is enabling a student to overcome a difficult obstacle, with the knowledge that the teacher's role in the process was crucial. Unfortunately, high student/teacher ratios often make such rewards a rarity.

Inability to Spend Adequate Time Planning and Developing Instruction   Teachers are usually allotted less than one hour per day during which to grade student work, develop instructional materials, and plan future activities. One hour per day is probably inadequate for *any one* of these activities. Student work is often evaluated at the expense of teachers' private lives. Development of instructional materials and planning for the future, however, tend to receive minimal attention beyond what is absolutely required.

Inability to Grade and Track Student Performance Efficiently   The process of tracking the performance of students through several academic subjects is a formidable task. Teachers are ill equipped for this job, especially when compared with the computer's tireless ability to evaluate and track student performance.

Inability to Evaluate Student Performance Objectively   It may be impossible for a teacher to separate feelings for a student from ratings of the student's ability to perform. When teachers evaluate students, an answer from a bright or likeable student may be more likely to be considered correct than the same answer offered by a troublesome individual. Conversely, responses from a less affable student may be judged more harshly.

Ability to Experience Frustration   When a teacher attempts to work with an individual student who is experiencing learning problems, there is a tendency for the teacher to become frustrated. If subsequent attempts are still unsuccessful, this frustration mounts, and success becomes even less probable. Frustration is due in part to demands placed on the teacher's time and in part to the teacher's unsuccessful attempts to communicate the information more effectively. In the end, it is the student who is often the victim of teacher frustration.

Ability to Experience Boredom   Teachers often teach the same courses or grade levels from semester to semester or year to year. After having taught a course several times, teachers may become bored. This may result in a loss of enthusiasm, which may inadvertently reduce student interest in the topic. Computers can deliver lessons repeatedly without becoming bored.

The Role, Strengths, and Weaknesses of Computers

THE COMPUTER'S ROLE

Computers have been employed in classrooms to perform a variety of tasks. They are often used in diagnosing student needs, delivering instruction, drilling students in need of practice, grading student responses, reporting student progress, and simulating expensive equipment or dangerous experiments. In addition, computer time is sometimes distributed as a reward to motivate students to perform during conventional lessons.

The computer, when equipped with well-written software, has several strengths that combine to make it appropriate for instructional use. The computer also has weaknesses that must be taken into account when attempting to convey a particular educational message. These strengths and weaknesses are summarized in Table 3.2 and discussed briefly here.

THE COMPUTER'S STRENGTHS

Ability to Perform at High Speed   Even microcomputers are now capable of processing several million instructions per second. Although it may take several hundred computer instructions to comprise an instruction we might give another

Table 3.2
Strengths and Weaknesses of Computers

Strengths	Weaknesses
The ability to	*The inability to*
Perform at high speed	Respond spontaneously
Perform accurately	Teach large groups effectively
Collect and manage information	Teach or model certain behaviors
Motivate students to perform	
Perform repetitive tasks without boredom	
Maintain composure	
Individualize cost effectively	

human, the sheer volume of work a computer can produce more than compensates for this. The result of such rapid processing speed is that simple tasks like computing percentages are completed instantly, and large databases may be searched in a matter of moments. When compared to the time required for even the brightest humans, the computer's speed is a valuable asset.

Ability to Perform Accurately   Computers do not make mistakes—they are not smart enough. Although this may sound strange, computers simply follow very explicit sets of instructions provided by a programmer. They do not have enough intelligence to vary from the path they are programmed to follow. Computer errors are actually human errors, resulting from a faulty set of instructions, which the computer executes faithfully. Once a program has been tested to assure that it is "bug-free," the computer is certain to execute the program accurately.

Ability to Collect and Manage Information   The computer's speed and accuracy combine to produce an amazing ability to manipulate numbers and alphabetic characters. The ability to quickly and accurately manipulate characters and numbers makes the computer an excellent device for recording, managing, and reporting student performance during or after instruction.

Ability to Motivate   Currently, the computer is attractive to many students. The interest and excitement generated by computers often transfer to the topic being taught (Brown, 1986). The capability to teach via games, as well as other varied and interesting formats, bestows upon the computer strong motivational potential.

Ability to Perform Repetitive Tasks Without Boredom   Computers do not experience boredom. They do not know if they are executing the same commands repeatedly or never executing the same command twice. The boredom that often haunts teachers is not a factor when the teacher is a machine.

Inability to Experience Frustration   Because computers do not have feelings, they do not become frustrated when students experience difficulty. Whether the program is presented once or twenty times, the tenor of the instruction remains consistent. Because the computer cannot help but maintain composure, it does not become sarcastic or bitter or do things that damage the student's self-image.

Ability to Individualize Cost Effectively   Suppose a typical minicomputer system costs $2400. The life expectancy of a computer system should be about three to five years. Using the three-year estimate, the system's cost per year is $800. Assume the typical school year is composed of 180 days and the typical day consists of seven hours (although many computers are also made available before and after school); the computer is available 1260 hours. The cost for each hour of one-to-one student contact during the computer's life is approximately 64 cents. The cost for an hour of dedicated teacher time is many times higher. Although the teacher may be more cost-effective when dealing with groups, the computer has an advantage when working with individual students.

THE COMPUTER'S WEAKNESSES

Although computers do many things well, there are also limitations to consider. A brief overview of the computer's limitations is presented here.

Inability to React Spontaneously Teachers can react instantaneously from a complex base of knowledge and accrued wisdom based on years of varied experiences. They can even react appropriately to new experiences, drawing on similar events and on rules learned in other contexts. At this stage of its development, the computer acts only as instructed. It only knows what a programmer provided to it in order for it to perform specific tasks. With more sophisticated hardware and the advent of artificial intelligence, this will change.

Inability to Deal Effectively with Large Groups Because interaction and individualization are goals of effective CAI, the grouping of students at a CAI station can defeat major strengths. By providing several individualized sessions, large computer systems can teach many students simultaneously, but the burgeoning costs for hardware and software quickly elude the budgets of all but the most affluent school systems.

Inability to Teach or Model Certain Types of Behavior As Nygren (1983, p. 40) stated, "the most fundamental elements of an education—how people communicate with one another, how they experience one another, and how they share such joys as art and the humanities—will not happen at electronic terminals." Whether or not this prediction is upheld remains to be seen. It is important to note, however, that much of Nygren's concern is presently supported.

The Computer and Expert Teachers

Both teachers and computers have strengths that serve as logical solutions to educational problems. Neither can fully replace the other, nor can either be rejected categorically as ineffective or undesirable. Several heuristics can be followed that capitalize on the strengths, while minimizing the limitations, of teachers and computers.

Avoid settings that minimize contact with a live teacher. Students benefit from personal contact. Morris (1983) compared computer-intensive settings to the experiments in which baby monkeys were taken from their parents and raised by surrogate mothers made of cloth. According to Morris (p. 13),

> These surrogates provided the babies with all of their needs, except one: the chance to observe what it was like to be an adult monkey. When the babies survived they appeared to be severely psychotic. Similarly, it might be that a child trained largely by computer would lose precisely the ingredient that a good teacher must provide; a model of what it is like to be an ethical human being. This ethical element is far more important, in the long run, than most of the other things the child might learn—like the names of the states or a method for finding square roots.

Students are best served when teachers and computers are employed in combination, capitalizing on strengths and minimizing the effects of weaknesses. Table 3.3 summarizes the comparative strengths and weaknesses of teachers and computers. Computers should be used to provide the individualized instruction for

Table 3.3
Human Teachers vs. Computer Teachers: An Analysis of Teaching Tasks

Tasks	Advantage to	
	Teacher	*Computer*
Developmental		
Planning the course of study	X	
Evaluating and locating appropriate instructional materials	X	
Developing instructional materials	X	
Administrative		
Handling administrative details	X	X
Evaluating student progress	X	X
Recording indicators of student progress (grades, anecdotal comments, etc.)	X	X
Informing students, parents, administrators, and other teachers of student progress	X	X
Evaluating final performance of students		X
Evaluating the success of courses		X
Environmental/affective		
Modeling adult behavior and values	X	
Bonding	X	
Counseling students	X	
Motivating	X	X
Providing a safe environment for students	X	
Providing necessary discipline	X	
Instructional		
Presenting instruction to groups	X	
Presenting instruction to individuals	X	X
Cost efficiency when working with groups	X	
Cost efficiency when working with individuals		X
Responding to spontaneous student inquiries	X	
Adapting the course of study for individual students	X	X
Adapting to changing demands	X	
Synthesizing	X	

which teachers do not have time and to accomplish administrative functions such as testing, grading, reporting, and course scheduling. Computers should also be used to provide the teacher with more time for tutoring, planning, and developing new instruction. Landa (1984) viewed computers as a "cadre of teaching assistants" performing a variety of tasks, from presenting remedial instruction to introducing new topics to the capable, self-directed learners who are ready to proceed.

Incorporating Computers into Educational Settings

Once a decision is made to use computers to support education, computers are usually incorporated in one of the following ways.

THE COMPUTER-LAB APPROACH

In the computer-lab approach, several computers are centrally located in a room. There is usually one teacher or supervisor scheduled in that room at all times. This coordinator generally plans activities, schedules classes, designs curricula, and presents instruction during designated periods. In this regard, the lab teacher performs much like the music, physical education, and art teachers in many schools. In some computer laboratories, all students are scheduled. In other schools, only specified grades or classes attend. The laboratory schedule often contains one or two hours of open time, during which teachers can send students for specific remedial or enrichment activities.

There are several advantages to the computer-lab approach. It provides access for more classes and students, an expert available to answer questions, the ability to schedule group activities, and the ability to share peripheral devices such as printers and modems. In addition, the lab approach provides the teacher with additional time during which tutoring, planning, or development of instructional materials may take place.

There are also disadvantages to this approach. When placed in labs, computers are unavailable to students most of the time. Teachers and students often view them as "add-ons" and do not feel kinship for the computers or for the program. In such cases, teachers are not as likely to integrate computers into other activities. As a result, computers are often viewed as isolated curiosities rather than as tools with virtually limitless applications.

CLASSROOM MICROCOMPUTER CENTERS

Another alternative involves microcomputers as a standard piece of classroom equipment, much like a blackboard. In this arrangement, one or more microcomputers are generally placed around the perimeter of the classroom and are available to students during times that the teacher schedules or when work is finished early.

With computers directly in the classroom, they are always available for teacher and student use. The computers can be easily incorporated into daily routines, and students come to view computers as a basic part of their education. In many cases, teachers learn more about computers as well.

There are also disadvantages to the classroom computer center approach. There are seldom enough microcomputers to allow sufficient student/computer contact. Untrained teachers may not make effective use of the equipment, often letting the computers sit idle or using them indiscriminately.

THE ROVING MICROCOMPUTER

In this approach, microcomputers are not placed in a single location, but are moved about. A micro may be placed in one class for a month, moved on to another location for the following month, then to a third location, and so on.

A primary advantage of this approach is that more students will have contact with limited computer resources. An obvious disadvantage is that the computer will spend little time in any one place, and neither teachers nor students will receive enough contact to make significant progress.

Obstacles to Overcome If Computers Are to Impact Education

In many ways, the educational impact of computers in the United States has been minimal. The three obstacles minimizing the potential impact appear to be (1) the number of microcomputers available per student, (2) the number of teachers untrained in the use of microcomputers, and (3) the absence and/or poor quality of educational courseware.

Increasing the number of microcomputers should improve both the level of teacher training and the quality of the software available. Once computers are more accessible, teachers can spend more time with them and hands-on training will become possible. In addition to formal learning provided through universities and district in-service programs, teachers are likely to experiment and therefore improve their competency on the machines. Administrators will consider computer skills more seriously when hiring new teachers, and teacher training institutions will therefore commit to producing graduates with effective, marketable computer skills.

As more microcomputers become available, the economic incentive for producing quality educational software will increase. This potential for profit has already attracted several major publishers into the educational courseware market, allowing them to spend necessary amounts of money and time to develop quality courseware.

AVAILABILITY OF COMPUTERS IN SCHOOLS IN THE UNITED STATES

Microcomputers have become increasingly available. According to a survey conducted by Market Data Retrieval, the current growth is astounding. As their 1984 report stated (p. 5),

> It becomes almost trite to characterize the growth of microcomputers in U.S. public schools as explosive, astonishing, or phenomenal. But the fact is that the number of schools [using micros] in some categories actually quintupled from 1981 to 1983.

Their 1985 report showed that this rapid growth had continued. The graphs contained in Figures 3.1 through 3.4 illustrate the magnitude of this growth. Figure 3.1 illustrates that the percentage of school districts using microcomputers to teach more than doubled between 1981 and 1983 and that the percentage of districts using microcomputers had reached 94.2 percent by 1984. Figure 3.2 shows that the percentage of elementary, junior high, and high schools using microcomputers for CAI has more than quadrupled in the same four-year period. Neither use nor growth rate has been uniform across school type. As might be expected, Figure 3.2 also reveals that the percentage of high schools using computers is greater than the percentage of junior high schools, which is greater than the percentage of elementary schools, and that, although use in elementary and junior high schools has increased steadily, the increase in the percentage of high

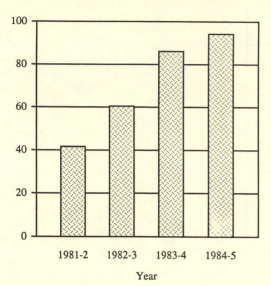

Figure 3.1
Percentages of school districts with microcomputers.

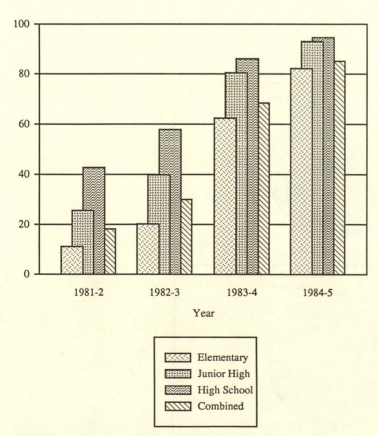

Figure 3.2
Percentages of individual schools with microcomputers, by school type.

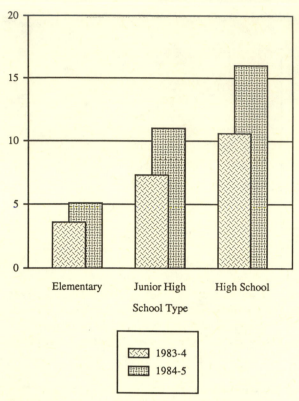

Figure 3.3
Average number of microcomputers per school.

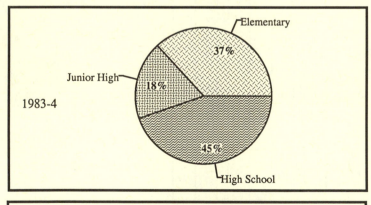

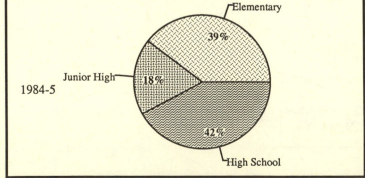

Figure 3.4
Distribution of microcomputers by school type.

schools is beginning to level off. The authors of the survey attribute this to the fact that the percentage is approaching 100 percent.

Analysis of Figures 3.3 and 3.4 reveals that the average number of micros available per building also varies according to school type and is also increasing rapidly. On the average, elementary schools had approximately three microcomputers each in 1983 and five by 1984. The number in junior high schools had increased from approximately seven to eleven, and high schools increased their numbers from approximately ten to approximately sixteen. Although a smaller percentage of elementary schools has microcomputers, and the number of microcomputers per building is also lowest, because there are approximately twice as many elementary schools as there are junior high and high schools combined, a surprisingly large percentage of the nation's microcomputers is located in elementary schools. Figure 3.4 illustrates how the total number of microcomputers was distributed among school types in 1983 and 1984.

Unfortunately, microcomputers are not spread uniformly across the country. Table 3.4 provides survey information on a state-by-state basis. Columns indicate the percentages of schools using microcomputers and micro-intensities. *Micro-intensity* is a term used by Market Data Retrieval to indicate the number of students per computer, a better measure of the availability of computers than a raw number per state. For example, a micro-intensity of 95 means that there are 95 students for each microcomputer used for instructional purposes in that state. Ranks for each of the three categories are displayed next to the percentages. Two years of data allow you to determine whether a given state is gaining ground or losing it as compared to other states.

Trends and Implications for the Near Future

Based on these figures, it seems safe to say that there will be adequate numbers of microcomputers in the schools to have a significant impact on education. Adequate teacher training and improved educational software are critical factors that will influence the speed and extent to which computers contribute to the field in the next few years. School districts, colleges, and universities must understand the importance of teacher training and develop programs that teach teachers (1) to use microcomputers in their classrooms and schools; (2) to identify quality courseware; and, in some cases, (3) to revise existing programs or produce original software to meet classroom-specific needs.

Chapter Summary

Computers cannot replace teachers, nor can teachers replace computers. When they are combined in a way that capitalizes on the strengths of each, teams of teachers and computers can become efficient, effective instructional systems.

Given enough time, teachers can become very good at every aspect of teaching. Computers, by identifying areas in which students need instruction, presenting instruction on a one-to-one basis, evaluating student progress, reporting on student progress, and evaluating courses, can provide the teacher with more time to excel

Table 3.4
State Rankings on the Availability of Computers in Schools for Instructional Purposes

	1983				1984			
State	Percent of Schools	Rank	Micro-intensity	Rank	Percent of Schools	Rank	Micro-intensity	Rank
Alabama	42.3	49	157.1	49	75.7	43	89.5	45
Alaska	46.5	47	103.5	39	80.6	36	24.1	1
Arizona	64.0	31	71.1	13	83.3	31	45.8	7
Arkansas	56.2	40	75.0	17	84.0	30	51.3	18
California	82.9	6	125.6	42	93.4	5	81.2	42
Colorado	87.3	3	73.3	15	96.7	2	48.4	12
Connecticut	75.4	15	81.7	21	89.4	14	48.1	9
Delaware	77.9	12	95.6	36	80.0	39	63.7	32
Dist. of Col.	61.1	34	54.0	2	88.7	16	55.2	22
Florida	68.2	24	92.8	33	90.3	11	59.7	25
Georgia	54.9	45	152.2	48	80.8	35	107.1	50
Hawaii	26.6	51	264.4	51	67.1	48	180.5	51
Idaho	66.0	26	83.2	22	87.8	17	62.7	30
Illinois	68.5	23	85.9	25	85.0	28	62.0	27
Indiana	80.3	7	83.8	23	92.9	8	48.2	10
Iowa	83.7	5	67.5	8	93.1	6	49.9	16
Kansas	71.1	22	62.1	6	90.7	10	49.9	16
Kentucky	55.1	44	99.9	37	80.4	37	65.3	36
Louisiana	45.4	48	135.6	45	65.5	50	96.9	46
Maine	64.5	29	92.9	34	81.2	34	65.2	35
Maryland	59.7	35	150.3	47	85.7	25	98.6	48
Massachusetts	71.2	21	81.1	20	87.0	20	61.9	26
Michigan	78.4	11	90.6	28	89.3	15	63.6	31
Minnesota	92.8	1	56.5	4	98.3	1	35.8	3
Mississippi	36.2	50	135.1	44	66.5	49	97.1	47
Missouri	55.6	42	93.6	35	66.5	49	97.1	47
Montana	74.9	16	54.4	3	82.0	33	41.0	5
Nebraska	55.3	43	70.1	10	61.3	51	48.2	11
Nevada	50.2	46	91.9	29	74.5	46	64.5	34
New Hampshire	79.2	9	91.3	30	87.7	18	66.7	39
New Jersey	74.3	17	68.4	9	86.8	21	53.9	20
New Mexico	58.9	37	90.2	27	79.5	40	46.1	8
New York	78.7	10	91.9	32	90.2	12	65.3	36
North Carolina	72.9	19	141.2	46	92.6	9	83.8	44
North Dakota	74.0	18	65.2	7	86.7	22	48.6	14
Ohio	64.2	30	100.1	38	85.2	27	73.4	40
Oklahoma	55.8	41	70.9	12	74.7	45	57.0	23
Oregon	92.4	2	73.6	16	95.2	4	51.3	18
Pennsylvania	59.6	36	80.9	19	80.1	38	62.0	27
Rhode Island	67.0	25	108.5	40	86.5	23	44.2	6
South Carolina	57.3	39	162.8	50	77.5	42	105.6	49
South Dakota	65.0	28	49.2	1	73.9	47	33.2	2
Tennessee	61.2	33	123.9	41	83.2	32	82.5	43
Texas	57.6	38	87.8	26	74.9	44	64.0	33
Utah	85.7	4	83.9	24	96.1	3	57.9	24
Vermont	65.1	27	71.6	14	85.6	26	49.3	15
Virginia	71.6	20	127.3	43	87.6	19	80.0	41
Washington	77.4	13	70.8	11	90.2	12	48.4	12
West Virginia	61.5	32	91.4	31	84.9	29	62.4	29
Wisconsin	76.7	14	75.6	18	93.0	7	54.1	21
Wyoming	80.1	8	58.1	5	86.4	24	37.1	4

in important teaching functions. The teacher can use this time to do those things that only a teacher can do: planning, developing instructional materials, modeling adult behavior, counseling students, and bonding with students.

The availability of microcomputers is increasing rapidly. Within a few years, their numbers will be sufficient to have a profound impact on education in the United States. If computers are to attain their potential, teachers must be adequately trained, and higher quality educational software must be produced.

References

BROWN, J. W. (1986). Some motivational issues in computer-based instruction. *Educational Technology*, **26**(4), 27–29.

LANDA, R. K. (1984). *Creating Courseware: A Beginner's Guide*. New York: Harper & Row.

Market Data Retrieval. (1984). *Microcomputers in Schools, 1983–84: A Comprehensive Survey and Analysis*. Westport, CT: Market Data Retrieval.

———. (1985). *Microcomputers in Schools, 1984–85: A Comprehensive Survey and Analysis*. Westport, CT: Market Data Retrieval.

MORRIS, J. M. (1983). Computer-aided instruction: Toward a new direction. *Educational Technology*, **23**(5), 12–15.

NYGREN, B. M. (1983). Let's don't go gaga over computers. *Executive Educator*, **5**(5), 40.

SPILLER, R. and J. ROBERTSON (1984). Computer-based training: A major growth opportunity. *Technological Horizons in Education*, **11**(6), 75–76.

Related Reading

BARRETT, B. K., and M. J. HANNAFIN (1982). Computers in educational management: Merging accountability with technology. *Educational Technology*, **22**(3), 9–12.

BORK, A. (1981). *Learning with Computers*. Bedford, MA: Digital.

CHAMBERS, J. A. and J. W. SPRECHER (1983). *Computer-assisted Instruction: Its Use in the Classroom*. Englewood Cliffs, NJ: Prentice-Hall, Inc.

HANNAFIN, M. J., D. W. DALTON, and S. HOOPER (1987). Computers in education: 10 myths and 10 needs. *Educational Technology*.

———. (1987). Computers in education: Barriers and solutions. In E. Miller and M. L. Mosley (Eds.) *Educational Media and Technology Yearbook*. Littleton, CO: Libraries Unlimited.

SWADENER, M., and M. J. HANNAFIN (1987). Gender similarities and differences in sixth graders' attitudes towards computers: An exploratory study. *Educational Technology*, **27**(1), 37–42.

TAYLOR, R. P. (1980). *The Computer in the School: Tutor, Tool, Tutee*. New York: Teacher's College Press.

Chapter Review Exercises

COMPREHENSION

1. Discuss the strengths and weaknesses of teachers. (See pages 30–33 and Table 3.1.)
2. Discuss the strengths and weaknesses of computers. (See pages 33–35 and Table 3.2.)

3. Name and describe ways in which computers are often incorporated into educational environments. (See pages 36–37.)

4. Discuss the advantages and disadvantages of the computer-lab approach to placing micros in schools. (See page 37.)

5. Discuss the advantages and disadvantages of placing microcomputers in classrooms. (See page 37.)

6. Discuss the impact computers have had on education in the United States and why. (See pages 38–41.)

7. Discuss the extent to which microcomputers are currently available in high schools, junior high schools, and elementary schools in the United States. (See pages 38–41, Figures 3.1–3.4 and Table 3.4.)

8. Discuss trends in the availability of computers in schools and the impact these trends are likely to have on the ability for computers to contribute in the near future. (See page 41.)

9. Discuss the three critical obstacles to be removed if computers are to have a major impact on education in the United States. (See page 38.)

10. Discuss how your home state ranks on computer availability, whether availability is increasing or decreasing as compared to growth in other states, and your reactions to that ranking. (See Table 3.4.)

CHAPTER 4

Learning Foundations and CAI

Prospective CAI developers have been led to believe that developing CAI requires little knowledge. Workshops, in-service sessions, and publishers of courseware development tools have promoted the idea that producing effective CAI requires little background. People set out to develop courseware believing that the ability to transmit information to the computer monitor, accept and evaluate answers, and branch accordingly is all one needs to know.

This is a dangerous misconception—one that has contributed to the glut of substandard CAI software presently available. The design of good instructional material requires more than the ability to write. Although there are tools that minimize the computer-related knowledge required, successful designers need to understand both the subject upon which the lesson is based and the principles of learning.

The purpose of this chapter is to transfer what is known about how people learn to the design of effective CAI. The chapter presents well-established principles of educational psychology and discusses how to incorporate these principles into CAI lessons in order to maximize effectiveness.

OBJECTIVES

Comprehension

After completing this chapter you will be able to

1. Describe the difference between the behavioral and cognitive learning theories.
2. List and describe at least five principles derived from learning theory.
3. List and discuss the eleven implications for CAI design derived from these principles.
4. Discuss the characteristics of effective feedback.
5. Discuss the role of practice in learning.
6. Discuss the concept of congruence between objectives, instruction, and evaluation.
7. Discuss the use of learner control in CAI.

Principles of Educational Psychology and Computerized Instruction

We do not fully understand how people learn. Theories have been advanced attempting to explain how learning occurs, and principles derived from these theories have been employed to produce measurably better instruction. In this section, an overview of behavioral and cognitive learning theories and the principles of instructional design that have evolved from each theory will be presented. In addition, techniques for applying these principles during the design of CAI will be presented.

BEHAVIORAL LEARNING THEORY

Behavioral psychology, also known as Skinnerian or stimulus–response psychology, is based on the premise that learning results from the pairing of responses with stimuli. An example is the classic Pavlovian study, during which dogs learned to associate the presentation of food with the ringing of a bell. The stimulus (the bell) eventually elicited the learned response (salivation). A key concept in this theory is that of reinforcement. Reinforcement is viewed as an event that follows the response. *Positive reinforcement* is an event or condition that makes the associated response more likely, and *negative reinforcement* is an event or condition that makes the response less likely.

An educational example is the presentation of a flash card containing the problem 6×4 (the stimulus). The student may respond, "22," after which the teacher might provide negative reinforcement like "No, 6 times 4 is not 22. Try again." This negative reinforcement makes the student less likely to respond with the same answer but more likely to respond in a desired way. The student ventures another attempt at the problem and responds, "24." The teacher positively reinforces the answer. "Right! Six times four *is* 24." Following this exchange, the answer "24" is more likely to occur under the stimulus conditions.

Several principles guiding the design of instruction have been derived from behavioral learning theory. Gagné and Briggs (1979) discussed three: contiguity, repetition, and reinforcement. A fourth, prompting and fading, is also helpful to the designer of CAI.

> *Principle 1:* **Contiguity: The response should follow the stimulus without delay.**

The principle of contiguity implies that the stimulus to which the learner is to respond must be presented contiguously in time with the desired response (Thornburg, 1984; Houston, 1976). The stimulus is presented; the response follows. If longer periods of time elapse between the stimulus and the response, the probability that the response will be paired with the stimulus is diminished.

> *Principle 2:* **Repetition: Practice strengthens learning and improves retention.**

In order for learning and retention to be improved, the stimulus and response must be practiced. Practice strengthens the bond between the stimulus and response (Loree, 1965; Houston, 1976). The learning of multiplication facts is a good example of a case in which practice is essential. Merely saying the correct answer once does not guarantee that the correct response will always follow the stimulus. Repetition of the stimulus/response pattern strengthens learning.

Principle 3: **Feedback and reinforcement: Knowledge concerning the correctness of the response contributes to learning.**

The learner must gain information on the appropriateness of the response. Feedback provides the learner with knowledge of results, that is, whether the response was right, wrong, or neither. If the response becomes more or less likely to occur, then the feedback served a reinforcement function. Feedback may be especially valuable following incorrect responses, because without feedback the response is likely to be repeated (Loree, 1965; Kolesnik, 1976; Houston, 1976). Repetition of a correct response is desirable; repetition of an incorrect response is not.

Principle 4: **Prompting and fading: Learning may be achieved by leading the student to the desired response under decreasingly cued conditions.**

A response to a given stimulus may be shaped (Thornburg, 1984; Skinner, 1968; Houston, 1976). Consider, for example, the task of teaching a student to provide the correct word or phrase in response to a completion question. You may first show the whole sentence, including the desired response, perhaps even highlighting the response. Next you may have the student fill in the blank while the correct response is visible. Then you might remove the correct response from view but place the first three letters of the correct response in the blank. Finally, you may have the student fill in the blank with no assistance. The terms *prompting* and *fading* refer to the process of providing several or alternate stimuli to shape the desired response. Eventually the learner progresses from the point at which the desired response is provided under cued conditions to the point at which the response is elicited under the desired conditions.

Behavioral theory is restricted to external, observable behaviors, attempting to explain *why behaviors occur*. By observing the four principles just discussed, teachers and trainers have produced increasingly efficient instruction. In contrast with behavioral theory, cognitive theory attempts to determine *how learning takes place*, based on processes believed to occur *within* the learner.

COGNITIVE LEARNING THEORY

Solso (1979, p. 1) describes cognitive psychology as studying "how we gain information from the world, how such information is represented and transformed as knowledge, how it is stored, and how that knowledge is used to direct our attention and behavior." According to cognitive theorists, learning is composed of the reception, short-term storage, encoding, long-term storage, and retrieval of information.

According to cognitive theory, stimulation affects the learner's sensory receptors and produces patterns of neural activity. The neural activity is transformed, and salient features are recorded in short-term memory. The capacity of short-term memory is limited, both in the number of items it may contain and in the length of time an item may remain. Encoding takes place as the meaningful information moves from short-term memory to long-term memory, where it is stored *according to its meaning*. In effect, the meaningfulness of information is a primary variable affecting the strength of learning. Where meaning has been already established, little effort need be expended; where information lacks meaning, the task is to aid students in determining and assigning individually relevant meaning.

When existing information is retrieved, it is either returned to short-term memory, where it may be combined with incoming information to form new learned capabilities, or is passed to a mechanism that transforms the information into action. Performance based on the retrieved information sets in motion a learning process (similar to that demonstrated by the behaviorists) subject to the principles of feedback and reinforcement.

The selection and initiation of cognitive strategies related to learning and remembering and the modification of information flow within the learner are handled by presumed executive control processes. They are presumed to control such things as attention, the encoding of incoming information, and the retrieval of what has been stored.

Since cognitive theory provides a working model of learning, it is possible to derive principles from the theory that, when applied, may either enhance or interfere with learning. Three principles may be added to those already discussed.

***Principle 5:* Orientation and recall: Learning involves the synthesis of prior information that must be recalled to active memory.**

According to cognitive theory, learning is the combination of existing information and new information (Gagné, 1970; Gagné and Briggs, 1979). In order for this to take place, the required existing information must be resident in the learner's short-term memory. This information may be provided at the time of instruction or may have been learned previously and be recalled by the learner from long-term memory. A review or discussion of prerequisite information or skills tends to improve the probability that learning will take place.

***Principle 6:* Intellectual skills: Learning is facilitated by the use of existing processes or strategies.**

Intellectual skills are different from information, in that these skills are the *formulas or processes* with which the learner has achieved similar objectives, not learned specific data (Gagné and Briggs, 1979). By recalling how similar learning objectives were achieved, the student may employ existing methods to learn new information, improving the efficiency of the learning process (Gagné, 1970; Gagné and Briggs, 1979).

***Principle 7:* Individualization: Learning may be more efficient when the instruction is adapted to the needs and the profiles of individual learners.**

Since learning is closely tied to the knowledge and skills of an individual learner, lessons are more likely to be successful and will be more efficient when the teaching is modified to match the learner's skill/knowledge profile (Thornburg, 1984, Kolesnik, 1976). Efficiency in teaching is achieved by focusing on only appropriate information, using examples that draw existing knowledge and strategies into short-term memory, and providing practice that is adequate but not excessive.

PRINCIPLES CROSSING BEHAVIORAL/COGNITIVE BOUNDARIES

Additional principles improving the design of effective instruction do not fall neatly into the behavioral or cognitive categories. The following two principles cross theoretical boundaries.

> *Principle 8:* **Academic learning time: Increasing the time a student spends actively engaged in profitable instructional activities will result in more learning.**

Bright (1983), in explaining the efficiency of CAI, employed a concept called academic learning time, which prior research has shown to be correlated to achievement. Academic learning time is defined as time during which the learner is engaged in a learning activity and is responding successfully. Keeping the student alert, interested, and responding will motivate the learner to continue with the instruction. The student will be willing to spend more time engaged in the learning activity, thereby increasing the time available for learning to occur. If both the available learning time and the student's willingness and desire to learn are increased, more learning should result.

> *Principle 9:* **Affective considerations: "The attitudes of participants in an activity are important to its success" (Clement, 1981, p. 28).**

When students want to learn and feel successful, they are more likely to learn. Motivation and attitude, among other factors, influence the probability that learning objectives will be met (Kolesnik, 1976). Much has been written about the powerful role of affective variables in the learning process. Thornburg (1984) discusses this topic in detail, describing the roles of intrinsic, extrinsic, achievement, task, aspirational, competitive, affiliative, anxiety, avoidance, and reinforcing motivation. Although a thorough discussion of the topic is beyond the scope of this text, it should be stated that attention to affective variables and attempts to assure that productive attitudes are fostered during instruction will enhance the effectiveness of CAI.

Implications for CAI Design

The primary goal of this book is to develop individuals capable of producing better CAI. The eleven implications for the design of CAI listed in Table 4.1 have been derived from the foregoing principles. If one uses them as guidelines for CAI development, the probability of designing successful lessons should improve.

1. *Develop CAI in accordance with the internal processes of learning.* Based on cognitive learning theory, Gagné, Wager, and Rojas (1981) have identified internal learning processes corresponding to nine different phases of the learning cycle: (1) alertness, (2) expectancy, (3) retrieval to working memory, (4) selective perception, (5) semantic encoding, (6) retrieval and responding, (7) reinforcement, (8) cueing retrieval, and (9) generalizing. They have associated an external instructional event with each. These external instructional events are designed to ensure that the corresponding internal learning process occurs. If the nine external

Table 4.1
Implications of the Principles of Learning for CAI Design

1. Develop CAI in accordance with the internal processes of learning
     Gain the learner's attention
     Inform the learner of the lesson's objectives
     Stimulate recall of prior learning
     Present stimuli with distinctive features
     Guide the learning
     Elicit the desired performance
     Provide informative feedback
     Assess performance
     Enhance retention and learning transfer
2. Individualize
3. Make CAI lessons interactive
4. Use feedback effectively
5. Guarantee success
6. Assure congruence among objectives, instruction, and assessment
7. Allow an appropriate amount of learner control
8. Account for, monitor, and evaluate affective considerations
9. Evaluate based on objectives, attitudes, and adequacy of programming
10. Design screens carefully
11. Use additional media as appropriate

events are included in each module of a CAI lesson, a greater degree of confidence in the performance of the lesson may be attained.

For something to be learned, it must first be perceived. To direct the learner's attention to the material to be presented and to attract the learner to the learning process, use such things as attractive, captivating, graphic sequences and intellectual challenges.

When students are aware of lesson expectations, they are more likely to learn what is expected. Their expectations influence the information, skills, and strategies that will be recalled to working memory for use during acquisition. Objectives should be communicated to the student in everyday language, not in the technical way written by instructional designers to meet instructional demands.

Since learning requires the integration of existing with new information, the learner should be informed or reminded of any prerequisite skills, knowledge, or strategies. These prerequisites may be tested; if they are absent, remediation should take place before the lesson begins. Perception is selective. To direct the learner's perception and draw attention to key elements, add distinctive features to highlight crucial elements. For example, use color, flashing text, underlining, or other means to focus the learner's attention.

Storage alone is of little value. The goal of most lessons is to make *retrieval and performance* possible. Practice in retrieval and subsequent performance demonstrates that the desired behaviors have been acquired, improving the probability that these behaviors will be available at a later date. Provide adequate amounts of practice. Do not underrate the amount of practice required to make what is learned either automatic or permanent. Feedback may be used to shape desired behaviors and to reinforce successful responses. Feedback, discussed in more detail subsequently, is often more valuable following an incorrect response than following a correct response, especially when the student's response confidence is higher. However, most lessons incorporate feedback of some type for both correct and incorrect responses.

Students need to apply learning in novel situations. Inform students how the information, skill, or strategy they are about to learn might be useful in the future.

2. *Individualize.* Since information and prior experiences are involved in the learning process, it is no surprise that computerized instruction designed to adapt to the individual learner has been shown to improve educational outcomes (Ross, 1984). Learner characteristics such as interests, reading rate, prior experience and knowledge, and job interest have all been used by CAI designers to determine appropriate instructional characteristics. Characteristics adjusted according to learner variables have included the content of the lesson, the pace of the lesson, the presence or absence of music as reinforcement, the amount of practice provided, the amount and nature of feedback, the amount of information appearing on the screen at a given time, and the selection of relevant examples during instruction.

Ross (1984) noted that individualization may aid learning by (1) increasing interest, (2) activating relevant past experiences as conceptual anchoring for new information, and (3) associating rules with a meaningful, integrated set of ideas.

3. *Make CAI lessons interactive.* One of CAI's salient features is its ability to *involve* the learner. Interaction may contribute to learning in several ways.

a. *Interaction assures that messages are received and that critical attributes of the lesson are attended to.* Unlike lectures, videotapes, and most other media, a computerized lesson generally requires frequent responses from the learner to control lesson execution. When the student's mind wanders, the computer patiently waits (unless it has been programmed to regain the student's attention after a lengthy pause); information need not be presented to an inattentive audience. In addition, the computer can frequently query students and monitor responses to ascertain that the student has received and processed the intended educational message.

b. *Interaction encourages responses to strengthen cognitive ties and facilitate recall of the response.* When a student physically responds to a question or demonstrates a desired behavior within the context of a lesson, the act of responding may itself be remembered, providing an additional method by which the desired learning may be recalled.

c. *Interaction allows for remediation of incorrect responses.* Interaction between the computer and the learner allows the CAI program to identify and remediate incorrect learning and to identify misconceptions so they do not endure in place of the desired learning outcome.

d. *Interaction increases academic learning time.* Learners are willing to spend more time with CAI than learners employing more traditional educational media (Bright, 1983). Interaction, by definition, requires learner involvement. This involvement may lead to feelings that the learner controls the instruction, which may, in turn, be responsible for the willingness to spend more time with CAI lessons.

Alternatively, interaction helps to assure success. Many CAI designers incorporate mastery learning concepts in which the learner does not proceed until success has been achieved. This perception of success may produce positive attitudes within the learner, which maintain the student's interest and increase academic learning time.

4. *Use feedback effectively.* Kulhavy (1977) summarized the research on feedback and reached the following conclusions:

a. Positive feedback (given when the response is correct) is less helpful than negative feedback (provided when the response was incorrect). When a learner responds correctly, the correct response will probably be repeated with or without feedback. Negative feedback informs the student that previous responses must be modified to prevent the response from recurring. Negative feedback is most valuable when student confidence in responses is strong.
b. Feedback is not necessary after every correct response; in fact, it may be best when provided intermittently. Feedback following correct answers may, on occasion, be counterproductive. Feedback requires time, slowing progress during an instructional session. When given the opportunity, students often choose to bypass feedback and/or reinforcement following correct responses.

Cohen (1985) extended Kulhavy's conclusions, noting that CAI feedback timing depends on several factors, such as the mastery level of students, the short- versus long-term retention requirements of the learning, and the availability of prior knowledge to support learning. The progress of students who demonstrate high mastery levels may be slowed unduly by continuous immediate feedback. On the other hand, immediate feedback helps to support short-term retention of lesson content, while delayed feedback supports long-term retention. Students with limited background knowledge in the lesson content may require continuous immediate feedback in order to gain initial competence.

In addition, Cohen (1983) presents the following advice to CAI designers concerning the use of feedback:

a. Do not use feedback to "yell at" the learner.
b. Provide feedback immediately.
c. Provide feedback that states *whether* the answer was correct or incorrect.
d. Provide feedback that explains *why* the answer was correct or incorrect.

In addition, feedback for an incorrect response should not be more attractive than for a correct answer. In some cases, students provide incorrect answers in order to see more entertaining negative feedback, defeating the purpose for which the lesson was developed (Caldwell, 1980; Cohen, 1983).

Feedback should be based on characteristics of the learner and the learning task. As examples, younger learners might require more elaborate feedback than more experienced learners, and constructed response questions generally require more elaborate feedback than questions in which the student selects a response from several options. MacLachlan (1986) proposed that CAI designers consider withholding feedback from more skilled learners, causing them to question decisions, thereby strengthening learning.

5. *Ensure success.* Success can be motivating. Responding correctly strengthens the desired response patterns. Use the computer's ability to monitor performance to provide instruction appropriate for each student. Move from simple to complex topics, assuring that prerequisites have been mastered before entering each new topic. Make the size of instructional steps appropriate, based on the characteristics of the learner and the content.

Informing the student of the objectives, discussed under implication 2, will also help to ensure success.

6. *Assure congruence among objectives, instruction, and assessment items.* Unfortunately, it is too common for a student to complete an instructional unit, return to the target environment, and be unable to perform the desired behaviors. The most common reason for this is a lack of congruence among the objective, the instruction, and the way in which the learning is evaluated during instruction (Jurgemeyer, 1982).

For example, if the objective is for the student to list the five steps in an assembly process, the instruction should teach and provide practice to enable him or her to do just that. The assessment should then require the student to list the five steps. It is inappropriate to ask the student to select the five steps from a list of eight or to place the five steps in the correct order, since the intent of the lesson was to list the steps.

Another common trap is to write objectives according to the media used to deliver instruction rather than the actual behavior to be exhibited in the target environment. For example, when the target objective is to assemble a carburetor, listing the steps involved is inadequate. Listing the steps, an objective achievable using CAI, may be taught as an enabling objective. However, the ability to perform the actual assembly cannot be assumed based solely on the ability to list the required steps. If this were true, every person who passed a written driver licensing examination would be a competent driver. We know this is not the case.

Although the previous examples dealt with overestimating the student's ability to perform, the reverse is also a common error. In CAI, a frequent mistake is to confuse the student's inability to type with ignorance of the correct answer. For example, when the objective is for the student to name the reference book in which to find the capitol of Bolivia, asking the student to type *e* or *d* would be better than asking the student to type *encyclopedia* or *dictionary*.

Another CAI problem is overprompting. The correct answer often flashes or is printed in a contrasting color, allowing the student to provide the answer without even reading the entire screen, let alone learning the information. As with programmed instruction, prompting may be useful initially, but fading of cues not present in the target environment should be complete before the performance is evaluated.

When presenting questions, use consistent question formats. Students should not spend inordinate amounts of time determining the required method by which to respond. Separate response options into a columnar listing rather than embedding them into sentences or paragraphs so that the options may be readily identified by the learner.

Judge answers as an expert teacher would. Anticipate as many answers as possible so that each appropriate response may be reinforced, while inappropriate responses may be remediated (Eisele, 1978). Where possible, use a bank of questions from which the computer selects randomly so that the test appears different each time. Students repeating the lesson must respond according to the concepts taught rather than memorizing the answers to a static list of questions.

7. *Allow an appropriate amount of learner control.* The issue of learner control is still unresolved. Although early guidelines for CAI promoted extensive learner control, including the ability to select the sequence of instructional modules and the amount of practice to be provided, current research indicates that learner control may not be advisable with certain categories of learners (Garhart and Hannafin, 1986; Hannafin, 1984; Tennyson, 1984). An "appropriate amount" of learner control implies that matters of instructional integrity, such as important sequence decisions and presence of prerequisites, be controlled by the designer and not the learner. Matters of convenience and preference, such as the ability to review, exit, turn off music, or test out of certain instructional modules may be left to the learner.

To make effective use of learner control, consider incorporating the following characteristics into CAI lessons:

a. Make the modularity and any hierarchical arrangement of topics obvious to the learner (Caldwell, 1980).
b. To facilitate review, allow easy access to lesson segments.
c. Monitor progress and allow the learner to continue where a previous session ended or to restart the module or the entire lesson.
d. Provide estimates of the time required to complete each module.

8. *Account for, monitor, and evaluate affective considerations.* Students generally have positive attitudes toward CAI because it (a) is self-paced, (b) is less threatening and less embarrassing when mistakes are made, (c) provides immediate feedback, (d) provides students with the impression that they learn better, and (e) is objective, basing its responses on the student's performance rather than on personal characteristics of the student. However, the designer of a major CAI system must still be sensitive to affective concerns when implementing a CAI course (L'Allier and Tennyson, 1980). Assess attitudinal data and respond appropriately to apparent attitudinal problems.

During the CAI sessions, the computer's ability to store information can be useful in collecting comments from the learners. Allowing the students to comment on the lesson serves two purposes: (1) it provides valuable information to the designer, so that the lesson may be revised for improved effectiveness, and (2) it may serve as a release for frustration or anxiety the student experiences during the lesson.

To maintain student interest, design attractive screens, incorporate graphics to minimize the amount of text to be absorbed, eliminate unnecessary words, use motivational techniques, and design the instruction to guarantee success.

One word of caution regarding the use of humor. What one person finds funny, another may find condescending. According to Jay (1983), humor has no consistently beneficial effect on information acquisition. The use of humor should be tempered and avoided where effects cannot be uniformly predicted.

9. *Evaluate CAI often, based on instructional, cosmetic, curricular, and programming adequacy.* Evaluation of CAI lessons assures that the instruction is effective. Three levels of evaluation are generally recommended for instructional units: one-to-one testing, small-group testing, and field testing. In one-to-one testing, an evaluator usually observes as a student works through a first-draft version of the lesson. The evaluator takes extensive notes and asks the student to think out loud during the session. The lesson is revised based on the findings of the one-to-one testing, after which small groups are observed. These groups should represent the target population, and enough people should participate to assure that the lesson achieves its goals for any significant subgroups within the target population. Data gathered from these small groups form the basis for the revision of the lesson before general distribution. In field testing, the goal is to evaluate the lesson in actual end-user environments. Because the purpose of evaluation is to confirm that the lesson works as planned, it should include analysis of (a) objective-based data—Did the lesson meet its objectives? (b) affective data—Did the students like it? Would they use another lesson like it? and (c) programming attributes—Did the computer program run well? Were there any unresolved branches? Was the speed at which the program ran acceptable? Evaluation is discussed in detail in Chapter 18.

10. *Design screens carefully*. Although the recommendations of many authors discussing screen design appear to be arbitrary, many of the guidelines are justifiable. Heines (1984), for example, has developed several guidelines for the designer of computer frames. Additional guidelines have also been reported by Burke (1982).

Limit the amount of text on the screen. The relatively low resolution of current video monitors can curtail the appropriateness of CAI for displaying textual information. Cohen (1983, p. 11) noted that most video monitors have about half the resolution quality we are accustomed to in printed form:

> Because the print is inherently difficult to read, it is especially important that the formatting and frame display not add to the viewing difficulty. Lines of text must have space between them, long passages should be left to textbooks and magazines, and the screen should be completely clear before each new display, rather than have frames fill up line by line.

In addition to the limits of perception, the desire to motivate students to spend time with CAI instruction and the desire to communicate effectively have implications for screen design as well. Jay (1983) presented the following guidelines for presenting information via CAI:

a. Present one idea at a time, then clear the screen. (An idea, according to Jay, is probably one or two sentences long.)
b. Since processing takes time, either give the learner control of the pacing or allow sufficient time for processing.
c. Eliminate scrolling—people like to think of the screen as turning pages.
d. Use supplemental materials for text-intensive communications.
e. Use concrete rather than abstract language.
f. Use boxes, color, and/or highlighting to accent important information.

11. *Use additional media as appropriate*. Although most learners know how to interact with a textbook, the methods used to access and interact with CAI lessons vary from lesson to lesson. A clear, concise, step-by-step, text-based procedure for lesson implementation is often necessary. Once the student is within the lesson, a reference card should be provided informing the user how to review, exit the lesson, or perform other significant tasks.

Since it is generally inconvenient or impossible to regain access to the CAI lessons after they have been completed, a text-based summary and/or comprehensive notes should be provided for review and reference purposes.

Chapter Summary

We do not know precisely how learning occurs. There are two theories of learning that have provided principles that have been employed to produce more effective instruction.

Based on behavioral and cognitive learning theories, a set of principles was derived that may be used to improve the design of instructional materials. From these principles, implications for the design of effective CAI were derived.

References

BRIGHT, G. W. (1983). Explaining the efficiency of computer assisted instruction. *AEDS Journal*, **16**(3), 144–153.

BURKE, R. L. (1982). *CAI Sourcebook*. Englewood Cliffs, NJ: Prentice-Hall.

CALDWELL, R. M. (1980). Guidelines for developing basic skills instructional materials for use with microcomputer technology. *Educational Technology*, **20**(11), 7–12.

CLEMENT, F. J. (1981). Affective considerations in computer-based education. *Educational Technology*, **21**(10), 28–32.

COHEN, V. B. (1983). Criteria for the evaluation of microcomputer courseware. *Educational Technology*, **23**(1), 9–14.

——— (1985). A reexamination of feedback in computer-based instruction: Implications for instructional design. *Educational Technology*, **25**(1), 33–36.

EISELE, J. E. (1978). Lesson design for computer-based instructional systems. *Educational Technology*, **18**(9), 14–21.

GAGNÉ, R. M. (1970). *The Conditions of Learning* (2nd ed.). New York: Holt, Rinehart, & Winston.

———, and L. J. BRIGGS (1979). *Principles of Instructional Design* (2nd ed.). New York: Holt, Rinehart & Winston.

———, W. WAGER, and A. ROJAS (1981). Planning and authoring computer-assisted instruction lessons. *Educational Technology*, **21**(9), 17–26.

GARHART, C., and M. J. HANNAFIN (1986). The accuracy of cognitive monitoring during computer-based instruction. *Journal of Computer-Based Instruction*, **13**(3), 88–93.

HANNAFIN, M. J. (1984). Guidelines for determining locus of instructional control in the design of computer-assisted instruction. *Journal of Instructional Development*, **7**(3), 6–10.

HEINES, J. M. (1984). *Screen Design Strategies for Computer-Assisted Instruction*. Bedford, MA: Digital Press.

HOUSTON, J. P. (1976). *Fundamentals of Learning*. New York: Academic Press.

JAY, T. B. (1983). The cognitive approach to computer courseware design and evaluation. *Educational Technology*, **32**(1), 22–26.

JURGEMEYER, F. H. (1982). Programmed instruction: Lessons it can teach us. *Educational Technology*, **22**(5), 20–21.

KOLESNIK, W. B. (1976). *Learning: Educational Applications*. Boston: Allyn & Bacon, Inc.

KULHAVY, R. W. (1977). Feedback in written instruction. *Review of Educational Research*, **47**, 211–232.

L'ALLIER, J. J., and R. D. TENNYSON (1980). Principles of instructional design applied to an introductory course on educational computing. *Journal of Computer-Based Instruction*, **7**(2), 26–32.

LOREE, M. R. (1965). *Psychology of Education*. New York: The Ronald Press Company.

MACLACHLAN, J. (1986). Psychologically based techniques for improving learning within computerized tutorials. *Journal of Computer-Based Instruction*, **13**(3), 65–70.

ROSS, S. M. (1984, April). Matching the lesson to the student: Alternative adaptive designs for individualized learning systems. *Journal of Computer-Based Instruction*, **11**, 42–48.

SKINNER, B. F. (1968). *The Technology of Teaching*. New York: Meredith Corporation.

SOLSO, R. L. (1984). *Cognitive Psychology*. New York: Harcourt Brace Jovanovich, Inc.

TENNYSON, R. (1984). Application of artificial intelligence methods to computer-based instructional design: The Minnesota Adaptive Instructional System. *Journal of Instructional Development*, **7**(3), 17–22.

THORNBURG, H. D. (1984). *Introduction to Educational Psychology*. Saint Paul, MN: West Publishing Company.

Related Reading

DENCE, M. (1980). Toward defining the role of CAI: A review. *Educational Technology*, **20**(11), 50–54.

GOETZFRIED, L. L., and M. J. HANNAFIN (1985). The effects of embedded CAI instructional control strategies on the learning and application of mathematics rules. *American Educational Research Journal*, **22**, 273–278.

HANNAFIN, M. J., T. L. PHILLIPS, L. P., RIEBER, and C. GARHART (in press). The effects of orienting activities and cognitive processing time on factual and inferential learning. *Educational Communication and Technology Journal*.

KRAHN, C. G., and M. C. BLANCHAER (1986). Using an advance organizer to improve knowledge application by medical students in computer-based clinical simulations. *Journal of Computer-Based Instruction*, **13**(3), 71–74.

RIEBER, L. P. and M. J. HANNAFIN (1986). The evolution of computer-based instruction: From behavioral to cognitive. *Proceedings of the 28th international conference of the Association for the Development of Computer-Based Instructional Systems*. Bellingham, WA: ADCIS.

SCHLOSS, P. J., P. T. SINDELAR, G. P. CARTWRIGHT, and C. N. SCHLOSS (1986). Efficacy of higher cognitive and factual questions in computer assisted instruction modules. *Journal of Computer-Based Instruction*, **13**(3), 75–79.

Chapter Review Exercises

COMPREHENSION

1. Describe the difference between the behavioral and cognitive learning theories. (See pages 46–49.)

2. List and describe at least five principles derived from learning theory. (See pages 46–49.)

3. List and discuss the eleven implications of principles of learning on the development of CAI. (See pages 49–55 and Table 4.1.)

4. Discuss the characteristics of effective feedback. (See page 52.)

5. Discuss the role of practice in learning. (See page 51.)

6. Discuss the concept of congruence between objectives, instruction, and evaluation. (See page 53.)

7. Discuss the use of learner control in CAI. (See pages 53–54.)

CHAPTER 5

Instructional Systems Design and CAI

Confusion often occurs because many new teacher/authors encounter for the first time both a relatively new approach to instructional design and a new delivery vehicle. The result of this combination seems to be a lack of confidence about where to begin and a misunderstanding of which of the two—instructional design or computer systems—should provide the basis for development of (CAI) materials.

(Eisele, 1978, p. 14)

In Chapter 4 we examined principles derived from educational psychology and their implications for CAI design. Instructional design systems, systematic approaches to the development of instruction in any medium, provide sets of procedures that designers can follow in order to produce instruction based on these principles.

We are strong supporters of instructional design systems. However, development of the knowledge and skill required to understand and apply instructional design creatively and to several media is beyond the scope of this book. Attempts to teach instructional design and other aspects of CAI development have resulted in the problems Eisele described. Many colleges and universities offer one or more courses in the design of instruction. We recommend such courses for the professional designer.

The goal of this chapter is to provide a working knowledge of instructional design, applied specifically to the task of creating computerized instruction. A checklist has been provided, which applies instructional design to CAI. A carpenter doesn't need to know how to build the tools of the profession. The master carpenter modifies tools and becomes expert in using those tools to produce the desired results. In much the same way, by learning to use the tools provided in this book and adjusting them to work most effectively, you will be able to produce sound CAI lessons.

OBJECTIVES

Comprehension

After completing this chapter you will be able to

1. Discuss the meaning of the term *instructional design system*.
2. Name and diagram the phases of the CAI Design Model (CDM).

3. Discuss the flow from phase to phase within the CDM.
4. List at least five activities to be completed or questions to be answered in each phase.
5. Discuss when and how to use the CAI Design Checklist (CDC).
6. Discuss the advantages and disadvantages of a team approach to CAI development.

Application

After completing this chapter you will be able to

Complete sections 1.1–1.4 of the CAI Design Checklist based on a CAI project you are likely to undertake in the near future.

Systematic Approaches to the Design of Instruction

Is it possible to use a single plan to develop instruction on topics as diverse as learning chemical formulas, learning to play a musical instrument, learning to drive an automobile, learning to divide fractions by mixed numbers, and understanding the implications of nuclear war? Is it possible to use a single plan that will produce effective instruction for pre-school children as well as for graduate students and senior citizens? Can it be used in schools, homes, and businesses? For print-based, video-based, or computer-based delivery? Experts would answer yes to all of these questions.

Individuals in the field of instructional systems design (ISD or ID) have developed procedures to produce efficient, effective instruction for a variety of outcomes, learners, environments, and media. Several models have been developed to lead the designer through the process (Briggs and Wager, 1981; Davis, Alexander, and Yelon, 1974; Dick and Carey, 1985; Gagné and Briggs, 1979; Smith and Boyce, 1984). These models differ in a number of ways, but their differences are slight when compared to their similarities.

Instructional design *systems*, as the name implies, are composed of a series of interrelated steps based on principles derived from educational research and theory. Table 5.1 lists steps generally found in instructional design systems.

The initial step in solving any problem is to gain a thorough understanding of it. In solving instructional problems, this involves determining goals and objectives. It then becomes possible to break each objective down further, uncovering several levels of tasks. Once an understanding of all of the skills and knowledge required has been gained, the designer must decide which of these will be included in the lesson and which will be assumed as prerequisites before the lesson begins.

Understanding the instructional task is critical, but so is understanding the constraints under which development and production are to occur. Knowledge of the target population for which the lesson is to be developed, as well as awareness of deadlines, budget, equipment, and human resource availability are also required. After gaining an understanding of the instructional task and the constraints within which work will proceed, the designer generates multiple alternative methods for solving each aspect of the problem. Several ways to achieve each objective are identified, after which the designer selects those with the best probability of

Table 5.1

Steps Generally Included in Instructional Design Systems

- Identification of instructional goals and objectives
- In-depth analysis of the tasks and subtasks involved
- Determination of the prerequisite skills and knowledge required for the lesson to be successful (which skills will be taught and which will be assumed before the lesson begins)
- Identification of the constraints (such as time and budget) within which the product must be developed
- Generation of instructional alternatives
- Selection from among the alternatives generated
- Determination of the sequence in which the tasks are to be achieved
- Development of the instruction
- Testing the accuracy of the program execution
- Evaluation of the instruction
- Revision of the instruction

succeeding, given the task and constraints identified. After the sequence in which the instructional events will occur is determined, development begins. Evaluation of the product occurs during as well as after development, and revisions may be made to the plan or the product at any time.

The steps are generally combined into phases. The number of steps and the number of phases into which the steps are grouped differ from model to model. The CAI design model (CDM) presented in Figure 5.1 combines these activities into four phases: needs assessment, design, development and implementation, and evaluation and revision.

The model generally flows from left to right. Notice that the only pathway from phase to phase is through "Evaluation and Revision." When each of the three phases has been completed, progress is evaluated, and the project may move to the next phase, may return to the current phase for additional attention, or may be returned to a previous phase for modification. Notice also that there is no stopping point. During CAI development, a good deal of time is spent cycling between implementation, evaluation, and revision.

PHASE 1: NEEDS ASSESSMENT

The purpose of needs assessment is to define clearly the specifications of a project. During this phase, the designer develops an understanding of the student for whom the program is to be developed, the environment in which the program will

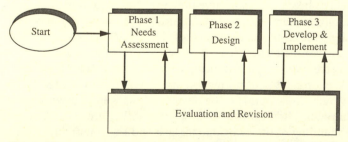

Figure 5.1

The CAI design model (CDM).

be used, the constraints within which the program will be developed, the goals and objectives the program is to achieve, and the assessment items that will be used to determine the extent to which objectives have been met. The designer identifies the skills and knowledge the student is to acquire during the lesson, as well as those the student must possess *prior to beginning* the lesson. Chapters 7 and 8 present more detailed accounts of task analysis and the writing of objectives.

When needs assessment has been completed, attention is shifted to the evaluation and revision phase, where needs assessment findings are scrutinized. If necessary, the project is returned to the needs assessment phase for additional information.

PHASE 2: DESIGN

After completing the needs assessment, the designer understands the problem more completely. Expectations have been clarified, resources and constraints have been identified, and other parameters of the problem have been defined. The purpose of phase 2 is to identify and document the best means of achieving the desired results.

The first step is to determine the sequence in which the objectives will be met. After the sequence has been determined, several potential solutions are considered *for each objective identified during the needs assessment.* After potential solutions have been identified for an objective, the best solution is selected, given the nature of the problem. For example, the options generated for a unit on adding fractions might include illustrating the concept using a number line, illustrating the concept using segments of a pie, or conveying the concept using only text without any illustrations. Once these options have been identified, one may be selected based both on the information gained during needs assessment and on the probability of success.

During this phase, the designer determines the sequence in which the objectives will be met, expands the list of objectives and assessment items to include a description of the activities that will meet each objective, and transfers the entire lesson to storyboards. Storyboards are illustrations depicting each change to the computer screen and conveying other important information to the reviewers and programmers. A sample storyboard is depicted in Figure 5.2.

At the top of the storyboard, the designer indicates the number of the objective that the screen supports, the screen number, and the number of screens that relate to the objective. The screen depicted is the third of seven screens used to achieve objective number four. In this example, the body of the storyboard illustrates how the screen will look *at the end* of the sequence. This screen has a title, "Dividing by Fractions," which is repeated on all of the screens for this objective. Below the title, the rule is stated, after which two examples are displayed. As the comments to the programmer indicate, the examples are displayed using a technique sometimes called progressive disclosure, in which sections of the screen are displayed in sequence. In this example, the title and rule are displayed first. The student reads the title and rule and then presses the spacebar. Initially, only the problem is displayed. After a three-second pause, the solution begins by flashing the multiplication sign and the inverted fraction. After three more seconds, the problem is completed, and the "Press Spacebar to Continue" prompt returns. When the student responds, a second problem is displayed in the same manner. Although the notes to the programmer are quite complete in this example,

Figure 5.2
A sample storyboard.

Objective # __4__   Board # __3__ of __7__

DIVIDING BY FRACTIONS

RULE: DIVIDING BY A FRACTION PRODUCES THE

SAME RESULT AS MULTIPLYING BY ITS INVERSE.

FOR EXAMPLE: $\dfrac{3}{4} \div \dfrac{1}{8} = \dfrac{3}{4} \times \dfrac{8}{1} = \dfrac{24}{4} = 6$

ANOTHER EXAMPLE: $\dfrac{2}{3} \div \dfrac{5}{6} = \dfrac{2}{3} \times \dfrac{6}{5} = \dfrac{12}{15} = \dfrac{4}{5}$

—PRESS SPACEBAR TO CONTINUE—

Preceding Storyboard(s): _____4 - 2_____

Following Storyboard: _____4 - 4_____

Action Required to Advance: _____SPACEBAR_____

Comments: *Step 1 = Title + Rule only — Student presses spacebar*
Step 2 = "For example: ¾ ÷ ⅛ =" followed by 3 second
pause
Step 3 = "¾ × 8/1" with "× 8/1" flashing — 3 second pause
Step 4 = complete solution to first problem — spacebar —
Step 5 - 7 = Display second problem in same manner.

abbreviations and other conventions allow the designer and programmer to communicate more efficiently.

After illustrating the content of the lesson, the designer determines the extent to which performance will be monitored and reviews the storyboards to identify methods to maximize interaction and to increase the program's ability to account for individual differences.

Once phase 2 activities have been completed, the status is reviewed during the evaluation and revision cycle, where the quality and validity of activities from both phases 1 and 2 are assessed. Purcell (1984) recommends a "walk-through," where the design is explained to a team of evaluators who provide feedback before programming begins. The project may be redirected to either needs assessment or design phases if additional effort is deemed necessary, or it may proceed to phase 3 for development and implementation.

PHASE 3: DEVELOPMENT AND IMPLEMENTATION

As phase 3 begins, the lesson exists only on paper. The activities in phase 3 convert the lesson from paper to the point at which it is actually used by students in the target environment. Activities during this phase include flowcharting, authoring and/or programming, testing and debugging, documenting lesson procedures, formative evaluation, summative evaluation, and revision. The computer program is produced during this phase. The final product is a CAI lesson in the form of a computer program or set of programs that accomplishes the prescribed goals and objectives within the constraints identified during needs assessment.

The first step during phase 3 is the development of a flowchart, a diagram indicating the possible paths through the lesson. Although sophisticated flowcharting conventions are often used by experienced programmers, the primary goal is for both programmer and designer to understand the lesson execution "blueprint."

After completing a lesson flowchart, authoring or programming the lesson may begin. This step involves the writing of commands needed to accomplish the conditions and actions prescribed in the flowchart and illustrated in the storyboards. Authoring, an alternative to programming which results in an educational computer program without requiring a general-purpose programming language, is discussed in depth in Chapter 14.

After the program has been developed, it must be tested thoroughly. Testing in this context refers to an evaluation of program execution, not to the ability to produce desired educational outcomes.

Lesson developers must also inform potential users of the objectives of the lesson, the prerequisite skills and knowledge required to be successful, lesson use, the computer system(s) on which the lesson will run, and any additional instructions required to implement the lesson. By developing the clear, concise documentation prior to evaluation, it becomes possible to test the effectiveness of the documentation as well as the lesson.

After verification that the program executes flawlessly and that necessary documentation has been developed, the goal is to evaluate the lesson's ability to meet the prescribed objectives. *Formative evaluation* refers to evaluation that takes place *while the program is being developed*. By allowing the evaluator to watch closely while actual members of the target population use the product, formative evaluation identifies areas of the lesson that are in need of revision, while it is still relatively simple and inexpensive to modify the lesson.

After the lesson has been revised according to the information gained during en-route evaluation, a final, or summative, evaluation validates the fact that the lesson performs as required. Several alternatives used in CAI lesson evaluation are discussed in Chapter 18.

The CAI Design Checklist

There are many steps involved in the successful design and development of a CAI lesson. The CAI Design checklist (CDC), included as Figure 5.3, prescribes the principal steps of the process.

Modify the CDC to meet your needs by adding, deleting, and rearranging steps.

Figure 5.3
The CAI design checklist (CDC.)

Phase 1.   Needs Assessment
   1.1.   Describe the student for whom the lesson will be written.

   1.1.1.   Age range: __12__ to __16__

   1.1.2.   Reading level: 1   2   3   4   5 (6) 7   8   9   10   Adult

   1.1.3.   Other significant characteristics:

   They like game formats and animated graphics.

   1.2.   Describe the environment in which the lesson is to be used.

   1.2.1.   Is supervision available to start the lesson? Y (N)

   To answer questions? Y (N)

   1.2.2.   Would music or sound pose a problem for others? Y (N)

   1.2.3.   Describe the setting(s) in which the lesson will be used:

   ① Computer labs
   ② Classrooms
   ③ Student can take the lesson home

   1.2.4.   On what computer system(s) must the lesson run? _____
   Apple II Microcomputers

   1.3.   Describe the constraints within which the lesson must be developed:
   1.3.1.   Time:
   1.3.1.1.   Date the project must be ready for

   distribution: __March 15th__

Figure 5.3 (*Continued*)

1.3.1.2. Date the project must be ready for summative

evaluation: <u>Feb. 1ST</u>

1.3.1.3. Date the project must be ready for

testing: <u>Jan. 3rd</u>

1.3.1.4. Date the design must be ready for

programming: <u>Nov. 20</u>

1.3.1.5. Date the needs assessment must be

complete: <u>Oct. 25</u>

1.3.2. Fiscal:
1.3.2.1. Total cost of the project not to exceed:

<u>$1,500⁰⁰</u>

1.3.3. Resource:
1.3.3.1. How many machines will be available for

development and testing? <u>1 for development, 10</u>

<u>for testing</u>

1.3.3.2. What people will be involved in the development of the lesson, and in what capacity?

Name:	Role:
Wilma Daniels	Subject Matter Expert
Sara Meagher	Inst. Designer
Doug Archer	Programmer
Carolyn McMain	Test Coordinator
Walt Wright	Evaluator

Figure 5.3 (Continued)

1.4. List the goals of the lesson:

① The student will understand how <u>chords</u> are formed.

② The student will learn to <u>name notes</u> as they are played.

③ The student will be able to understand how <u>scales</u> are formed.

1.5. List the objectives of the lesson and an assessment item for each.

Obj. # Objective (Conditions/Action/Quality)

1 Given the tonic note, the student will provide the third note of the major triad within two attempts.

Assessment item: "You are building a major triad. The tonic note is the note F below middle C. Find the third note of the triad."

Obj. # Objective (Conditions/Action/Quality)

2 Given the note upon which a scale is built, the student will provide the 4th note within 2 attempts.

Assessment item: "What is the 4th note of a scale built on the note D^b just above middle C?"

Figure 5.3 (*Continued*)

Obj. #   Objective (Conditions/Action/Quality)

3   Given the note upon which a 7th chord is built, the student will provide the 7th within 3 attempts.

Assessment item: "Find the 7th in a 7th chord built on the note A^b below middle C."

Objectives/Assessments: Page **1** of **4**

1.6.   List the skills and knowledge the student must bring to the lesson in order to be successful:

Must understand:
1. major triad
2. tonic note
3. layout of a piano keyboard

Must read at the 6th grade level or above.

Evaluation and Revision of Phase 1.

✓ Student characteristics are adequately understood.

✓ The environment(s) in which the lesson will be used is/are understood.

✓ The constraints under which the lesson is to be developed are understood and are reasonable.

✓ The objectives of the lesson are clear, measurable, and attainable.

Figure 5.3 (*Continued*)

✓ Assessment items are congruent with the objectives.

✓ List of prerequisite skills required of the learner is complete.

✓ The resources (human, fiscal, and computer) available are appropriate for the size of the task.

Phase 2. Design
   2.1. Sequencing the objectives
        2.1.1. Examine the objectives listed in section 1.5 and place the objective numbers below to indicate the sequence in which they will be met.

Lesson Sequence	Objective #	Lesson Sequence	Objective #	Lesson Sequence	Objective #
1	1	18	____	35	____
2	3	19	____	36	____
3	4	20	____	37	____
4	2	21	____	38	____
5	5	22	____	39	____
6	12	23	____	40	____
7	11	24	____	41	____
8	6	25	____	42	____
9	7	26	____	43	____
10	8	27	____	44	____
11	10	28	____	45	____
12	9	29	____	46	____
13	____	30	____	47	____
14	____	31	____	48	____
15	____	32	____	49	____

Figure 5.3 (*Continued*)

Lesson Sequence	Objective #	Lesson Sequence	Objective #	Lesson Sequence	Objective #
16	_____	33	_____	50	_____
17	_____	34	_____		

2.2. Description of Activities to Meet Objectives

✓ 2.2.1. Examine each objective, generate multiple methods of attaining that objective, and select the best.

✓ 2.2.2. Determine the method by which remedial instruction will be presented.

2.2.3. Record the decisions from steps 2.2.1 and 2.2.2 below:

Objective #: __1__ Topic: 3rd note of major triad

Primary means of achieving the objective: Student will control the movement of an animated figure across a keyboard on the screen, and will stop on the correct note. Computer will play the student's triad and the correct answer.

Method in which remediation will be presented: Correct answer will be presented graphically, by highlighting appropriate keys as the notes are played. A brief explanation will follow.

2.3. Storyboarding
2.3.1. Using the forms provided, develop a set of storyboards for each objective.
2.3.2. Conduct a "walk-through" with team members and designated others.

Figure 5.3 (*Continued*)

Storyboard Form for Presentation Frame

Objective # __2__   Board # __3__ of __7__

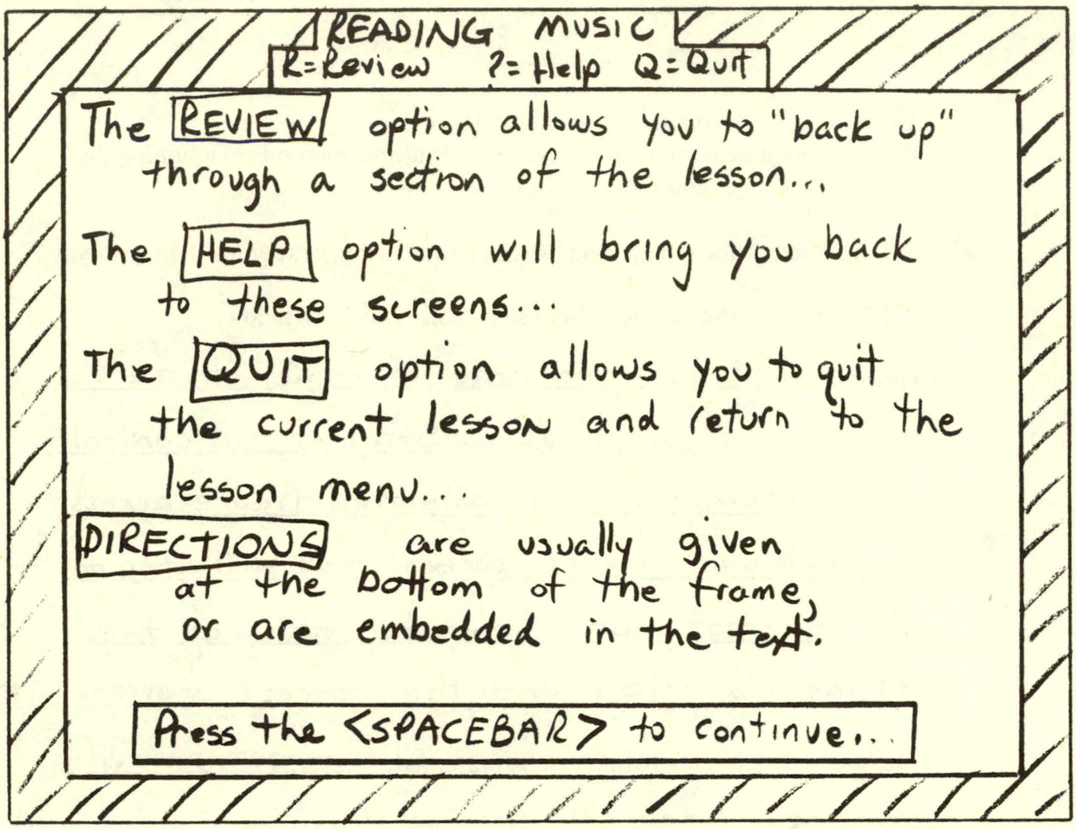

```
        READING MUSIC
       R=Review   ?=Help  Q=Quit

The REVIEW option allows you to "back up"
    through a section of the lesson...

The HELP option will bring you back
    to these screens...

The QUIT option allows you to quit
    the current lesson and return to the
    lesson menu...

DIRECTIONS      are usually given
    at the bottom of the frame,
    or are embedded in the text.

    Press the <SPACEBAR> to continue...
```

Preceding Storyboard(s): _____2 – 2_____

Following Storyboard: _____2 – 4_____

Action Required to Advance: __<SPACEBAR> (after each option)__

Comments: __Display each option statement__
__sequentially until the full screen is complete.__
__Keywords (REVIEW, HELP, QUIT, DIRECTIONS) to__
__be inversed for amplification effect.__

Figure 5.3 (*Continued*)

Storyboard Form for Menu/Question Frame

Objective # __8__   Frame # __4__ of __10__

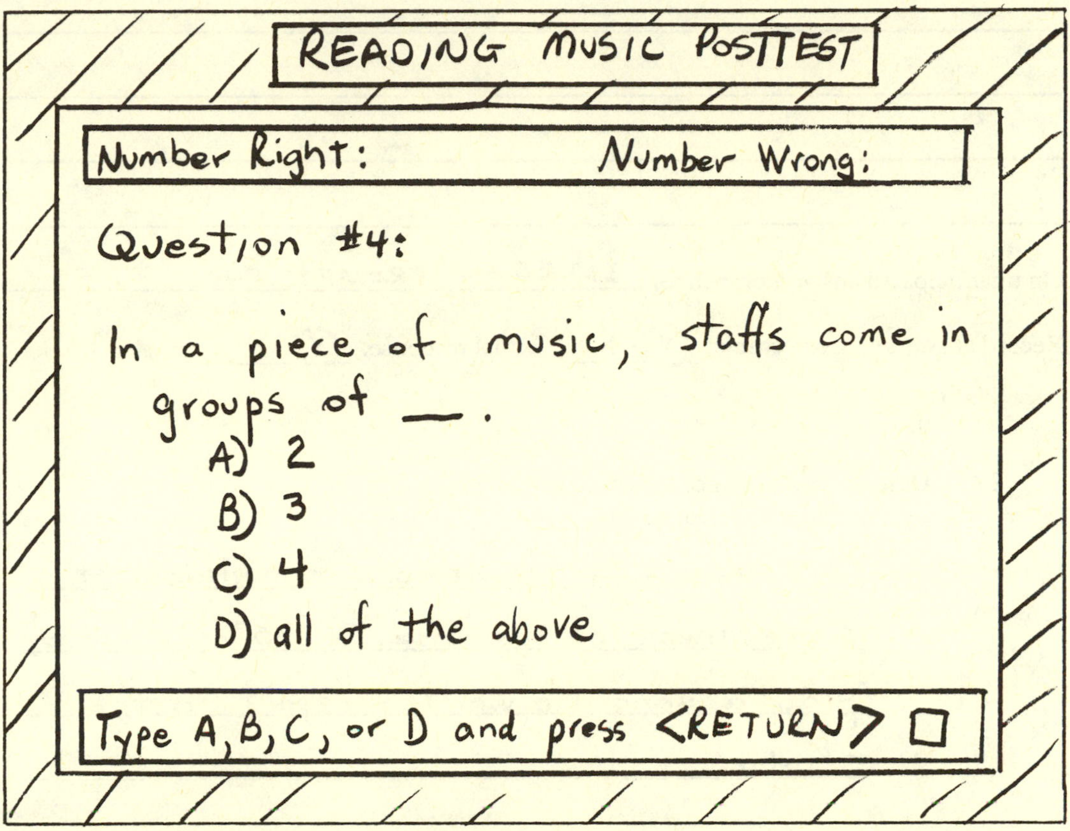

```
//////////////////////////////////////////////////////
//  ┌─────────────────────────────────────────┐  /
// /│    READING  MUSIC  POSTTEST    │  /
//  └─────────────────────────────────────────┘   /
//  ┌──────────────────────────────────────────┐  /
// / │ ┌──────────────────┐    ┌─────────────┐ │ //
//   │ │ Number Right:    │    │Number Wrong:│ │ //
//   │ └──────────────────┘    └─────────────┘ │ //
//   │                                          │ //
//   │  Question #4:                            │ //
//   │                                          │ //
//   │  In a piece of music, staffs come in     │ //
//   │     groups of __ .                       │ //
//   │        A) 2                              │ //
//   │        B) 3                              │ //
//   │        C) 4                              │ //
//   │        D) all of the above               │ //
//   │                                          │ //
//   │ ┌──────────────────────────────────────┐│ //
//   │ │Type A,B,C, or D and press <RETURN> □ ││ //
//   │ └──────────────────────────────────────┘│ //
//   └──────────────────────────────────────────┘ //
//////////////////////////////////////////////////////
```

Preceding storyboard(s): _____ __8 - 3__ _____

Anticipated answers:	*On this answer branch to:*
A	PART CORRECT → B/C SUBS
B	PART CORRECT → A/C SUBS
C	PART CORRECT → A/B SUBS
D	CORRECT SUB → 8 - 5

Figure 5.3 (*Continued*)

_____   _____

_____   _____

_____   _____

_____   _____

_____   _____

On unanticipated answer, branch to: _ILLEGAL   PROMPT   SUB_____

Record answers?   Correctness: ⓨ N   Actual response: ⓨ N

   2.4.   Describe performance reports to be provided:
       2.4.1.   Student Performance:

           2.4.1.1.   To the student: *Immediate knowledge of correctness of response. If 90% or better, play a song. No written report to the student.*

_____

_____

           2.4.1.2.   To the Teacher or Supervisor: _____ *NONE*

_____

_____

       2.4.2.   Lesson Performance:
           2.4.2.1.   To the Teacher or Supervisor: _____ *NONE*

_____

_____

_____

_____

Figure 5.3 (*Continued*)

2.4.2.2. To the lesson's Designer(s) <u>Track the number of responses each student makes for each item.</u>

✓ 2.5. Make another pass through the storyboards modifying them to increase inter-activity and individualization.

Evaluation and Revision of Phase 2.

✓ Sequence of objectives is appropriate (progresses from easy to more difficult, no unde-fined terms or necessary concepts covered later than needed, etc.).

✓ Activities listed for primary instruction and for remediation for each objective seem adequate to meet instructional needs.

✓ Storyboards communicate the designer's intent unambiguously so that the programmer will be able to faithfully execute the designer's plan.

✓ Requirements for performance tracking are conveyed clearly.

✓ Lesson involves the learner by requiring meaningful interactions as opposed to a series of automatic or contrived responses.

✓ The lesson adapts to the needs of individual students.

≈ The student is made aware of the lesson's objectives. (needs work)

✓ The student is made aware of prerequisite skills required.

✓ The lesson provides adequate remediation and re-teaching.

✓ The lesson provides an adequate amount of learner control.

✓ The lesson will maintain the student's interest.

✓ The instructions are clear.

✓ The actions required of the student are unambiguous and easy to understand.

✓ The student is made aware of the correctness of each response.

Figure 5.3 (*Continued*)

✓ Positive feedback is not overdone.

✓ Negative feedback is informative but not punitive.

✓ Feedback is varied.

✓ Feedback motivates the student to respond correctly.

✓ The lesson does not require an inordinate amount of Teacher / Supervisor involvement.

✓ Test items match instructional objectives.

✓ Questions are unambiguous and do not use unfamiliar terminology.

✓ Answer judging is thorough. Correct alternatives to the most likely answer are considered correct, anticipated incorrect answers are considered incorrect, and the student is asked to redo unanticipated answers.

✓ Responses required do not interfere with the student's ability to answer. For example, inability to type is not misinterpreted as inability to generate the correct answer.

✓ The lesson uses graphics appropriately to eliminate overuse of text.

✓ Highlighting is used to direct the student's attention

✓ The lesson provides adequate opportunity to practice.

Additional Comments on Phase 2 Work:

Nice design! Good collaboration between subject matter expert and instructional designer.

Phase 3. Development and Implementation

✓ 3.1. Flowcharting

   ✓ 3.1.1. Develop the flowchart.

   ✓ 3.1.2. Programmer and Designer review the flowchart.

✓ 3.2. Determine the programming language or authoring system or language which will be used to produce the lesson. (Remember that the computer system on which the lesson is to run and cost constraints should be major considerations in this decision.)

Figure 5.3 (*Continued*)

    ✓ 3.2.1. Which programming language or authoring system or language will be

        used? <u>Super PILOT</u>

3.3. Set a date for preliminary review of first module of the lesson, to take place on the computer system for which the lesson is being developed. (12/15)

✓ 3.4. Produce first module.

✓ 3.5. Review first module to verify that designer's intentions are being implemented by the programmer, and that any questions are answered before the entire lesson is done incorrectly.

✓ 3.6. Make indicated revisions to the first module. (done 12/20)

✓ 3.7. Produce remaining modules.

✓ 3.8. Test program to assure flawless program logic.

✓ 3.9. Designer takes entire lesson to validate that the plan was implemented as intended.

✓ 3.10. One to one formative evaluation (See Chapter 17 for more detail on evaluating CAI)

    ✓ 3.10.1. Evaluate

    ✓ 3.10.2. Report results

    ✓ 3.10.3. Identify problems

    ✓ 3.11. Revise as indicated

    ✓ 3.12. Small group evaluation

    ✓ 3.12.1. Evaluate

    ✓ 3.12.2. Report results

    ✓ 3.12.3. Identify problems

    ✓ 3.13. Revise as indicated

    ✓ 3.14. Field test

    ✓ 3.14.1. Evaluate

    ✓ 3.14.2. Report results

    ✓ 3.14.3. Identify problems

Figure 5.3 (*Continued*)

✓ 3.15. Revise as indicated

✓ 3.16. Revise the flowchart to reflect any changes made since it was first developed

✓ 3.17. Revise the storyboards to reflect any changes

✓ 3.18. Develop appropriate documentation to accompany the lesson.

    ✓ 3.18.1. Teacher/Supervisor level documentation

    ✓ 3.18.2. Student level documentation

    ✓ 3.18.3. Programmer level documentation (for maintenance purposes)

Evaluation and Revision of Phase 3.

✓ The lesson design has been implemented faithfully. (as modified)

✓ The lesson has been thoroughly tested and has been proven to run adequately on the desired computer system(s) and to be free from errors of program logic.

✓ The documentation accompanying the lesson provides adequate information for the Teacher/Supervisor to determine appropriate uses for the program.

✓ The instructions allow the student to use the lesson with minimal or no Teacher/Supervisor involvement.

✓ The lesson has been adequately evaluated and meets its objectives.

✓ Students like the lesson.

Individual Development vs. the Development Team

There has been considerable discussion concerning the benefits associated with a team approach to the development of CAI. Teams generally consist of one or more instructional designers, content experts, programmers, and evaluators. Proponents of development teams (Applebaum, 1985; Bork, 1984; Dimas, 1978; Hartman, 1981; Roblyer, 1983) believe that a team approach to CAI design offers the ability to divide responsibility, resulting in shorter development times and reduced individual burdens. The use of experts in each aspect of product development provides a system of checks and balances, which tends to yield better products.

Disadvantages have also been associated with a team approach. Such disadvantages have included higher development costs, a lack of "ownership" felt by team members, divergence of opinion, and quality dragged down by the weakest member of the team. There may also be communication problems among different team members, as well as scheduling complications.

Since many of the disadvantages may be avoided, the advantages of a team approach often outweigh the disadvantages. Few people are qualified to assume multiple roles, and even fewer have the time to do so. A team approach capitalizes on the strengths of the team members, and the momentum provided by the team can maintain progress on projects that might have faltered due to waning interest or energy.

In instances where local resources preclude the use of a development team, consider involving another person to evaluate decisions made during each phase. Even an evaluator with no knowledge of CAI design but an understanding of the educational process can identify shortcomings and provide helpful suggestions to improve the lesson and reduce time-consuming revisions. If it is impossible to assemble a team or even an additional evaluator, the quality of CAI products can be improved if you, as the sole designer, consciously perform the functions normally assigned to different experts to the best of your ability.

Chapter Summary

According to Roblyer (1981, p. 174), "Even now, when it is widely recognized that programming expertise alone is not enough in courseware development, there still appears to be an emphasis on 'authoring CAI programs' rather than on 'designing instructional courseware.'" If computers are to have significant impact on education, the quality of available courseware must improve. Use of an instructional system design model can help to improve the quality of the CAI produced.

This chapter described instructional design systems as a series of interrelated steps based on principles derived from educational research and theory. By following these steps, the designer can be more confident that the resulting instruction will be appropriate for the students, environments, and computer systems for which it was designed.

The CAI design model (CDM) classified the steps of instructional design systems into four phases: needs assessment, design, development and implementation, and evaluation and revision. Adherence to the CAI design checklist (CDC), a set of activities that proceeds from planning through design and development, can also improve CAI lessons. It is suggested that this tool be modified to meet your needs by adding items, deleting items, and modifying the sequence of items as appropriate.

For some time, CAI authorities have warned that more attention must be paid to instructional design (Hazen, 1985; Kearsley, 1984; Leiblum, 1984; Splittgerber, 1979). CAI will be successful or will fail depending on the lesson design. Devote the effort required to ensure success.

References

APPLEBAUM, W. R. (1985). Course-centered development: A team approach to CBT. *Data Training*, **4**(4) 26–27.

BORK, A. (1984). Producing computer-based learning material at the educational technology center. *Journal of Computer-Based Instruction*, **11**(3), 78–81.

✳ BRIGGS, L. J., and W. W. WAGER (1981). *Handbook of Procedures for the Design of Instruction* (2nd ed.). Englewood Cliffs, NJ: Educational Technology Publications.

DAVIS, R. H., L. T. ALEXANDER, and S. L. YELON (1974). *Learning System Design: An Approach to the Improvement of Instruction*. New York: McGraw-Hill.

✳ DICK, W., AND L. CAREY, (1985). *The Systematic Design of Instruction*. Glenview, IL: Scott, Foresman and Co.

DIMAS, C. (1978). A strategy for developing CAI. *Educational Technology*, **18**(4), 26–29.

EISELE, J. E. (1978). Lesson design for computer-based instructional systems. *Educational Technology*, **18**(9), 14–21.

✳ GAGNÉ. R. M., and L. J. BRIGGS (1979). *Principles of Instructional Design* (2nd ed.). New York: Holt, Rinehart and Winston.

HARTMAN, J. (1981). A systematic approach to the design of computer assisted instruction materials. *Technological Horizons in Education*, **8**(2), 43–45.

HAZEN, M. (1985). Instructional software design principles. *Educational Technology*, **25**(11) 18–23.

KEARSLEY, G. (1984). Authoring tools: An introduction. *Journal of Computer-Based Instruction*, **11**(3), 67.

LEIBLUM, M. D. (1984). Some principles of computer-assisted instruction, or how to tame the flashing beast. *Educational Technology*, **24**(3), 16–18.

PURCELL, G. A. (1984). Walking it through: Preventitive planning for cbt courses. *Training News*, **6**(3), 11.

ROBLYER, M. D. (1981). Instructional design versus authoring of courseware: Some critical differences. *AEDS Journal*, **14**(4), 173–181.

———. (1983). The case for and against teacher-developed microcomputer courseware. *Educational Technology*, **23**(1), 14–17.

SMITH, P. L., and B. A. BOYCE (1984). Instructional design considerations in the development of computer-assisted instruction. *Educational Technology*, **24**(7), 5–10.

SPLITTGERBER, F. L. (1979). Computer-based instruction: A revolution in the making? *Educational Technology*, **19**(1), 20–26.

WAGER, W. (1982). Design considerations for instructional computing programs. *Journal of Educational Technology Systems*, **10**, 261–270.

Chapter Review Exercises

COMPREHENSION

1. Discuss the meaning of the term *instructional design system*. (See pages 59–60.)

2. Name and diagram the phases of the CAI design model (CDM). (See Figure 5.1.)

3. Discuss the flow from phase to phase within the CDM. (See page 60.)

4. List at least five activities to be completed or questions to be answered in each phase. (See Figure 5.3.)

5. Discuss when and how to use the CAI design checklist (CDC). (See page 64.)

6. Discuss the advantages and disadvantages of a team approach to CAI development. (See pages 76–77.)

APPLICATION

1. Choose a topic for which you are about to develop a CAI lesson. Complete sections 1.1–1.4 of the CAI design checklist based on this topic. (See Figure 5.3.)

III

Planning for CAI

Several studies have demonstrated CAI to be more efficient and effective than traditional methods of instruction. Why should this be true?

Several factors combine to produce such results, many of which were discussed in Section I. But perhaps the most significant factor in these studies has been the careful planning used in the preparation of CAI materials. In most cases, studies were conducted by professional educators or researchers, who developed the lessons based on years of relevant training and experience.

In this section, we introduce techniques to guide you through phase 1 of the CAI design model, the planning of CAI lessons. Although aimed specifically at CAI development, the activities are applicable to the development of instruction using other media as well.

SECTION GOALS

After completing this section you will

1. Determine, before development begins, whether CAI will be an appropriate solution to a specific instructional problem.
2. Analyze learning tasks to ensure that all important topics are identified and addressed during the lesson.
3. Write sound instructional objectives that identify what will be accomplished and communicate lesson intent to other members of the development team as well as to the students and teachers who use the lesson.

CHAPTER 6

Determining the Appropriateness of Computers in Instruction

To a man with a hammer every problem tends to look like a nail.

Anonymous

CAI cannot be the answer to all educational problems. As discussed earlier, CAI is a delivery system with unique sets of advantages and disadvantages. Even when CAI is a viable instructional alternative, there may be more cost-effective methods. Critics of CAI often cite simpler solutions that might be used to reach the same goal, suggesting that CAI proponents often apply "$20,000 worth of computer and program to solve a $200 problem" (Roblyer, 1981, p. 49).

This chapter focuses on methods for the identification of educational problems for which CAI is an appropriate solution, those for which it is not, and those for which a combination of CAI and other educational media is most appropriate.

OBJECTIVES

Comprehension

After completing this chapter you will be able to

1. List at least five questions to ask in determining whether or not CAI is a viable instructional medium.
2. List at least four categories of cost savings often associated with the use of CAI.

Application

After completing this chapter you will be able to

1. Use a quick screening device to determine whether CAI is a viable alternative for the solution of an instructional problem.
2. Use the media selection guide to determine the best medium for a given instructional task.

The selection of appropriate educational media can be deceptively complex. Long before CAI was available, instructional developers grappled with the question of which instructional option to use. Many factors are involved in determining the "best" option, and the importance of these factors varies according to environmental, student, and task characteristics. To automate the decision-making process, guidelines and checklists were developed (Reiser and Gagné, 1982). In this chapter, we present two methods for determining the appropriateness of CAI: The first is a quick test; the second, a more complete analysis of the benefits of CAI as compared to other instructional media.

A Quick Assessment of the Appropriateness of CAI

Yarusso (1984, pp. 24–25) identified two basic considerations in determining the appropriateness of CAI for training applications: (1) the objectives of the training and (2) cost effectiveness. According to Yarusso, if the answer is yes to the following questions, then the defined objectives may be appropriately taught through CAI.

1. *Will the training be relatively stable?* Yarusso proposes that topics requiring frequent revision are not well suited for CAI. The longer development times for CAI suggest that the content of a volatile lesson may change while the lesson is being developed or shortly after it has been released. The contents of a slide/tape program, for example, may be modified more easily, often by a single developer. By adding or deleting a few slides, recording some new information, and rerecording the sound track, the lesson may be updated. Changes in CAI lessons, on the other hand, require the efforts of a team of people and reintroduce the requirement for extensive testing to ensure that all aspects of the lesson function properly.

2. *Do the objectives imply that knowledge (as opposed to skills, concepts, or rules) is a secondary focus of the training content?* Yarusso noted that a knowledge-based program is not likely to make use of the unique capabilities of CAI. When computers are employed to deliver knowledge, they are often underutilized as glorified page turners. Unless the computer's ability to track and manage the student progress through the course is critical, there may be easier and less expensive alternatives to deliver knowledge-based training. The development of concepts or skills, on the other hand, is often a challenge that requires designers to capitalize on CAI's ability to involve the student. Such lessons generally result in meaningful exchanges between the student and the computer, through which learning is enhanced significantly to justify the additional time and expense involved in the design and production of CAI.

3. *Do the objectives imply that significant instructor/trainee or trainee/trainee interactions will have minimal impact on achieving the desired outcomes?* If interaction among people plays a critical role in the learning process, as is the case with topics such as interviewing, negotiating, sales training, or management development training, then CAI by itself may not be the best alternative. Consider combining methods. In interviewing skills training, for example, the designer may choose to

use CAI to teach the skills and concepts; may employ text-based training or a job aid such as an interviewing form or list of questions to communicate knowledge of what to ask; and may incorporate role-play situations, during which an instructor and the student simulate the interviewing process. The instructor may then review progress and assist the student with difficulties encountered during any aspect of the lesson.

4. *Do the objectives suggest that trainees could take a branching path through the content?* One of CAI's principal advantages is its ability to individualize. When this capability is not important, the topic should be handled appropriately with conventional linear approaches which are easier and less expensive to develop. Because branching may be employed to provide remediation when a student has not mastered an objective and to eliminate instruction on topics the student has mastered before the lesson began, it is difficult to identify instances in which branching could not make instruction more efficient or more effective. The question really becomes whether linear alternatives could produce learning that is acceptable when cost and time are taken into account.

5. *Do the objectives require the trainee to learn something other than physical skills?* It is difficult, if not impossible, to teach certain physical skills through CAI. For example, imagine the effort involved in teaching a student to dance, to swim, or to use a complex tool with CAI. Even where possible, it may be more efficient to use modeling or hands-on training to achieve such results.

6. *Is CAI a cost-effective alternative?* When one is using CAI, costs may be deceptive. Development time for CAI is often surprisingly long. Hardware costs are often considerably higher than expected, especially when they include support features such as special tables for the equipment and optional peripheral devices such as touch screens, disk drives, or printers.

On the other hand, cost savings provided by CAI are also deceptive. Remember to include savings in teacher time. When the student is an employee paid during training, savings in the areas of salary, travel expenses, lodging, meals, and time during which the employee's job goes undone may also be considered. Additional cost savings may be realized during the duplication and distribution of CAI materials. It is often much cheaper to duplicate a diskette than to print a text-based lesson, and it is less expensive to mail a diskette or to communicate its contents electronically than to ship text, video, or slide-based lessons. Facilities and equipment cost savings may also be realized when CAI eliminates the requirement for classrooms or expensive equipment simulated by inexpensive microcomputers.

Figure 6.1 combines these questions to evaluate the viability of CAI for a given project. Do not consider a single "no" as an indication that CAI is inappropriate. Even several negative answers should not necessarily preclude the use of CAI. Such answers simply indicate that care should be exercised to consider alternatives, such as combining CAI with other media to achieve the desired results.

A More Complete Assessment

By answering the preceding questions and looking at cost effectiveness, it is possible to determine whether or not CAI is a viable alternative. However, only through a more extensive examination can it be determined whether or not CAI is the *best* option available. In the remainder of this chapter, we focus on the demands

Figure 6.1
A quick test of the viability of CAI

Complete this form by circling *Y* for *Yes* or *N* for *No* for each question. If responses are negative, consider the combination of CAI with other media or the use of other media instead of CAI.

Objectives

(Y) N   Is the topic relatively stable?

(Y) N   Is the transmission of knowledge of *secondary* importance?

(Y) N   Is the role of person-to-person interaction *minimal* in achieving the objectives?

(Y) N   Does the topic suggest a branching path through the lesson?

(Y) N   Does the lesson require learning *other than* physical skills?

(Y   N)   Can the learner read well enough to make CAI a plausible solution?
               (We'll need to watch out for reading level!)

Cost Effectiveness

(Y) N   Does initial analysis of development, production, distribution, and delivery costs seem to indicate the use of CAI?

that learning tasks place on instructional media and on the capacity of media to meet these demands.

Media Selection

Locatis and Atkinson (1976, p. 19) analyzed the appropriateness of instructional media according to three sets of criteria: (1) the "capacity of media to accommodate instruction" (their ability to achieve instructional objectives), (2) "the compatibility of media with the user environment," and (3) "trade-offs that must be made between media effectiveness and media costs."

After information has been accumulated during needs assessment, the designer matches characteristics of the learning task with characteristics of instructional media. Once the lesson objectives have been categorized as developing some combination of physical skills, knowledge, concepts, or rules, the designer may begin to evaluate a medium's appropriateness. For example, neither text-based nor computerized instruction is an effective way to achieve the acquisition of physical skills. The designer also selects from among the different ways in which information may be presented, determining whether the communication will be largely verbal, auditory, or visual and whether motion is required. If the communication is largely verbal or visual but does not require extensive use of written text or use of realistic images or motion, CAI may be an effective alternative.

The responses to be provided by the learner must also be defined. The designer must determine whether the student is to perform a physical act, to respond verbally, to respond in writing, or to respond in yet another manner. Because CAI may accept and evaluate a variety of inputs from the student, it generally gains favor when the designer determines that student response serves an important function during learning. The designer must also consider the importance of providing the student with knowledge of results during and after the instruction. When students are responding during learning, the instructional medium should be capable of returning information about the correctness of the response. The designer must also consider the importance of the ability to adapt the instruction to differing levels of preparedness and performance. If the ability to provide flexible, adaptive instruction is important, then instructor-led, CAI, and programmed learning activities gain favor.

Next the designer evaluates the environment in which the lesson will be used. The location in which the lesson is to be used, the amount of time the lesson is likely to require, and the time of day during which the lesson will generally be used influence the appropriateness of educational media. For example, if the instruction is to be completed by the student outside the classroom environment or at times when equipment is not available, CAI and other equipment-constrained media may be less appropriate than text-based instruction.

Characteristics of the learner are also important during media selection. The presence or absence of strong verbal and reading skills and the willingness and ability to learn independently will influence the designer's media-selection decision.

Constraints often prohibit the use of the optimal instructional medium. In discussing costs, benefits, and tradeoffs, Locatis and Atkinson noted that, although a given medium may be superior for a given instructional task, the costs associated with that medium may also be correspondingly higher, making another alternative more attractive. This may often be the case with CAI. It is likely that the advantages associated with CAI will often make it the best medium when considering efficiency of instruction and enviromental and administrative factors. However, if other media will ultimately produce the desired instructional results and can be developed more quickly and implemented at a lower cost, secondary or tertiary alternatives may be more attractive.

The selection process proposed by Locatis and Atkinson illustrates how analysis of information gained during needs assessment may be used by the designer to make wise decisions concerning media selection. However, the process does not provide information to assist novice designers in evaluating the tradeoffs to be made when no single medium dominates the analysis. The considerations just described are not of equal importance, and their importance changes depending on the characteristics of the lesson to be developed.

Leiblum (1980, 1982) identified 36 "attributes of learning mechanisms," including attributes unique to CAI, and developed a matrix for designers to compare the appropriateness of different media for instructional purposes. Leiblum's media selection process consisted of (1) determining the importance of each attribute for the instructional task ahead, (2) determining the degree to which each medium possessed each attribute, (3) multiplying the weight (importance) of the attribute by the extent to which the medium possessed the attribute, and (4) adding the columns to provide a score indicating the appropriateness of the medium for that instructional task. By taking the importance of each attribute into account, this model assists the novice designer in quantifying the appropriateness of instructional media.

The Media Selection Guide (MSG)

Table 6.1 illustrates the media selection guide, a tool developed to determine the best medium or combination of media for an instructional task. By assigning a degree of importance to characteristics affecting the appropriateness of instructional media for a given lesson and by evaluating each candidate medium's ability to fulfill the requirement, it becomes possible to quantify the medium's ability to

Table 6.1
Media Selection Guide

Media Selection Guide	Importance Factor	Medium #1 CAI	Medium #2 SLIDE/TAPE	Medium #3 VIDEO	Medium #4 TEXT
Task Requirements:					
1) Ability to teach more than two students simultaneously	O				
2) Ability to teach a physical skill	O				
3) Ability to provide human interaction	O				
4) Ability to identify readiness for the lesson	O				
5) Ability to adapt to individual needs	7	3 / 21	O / O	O / O	1 / 7
6) Ability to accept responses from students	10	3 / 30	O / O	O / O	O / O
7) Ability to evaluate responses	10	3 / 30	O / O	O / O	O / O
8) Ability to provide immediate feedback	10	3 / 30	O / O	O / O	O / O
9) Ability to adapt based on learner responses	10	3 / 30	O / O	O / O	O / O
10) Ability to produce lifelike images	2	1 / 2	3 / 6	3 / 6	2 / 4
11) Ability to produce high-quality audio	2	O / O	3 / 6	3 / 6	O / O
12) Ability to portray motion	5	1 / 5	2 / 10	3 / 15	O / O
13) Ability to telescope time (time-lapse or slow motion)	O	1	2	3	O
Subtotal for Page #1		148	22	27	11

Table 6.1 (*Continued*)

Media Selection Guide: Page 2

Learner Requirements:	Importance Factor	Medium #1 CAI	Medium #2 SLIDE/TAPE	Medium #3 VIDEO	Medium #4 TEXT
14) Ability to gain attention and to motivate	7	3 / 21	2 / 14	2 / 14	1 / 7
15) Ability to adapt to learner preferences	2	3 / 16	0 / 0	0 / 0	2 / 4
16) Ability to minimize demands on verbal & reading skill	9	1 / 9	3 / 27	3 / 27	0 / 0
Administrative Requirements:					
17) Ability to calculate	0				
18) Ability to record indicators of student performance	5	3 / 15	0 / 0	0 / 0	0 / 0
19) Ability to report on student and lesson performance	3	3 / 9	0 / 0	0 / 0	0 / 0
Environmental Requirements:					
20) Availability when it is needed	5	1 / 5	1 / 5	1 / 5	3 / 15
21) Availability where it is needed	5	0 / 0	1 / 5	0 / 0	3 / 15
22) Ability to co-exist with other simultaneous activities	3	2 / 6	1 / 3	2 / 6	3 / 9
Subtotal for Page #2		71	54	52	50

Media Selection Guide: Page 3

Cost Requirements:	Importance Factor	Medium #1 CAI	Medium #2 SLIDE/TAPE	Medium #3 VIDEO	Medium #4 TEXT
23) Development/Acquisition costs must not exceed $ 2 per STUDENT.	8	2 / 16	2 / 16	2 / 16	3 / 24
24) Equipment costs must not exceed $2,000 per SCHOOL.	10	2 / 20	3 / 30	3 / 30	3 / 30
25) Delivery costs must not exceed $20 per SCHOOL.	8	3 / 24	2 / 16	1 / 8	3 / 24
Other Requirements:					
26) ABILITY TO PRODUCE MUSICAL NOTES	10	2 / 20	3 / 30	3 / 30	0 / 0
27)					
28)					
29)					
30)					
Subtotal from **this** page		80	92	84	78
Subtotal from **page 1**		148	22	27	11
Subtotal from **page 2**		71	54	52	50
GRAND TOTAL:		299	168	163	139

handle the instructional task. The process of completing the MSG, similar to that developed by Leiblum (1980), consists of the following steps:

Step 1: Complete the list of requirements.
  a. The list of requirements presented in the left-hand column is a synthesis of those commonly considered when selecting instructional media (Briggs and Wager, 1981; Dick and Carey, 1985; Gagné and Briggs, 1979; Locatis and Atkinson, 1976; Leiblum, 1980). Read the list of requirements presented in the left-hand column.
  b. Determine whether additional items are important to the lesson you are about to develop. If so, place additional items on page 3 of the list.
Step 2: Determine the importance of each requirement.
  a. Some of the items on the list will be more important than others. Determine the importance of each item on the list on a scale of 0 to 10, with 0 indicating that the requirement is of no importance (should not be considered) and 10 indicating that the requirement is critical.
  b. Write the number (0–10) reflecting your rating of the importance of each item in the "Importance" column. This number will be multiplied by each medium's ability to meet the requirement, to provide a score for that requirement. These individual item scores will be added to produce a rating for each medium.
Step 3: Identify potential media.
  a. Based on the information gathered during needs assessment, propose several media *or combinations of media* that appear to be capable of producing the desired instructional outcomes. Write the names of the media or combinations to be evaluated at the tops of any (or all of) the last four columns. If more than four are to be evaluated, use additional copies of the MSG.
Step 4: Estimate each medium's ability to meet each requirement.
  a. For each requirement, determine each medium's ability to meet the requirement on a scale of 0 (cannot meet the requirement) to 3 (meets the requirement effectively).
  b. Write the number (0–3) in the top half of the rows for each requirement.
Step 5: Eliminate unacceptable media.
  a. Look through the data, identifying instances where the requirement's importance factor is high and the medium's rating is low.
  b. Eliminate each medium unable to meet critical requirements by crossing out the entire column.
Step 6: Multiply the importance of the requirement by the medium's ability to meet the requirement.
  a. The product of the requirement's importance and the medium's ability to meet that requirement is a reflection of the appropriateness of the medium for the designated instructional task. For each requirement, multiply the importance of the requirement by the score for each medium's ability to meet the requirement. Write this product in the bottom half of each box.
Step 7: Calculate the totals for each medium.
  a. The sum of all of the products just calculated indicates the medium's overall appropriateness. Add the products in each column to produce subtotals for each page.

      b. Transcribe the subtotals from pages 1 and 2 to page 3.

      c. Add the three subtotals to produce a grand total for each medium.

Step 8: Rank the media.

      a. Compare the grand totals. Rank them by assigning a rank of 1 to the medium with the highest grand total, a 2 to the second highest total, and so on.

      b. Transcribe the rankings to page 1.

Combining media may reduce or eliminate weaknesses present in any single medium. For example, a live instructor may motivate students, CAI may deliver instruction referring the student to photographs contained in a student handbook provided for the lesson, and a group session may follow the instruction to discuss how the new information and skills may be transferred to other challenges. Each component of the delivery system provides unique strengths and minimizes the potential limitations of the others.

CAI will play many different roles in the instructional process. CAI may be the sole source of instruction, may provide instruction that supplements primary instruction delivered by other means, may provide reinforcement or practice of prior learning, or may be used for testing and record-keeping functions.

Chapter Summary

CAI is not always the best solution to an instructional problem, nor is it always the most cost-effective. The appropriateness of CAI or any instructional medium depends on

- The type of learning outcome(s).
- Characteristics and requirements of the teaching task.
- Learner characteristics.
- Environmental characteristics.
- Cost effectiveness.

A quick test of the viability of CAI was presented to allow the designer to eliminate CAI in cases where it is clearly inappropriate. A more thorough tool, the media selection guide (MSG) allows the designer to determine which medium or combination of media is best suited for a given instructional task. The MSG allows the evaluator to assign values indicating the importance of instructional requirements and to use these estimates to determine which medium or combination of media best meets a task's needs.

Media may be combined to minimize the weaknesses of an individual medium. For example, a computer simulation may be used to orient and motivate students before an instructor-led discussion of economics. The instructor's presentation might be followed by videotapes, newspaper articles, and/or programmed instruction; and student performance and the success of the course itself may be evaluated by the computer.

References

BRIGGS, L. J., and W. W. WAGER (1981). *Handbook of Procedures for the Design of Instruction* (2nd ed.). Englewood Cliffs, NJ: Educational Technology Publications.

DICK, W., and L. CAREY (1985). *The Systematic Design of Instruction*. Glenview, IL: Scott, Foresman and Co.

GAGNÉ, R. M., and L. J. BRIGGS (1979). *Principles of Instructional Design* (2nd ed.). New York: Holt, Rinehart and Winston, pp. 178–194.

LEIBLUM, M. D. (1980). A media selection model geared toward CAL. *Technological Horizons in Education*, 7(2), 29–33.

———. (1982). Factors sometimes overlooked and underestimated in the selection and success of CAL as an instructional medium. *AEDS Journal*, 15(2), 67–79.

LOCATIS, C. N., and F. D. ATKINSON (1976). A guide to instructional media selection. *Educational Technology*, 16(8), 19–21.

REISER, R., and R. M. GAGNÉ (1982). Characteristics of media selection models. *Review of Educational Research*, 52, 499–512.

———., and R. M. GAGNÉ (1982). *Selecting media for instruction*. Englewood Cliffs, NJ: Educational Technology Publications.

ROBLYER, M. D. (1981). When is it "good courseware"? Problems in developing standards for microcomputer courseware. *Educational Technology*, 21(10), 47–54.

YARUSSO, L. (1984). The decision to use a computer. *Performance and Instruction Journal*, 23(5), 24–25.

Chapter Review Exercises

COMPREHENSION

1. List at least five questions to ask in determining whether or not CAI is a viable instructional medium. (See pages 82–83 and Figure 6.1.)

2. List at least four categories of cost savings often associated with the use of CAI. (See page 83.)

APPLICATION

1. Use the quick test of the viability of CAI to determine whether CAI is a viable alternative to an instructional problem of your choice. (See Figure 6.1.)

2. Use the Media Selection Guide to determine the best medium for an instructional task of your choice. (See Table 6.1.)

Analyzing the Learning Task

Have you ever repaired something, only to have it malfunction again shortly after you had finished? You probably attended to the wrong component. Although the component repaired or replaced may in fact have been malfunctioning, another problem may have been responsible for the poor performance or breakdown. Based on a superficial knowledge of what was needed, the *symptom* rather than the problem was addressed.

Why does instruction fail? Although many valid answers to this question exist, the most likely answer is that the designers, instructors, and/or students do not accurately identify the problem. In instructional design, as in other fields, solving a problem is often simple, once it is thoroughly understood.

Needs assessment, phase 1 of the design model, is critical in determining the success of CAI products. The following chapters assist in completing phase 1 tasks by teaching how to analyze instructional problems and how to communicate findings to designers, developers, instructors, and students. In this chapter, we move from broad educational goals to complex sets of interrelated skills and knowledge upon which instruction will be focused.

This chapter provides techniques for analyzing instructional problems to determine what the learner needs to know at the outset of a lesson; what a lesson must cover; and what parts of a lesson may be optional, based on student needs and preferences. Once determined, lesson objectives may be developed with confidence that the instruction produced will achieve the desired educational outcomes.

OBJECTIVES

Comprehension

After completing this chapter you will be able to

1. List the four steps in analyzing learning tasks.
2. List and describe the activities performed during each of the four steps.

Application

After completing this chapter, you will be able to

1. State instructional goals.
2. Complete a task description for a specified instructional task.

3. Prepare a hierarchical listing of enabling skills and knowledge for a specified instructional task.
4. Diagram the hierarchical list of enabling skills and knowledge.
5. Appropriately categorize required skills and knowledge into *assumed, taught,* and *optional* categories for a specified student population.

Before development can begin, the instructional problem ahead must be understood. The process of understanding the instructional problem begins by defining the general purpose of the instruction. After an understanding of the purpose has been established, the designer must probe to develop a set of terminal objectives that defines the set of behaviors the student will be able to produce following successful instruction. The understanding of the instructional problem *does not*, however, end once terminal objectives are defined. For each terminal objective there may be several additional enabling objectives that describe prerequisite skills, knowledge, or strategies the student must possess in order to progress. Once the complex network of enabling and terminal objectives has been identified, the designer must determine which of the identified objectives will be covered by the lesson and which will be considered prerequisite. *This process of understanding the instructional problem and defining lesson content is called task analysis.*

Several approaches to task analysis have been proposed (Davis, Alexander, and Yelon, 1974; Gagné and Briggs, 1979; Dick and Carey, 1985). Dick and Carey proposed a procedural approach, which is recommended when the behaviors to be taught are to be performed in a predefined sequence; a hierarchical approach, which is recommended when layers of subordinate and superordinate skills are involved; and a combination of these two approaches, which is recommended when the behaviors to be acquired represent a complex psychomotor skill or a complex linear chain of cognitive tasks. A similar process, proposed by Gagné and Briggs, involved identifying the purpose of the course; performing an information-processing analysis, which results in a clear description of target objectives; classifying these target objectives according to the type of mental processing the task requires; and performing a learning task analysis to determine the prerequisites for the identified objectives.

Like the topic of instructional design itself, the development of a thorough understanding of the principles of task analysis is beyond the scope of this text. Use of the procedures and tools provided in this chapter will apply the fundamentals of task analysis to your projects.

Analyzing Learning Tasks: A Four-Step Process

The process of analyzing learning tasks consists of four steps: (1) stating educational goals, (2) describing the task, (3) listing enabling skills and knowledge, and (4) differentiating between skills and knowledge to be taught and those to be assumed.

STATING EDUCATIONAL GOALS

Educational goals are general statements of what is to be learned. Examples of educational goals include "Learning to multiply whole numbers," "Learning to drive safely," "Learning to budget," "Learning to appreciate impressionistic art," or "Learning to power up a microcomputer." Goals describe what is to be accomplished in general terms but are insufficient to guide the development of instruction. They serve as a springboard from which an in-depth analysis of the instructional task can occur. As the first step in developing an instructional unit, one should determine and record the goals that the lesson is to achieve. For example, the goal for a unit on powering up a popular microcomputer might be "To enable the computer's user to turn the computer on."

DESCRIBING THE TASK

The second step in instructional task analysis is to produce a task description. The result of this process is a sequential list of all of the activities, *both visible and cognitive*, that the student must go through in performing the desired behavior. To compile this list, it may be useful to observe competent people perform the desired task, recording observations. After compiling the list, it might be helpful to have competent subjects repeat the procedure slowly while explaining the steps.

In the example of turning on the computer, the following steps were identified by observing and talking with competent operators.

> Step 1. Insert the operating system diskette in drive A.
> Step 2. Turn the computer's power switch to "on."
> Step 3. Turn the monitor's power switch to "on."
> Step 4. Respond to date and time prompts displayed.

Typically, the process is more complicated than it appears initially. The next step, listing the enabling skills and knowledge, provides the additional level of detail required to produce effective instruction.

LISTING ENABLING SKILLS AND KNOWLEDGE

Most learning requires that previously learned skills and knowledge be present in order for instruction to be effective. Lack of attention to prerequisite skills has been the downfall of many lessons. Imagine attempting to read before having learned to speak or to understand spoken language. Imagine trying to multiply large numbers without having learned to add or trying to run before having learned to walk. Most educational examples are less obvious but equally important. By definition, enabling skills are necessary for subsequent learning.

Enabling skills and knowledge surface as a result of in-depth analysis of each task identified during the task description. First determine all of the subtasks involved in completing each task identified in the task description. Then repeat the process, identifying additional subtasks below previously identified subtasks. Repeat the process until all identified tasks and subtasks may be assumed as part of the target audience's base of prior knowledge.

To identify enabling skills and knowledge, it is usually wise to have competent people perform the procedure, describing not only the process but each decision made and the bases for the decisions. The notes taken during these discussions will improve the understanding of what the process actually entails. The following list depicts the subtasks identified for each task specified in the computer power-up example. Indentation indicates the hierarchical nature of the list, with prerequisites indented under items for which they are required.

Step 1. Insert the operating system diskette in drive A.
    a. Identify the operating system diskette.
        (1) Identify a diskette.
        (2) Identify the diskette label.
        (3) Know discriminating information appearing on the operating system diskette label.
    b. Identify drive A.
        (1) Identify a diskette drive.
        (2) Know the position of drive A.
    c. Open the diskette drive door.
        (1) Identify the latch.
        (2) Know how to open and close the latch.
    d. Orient the diskette correctly before insertion.
        (1) Determine the top of the diskette.
            (a) Locate the label.
        (2) Determine the leading edge of the diskette.
            (a) Identify read/write opening.
    e. Insert the diskette.
    f. Close the diskette drive door.
Step 2. Turn the computer's power switch to "on."
    a. Flip the computer power switch.
        (1) Locate the switch.
Step 3. Turn the monitor's power switch to "on."
    a. Flip the monitor power switch.
        (1) Locate the switch.
Step 4. Respond to the date and time prompts as they appear.
    a. Learn to respond to the date prompt.
        (1) Recognize the date prompt.
    b. Learn to respond to the time prompt.
        (1) Recognize the time prompt.

This list could have been made longer by adding such things as the concepts of *date, time, open,* and *close.* The listing process for a given branch of the analysis should end when it may safely be assumed that all members of the target population possess the subtask identified. In this case, it is assumed that computer users all understood the concepts of date, time, open, closed, top, bottom, left, right, and many others.

When the list of skills and knowledge has been compiled, review the list in an attempt to identify overlooked items. Once you are satisfied with the completeness of the list, diagram the list to illustrate the hierarchy of tasks and subtasks. A diagram for the computer example is included as Figure 7.1.

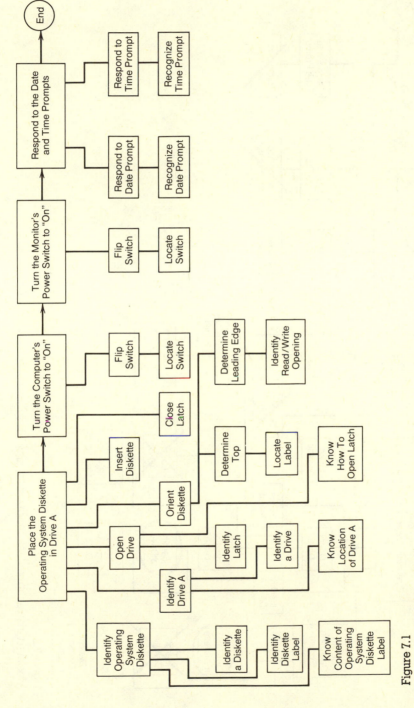

Figure 7.1

Instructional task diagram for powering on a microcomputer.

96

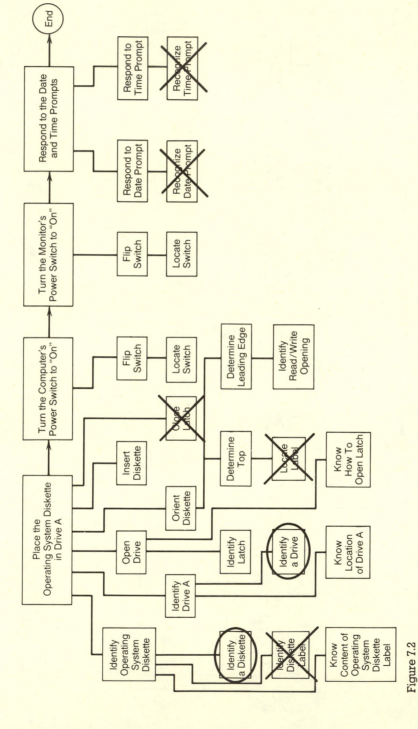

Figure 7.2
Modified instructional task diagram for powering on a microcomputer.

DIFFERENTIATING BETWEEN TOPICS ASSUMED AND TAUGHT

The final step in instructional task analysis is to decide what will be presented during the lesson. To do this, inspect the expanded task diagram. Decide which tasks to assume that *all* learners already know, which task *some* of the learners know, and which tasks it is reasonable to believe *few if any* of the learners know.

Cross out tasks all learners already know. The lesson need not cover these. List these tasks and set the list aside for use when writing a lesson summary. By inspecting this list, the teacher can determine whether the prerequisite skills and knowledge make it appropriate for individual students. Or you may wish to use this list as the basis for the development of a pretest, which is used as a screening device to test whether students using the lesson possess the required skills.

Circle the topics that some of the learners will have mastered before entering the lesson. Instruction on these topics might be optional. Pretest results could be used to route individual students through these modules if necessary. Tasks not crossed out or circled become standard lesson modules.

Figure 7.2 illustrates how the diagram developed earlier has been modified to illustrate the topics that will be eliminated (crossed out), optional (circled), and standard lesson modules (unchanged).

Note that it has been assumed that the target audience needs no instruction on the tasks "identify diskette label," "locate label," "close latch," "recognize date prompt," and "recognize time prompt." The two optional instructional segments, "identify a diskette" and "identify a drive," may be located and taught together. These will not become a standard part of the lesson but will be made available if the student indicates a desire or need for instruction in these topics.

Defining an Effective Instructional Task Analysis

An instructional task analysis is used to generate the objectives of the lesson. It is successful if adequate information is provided to write the objectives required for effective instructional design. The analysis is unsuccessful, however, if such information cannot be extracted.

Different instructional designers would likely generate slightly different task analyses for the same instructional task. Perhaps the best way to assess the quality of a task analysis is by examining the success of the instructional unit as a whole. If the instruction produces the desired outcomes, then the instructional task analysis was probably adequate. If, on the other hand, the instruction fails to meet its objectives, then the task analysis is one possible source of the failure.

Chapter Summary

Instructional task analysis provides the necessary detail to design effective instruction, whether in CAI or other educational media. The process described involves four steps:

1. Stating educational goals: Identifies the lesson's purpose in general terms.
2. Describing the task: Identifies the steps involved in the desired behavior.

3. Listing enabling skills and knowledge: Identifies the hierarchy of skills and knowledge that enables the student to achieve the desired results.
4. Differentiating between skills and knowledge to be taught and those assumed present before instruction: Separates the identified topics into those that will not be taught, those that will be provided as needed, and those that are standard lesson modules.

The product of these steps is a functional picture of the hierarchy of skills and knowledge involved in the desired set of behaviors. Based on the knowledge gained during task analysis, the designer can make intelligent decisions about what the lesson must achieve to ensure success.

References

DAVIS, R. H., L. T. ALEXANDER, and S. L. YELON (1974). *Learning System Design: An Approach to the Improvement of Instruction*. New York: McGraw-Hill.
DICK, W., and L. CAREY (1985). *The Systematic Design of Instruction*. Glenview, IL: Scott, Foresman and Co., pp. 24–47.
GAGNÉ, R. M., and L. J. BRIGGS (1979). *Principles of Instructional Design* (2nd ed.). New York: Holt, Rinehart and Winston, pp. 97–115.

Chapter Review Exercises

COMPREHENSION

1. List the four steps in analyzing learning tasks. (See page 92.)
2. List and describe the activities performed during each of the four steps. (See pages 93–97.)

APPLICATION

Assume that you are about to develop a lesson to teach sixth-grade students to simplify improper fractions (to change fractions with numerator larger than the denominator to mixed numbers; for example, $\frac{7}{5} = 1\frac{2}{5}$). Perform the following tasks.

1. State the instructional goals. (See page 93.)
2. Complete a task description. (See page 93.)
3. Prepare a hierarchical listing of enabling skills and knowledge. (See pages 93–94.)
4. Diagram the hierarchical list. (See Figure 7.1.)
5. Modify the diagram to indicate the topics that are assumed, optional, and taught. (See pages 96–97 and Figure 7.2.)

Developing Instructional Objectives

Chapter 7 presented techniques for identifying instructional tasks. In this chapter, you will learn to translate instructional tasks into measurable, understandable, achievable objectives.

The relatively simple task of writing sound instructional objectives may well be the most important step in the development of effective instruction. Instructional objectives guide the development of the lesson, inform prospective users of the content of the lesson, allow students to focus on the most important aspects of the lesson, and serve as the basis upon which to judge both student progress and the success of the lesson.

OBJECTIVES

Comprehension

After completing this chapter you will be able to

1. List at least three ways in which objectives contribute to the learning process.
2. List the three parts of a well-written objective.
3. Identify poorly written objectives.
4. Name the missing parts of incomplete objectives.
5. Discuss the difference between the wording of objectives written for the designers and developers of a lesson and the same objectives written for presentation to students.

Application

After completing this chapter you will be able to

1. Rewrite poorly written objectives.
2. Write effective instructional objectives.

The Purpose of Objectives

An experienced pilot will not leave the ground without knowing the final destination, nor will a carpenter begin construction without a detailed understanding of the structure to be built. Should an instructor or trainer begin teaching without understanding what the student must be able to do after the lesson is complete?

Consider the following scenario. A dynamic speaker presents an enlightened monologue for approximately one hour to an audience that listens intently. At the end of the session, the speaker asks the audience for questions. The few questions that surface are handled quickly and to the audience's satisfaction. After the presentation, complimentary comments abound. One observer is heard to say, "She really knew the topic!" Another responds, "And presented it in a well-organized, entertaining manner." A third participant adds, "I hope the rest of the speakers in this course do as well!"

Should this session be described as successful? While some lessons fail obviously, others fail silently. Although the audience was pleased with the presentation, the session may or may not have been successful. Success and failure are relative to the intent of the lesson. Based upon the information provided, it cannot be determined whether the lesson performed as desired. If the intent of the lesson was simply to please the audience, to motivate them to return for other lessons, or to model effective presentation skills, then the lesson was probably successful. If, on the other hand, the intent of the lesson was to transfer specific knowledge from the presenter to the student, to teach the students to use new information in different settings, or to teach them to actually *become* effective presenters, the lesson may have failed.

Lesson intent is defined by lesson objectives. By describing lesson intent, objectives contribute to learning in several ways. Instructional objectives guide the development of the lesson, inform prospective users of the content of the lesson, allow students to focus on the most important aspects of the lesson, and serve as the basis upon which to judge both student progress and the success of the lesson.

1. *Objectives guide the development of the lesson.* Reconsider the previous example. If the objective was to transfer knowledge from the presenter to the student, activities should have been incorporated to maximize the probability that transfer occurred. For example, the presenter may have used 35-millimeter slides highlighting key words to imprint the knowledge in the student's mind. Or a mnemonic device or visual imagery techniques could have been employed to help students recall the information. A simple handout could have summarized the information to allow students to study or review it at a later date. Once objectives are known, it is possible to develop instruction that includes activities devoted to achieving those ends.

2. *Objectives help potential users determine lesson appropriateness.* By reading the list of lesson objectives, potential users (both teachers and students) can determine whether they are likely to benefit from the lesson. If the objectives describe skills and activities that are not yet mastered and that are of value to the student, then the lesson has much to offer and should be used. If the objectives describe valuable skills and knowledge that are missing from a knowledge base but that are of such difficulty that attaining them would be impossible, student time and effort should

be spent on other topics. Titles and course descriptions provided for lessons, films, books, or CAI modules are insufficient. Only when the lesson's objectives are specified is it possible to make accurate judgments.

3. *Objectives allow the student to focus on important learning tasks.* Objectives may help the student by communicating priorities. When students know what is expected, it becomes easier to meet expectations. If, for example, the student is aware that an objective requires the listing of the planets in the solar system in order by distance from the sun, the student is likely to attend more intently when this topic is presented. On the other hand, when students are aware of objectives and know that assessment will be based solely on the objectives, students pay *less* attention to information not directly related to the achievement of objectives. The presentation of objectives tends to increase learning of objective-related information, but it may limit the amount of incidental learning that occurs (Hamilton, 1985).

4. *Objectives define the evaluation of student performance.* Student progress may be evaluated by determining whether or not the student has mastered lesson objectives. Students meeting the objectives have completed the lesson successfully; others have not.

If the objective was to list the names of the planets in order by distance from the sun, then the test item should employ virtually the same wording. Each objective should be translated into one or more test items, and the test should not include items not directly related to lesson objectives.

5. *Objectives can be used to evaluate the success of the lesson.* By examining performance across several students, objectives permit the evaluation of the lesson itself. For example, most students might achieve lesson objectives most of the time. However, very few students may successfully attain a particular objective. This information allows the designer to reexamine the instruction and questions used to evaluate attainment of the objective. The instruction may have been faulty, or the objective or assessment item may have been poorly worded.

Components of Effective Instructional Objectives

Mager (1962) identified three components of a well-written instructional objective:

- The behavior to be exhibited.
- The conditions under which it is to be exhibited.
- The criteria by which acceptable performance will be judged.

By writing objectives that include these three components, designers know what the lesson must achieve, developers know what to build, and evaluators can determine whether or not the lesson was successful. Each of the three components is discussed in detail here.

COMPONENT 1: AN OBSERVABLE BEHAVIOR

An effective instructional objective specifies an observable task that the student will perform. Consider the following instructional objective for a science lesson in

Table 8.1
Sample Verbs for Use in Instructional Objectives

adjust	assemble	build	calculate
categorize	choose	circle	classify
clean	cook	count	create
demonstrate	describe	develop	discriminate
discuss	execute	explain	generate
identify	label	list	match
operate	perform	play	program
provide	recall	recite	repair
run	select	sort	state
summarize	type	use	write

an elementary school: "The student will understand how various drugs affect the human body." Is that statement of intent sufficient to guide the development of a lesson? Does it help the learner know what is considered important? Is it sufficiently clear to guide evaluation? The answer to all of these questions is no.

For an objective to be useful, it must specify the observable behaviors that the student must exhibit. Once these behaviors have been identified, the designer understands the instructional problem, and the student may focus attention on meeting the lesson's objectives.

Although the words *understand, know, appreciate, believe*, and *feel* are verbs, they do not imply an *observable action*. For this reason, they are not sufficient for use in instructional objectives. Table 8.1 contains some of the many words that may be appropriately used in instructional objectives.

Note that, although the use of such words will improve the probability of producing observable, measurable outcomes, their use alone is no guarantee of a successful lesson. These verbs are often combined to produce more accurate and descriptive objectives. Let's return to the insufficient objective: "The student will understand how various drugs affect the human body." By using words from the preceding list, we can write several observable objectives that better describe the intent.

The student will be able to

- List at least five drugs that have harmful effects on the human body.
- Classify each item on a list of drugs as an amphetamine, a barbiturate, or hallucinogen.
- Write the names of three hallucinogens and list and describe at least three harmful side effects for each.
- Identify alcohol as a drug.
- Match the street names for common drugs with the corresponding scientific names.
- Discuss the effects of prolonged abuse of alcohol.
- Summarize, in writing, his or her position on the use of drugs by adolescents.

The use of verbs that identify required performance reduces the ambiguity substantially. When the remaining components are provided, objectives communicate the instructional intent even more clearly.

COMPONENT 2: THE CONDITIONS UNDER WHICH PERFORMANCE IS TO TAKE PLACE

Effective objectives specify the conditions under which the behavior is to take place. The preceding objectives, though superior to the vague initial statements, still leave much to be desired. Are the identified behaviors to be performed individually or in groups? With or without the use of notes and textbooks? Within a certain period of time? At home or in school?

By specifying the conditions under which the behavior will be performed, it becomes possible to eliminate ambiguity and to move closer to defining and communicating lesson intent to designers, developers, and students.

The following is the list of objectives developed earlier, modified to include conditions under which the performance of each is to take place:

- Without access to books, notes, or other aids, the student will list at least five drugs that have harmful effects on the human body.
- While a list of ten drugs appears on the computer's screen, the student will classify each item on the list as an amphetamine, a barbiturate, or hallucinogen by typing *A*, *B*, or *H* without access to books, notes, or other aids.
- Using books, notes, or other aids as necessary, the student will write the names of three hallucinogens and list and describe at least three harmful side effects for each.
- In response to the question "Is alcohol a food or a drug?" the student will identify alcohol as a drug.
- When presented with a two-column list with ten randomly ordered street names for common drugs in the first column and ten randomly ordered scientific names for the same drugs in the second column, the student will use the light pen attached to the computer system to draw lines matching the street names with the corresponding scientific names.
- Given two weeks from assignment to due date, the student will discuss the effects of prolonged abuse of alcohol in a research paper, citing at least three credible references.
- Immediately following a fifteen-minute discussion on the topic, the student will summarize in writing his or her position on the use of drugs by adolescents. The response will answer the following questions, which will appear on the blackboard during the assignment: (1) Are drugs more harmful to adolescents than to adults? (2) Why do adolescents use drugs? (3) Are there conditions under which it is acceptable for adolescents to use drugs? (4) Should adolescents use drugs?

Three points become apparent at this stage: (1) As the objectives become clearer, the method to use to evaluate attainment of the objective also becomes clearer. (2) Objectives that once were simple sentences can become complex sentences and even paragraphs. (3) Certain objectives do not lend themselves well to CAI.

By adding the third component, the criteria by which performance will be judged, it becomes possible to determine when the objective has been met.

COMPONENT 3: THE STANDARDS AGAINST WHICH PERFORMANCE WILL BE JUDGED

Effective instructional objectives specify the standards against which performance will be evaluated. Is the intent in the previous objective to summarize a position, or is it to have specific viewpoints reflected in that opinion? When classifying the ten listed drugs, is a score of nine out of ten acceptable, or must the student respond correctly to all ten to achieve the objective?

Learning is seldom an all-or-nothing activity. In most cases, learning happens gradually, but perfection is seldom attained. In many cases, perfection is not required, and the expense of seeking perfection is not worth the effort. In other cases, such as pilot training or surgical training, perfection is the only acceptable goal.

When writing objectives for CAI, the specification of standards becomes even more important. In conventional forms of instruction, standards are often used only after the instruction is complete, in order to evaluate student and sometimes lesson performance. In CAI, the standards often determine *when* instruction is complete. Many CAI lessons use *mastery learning,* in which instruction continues until objectives are achieved. The setting of appropriate standards assures that skills are learned without expending more time or effort than is required.

Standards for instructional objectives are often based on either the *quality of the response* or the *time within which the behaviors must occur,* or both. Quality standards often include the definition of *successful completion* and the percentage of attempts that must be completed successfully. Time constraints are often expressed as the number of successful completions in a specified amount of time.

The first objective on our sample list already includes a performance standard.

- Without access to books, notes, or other aids, the student will list at least five drugs that have harmful effects on the human body.

The phrase *at least five* indicates what is required for an acceptable performance. Another objective also included performance standards.

- Using books, notes, or other aids as necessary, the student will write the names of three hallucinogens and list and describe at least three harmful side effects for each.

A third objective indicated only one question and one correct answer, thereby implying an acceptable standard with which to evaluate performance.

- In response to the question "Is alcohol a food or a drug?" the student will identify alcohol as a drug.

Notice that, although these objectives were considered to have acceptable standards, none imposed a time limit for successful completion. Time was not a critical element in these cases. The remaining sample objectives have been modified to include standards:

- While a list of ten drugs appears on the computer's screen, the student will classify each item on the list as an amphetamine, a barbiturate, or a hallucinogen by typing *A*, *B*, or *H* without access to books, notes, or other aides. A score of eight correct will be considered acceptable performance.

- When presented with a two-column list with ten randomly ordered street names for common drugs in the first column and ten randomly ordered scientific names for the same drugs in the second column, the student will use the light pen attached to the computer system to draw lines matching the street names with the corresponding scientific names with 70% accuracy.
- Given two weeks from assignment to due date, the student will discuss the effects of prolonged abuse of alcohol in a research paper, citing at least three credible references. Acceptable responses will mention at least three of the following: destruction of brain cells, liver damage, psychological dependence, possible effects on the circulatory system, and the increased potential for social or emotional problems.
- Immediately following a fifteen-minute discussion on the topic, the student will summarize in writing his or her position on the use of drugs by adolescents. The response will answer the following questions, which will appear on the blackboard during the assignment: (1) Are drugs more harmful to adolescents than to adults? (2) Why do adolescents use drugs? (3) Are there conditions under which it is acceptable for adolescents to use drugs? (4) Should adolescents use drugs? Points will be awarded for matching the following anticipated responses:

Part 1 (two points possible)
   a. Drug use is more harmful to adolescents (1).
   b. Because of effects on physiological and emotional changes (1).

Part 2 (three points possible)
   a. Peer pressure (1).
   b. Emotional problems (1).
   c. Recreational aspects of drug use (1).

Part 3 (two points possible)
   a. Under medical supervision (1).
   b. As recommended on labels of over-the-counter drugs (1).

Part 4 (one point possible)
   a. Only under medical or adult supervision (1).

Examples

INCOMPLETE INSTRUCTIONAL OBJECTIVES

Examples of incomplete objectives are listed here, with an explanation of the shortcomings of each.

- "Upon completion of this lesson, the student will know how the American governmental system works." (Missing observable behavior, conditions, and standards.)
- "The student will know how electricity works and will score 85% or better on the posttest." (Missing observable behavior and conditions.)
- "Using the help key provided in this CAI lesson and a quick reference card, the student will learn about operating popular microcomputer systems in less than forty-five minutes." (Missing observable behavior and standards.)

- "Upon completion of this lesson, the student will be able to match countries with the continents on which they are located." (Missing conditions and standards.)
- "The student will be able to list in writing the steps required to parallel park a car. All steps must be provided, and the answer must be completed within five minutes." (Missing conditions.)
- "Using any resources available in the school library, the student will be able to locate the answers to three library trivia questions." (Weak standards. Although correctness of the answers is implied, a time limit would be helpful.)
- "Given unrestricted access to a microcomputer system and the accompanying documentation for a period of two weeks, the student will really understand the computer inside and out. Performance will be evaluated based on performance on a final examination, with 90% indicating a satisfactory score." (Missing observable behavior.)

WELL-WRITTEN OBJECTIVES

The following list provides examples of objectives for a CAI unit introduced in the previous chapter. Obviously, a CAI lesson on turning the power on to a microcomputer assumes that a competent operator will start the lesson. The goal of the lesson is to teach the student to be self-sufficient after the lesson is complete. The following objectives all include the observable behaviors the student will exhibit, the conditions under which the behaviors will be displayed, and the standards by which the behaviors will be judged as satisfactory.

- "Given a CAI frame containing a line drawing of a diskette, a numbered list of the parts of a diskette, and appropriate directions, the student will be able to type the number of each part in the appropriate blank as the cursor moves from blank to blank on the diagram. Numbered parts will include (1) the diskette label, (2) the read/write opening, (3) the write-protect notch, and (4) the protective covering. The task will be considered successful only if all part numbers are placed in the correct blanks within a three-minute period."
- "Given a frame showing the front of the microcomputer and appropriate directions, the student will touch the area representing diskette drive A. This task must be completed successfully the first time. Touching any other area will be considered incorrect."
- "Given a frame showing a series of three illustrations of a hand about to place a diskette in a diskette drive and appropriate directions, the student will identify (by touching the appropriate section of the screen) the drawing that represents the correct orientation of the diskette. To minimize the possibility of a correct answer by chance, the task will be considered correct only if the student can repeat the process three times without error as the drawings are shuffled and redisplayed in different locations."
- "Given a frame showing five diskette labels and appropriate directions, the student will identify (by typing the letter associated with the correct label) the label that is found on the operating system diskette. To minimize the possibility of a correct answer by chance, the process will be considered correct only if the student can repeat the task three times without error as the labels are displayed in different locations."

- "During an interactive sequence simulating the date and time prompts, the student will successfully respond to these prompts. Successful responses will include any that the computer would consider acceptable. On the first two incorrect responses, the session will react by displaying an error message identical to the message that would have been provided by the computer. On a third incorrect response to either prompt, the task will be considered as failed."
- "Once the preceding objectives have been met, the student will demonstrate knowledge of the location and function of the power switch by powering the computer off. If the computer has been turned off within one minute after the instructions to do so appeared on the computer screen, the task will be considered successfully completed."
- "The student will be provided a set of five diskettes, one of which is the operating system diskette, and a computer in working order identical to the one for which the lesson was developed. Using these and no documentation or notes of any kind and with no help from anyone, the student will demonstrate the process of actually powering up the target computer system. The process will be considered successful if the student is able to gain access to the operating system prompt within three minutes without damaging the computer or any of the diskettes."

Classifying Instructional Objectives

Bloom (1956) categorized objectives in three domains: cognitive, affective, and psychomotor. Cognitive objectives deal with the acquisition of knowledge and the development of intellectual skills. Affective objectives attempt to modify student attitudes, values, or emotions. Psychomotor objectives are concerned with the development of physical, muscular abilities. Within each of these domains, there are additional classifications. In the cognitive domain, the one at which a good deal of CAI is targeted, six additional levels are proposed. These levels are considered hierarchical, that is, achievement of objectives at a higher level presumes achievement at a lower level.

The lowest level in the cognitive domain is the knowledge level. Objectives written at this level focus on recall. The student is required to acquire information and subsequently recall that information. The next level is the comprehension level. At this level, students are asked to paraphrase or summarize information rather than simply repeating the information. If a student is able to paraphrase information, it has been internalized, implying that higher-level processing has occurred. The third level is application. At this level, students are asked to generalize what they have learned to novel situations. The fourth level is analysis. When students reach this level, they are able to analyze new information into its components and to understand and describe the organization of the information. Next is the synthesis level. At this level, the student can assemble pieces into cohesive, functional units. The highest level, according to Bloom, is evaluation. At this level, the student is asked to make judgments about the value or importance of information.

What makes classification of objectives important to the designers of instruction? Most instruction, including CAI, tends to focus on attainment of lower-level objectives. Attention to this hierarchy encourages designers to focus on what is actually important. Important behaviors are usually described by higher-level objectives. It is seldom important that students acquire information for its own sake. The information becomes important when it is understood and applied.

When you have completed the list of objectives for a lesson, examine each objective to determine its position on the hierarchy. For each objective written at the knowledge or comprehension level, verify either that another, higher-level objective exists in the lesson for which the knowledge is required, or that the objective provides prerequisite information or skill for an upcoming lesson.

Procedures for Writing Instructional Objectives

As experience writing sound instructional objectives is gained, the process becomes second nature, and the modest amounts of additional time required is recovered many times over during development, evaluation, and revision. Until considerable experience writing objectives has been obtained, the sequence of steps listed in Table 8.2 may be employed to promote the efficient writing of effective objectives.

Rewriting Instructional Objectives for Students

As indicated in the beginning of this chapter, objectives serve many purposes and several audiences. Just as instruction must be developed with learner characteristics in mind, objectives must be tailored to suit the different audiences they serve.

Table 8.2
Procedures for Writing Sound Instructional Objectives

1. Determine the verb that the objective will use to describe the desired observable behavior.
2. Determine the conditions under which the behavior is to be exhibited.
3. Draft the objective by writing a sentence that includes both the conditions and the description of the action the student will exhibit.
4. Write a second sentence describing the standards against which the behavior will be evaluated.
5. Rewrite the sentences in an attempt to make your draft communicate more clearly.
6. Ask yourself the following questions about the objective:
    Does the objective adequately describe conditions, behavior, and standards?
    Will the designers of the lesson be able to use this objective to develop adequate instruction?
    Does the objective dictate the evaluation item(s) that will be used to determine whether the objective has been met?
    Would several independent evaluators come to the same conclusion when attempting to judge whether a single student had mastered the objective?
7. If the answer to any of these questions was no, go back to step 1 and revise the objective as necessary.

The objectives presented thus far are appropriate for communicating lesson design to developers and evaluators, and perhaps even to instructors who need to determine whether to purchase and use the lesson. But the student does not need this level of detail and may become confused or hesitant if confronted with objectives stated in this way.

It is useful to present the objectives to the student. Knowledge of objectives helps to focus student efforts to improve performance. However, it is generally appropriate to modify the objectives first. Student-level objectives should use the same action verb and should provide insight into the way in which achievement will be evaluated. The objectives listed for the microcomputer module might be reworded as follows for presentation to students:

After completing this lesson, you will be able to

- Identify the parts of a diskette.
- Locate the primary diskette drive (called "drive A").
- Correctly insert a diskette into a diskette drive.
- Identify the operating system diskette used when the system is first powered on.
- Power on both the computer and the monitor.
- Respond to the initial prompts the computer provides.
- Perform all of the necessary steps to get the computer up and running.

As additional examples, consider the objectives listed at the beginning of each chapter of this book. Sufficient detail is provided to guide student effort without overwhelming the student with unnecessary detail.

Chapter Summary

The ability to write sound instructional objectives may be the designer's most valuable skill. Effective instructional objectives contribute to the instructional process by guiding the development of the lesson, helping potential users determine the appropriateness of the lesson, allowing the student to focus on important learning tasks, defining the methods to be used in student evaluation, and making it possible to determine whether the lesson was successful.

By following the step-by-step procedure presented in this chapter, even designers with little or no experience in writing instructional objectives can develop sound objectives that successfully communicate lesson intent.

Instructional objectives written for designers, developers, and evaluators are not necessarily appropriate for students. However, knowledge of objectives has been shown to improve student performance. Rewriting objectives will make them appropriate for use by students.

Chapter 7 taught how to identify topics for which instruction must be developed. This chapter taught how to refine those topics into statements that focus and coordinate the efforts of the designers, developers, students, instructors, and evaluators. Well-written objectives save considerable time and effort that would otherwise be expended during subsequent stages of development, and they go a long way toward assuring the success of CAI lessons.

References

BLOOM, B. S. (1956). *Taxonomy of Educational Objectives. Handbook I: Cognitive Domain.* New York: McKay.

HAMILTON, R. J. (1985). A framework for the evaluation of the effectiveness of adjunct questions and objectives. *Review of Educational Research*, 55, 47–85.

MAGER, R. F. (1962). *Preparing Instructional Objectives.* Belmont, CA: Fearon Publishers.

Related Readings

BRIGGS, L. J., and W. W. WAGER (1981). *Handbook of Procedures for the Design of Instruction* (2nd ed.). Englewood Cliffs, NJ: Educational Technology Publications (pp. 39–65).

GAGNÉ, R. M., and L. J. BRIGGS (1979). *Principles of Instructional Design* (2nd ed.). New York: Holt, Rinehart and Winston (pp. 117–135).

Chapter Review Exercises

COMPREHENSION

1. List at least three ways in which objectives contribute to the learning process. (See pages 100–101.)

2. List the three components of a well-written objective. (See page 101.)

3. Five objectives are listed here. Identify those that do not contain *all three* components. (See pages 101–107.)

    a. After completing between twenty and thirty hours of rigorous instruction and watching two films on the subject, the student will be able to intelligently discuss the dangers presented by acid rain.

    b. Given an assembled human skeleton, the student will be able to name correctly nine of ten bones within ten seconds after the instructor points to them.

    c. Given an atlas and allowed access to class notes, the student will know at least forty-five of the fifty states in the United States and at least forty state capitals.

    d. The student will be able to demonstrate the use of at least three computer software programs.

    e. Provided a bale of straw and a spinning wheel, the student will be able to spin straw into gold within thirty days.

4. Name the missing components (if any) of the following objectives. (See pages 101–107.)

    a. Given a list of ten computer-related acronyms, the student will type the name represented by each acronym.

    b. Given only a pair of pliers and a roll of duct tape, the student will be able to survive in the jungles of Mexico without any human contact for the entire month of June.

    c. The student will be able to disassemble, clean, and reassemble the carburetor of a 1957 Chevy.

    d. Without the use of books, notes, or reference materials of any sort, the student will be able to successfully complete the posttest following a CAI lesson on marine biology.

    e. Upon completion of this lesson, the student will really understand the principles governing economics in America.

5. Discuss the difference between the wording of objectives written for the designers and developers of a lesson and the same objectives written for presentation to students. (See page 109.)

APPLICATION

1. Three incomplete objectives are listed here. Rewrite each objective so that it includes the three components of effective instructional objectives. (See Table 8.1. Note: There are many acceptable answers for each objective.)

    a. Upon completion of this lesson, the student will be able to name the symptoms of swine flu.

    b. The students will learn to appreciate classical music.

    c. By completing this CAI simulation, the students will learn what it is like to use word processing software.

2. Assume that you are about to develop a CAI lesson on multiplying two two-digit numbers. Write at least three complete (3-component) instructional objectives. (See pages 101–105.)

Analyzing and Selecting Options in CAI

The computer offers a virtually unlimited number of options for varying the structure, features, and nature of CAI lessons. Often, however, we become so fascinated with the computer itself, and the incredible power and capability it possesses, that we lose sight of the basic instructional purposes for which lessons are designed. Lessons often become testimonials to the power of the computer per se, rather than exemplifying the features of well-designed instruction. The focal point of many lessons inadvertently becomes "What can the *computer* do?" rather than "How can students learn well from the computer?"

This does not suggest that the formidable capabilities of the computer are necessarily inappropriate for CAI applications. Instead, the capabilities of the computer should be utilized intelligently and with a sense of purpose. We must differentiate those features of the computer that support the teaching and learning process from those that do not.

In this section, techniques and guidelines for analyzing and selecting options in CAI will be presented. The purposes of this section are to provide methods of harnessing the capabilities of the computer for instructional purposes and of promoting the intelligent and systematic use of the computer in the delivery of instruction.

SECTION GOALS

After completing this section you will

1. Understand the process of flow charting.
2. Represent CAI lesson designs in flow-chart form.
3. Become familiar with the CAI designs and modes most commonly used in educational settings.
4. Become familiar with the kinds of lesson frames used in CAI.
5. Develop skills in frame design techniques.
6. Understand the importance of interactivity in CAI lessons.
7. Develop several methods for designing interactive CAI lessons.
8. Understand the importance of obtaining and using student input in CAI lessons.
9. Identify several techniques for managing user input.

Flowcharting and Branching

If all lessons were executed in exactly the same manner, in the same order, and in the same sequence, then perhaps flowcharting would not be so important. It is relatively easy to design lessons where all learners receive the same instruction, at the same rate, and in the same sequence. Basically, the decisions adopted for one learner are the same decisions governing lesson execution for all learners.

However, this is unsatisfactory for many CAI applications. CAI lessons often require different consequences under one set of prescribed conditions than for others. We develop lessons that execute in uniquely different ways, depending on defined, specified conditions: If the student has missed the question, repeat the lesson; if the student has missed the past three questions, exit the lesson; if the student has answered the question correctly and cumulative accuracy is greater than 90 percent to this point in the lesson, skip the remainder of the lesson; and so on. Clearly, the number and type of conditions that affect lesson execution for any individual student are varied but are very much within the capabilities of the computer.

How best to represent the many decisions that affect lesson execution, to provide an overview of lesson execution that can be readily understood by others, and to develop a strategy to account for the number and type of lesson execution options is critical to the lesson design process. The computer offers enormous potential for CAI lessons *if* designers can effectively conceptualize the complex conditions governing lesson execution effectively and can communicate these complex conditions adequately to others.

Perhaps no single aspect of CAI planning does more to communicate design decisions that concretize the abstract process of lesson execution than flowcharting. The lesson flow chart is a concise map that allows each piece of the lesson puzzle, as well as the overall relationships among different lesson segments, to be scrutinized. It is a concrete visual representation of what will happen during a lesson. It is, arguably, the single most important device through which instructional designers, subject matter experts, and computer programmers communicate in mutually understandable terms.

In this chapter, we present simplified techniques and procedures for flow-charting various design decisions in CAI lessons. We focus on methods for representing what is presented to the student, when the student enters responses, when the computer evaluates student input, and what lesson execution options will be provided. We also address branching as it applies to CAI lesson design and examine techniques for representing branching conditions in flowchart form.

OBJECTIVES

Comprehension

After completing this chapter you will be able to

1. Describe the operational functions of each of the major flowcharting conventions.
2. Describe the importance of lesson flowcharting for lesson design, planning, and communication.
3. Describe the different types of branching.
4. Describe the principal differences between linear lessons and the different types of branched lessons.
5. Describe the circumstances in which each type of branching might be appropriate.
6. Describe the differences between physical and instructional branching.
7. Describe the phenomenon of the infinite loop.
8. Describe the differences between program-based and conceptually based infinite loops.
9. List and describe several techniques for eliminating conceptual loops.

Application

After completing this chapter you will be able to

1. Design lesson flowcharts that incorporate flowcharting symbols accurately.
2. Design lesson flowcharts that include linear design features.
3. Design and develop lesson flowcharts that utilize physical branching.
4. Designs lesson flowcharts that incorporate instructional branching.
5. Design lesson flowcharts that are free from both program-based and conceptually based infinite loops.

The Importance of Lesson Sequence

When a student reads a textbook, judgments are made as to the importance of the information, whether or not to review or to skip ahead, and other aspects related to the perceived importance of the instruction. With the textbook, it is possible simply to follow the text page by page, look back over pages from the preceding chapters, determine that information is already known and unnecessary to read again, and maneuver throughout the textbook as desired. In effect, the student controls the instructional sequence and activities based upon individual learning needs.

In much the same way, the computer offers the potential for maneuvering within lessons, following a fixed sequence, or doing both. CAI lessons can be designed to proceed absolutely through fixed program sequences; to skip unnecessary information within a lesson; to review past information; or, at the designer's discretion, provide each option. The decision-making capability of the computer permits a range of sequence options that may be useful for different lessons.

Top-Down Planning in Programming

For programmers, the concept of top-down programming is important in order to understand the nature and complexity of a programming task. Essentially, top-down planning is the computer programmer's counterpart to instructional task analysis. The top level, or terminal task, is identified initially, and each subtask required to complete the terminal task is subsequently identified, evaluated, and ordered. Top-down planning enables the programmer to plan *program* execution sequences in accordance with the sequence and options prescribed among the identified tasks and subtasks.

CAI designers are also interested in identifying and depicting specific lesson execution plans. It is necessary to plan not only for the major steps and substeps of a lesson, but also to identify important design features such as when specific lesson options will be available, what the consequences of correct and incorrect answers will be, when student responses should be saved permanently or retrieved from a permanent file, and a host of other instructional control decisions. The instructional aspects of the lesson—their simplicity or complexity—require planning skills and techniques beyond simply identifying the top-down sequence of tasks and subtasks.

Flowcharting CAI Lessons

Flowcharting is a process whereby the sequence, options, and conditions affecting lesson execution are identified and represented graphically (Edwards and Broadwell, 1974). Flowcharts are the vehicles through which the structure of a lesson is established, the specifications for a lesson are translated, and the flow of a lesson is visualized in concrete images.

Conceptualizing the logic of a lesson is the first and primary task for any lesson designer. Detailed flowcharts are used by lesson designers to represent the features and options of a lesson (Burke, 1982). We specify certain portions of a lesson to display information, others to present questions and solicit responses, and still others to skip, repeat, or continue lesson execution based upon the accuracy of a student response. We translate the lesson into an accurate and understandable plan that specifies the conditions and procedures of the lesson.

Lesson flowcharts are also used by computer programmers to identify all relevant input, output, and decision points of a lesson (Huntington, 1979). Both designers and programmers can use the same basic conventions for prescribing lesson execution, though programmers typically apply top-down methods to convert the lesson execution specifications to modular, efficient, programmable sequences. If the lesson designer adequately represents the lesson in flowchart form, then the task of programming the lesson is simplified appreciably.

The methods used for flowcharting can be as simple or as complex as necessary. For CAI purposes, however, the process and methods for flowcharting are very straightforward. Figure 9.1 illustrates the basic shapes required to flowchart most CAI lessons.

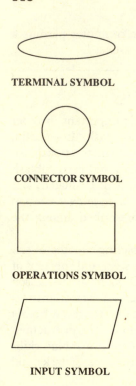

TERMINAL SYMBOL

CONNECTOR SYMBOL

OPERATIONS SYMBOL

INPUT SYMBOL

DECISION SYMBOL

Figure 9.1
Symbols used in CAI flowcharting.

Each of the flowchart symbols will be illustrated throughout this chapter to represent different lesson sequence and presentation options. As a brief introduction, however, let's consider the function of each.

TERMINAL SYMBOL

Terminal symbols are used to indicate the start or end of a lesson. The very first entry in most CAI flowcharts is a terminal symbol with the accompanying phrase "Start" or "Begin." Similarly, virtually all CAI flowcharts conclude with a terminal symbol with the phrase "End" or an equivalent term.

CONNECTOR SYMBOL

The connector is usually indicated by a circle with relevant information specifying the connection to be made. It is usually used to indicate connecting points with other lessons or lesson sections not included on the same flowchart. For example, if a student successfully completes a unit posttest, the designer might wish to begin the next unit in the sequence, so indicating with the appropriate connector symbol.

OPERATIONS SYMBOL

The purpose of the operations symbol is quite specific. In CAI, the operations symbol usually designates information that is displayed on the computer monitor. Operations symbols are often used to indicate the fact that instruction is being presented or that other information is to be shown to the student. The information may be a computer graphic, definitions of key terms, or almost any other output.

INPUT SYMBOL

The symbol we use to designate input points in a lesson is a parallelogram. The input symbol designates points in a lesson where the student is to provide a response. Input may be obtained to identify student name, to evaluate learning, or to respond to choices embedded within the lesson.

DECISION SYMBOL

The diamond-shaped symbol is used to designate points where a lesson execution decision is to be made by the computer, such as bringing about different consequences for correct or incorrect responses.

Although we have described flowcharting conventions that we use throughout this text, the important concern should not be for the specific symbols. If adopted, the conventions we use are sufficiently simple to be effective in representing lessons with relative ease. However, our advice is simple: Use those flowcharting conventions that are most effective in representing your lesson and in communicating your lesson plan to others, but *be consistent in their use*.

CAI lessons have an enormous range of lesson execution options, ranging from the simplest of progressions to the most complex of branching sequences. Let's examine how flowcharting is applied to plan for the different types of lesson execution.

Controlling Lesson Execution

LINEAR DESIGNS

Perhaps the easiest programming concept to comprehend is that of linearity. Linear designs, such as the one illustrated in Figure 9.2, are those in which all learners proceed through the same instruction in the same order. For example, the learning task may be so new that no need exists to skip information in the lesson. Or the information to be learned may require a highly specific set of procedures, each of which must be taught in a given order. Maybe the learning task requires the kind of instructional precision that can be best assured by maintaining control of the sequence across all students. In each of these cases, linear CAI may be indicated.

Consider the case of the student who must learn right-to-left procedures to compute products for complex multiplication problems, such as 3788 times 233. For students to demonstrate the skill, a series of steps must be taken in a fixed

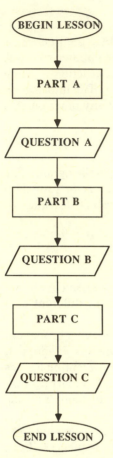

Figure 9.2
A simple linear CAI lesson flowchart.

order. In effect, an expert system has been devised, whereby students can be taught a specific method thought to be most effective in computing products of multiplication problems. All students must perform each step of the process in the same order to demonstrate mastery. In such a case, the order of the instruction must remain fixed across students, since each step must be taught and learned in a prescribed order.

Advantages and Limitations of Linear Designs   The principal advantage of linear designs is the capacity to maintain control over the sequence of the instruction. In addition, linear CAI is generally less complicated to program, requiring few conditions that affect program operation. Linear CAI is effective when students are homogeneous in entry skills and acquisition rate and for tasks that are procedural.

   Linear designs do not, however, account effectively for differences in acquisition rate or other learner differences. There is no opportunity for faster learners to skip unnecessary instruction or for slower learners to review previous instruction. It is also difficult to accommodate learner differences effectively—especially with regard to entry-level skills. Students who have already learned all, or part, of the information included in the lesson must still proceed through the entire lesson.

Some authorities contend that linear CAI is simply unnecessary, since the important concepts involved in the design of learning sequences can be adapted to more flexible lesson designs. Others maintain that linear CAI does not utilize the decision-making capabilities of the computer very well and that instruction requiring only linear presentation probably does not need the formidable capabilities of the computer. Finally, linear CAI may be inefficient in many cases. Since opportunities for review are not available in linear CAI, the precision and detail of the lesson are often overstated, causing many learners to proceed through substantially more detailed instruction than necessary.

As we will see in the study of branching techniques, some of the issues concerning the use of linear designs are valid, and others are without merit. Linear program designs have a great deal of utility when used appropriately, but they cannot provide the kind of flexibility necessary for the vast majority of CAI applications. Instead, models that provide greater flexibility and that rely on the talents and expertise of the designer to avoid possible trappings are often used in CAI.

BRANCHING PROGRAM DESIGNS

An important asset of the computer is the capacity to individualize instruction. This capacity is demonstrated by the way the computer evaluates responses, determines whether to proceed or to repeat sections of a lesson, and accommodates different learning rates within a CAI lesson. Different students sit before the computer and receive the same basic lesson in very different ways.

Actually, the reason for individualization and for any other options provided is that the lesson designer has determined that certain capabilities of the computer should be exercised in particular ways under prescribed conditions. The computer provides the capability, but the designer prescribes how that capability will be used.

Branching options are perhaps the single most important factor affecting the degree to which CAI will or will not be individualized. Branching refers to the capacity of a lesson to skip information or to backtrack, as deemed desirable. Branching makes possible the review of previous instruction for slower learners, the skipping of already learned information by faster learners, the use of menus from which students can select aspects of a lesson, and any of a host of additional options related to the individual needs, preferences, or performance differences among students.

Instructional Versus Physical Program Branching   It is difficult to imagine computer applications where physical program branching is not an integral part of program execution. Physical program branching refers to the jumping or skipping of adjacent program segments, as shown in Figure 9.3. In such an instance, the *program* has branched physically, since the commands were read and executed in a nonlinear order.

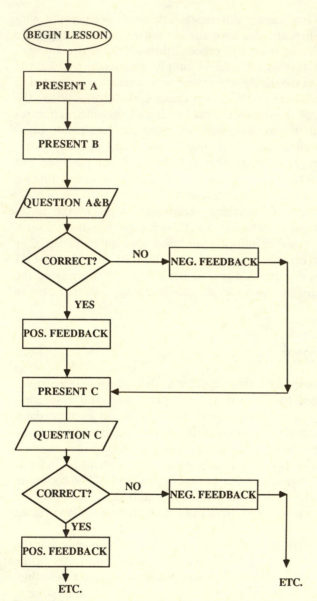

Figure 9.3
Physical or program-branching flowchart.

From a programming standpoint, physical branching is often a very efficient process. Different parts (called *procedures* or *subroutines*) of a program can be executed repeatedly without being duplicated throughout the program. Most computer programs of any size or consequence utilize physical branching.

In CAI, however, it makes more sense to think of branching as it pertains to lesson information. Branching in CAI may be best thought of as the skipping of adjacent instructional information rather than the physical process of program execution. An example of branching occurs when a student skips the practice section of a lesson in order to take a posttest.

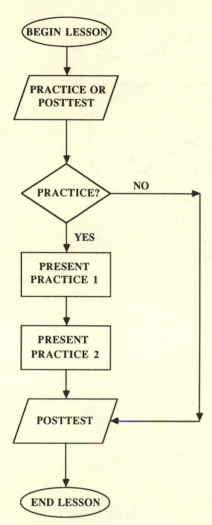

Figure 9.4
Instructional branching flowchart.

An example of instructional branching is shown in Figure 9.4, and a combined example is shown in Figure 9.5. Notice that physical program branching can, and often does, take place even when instructional branching does not.

TYPES OF BRANCHING IN CAI

In a simple sense, branching occurs either forward, backward, or randomly, depending upon the purposes served. We will review each of these branching options and examine how and when each might be applied in CAI.

Forward Branching Forward branching is the skipping of information between the current position in the lesson and a point further into the lesson.

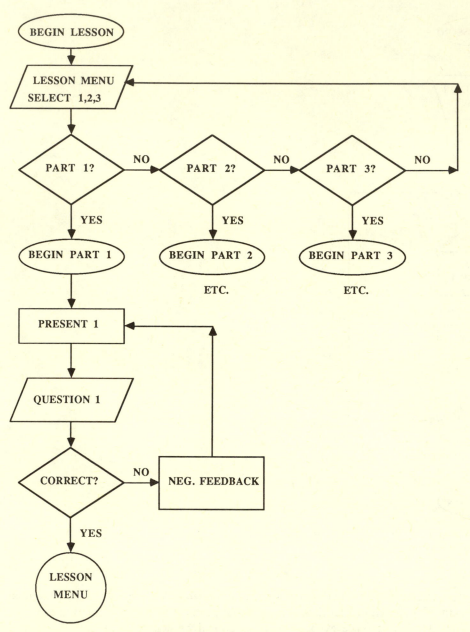

Figure 9.5
Combined physical and instructional branching flowchart.

Branching execution can be placed under either lesson or student control, depending upon the demands of the lesson and the dictates of the designer. Forward branching is commonly used to allow students to skip lesson portions at their discretion. In some cases, forward branching may be embedded as a designer-imposed lesson feature, such as skipping sections of a lesson based upon favorable pretest performance.

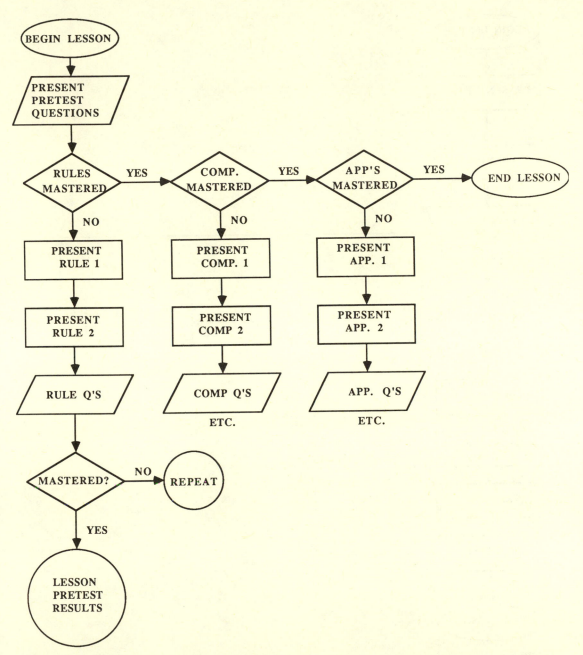

Figure 9.6
Forward-branching flowchart based on pretest score.

Figure 9.6 illustrates forward branching based upon pretest performance. As shown, the student may begin at several points in the lesson. If the student comprehended the rules necessary for completion of the task and possessed the computational skills requisite for effective performance during the pretest, he or she would be branched forward to the section focusing on applications. A different

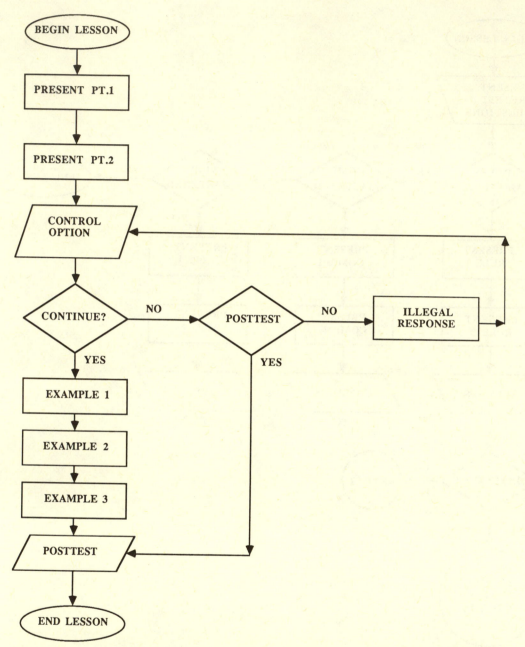

Figure 9.7
Forward-branching flowchart based on learner choices.

student might require the entire lesson, beginning with the rule section, while still another might begin the lesson with the computation section.

Now consider a forward branching example that might be placed under learner control. Figure 9.7 is such an example, where the student determines whether to continue or skip to the posttest, based upon the presentation of a menu.

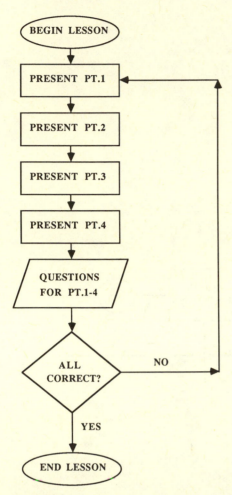

Figure 9.8
Backward-branching flowchart based on response
accuracy.

Backward Branching In many cases, it is necessary to move backward from
the current position in a lesson to a previous position. The process of skipping
adjacent lesson information to return to an earlier portion of a lesson is called
backward branching. Backward branching is commonly used in CAI to repeat
segments of a lesson, to return to a lesson menu, to start a lesson over again, or to
permit review of specific portions of a lesson.

Examine the flowchart shown in Figure 9.8. Notice how the lesson branches
back if the question is answered incorrectly. The lesson will continue to branch
back until the student provides the correct response. This is a fairly common
application of backward branching in mastery learning.

Random Branching Random branching is a special case of branching used
when the order or sequence among a group of lesson segments is unimportant.
Random branching allows any of a group of branching possibilities to occur
without concern for the sequence of the presentation. Such branching often makes

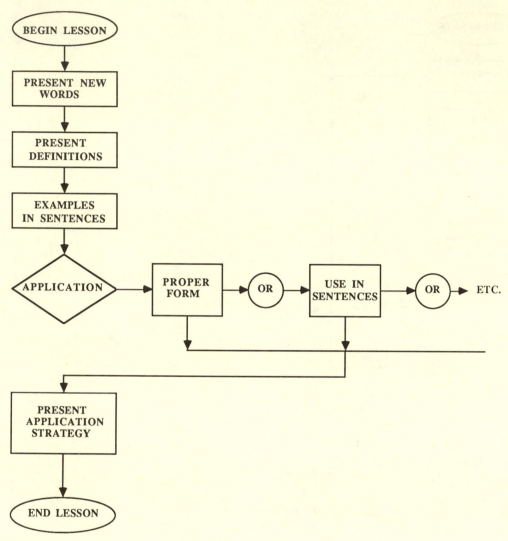

Figure 9.9
Random-branching flowchart.

the same lesson look different from one use to the next, since the order of execution is randomly altered each time.

Figure 9.9 is a flowchart illustrating random branching. Notice that at the application step, the program will branch randomly to any of the five sections available for application examples. For instance, a CAI lesson was developed to provide a variety of practice applications for a group of Spanish verbs. Once the verb had been taught in isolation, the student practiced a variety of applications: use in sentences, comprehension in written form such as newspapers, use of proper form, and so on. The designer determined that no particular order of presentation was required. In fact, the use of a variable order might be desirable, since the same student may use the lesson several times. The application lesson provides each of the options shown in Figure 9.9, but varies the order randomly.

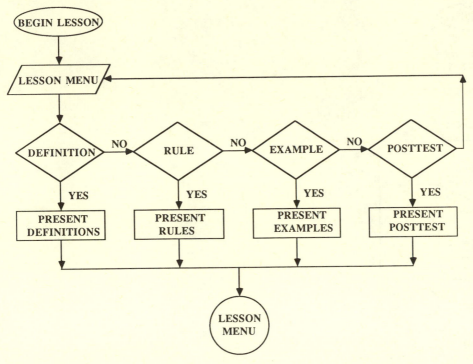

Figure 9.10
Absolute branching flowchart.

ABSOLUTE VERSUS CONDITIONAL BRANCHING

Branching usually occurs under two circumstances: The branching is either fixed within the lesson and will occur in all cases, or the branching is conditional and will occur only under certain prescribed conditions. Both are common and quite useful in the design of CAI. Let's examine examples of both absolute and conditional branching.

In absolute branching, all learners jump to the same specified section of a lesson. A common application of absolute branching is seen when, at the end of each lesson section, all learners return to a controlling lesson menu. This branching option is illustrated in Figure 9.10. It occurs irrespective of learner performance, any desire the student may have to repeat the last frame, or any other condition. The branching will *always* occur at each point shown in the lesson flowchart.

Conditional branching, on the other hand, executes only under prescribed circumstances. If a student were experiencing difficulty understanding the definitions in the preceding example, it might be useful for the student to repeat the section. If no difficulty were encountered in this section, perhaps the student should return to the lesson menu. This conditional branching option is shown in Figure 9.11. It occurs under varying conditions, prescribed by the designer.

Obviously, conditional branching offers a wealth of possibilities for CAI. Designers can prescribe relative mastery levels for a lesson, each of which results in unique branching. Instruction can possess a maximum degree of sensitivity to

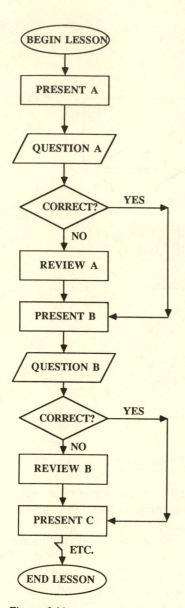

Figure 9.11
Conditional-branching flowchart based on response
accuracy.

differences in student performance. Conditional branching can also be used to permit either student or lesson control of the branching. Students routinely exercise this control when responding to lesson menus. Lesson branching, corresponding to student responses, is controlled conditionally, depending upon student choice. Absolute branching, on the other hand, permits physical jumping among program statements and procedures where conditional branching is unnecessary or undesirable.

ADVANTAGES AND LIMITATIONS OF DIFFERENT BRANCHING DESIGNS

Branching provides the opportunity to make CAI lessons as conditional in their execution as desired, as individualized as required, and as efficient as possible. Conditional branching designs allow a virtually unlimited number of lesson execution options. Meaningful standards can be prescribed to govern the sequence of the lesson. These standards allow students to receive instruction uniquely adapted to individual needs.

There are, however, potential limitations to the effective use of branching techniques. Skipping lesson segments based upon student choice or pretest scores might be intuitively sound, but it can weaken the base of prerequisite information required during a lesson. Some designers employ branching indiscriminately, seemingly reinforcing the notion that "If it can be done, it should be done." If branching does not aid or support overall learning, in terms of accuracy, efficiency, strength, and depth, then it cannot be justified.

OVERCOMING THE APPARENT LIMITATIONS OF BRANCHING DESIGNS

The limitations of branching designs are usually attributable to shortsightedness in the lesson plan and not to an inherent limitation of branching. For example, concern for the sequence of instruction can be readily accommodated through combining linear and branching features. In addition, conditional branching makes possible the specification of relevant criteria to control branching contingencies. In effect, the performance guarantee achieved in linear designs can be integrated as a branching condition. If it is deemed appropriate, students cannot proceed through a lesson unless *all* mandated performance standards have been met.

Many of the conditions resulting in the effective use of branching are little more than good common sense. In a case where all steps of a particular task must be learned in a prescribed sequence, it makes little sense to design learner-controlled branching options. This does not, however, presume that the design must be linear. The benefits of linearity can be captured through intelligent application of branching desings. Mastery can be assured for both fast and slow learners, but the activities and frame sequences need not be identical for all.

Infinite Programming Loops

Infinite loops, such as the one shown in Figure 9.12, are created by program branching statements that jump the lesson to and from the same points, resulting in a "loop" that continues infinitely if permitted to do so. For example, suppose a program were written to branch from the beginning of the lesson, "Instructions," to a different portion, such as "Posttest." Once the branching takes place, the next command is to branch to "Instructions." The computer dutifully executes this command, branches to "Instructions," then back again to "Posttest," and so forth

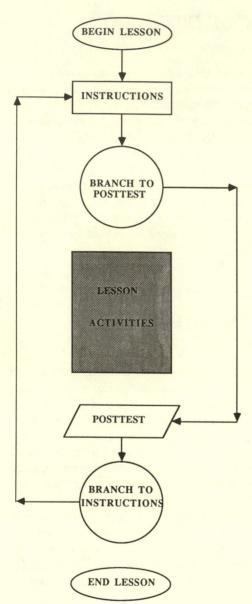

Figure 9.12
Infinite program loop.

until it is turned off or the lesson execution is somehow interrupted. The cause of an infinite loop is an oversight in programming, where two or more programming commands exchange lesson control indefinitely.

Infinite Conceptual Loops

Programming errors, however, are not the only cause of infinite loops in a lesson. In many cases, looping occurs when a student is unable to produce the response

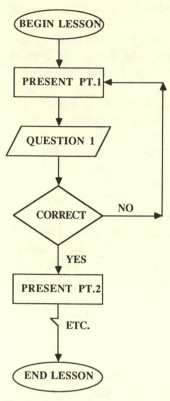

Figure 9.13
Conceptually based infinite loop.

required for lesson continuation. This phenomenon is sometimes referred to as a *conceptual loop.*

Consider the branching conditions prescribed in Figure 9.13. Upon completing a short lesson, the student must provide an answer based upon the recently completed instruction. If the student provides the correct answer, the lesson will proceed to Part 2; therefore, there is no infinite loop of a purely programming nature.

On the other hand, if the student does not provide the correct answer, the lesson information is repeated, and the student is again faced with the task of providing a correct response. If the student is unable to provide the correct response, this branching cycle will reoccur infinitely, alternately repeating instruction and requesting a response. In this case, the cause of the infinite loop is the student's inability to provide the information necessary to continue; it is not faulty programming logic.

SOME CAUSES OF CONCEPTUAL LOOPS

The probability of conceptual loops increases as the complexity of the information to be learned increases and the nature of the required response becomes more sophisticated. Information that is fairly simple and straightforward can generally be evaluated easily. The answer to the problem "2 + 2" has a significantly smaller domain of possible responses than "Describe how the concept of number-to-object association develops through the preschool years."

Test items that use multiple-choice, true–false, or other forced-choice formats are also less prone to infinite conceptual loops, since the domain of possible responses is narrowly prescribed. Through deduction alone, the student can avoid the probability of a conceptual loop.

Conceptual loops can be particularly troublesome, however, in constructed-response formats. Students do more than select among given responses, which increases the chance that the information required for lesson continuation will not be provided accurately by the student. Perhaps the student is a poor speller or is simply unclear as to how much information is required. It can be very difficult to produce the necessary responses under these conditions.

Conceptual loops are also more common for tasks that are difficult conceptually for the student to comprehend. Assume, for example, that you are asked to infer something that was not explicitly stated or written during a lesson. After you miss the initial attempt, you examine the instruction again and attempt another response. Upon missing your second attempt, you realize that you either do not understand the information or the question, or you are not typing the information correctly. You venture a third try, but you still cannot respond correctly. You would like to go on, to repeat the lesson, to quit the lesson, or almost anything other than repeating the same instruction and question over and over.

In virtually every case, conceptual loops are the result of inadequate planning by the designer. Good planning results in the necessary programming statements; poor planning does not. A simple recognition of the nature of the response format, the limitations as well as advantages, and the methods for compensating for potential limitations could certainly help to avoid most infinite conceptual loops.

TECHNIQUES FOR AVOIDING CONCEPTUAL LOOPS

1. *Build in error counters for conditional branching.* Usually designers do not force learners through a particular question more than two or three times. If the student is unable to produce accurate responses fairly readily with instruction and remediation, then the information may be too difficult. Typically, the designer includes *error counters* to tally the number of incorrect responses to a particular question and embeds a provision to exit the question or the entire lesson if excessive numbers of errors are made. By establishing conditions for alternate branching, error counters and conditional branching assure that students do not become the victims of infinite conceptual loops.

2. *Judge responses intelligently.* When responses are provided by the learner, the computer typically compares them to the correct answer prescribed by the lesson designer. The correct answer may consist of a single letter or number, as in multiple-choice items, or it may require several words in a set sequence. Whereas simple input can be judged readily, the constructed-response format poses several concerns for the designer. Should spelling errors be counted? What if the student includes more than the minimally prescribed information for correct answers? Are there alternative responses that are correct? Should the response be judged qualitatively, according to the degree of correctness, or simply as right or wrong? Depending upon the nature of the response and how it is to be judged, the designer

can anticipate multiple responses, accept certain spelling errors, and create virtually any condition affecting the judging of student input. These conditions can only be included, however, if the nature of the response, the alternatives for correctness, and the programming options that permit the alternatives are considered.

3. *Prompt students for required input.* In most unstructured response formats, it is essential that students be given sufficient guidance as to the type of information required. Consider the test item: "Describe the causes of the War of 1812." From the student's perspective, what type of information is to be provided? How much detail is needed? How much should the historical versus immediate causes be addressed? If the response is to be evaluated or judged by the computer, then criteria and standards for correctness must be adopted by the designer. The question could be prompted to reflect the types of information necessary, such as by rewording the sentence to read

Describe the causes of the War of 1812. Be sure to include the following:

- economic influences within the United States.

- the French–American alliance.

- the strategic value of the Port of New Orleans to both the United States and England.

While still posing tremendous answer-judging challenges, the additional prompting would clarify the nature of the required response while enabling the designer to focus the range of response judging to define areas.

Chapter Summary

The branching capability of the computer and the ability of designers to use this capability with intelligence and discretion are genuine concerns. It has become common for designers to use branching in ways that make little sense from an instructional perspective. Unlike the alpine enthusiast who, when asked why he climbed Mount Everest, proclaimed, "Because it was there," we cannot design lessons with branching patterns simply because they exist. It is insufficient to base an instructional strategy solely on the capability of any technology. We must identify those capabilities that make the most sense, given the nature of the instructional problem, and implement those that support the lesson objectives most effectively.

Through the application of systems approaches in the design of CAI lessons, we are able to understand better the nature of the learning task, the relationships among past and present information and concepts, and the extent to which options for skipping or repeating are appropriate. This information must be used to determine the appropriateness of associated branching schemes as well. If we cannot support the skipping of necessary information in a lesson, do we really want to provide a branching option that will allow a student to do just that? If the importance of a particular instructional sequence has been established, is it wise to allow learners to determine their own instructional sequence? When information obtained during the needs-assessment process is applied to the lesson design and development process, lesson branching decisions are based more appropriately on the learning task itself than on the technology used to teach.

Branching provides the means through which CAI lessons execute differently, under varied conditions, for individual learners. The variety of models described in this chapter represents but a small sample of the complex branching applications possible for lesson design and execution. From a technological perspective, almost any branching scheme that can be conceptualized can be executed through the computer. From an instructional perspective, however, we must be continually diligent to ensure that the branching used in CAI lessons is done to support learning and is not simply adopted because it is physically possible.

References

BURKE, R. L. (1982). *CAI Sourcebook*. Englewood Cliffs, NJ: Prentice-Hall, Inc.
HUNTINGTON, J. F. (1979). *Computer-Assisted Instruction Using BASIC*. Englewood Cliffs, NJ: Educational Technology Publications.

Related Reading

ALESSI, S. M., and S. R. TROLLIP (1985). *Computer-Based Instruction: Methods and Development*. Englewood Cliffs, NJ: Prentice-Hall, Inc.
DYER, C. A. (1972). *Preparing for Computer-Assisted Instruction*. Englewood Cliffs, NJ: Educational Technology Publications.
EDWARDS, P., and R. BROADWELL (1974). *Flowcharting and BASIC*. New York: Harcourt Brace Jovanovich.
MACK, B., and P. HEATH (1980). *Guide to Good Programming*. New York: Halstead Press.
STERN, N. B. (1975). *Flowcharting: A Tool for Understanding Computer Logic*. New York: John Wiley.

Chapter Review Exercises

COMPREHENSION

1. Describe the operational functions of each of the following flowcharting symbols: (See pages 118–119 and Figure 9.1.)
   a. Terminal symbol.
   b. Operations symbol.
   c. Input symbol.
   d. Decision symbol.
   e. Connector symbol.
2. Describe the importance of effective flowcharting in lesson design, planning, and communication. (See pages 116–117.)
3. Describe each of the following types of branching: (See pages 123–130 and Figure 9.6–9.11.)
   a. Forward.
   b. Backward.

    c. Random.

    d. Absolute.

    e. Conditional.

4. Describe the principal differences between linear lesson designs and branched lessons designs. (See pages 119–123 and Figures 9.2 and 9.3.)

5. Describe situations where each of the branched lesson designs might be appropriate. (See pages 121–130.)

6. Describe the differences between physical or program branching and instructional branching. (See pages 121–123 and Figures 9.3–9.5.)

7. Describe what is meant by the expression *infinite loop*. (See pages 131–132.)

8. Describe the differences between program-based and conceptually based infinite loops. (See pages 131–133.)

9. List and describe the techniques for eliminating conceptual loops. (See pages 134–135.)

APPLICATION

1. Design a lesson flowchart that incorporates each of the flowcharting symbols accurately. (See Figures 9.1–9.11.)

2. Design a lesson flowchart that features linear instructional sequencing. (See Figure 9.2.)

3. Design a lesson flowchart that features physical branching sequences. (See Figure 9.3.)

4. Design and develop a lesson flowchart illustrating instructional branching sequences. (See pages 123–131 and Figure 9.4.)

5. Design a lesson flowchart illustrating each of the different branching options, making certain that both program-based and conceptually based infinite loops are avoided. (See Figures 9.12 and 9.13.)

CHAPTER 10

Modes and Designs of CAI

Different teaching systems are characterized by variations in both their components and use. Within each teaching system, however, considerable variability also exists. It is impossible to muster global, unconditional support for one technology or another simply because each can be applied in so many different ways.

Print-based instruction, for example, takes many different forms, each with distinct functions. Textbooks are usually the principal source of information for a course or curriculum. Worksheets are also print-based, but they typically reinforce information rather than teaching information initially. It makes little sense either to support or to criticize printed instruction per se, because the applications of print-based teaching systems are so diverse that each is a teaching system by itself.

Computer-based instruction should be considered in much the same manner. We can neither support nor criticize the computer as a teaching system per se because so many variations of computer applications exist. As with most teaching systems, computers may be used as a primary teaching tool, to reinforce prior learning, to stimulate and motivate learning, or for any of a variety of other possibilities.

In this chapter, we examine the major CAI modes and designs, differentiating each by functions, features, and basic assumptions. The purposes of this chapter are to introduce the various design options and to provide examples of each.

OBJECTIVES

Comprehension

After completing this chapter, you will be able to

1. List and describe the major CAI designs.
2. Describe the assumptions typically made in the development of each design.
3. List and describe the major advantages and limitations of each design.
4. List and describe the features of effectively designed lessons for each design.
5. Describe the implications of each design for program complexity, hardware considerations, learner characteristics, and related instructional needs.

Application

After completing this chapter you will be able to

1. Evaluate the applicability of different designs for a selected learning problem.
2. Select an appropriate lesson design, given the learning requirements of the identified need.
3. Select an appropriate lesson design that can be implemented with available hardware.
4. Design the activities and materials necessary to support the selected CAI design.

Modes and Designs

The major classifications of CAI lessons include *tutorials, drill and practice, simulations,* and *instructional games* (Alessi and Trollip, 1985). A number of other classifications, such as problem-solving and inquiry lesson designs, have been discussed, but the overwhelming majority of CAI lessons fall within the previous four classifications. Each basic design provides a unique method for using the computer to teach, reinforce, practice, or apply information. In many cases, various design combinations, called *hybrid designs,* are developed to utilize the advantages and, in some cases, to minimize the disadvantages, of each design option. Let's consider each of the basic design options and then examine some of the hybrid designs that might be developed.

TUTORIALS

Basic information to be learned must be presented initially in some form. Traditionally, this presentation has taken the form of textbooks, lectures, videotapes, and other teaching systems. Generally, it is assumed that the teaching system should make the learning experience interesting and effective.

In tutorials, information is taught, verified, and reinforced through interaction with the computer. In this regard, tutorials may be seen as replacing the bulk of the teaching function of textbooks, filmstrips, lectures, or other systems in which new information is presented. Tutorials, in effect, model the best techniques available for tutoring students (Bramble and Mason, 1985).

In CAI, tutorials are generally used to present new information to learners—particular skills, information, or concepts. In many cases, the instruction is designed to be self-contained, that is, the teaching and learning of all relevant information are accomplished within the lesson. Students are typically questioned during the tutorial to verify comprehension. Lesson information may be further reinforced using computer-based or traditional teaching systems, but tutorials should teach well-defined objectives thoroughly enough to eliminate the need for repetition through another teaching system.

Features of Effective Tutorials Effective tutorials include lesson orientation information, learner guidance during the lesson, appropriate feedback and remediation, and strategies for making the instruction more meaningful to the

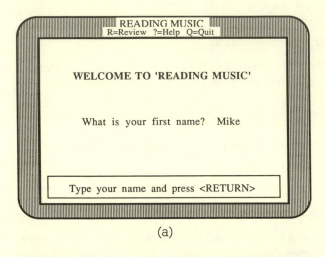

(a)

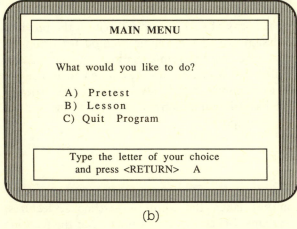

(b)

Figure 10.1
Screen faces from a CAI tutorial.

learners. Figures 10.1(a) through 10.1(h) illustrate the features important for the design of CAI tutorials.

Tutorials generally begin with activities designed to direct students to the screen or monitor in order to prepare for the instruction to follow. This is often accomplished by presenting an attractive graphic display; by using music; or, in some cases, by presenting a scenario that the student will recognize as meaningful, entertaining, or appropriate to his or her needs. In addition, lessons typically alert the student to the skill dependencies for the current lesson.

Students are usually informed of the lesson expectations prior to the presentation of new lesson content. New instruction should emphasize the unique, important, or differentiating features. The designer typically will use a variety of techniques, such as highlighting, to amplify key information.

Several techniques are used to aid learning. In some cases, an application of a concept will be presented, one piece at a time, to illustrate the process for the student. This provides support, hints, prompts, or other cues that will aid the

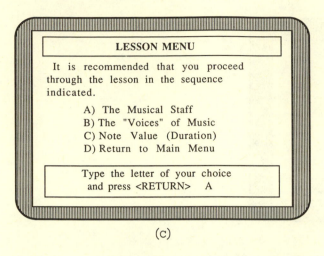

LESSON MENU

It is recommended that you proceed
through the lesson in the sequence
indicated.

     A) The Musical Staff
     B) The "Voices" of Music
     C) Note Value (Duration)
     D) Return to Main Menu

Type the letter of your choice
and press <RETURN>   A

(c)

Introduction: Musical Staff

This lesson is designed
to teach you how to read music.
Music is a language.
Like any language,
one lesson will not make you
completely fluent.

Press the <SPACEBAR> to continue...

(d)

Figure 10.1 (*Continued*)

student. A feature of virtually all tutorials is interaction between the student and the computer-based information. Computers are well suited for this feature, in that they can accept and evaluate responses according to the standards adopted by the designer and can perform any of a host of functions based upon the accuracy or inaccuracy of the response. By requiring students to respond, it is possible to determine whether the information can be retrieved effectively or whether additional instruction is indicated.

Feedback is usually provided to confirm accurate student responses or to correct inaccurate responses. Feedback may simply inform the student whether responses were correct, it may indicate the correct response, or it may provide substantially more elaborate and detailed information. Tutorials typically include an evaluation of the student's ability to perform the tasks established in the learning objective. Assuming that sufficient instruction, guidance, practice, and feedback have been provided during the tutorial, this step generally is a direct assessment of the outcome stated in the instructional objective. Students merely demonstrate for summative purposes the skills practiced to mastery during the lesson.

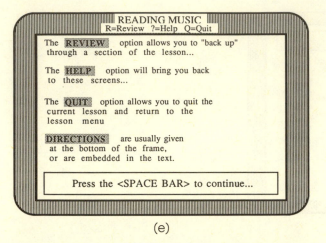

(e)

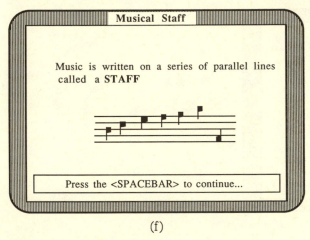

(f)

Figure 10.1 (*Continued*)

Finally, good tutorials attempt to deepen the level of processing of the instruction by providing different strategies to remember, making the instruction as relevant and meaningful as possible, and including aids for incorporating old with new information. This is a marked contrast to many tutorials, in which the information taught is treated singularly and without regard for other related knowledge. Effective tutorials provide strategies for students to remember the information taught and to relate new information to existing or to-be-learned information.

Advantages and Limitations of Tutorials   Tutorials are especially useful for teaching factual information, simple discriminations, rules, and simple applications of rules. Tutorials permit learners to move through instruction at their own rate, depending on considerations such as acquisition rate, reading fluency, utilization of learner options, and any of a variety of other factors. They tend to be most useful for verbal learning tasks in which large amounts of information must be presented.

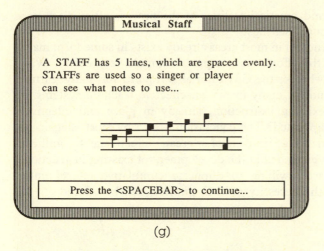

(g)

(h)

Figure 10.1 (*Continued*)

The principal limitations of tutorials are related to the time required to design and develop the lessons, difficulties in designing tutorials for higher-order objectives, and the duplication of instruction that is often available in other forms. When tutorials are to be self-contained, the instruction must be very comprehensive, accounting for a wide range of learners across all lesson objectives. The design must provide a good deal of embedded support for the learner, since the computer does not automatically provide the aids to which learners have grown accustomed. The computer must provide the activities and techniques that characterize a good tutor, and the options must be made available as a function of student responses or other options.

Although tutorials designed to teach higher-order skills such as problem solving have been developed, tutorials are more readily adaptable for other kinds of learning. The design and program requirements for higher-order skills are often sufficiently complex, and alternative methods are so readily implemented, that the computer is rarely called upon to teach such skills. It is possible, indeed common, in settings that provide technical training to use tutorials to teach higher-order skills, but the complexity and practical realities of the process often discourage such effort in most educational settings.

Finally, the fact that instruction in most areas already exists in some form makes the process of duplicating the efforts via computer tutorials very costly. When faced with the question of whether the CAI tutorial is *required* for many learning tasks, the answer is often no. In many instances, effective teaching systems are already in place. Should existing instruction, already in place and effectively meeting expectations, be duplicated? The conclusion drawn by most is again no. Though well-designed tutorials may be of equal or greater effectiveness, significant resources have already been expended in the development of existing instructional systems. The public is rarely willing to duplicate cumulative efforts unless compelling arguments for the necessity of CAI tutorials can be offered.

DRILL AND PRACTICE

Much of what is taught requires practice to promote proficiency and fluency. Practice provides an opportunity to establish that students are able to perform target skills, to provide feedback regarding performance, and perhaps to remediate those skills that students do not perform well. Practice, feedback, and remediation are partners in a continuous teaching cycle (cf. Siegel and DiBello, 1980).

Consider an all-too-common misapplication of practice. In elementary schools, students are given an enormous amount of practice for skills such as basic arithmetic facts, spelling, and writing. The drill work takes the form of worksheets, which are completed as either individual or group-assigned seat work. For many reasons, most of which are logistical, very little attention can be paid to an individual student response at the moment of the response. Students may respond with perfect accuracy, imperfect accuracy, or not at all. Generally, however, it is difficult for both the teacher and the student to monitor the process effectively, especially for individual responses. As students complete the practice, the worksheets are collected, marked right or wrong, and returned to the students within a few days.

Under ideal circumstances, the students should have received feedback quickly. This helps students to make necessary corrections or to reinforce correct responses. Immediate feedback also helps to assure that practice will have positive instructional value. The worst possible outcome is where a student repeatedly practices incorrectly or responds randomly due to confusion. Unfortunately, often due to the raw amounts of worksheet practice provided in many settings, the worst possible scenario is often the most common.

In CAI, drill and practice designs provide practice for defined skills, immediate feedback to the student for each response given, and usually some form of correction or remediation for incorrect responses. Drill and practice designs assume many of the same functions as traditional worksheets, but they avoid the problems of inadequate monitoring, unchecked error responses, and postponed feedback.

It is not typically the function of drills to teach new concepts, skills, or information. Generally, drill and practice designs are used to reinforce skills taught elsewhere via CAI tutorials or other teaching systems. Drill and practice should provide maximum interaction between the learner and the instruction.

(a)

(b)

Figure 10.2
Screen faces from a CAI drill.

Features of Effective Drills Drills should provide extensive opportunities for practicing well-defined skills. The student should have clear directions for responding; feedback appropriate to the nature of the response; and, in some cases, corrective or remedial instruction. Figures 10-2(a) through 10-2(g) illustrate each of these features.

Unlike tutorials, drill and practice designs usually assume that basic information has been taught elsewhere. The purpose of the drill is to provide an opportunity for reinforcing or strengthening correct responses, while identifying and correcting incorrect responses. Drills should permit the student to produce frequent answers to target questions and should minimize unrelated narrative, procedural complexity, and unnecessary information.

In general, drills are most effective when the nature of the response is brief and can be produced rapidly. This makes the focal point of the practice clear to the student, aids in increasing response frequency, and generally provides more practice on the target skills. In many cases, drills for more complicated tasks, such as correct verb tense in sentences, can be made more compact by requiring the

NAME THAT NOTE
Type '?' for Help or 'Q' to Quit

To move the tiny man, type:

R -> move to the right
L -> move to the left
U -> move up
D -> move down

Other options:

Q -> to quit the program
? -> to review the options
F -> when finished moving to play the note

Press the <SPACEBAR> to continue...

(c)

NAME THAT NOTE
Type '?' for Help or 'Q' to Quit

You are building a major triad.
The tonic note is the note F below middle C.
Find and play the THIRD note of the triad.

Move the man or type another option...

(d)

NAME THAT NOTE
Type '?' for Help or 'Q' to Quit

You are building a major triad.
The tonic note is the note F below middle C.
Find and play the THIRD note of the triad.

Listen now to the chord with your note...

Press the <SPACEBAR> to continue...

(e)

Figure 10.2 (*Continued*)

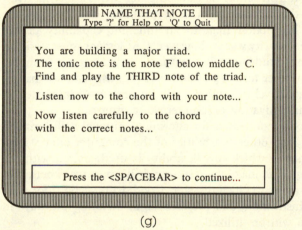

Figure 10.2 (*Continued*)

student to insert only those portions being drilled. In such a case, the drill might consist of an incomplete sentence, for which the student will select or type the necessary verb, rather than requiring the typing of entire sentences—a time-consuming and often unnecessary process.

Usually drills should focus on one or two well-defined skills rather than on several skills simultaneously. This is especially true during initial practice, where the drill activity should not be confounded by introducing information that is unrelated to the practiced skill. As proficiency develops, and as facility with subskills is demonstrated, it might be useful to integrate related skills in a separate drill. For example, the practice of multiplication facts may be best provided by isolating each of the specific multiplication factors initially, then integrating already learned factors in more complex forms.

Drills should offer both individual response feedback and other kinds of feedback that can be used to gauge performance. Individual response feedback provides an immediate cue as to individual response accuracy. Feedback may also provide richer elaborations of the correctness or incorrectness of responses, in order to explain more completely the accuracies or inaccuracies of an answer. Other kinds of program-level feedback, however, can also be made available. Cumulative performance within a drill can be used to give the student a running total of performance. Clarifying the relationship between lesson performance and the performance criteria for the practiced skill can also be very helpful features.

It is often useful to provide bail-outs for students, where very poor performance is identified during, rather than at the end of, a drill. If, for example, a student who was required to answer 18 questions out of 20 correctly to attain mastery of the practice skill misses the first three questions, the resulting score will inevitably fall below the criterion level after 20 questions. It is also likely that the three initial misses indicate that the student is not well prepared for the practice. It makes little sense to practice skills that are ineffective, but that is precisely what happens in programs where students have not yet acquired basic knowledge. In such instances, it is often useful to discontinue the drill and refer the students to more appropriate activities.

Initially, many students find instruction via the computer intrinsically motivating and appear seduced by the technology. This is probably due more to the novelty of computer-based instruction than to an inherent capability of the computer (Clark, 1985). When novelty wanes, however, CAI lessons must stand on merit. This is important, since students will eventually view learning from the computer as they would most other teaching systems: If the instruction is bad or lacking creativity or motivational value, students will become as disinterested in CAI drills as in any other unmotivating or uninteresting approach.

Computers offer a wealth of opportunities for altering traditional drill formats. The sound, color, animation, and other capabilities of the computer offer a good deal of flexibility. The manner in which this flexibility is used, paired with the fundamental logic of the design, can make the resulting drill a positive experience, a run-of-the-mill exercise, or an unqualified disaster. Good drills account for such variables as learner age, sophistication, and preferences in dictating the ways in which the computer features will be utilized.

In many cases, drills provide either the student or the instructor with options that control certain parameters of the lesson. For example, many drills permit the teacher to turn sound on or off, to print student performance reports or store student data to cassette tape or disk, or to select the number of problems to be presented. Still other drills allow either the teacher or the student to specify the complexity or difficulty of the drill questions by specifying particular problems to be provided, the difficulty of the problems presented, or the rate of display. Whereas these features are unnecessary for many drills, they are often very desirable as techniques for expanding the range of applicability for a drill.

Advantages and Limitations of Drill and Practice   Perhaps the principal advantage of CAI drills is the ability to provide an intensive, *controlled* opportunity for students to refine their skills. Unlike traditional worksheets, where significant time lapses separate responses from feedback, the quality of the practice can be monitored in an immediate sense. CAI drills provide an individual "teacher" for each student, capable of interacting with each student at the moment of response production. They do so with infinite patience and have virtually unerring accuracy in their assessment of student work (Dalton and Hannafin, 1985).

While some drill and practice activities are considered boring, the capacity to enliven the exercises through the incorporation of sound, color, and other computer features can make computer drills infinitely more appealing than alternative formats. Drills can also be designed to detect error patterns, to adapt the level of difficulty, and otherwise to manage the instructional process in ways that cannot be readily duplicated with other teaching systems. Record keeping can be instantaneously accomplished, student records updated, and progress reports generated at the discretion of the designer. The potential appears unlimited.

However, experienced designers of CAI drills are also aware of many of the realities of their application. Whereas the computer offers marvelous potential for practice, this potential is rarely applied. It is common for drills to be little more than electronic flash cards. As such, they do not in themselves teach; they only provide an opportunity to respond.

Another common criticism is that drills often appear more like tests than instruction. For example, the computer may present a math problem to a sixth grader, provide feedback for correct and incorrect responses, and perhaps even allow two or three attempts to produce a correct answer. This cycle by itself does not teach the student how to solve the problem. Instead, it merely informs as to correct answers—a feature also provided in many computer-based testing applications. If students produce incorrect responses, it would be more instructive to guide the student through the process of producing a correct response than to simply provide the answer.

Perhaps the most important issue in considering the assets and limitations of CAI drills is related to the potential versus the status of drill use. Most of the legitimate concerns pertaining to drills address status rather than potential. It is certainly true that many of the CAI drills presently available are poorly conceived, limited in their effectiveness, and uninteresting to students. These are not, however, a result of the limited *potential* of instructional drills. We have barely scratched the surface of what can be done using well-designed drills. The limitations cited usually result from inadequate methods and design. Many drills simply do not support learning well. We can and should reject such drills. However, we cannot reject the value and potential of intelligently designed CAI drills to support learning.

SIMULATIONS

CAI simulations approximate, replicate, or emulate the features of some task, setting, or context. Typically, simulations are used when the costs of alternative teaching systems are prohibitively high, when it is impossible to study the concepts of interest in "real time," or when the risks are considered sufficiently high to require demonstration of competence in a controlled, relatively risk-free environment (Alessi and Trollip, 1985; Ellinger and Brown, 1979). The procedures used in simulations vary considerably, but all represent a computer-controlled approximation of some other context.

Consider the following examples where computer simulations are used. Commercial airline pilots must be trained in a variety of procedures affecting the operation of aircraft, ranging from simply identifying and reading cockpit instruments to landing the aircraft safely during hazardous conditions. In many cases, it is far too costly to commit several expensive jet aircraft to much of the basic training, so computer-controlled simulators are often used. In addition, since the costs involved in preparing pilots to safely operate a commercial airline jet under hazardous conditions are potentially staggering, both in terms of aircraft costs and the human life risks, computers are often used to simulate various conditions.

Simulations are also used to study the effects of experiments that cannot be observed by the naked eye, due perhaps to the microscopic nature of the experiment or to the extreme speed or slowness of the elements to be observed. Imagine trying to observe the splitting of an atom in a nuclear reactor, a process that occurs instantaneously. Clearly, the only reasonable way to illustrate this process is to simulate the splitting. For these purposes, the process could be slowed down sufficiently to permit careful study. The same is true for processes that require long periods of time, such as phenomena studied in genetic research, which cannot be observed in "real time" for classroom instructional purposes. Students can splice certain genes under computer-simulated conditions and study the effects of the splicing over a period of years, decades, and even centuries.

Features of Effective Simulations   Good simulations provide a scenario or set of events, clear options for student participation, a range of plausible consequences for student responses to the scenarios, and guidance for completion of the scenario. Depending upon the nature of the simulation, the fidelity of the images used may be critical. High-fidelity visual images are necessary for CAI simulations of neurosurgical procedures because of the exactness of the required procedures. In other instances, the image fidelity may be of little or no consequence and may not even involve the use of sound or picture images. Lessons simulating the projected annual return on various bank loans are examples where the "thinking" power of the computer is required, but image fidelity is unimportant.

Good simulations present a believable set of circumstances, reasonable response options, logical consequences for responses, and a revised set of circumstances based upon the ongoing interaction of the student (cf. Rowe, 1981). Several of these features are illustrated in Figures 10-3(a) through 10-3(f), which are sample portions from different segments of a model rocket simulation.

As with all good CAI, students must have clear guidelines for participation. In some cases, the rules and directions are *front-loaded*, with all necessary information for participation provided before the actual simulation begins. In others, the directions and rules are distributed throughout the lesson and are introduced only where they are needed. Students require knowledge of the goals or objectives of the simulation, how the simulation is to be terminated, directions for responding, and any other information specific to the guidelines adopted for participation.

An initial scenario prescribes the givens of the situation being simulated, introduces the critical aspects of the simulation, provides limited coaching of the student, and prescribes the range of possible student responses. In effect, the initial scenario provides the baseline set of circumstances, into which different variations will be introduced, which the student must evaluate in order to produce the best possible response.

Once the initial scenario has been presented, the student must either choose an appropriate course of action from among the options provided or, in some cases, respond by entering the course of action in open-ended, typed entry format. The student should have a clear expectation of the anticipated consequences of the

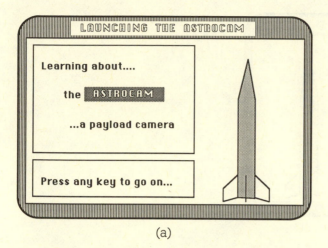

(a)

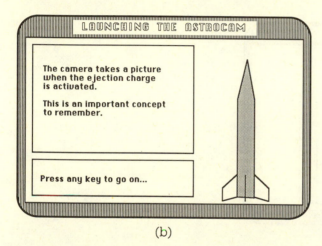

(b)

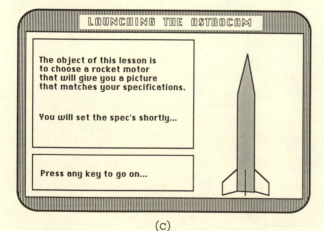

(c)

Figure 10.3
Screen faces from a CAI simulation.

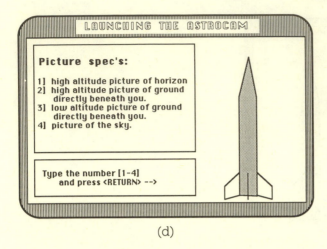

(d)

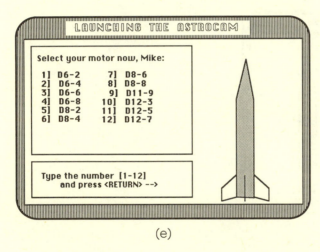

(e)

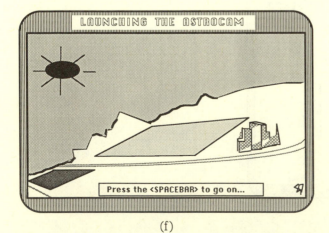

(f)

Figure 10.3 (*Continued*)

response, and, if appropriate, should be required to enter his or her expectation prior to continuation of the simulation. In this way, the simulation will incorporate both the scientific method and hypothesis testing concepts. This tends to enrich the instructional value of the simulation by permitting the student to evaluate projections relative to the consequences depicted in the simulation.

Good simulations identify changes in the critical elements of the scenario that result from student responses. In some cases, qualitative or quantitative evaluations of the consequences of the responses may also be provided. The purpose of clarifying the consequences is to provide immediate feedback on the effect of the input on the elements of the simulation and to allow the student to compare the observed consequences with those projected at the time of the response.

Typically, good simulations present a modified version of the initial scenario, based upon the cumulative responses of the student at each decision point. The modified scenario depicts the "new" situation and offers additional information necessary to produce an informed response. The modified scenarios should be readily identifiable as bringing the student closer to, or further from, the conclusion of the simulation.

Based upon the goals and rules of the scenario, the student completes the simulation effectively, ineffectively, or without judgment. Where possible and appropriate, students should receive a qualitative summary of their performances relative to the number of decisions made, the "losses" and "gains" incurred, or any other information related to the goals and elements of the simulation. In some cases, the simulation might also include further direction for the student. For example, responses may indicate a fundamental lack of comprehension, and the student might be referred to the necessary instruction. Since this is the final feature of the simulation, the completion portion should effectively bring closure to the simulation and provide as much overall feedback as possible to the student.

Advantages and Limitations of Simulations

Simulations offer perhaps the most unique application of the computer for instructional purposes. In many ways, CAI simulations represent the "thinking" and evaluative capabilities of the computer better than other designs. They permit the study of processes, procedures, and phenomena that either cannot be taught under *any* circumstances or cannot be easily taught using traditional methods. In some cases, it is possible to minimize or eliminate risks associated with certain learning tasks. In others, instructional simulations allow the study of things that cannot be observed directly in real time. Some simulations afford the learner a chance to apply skills in a nonthreatening simulation environment prior to the "real thing." In all cases, we are able to teach, learn, and practice skills in a computer world that more closely approximates real life than is otherwise possible. The current growth of interest is testimony to the increased awareness of designers of the power and potential of CAI simulations.

The limitations of simulations can be significant. Such problems, however, are related to the increased sophistication required to plan and program effective simulations and not to inherent limitations in simulations. Effective simulations often require advanced computer systems, as well as complicated computer programs. In many cases, complex phenomena must be simplified to the point that they are no longer valid representations of the actual circumstances.

Finally, well-designed simulations can pose a significant planning challenge for lesson designers. In some cases, it is not feasible to consider microcomputer CAI simulations due to the enormous time and expertise required to design and develop the lessons. It is important to note, however, that these are *human* shortcomings or, in some cases, specific computer limitations. The potential of CAI simulations as an alternative to high-cost, high-risk learning is most promising.

INSTRUCTIONAL GAMES

Games have been used for centuries to motivate individuals. Computer-based instructional games use the same basic concepts, except the purposes are defined more specifically as part of a teaching and learning context. Instructional games are high-motivational approaches to the reinforcement of already taught skills, concepts, and information (Malone, 1980, 1983). The game format offers possibilities that students often find appealing, but it must be emphasized that their purpose is first and foremost to develop, reinforce, and refine some aspect of learning. Unlike a simple noninstructional computer game, CAI games must retain instructional value as their primary goal. Whereas several skills are typically used to play an instructional game, the focal point of the game should be on the application of well-defined skills.

Usually instructional games emphasize some form of competition as the basic motivating component. The competition may be self-directed, as in exceeding a previous score. Perhaps the student is pitted against the computer, such as in games using imposed time limits or logic games. In certain cases, the student may oppose a character in the game, such as trying to avoid being devoured by a space creature. One student or group of students may be pitted against a different student or group. Virtually any instruction in which competition is a dominant procedural component can be considered an instructional game.

Instructional games are equated with arcade games, with the emphasis on elaborate graphics, sound, and motion. Certainly, many instructional games use this format since it is highly motivating to many students. However, instructional games and arcade games are not synonymous. Many instructional games use only words or numbers. The common denominator for CAI games is their capacity to provide practice in the application of skills, concepts, and information, using a motivating, competitive format (Crawford, 1984).

Features of Effective CAI Games Many of the features of games are similar to those of effective drills and simulations. Students must have clear directions for participation; the goal of the game must be understood by the student; and procedures for participation should be well defined, emphasizing frequent and easily generated responses. Figures 10.4(a–f) illustrate the features of CAI games.

For an instructional game to be effective, it must attract and enlist the enthusiasm of the student. If the game is not interesting, students will not invest effort in the lesson activities. Usually student motivation is piqued through the use of entertaining game scenarios; the incorporation of animation, color, and music; or the presence of competition as a basic element of the game.

Students must be given the information necessary to make sense of the lesson activities. For example, the goals of the game, the background related to game characters, the relationship between student responses and game consequences, and other information required to orient the student to the lesson are needed.

Well-designed instructional games use the orientation information as a way to sell the student on the activities that follow.

Guidelines for game participation must be provided. In addition, it is often necessary to make the rules and directions available during the game—especially for longer and more complex formats. The student must be given unequivocally clear guidance for lesson participation, except in cases where the discovery of the rules is an integral part of the game.

Instructional games must have an identifiable cause–effect relationship between student responses and game consequences. Correct answers should be acknowledged as correct, and game procedures should be executed that advance the scenario. Incorrect answers should be acknowledged as incorrect, and appropriate consequences should follow. It makes little instructional sense to design games that treat both correct and incorrect responses in the same manner (or randomly), since the game should aid in the development of prescribed skills.

Students should be advised continuously as to the quality of their performance. In addition, it is often useful for students to receive summaries of overall lesson performance. This summary should relate to both game consequences and student performance, since the game process is instructionally dependent. Well-designed instructional games equate response accuracy with game contingencies and occasionally prescribe the performance levels needed to improve game outcomes.

Advantages and Limitations of Instructional Games   Games offer instructional methods that capitalize on the competitive interests of students. Few other teaching approaches utilize this nature very frequently or effectively. Instead of relying on either the inherent interest of the lesson content or the diligence of individual learners to promote effective learning, instructional games incorporate methods that are as old as mankind.

Games formats are high in entertainment value and enlist the enthusiasm of students. Much of what must be taught is not inherently motivating to students. In many cases, the information is important, but it is perceived as uninteresting to many. Game formats can add entertainment value to instructional tasks that are

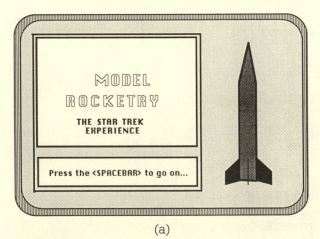

(a)

Figure 10.4
Screen faces from a CAI game.

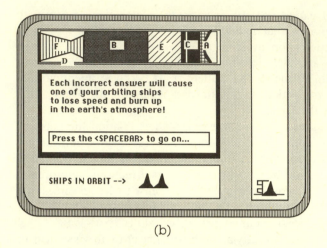

(b)

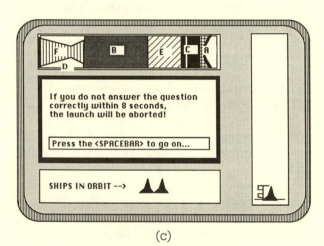

(c)

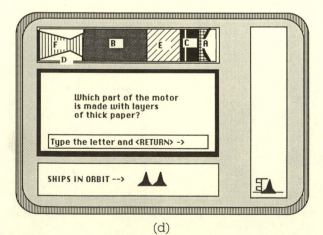

(d)

Figure 10.4 (*Continued*)

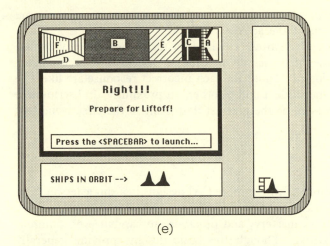

(e)

(f)

Figure 10.4 (*Continued*)

perceived negatively and can enlist the effort of many students for whom traditional methods are ineffective.

Computer-based instructional games also provide varied methods for learning that are different from most other approaches. In spite of differences in instructional hardware, many CAI lessons bear a remarkable resemblance to traditional lessons. This need not be true for CAI games. Computer-based instructional games offer presentation and participation formats that can be truly unique, and they represent the appearance of a new kind of instruction to many.

On the other hand, games have been criticized for several reasons. For instance, some games provide entertaining consequences for incorrect responses. Incorrect answers might be followed by an animated graphic with an accompanying raspberry sound that students find amusing. Game designers can unwittingly make incorrect answers more rewarding than correct responses.

Games have also been criticized for providing only incidental or minimal skill development in favor of the more elaborate game operation. For example, a single correct response might result in several minutes of game execution. Rather than providing a format for skill development, the visual and sound events of the game often become the focal point of the activity.

Finally, instructional games have been criticized for the excessive use of certain computer capabilities. Games that include a "Charge" melody for each correct response and a brief rendition of "Taps" for each incorrect response are likely to prove distracting, both to the student and to others in proximity. Indiscriminate use of computer capabilities can be the greatest detriment to the effectiveness of instructional games.

HYBRID DESIGNS

Hybrid designs include features of two or more CAI designs in a single lesson. The features of tutorials are often combined with drills or games, for example, to vary the lesson activities, to ensure mastery, and otherwise to capitalize on different methods of improving learning. Though the basic designs provide generally accepted classifications for CAI lessons, hybrid designs are perhaps the most common in CAI.

Many consider problem-solving and inquiry designs as hybrid designs, in that they often capture the functions of two or more basic designs rather than providing a truly unique and separate CAI design. This is probably an oversimplification. Problem-solving CAI is typically designed to encourage resolution of lesson-supplied dilemmas or problems through the systematic acquisition and application of lesson knowledge. Inquiry designs, on the other hand, encourage learning by permitting the student (or, in certain cases, the computer) to solicit information, explanations, and so on, based upon uniquely identified needs. In effect, the lesson is not designed to present sequentially arranged sets of frames but to permit the student to query the computer for needed information. While parallels among the basic designs, problem-solving lessons, and inquiry designs can be established, the functional intent of problem-solving and inquiry CAI designs is actually unique, and the procedures corresponding to each are typically quite different.

The applications of various hybrid designs are far reaching. It is often desirable, for example, to reduce the breadth of a lesson in favor of strengthening fewer skills—especially for young students. In such cases, tutorial and instructional game designs are often merged to provide the needed blend of knowledge and practice. In other cases, hybrid lessons will be developed to assure mastery via intensive drills prior to lesson continuation. The features of the different designs may then be incorporated into a single lesson strategy.

Each of the basic CAI designs can be used in combinations with one or more of the other designs. Tutorial designs, for example, are often combined with drills, as illustrated in Figures 10-5(a) and 10.5(b). This combination permits both the initial presenting of lesson content and the practicing of the skills taught until mastery has been attained.

It is also fairly common to combine tutorial and simulation designs. Figures 10.6(a) and 10.6(b) are samples from different portions of the same lesson. The figures illustrate information presented in preparation for ensuing simulation activities. In this case, one portion of the lesson focuses on the tutoring of concepts related to internal combustion. The information is presented, practiced, and reinforced in preparation for an engine-tuning simulation.

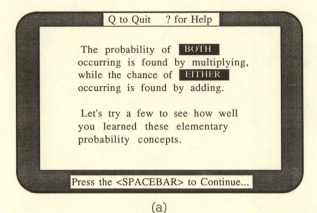

(a)

(b)

Figure 10.5
Hybrid design frames combining tutorial and drill modes.

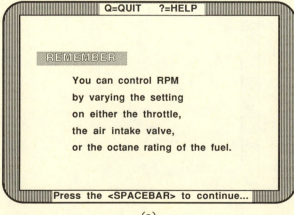

(a)

Figure 10.6
Hybrid design frames combining tutorial and simulation modes.

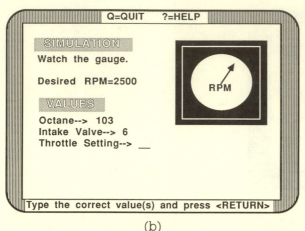

(b)

Figure 10.6 (*Continued*)

Figures 10.7(a) through 10.7(c) illustrate the combination of drill and game formats. The student is required to produce three consecutive correct responses to the math problems presented, after which he or she is permitted to make a move in the game. Since the game can only be played when the required performance has been demonstrated, a premium is placed on accuracy during the drill portion. In fact, students who do not attend to the drill feature effectively are forced to miss their turn, giving the advantage to those who work diligently during the drill.

It is not difficult to imagine hybrid applications for teaching foreign-language vocabulary, medical diagnostic procedures, or any of an infinite range of other instructional tasks. The possibilities are limited only by the designer's ability to recognize the appropriateness or inappropriateness of different hybrid combinations and to plan and implement such designs. As with any instructional strategy, confirmation of the appropriateness of the strategy must be a precondition for selection and development of hybrid designs.

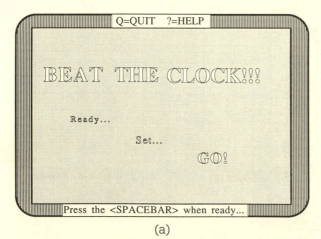

(a)

Figure 10.7
Hybrid design frames combining CAI game and drill and practice modes.

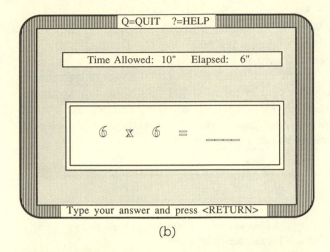

(b)

(c)

Figure 10.7 (*Continued*)

Although hybrid lessons are not unique CAI designs, they provide convenient methods for capturing the functions of different designs in a single lesson. They permit the development of comprehensive lessons that provide the complete set of instructional activities required for concept mastery. In certain cases, the development of a lesson featuring aspects of two or more designs can be most useful and effective.

Chapter Summary

In the introductory section of this chapter, we cautioned that all CAI is not the same. Each mode or design is uniquely adapted to provide different kinds of learning experiences, under different sets of assumptions. These options provide designers with an assortment of techniques that can be selected or modified to match a particular need.

From a systems perspective, meeting the defined need is the principal goal of the lesson development process. We plan and conduct needs assessments to clarify the nature of the problem, establish assumptions regarding the learning task, and otherwise obtain input that can be used in producing a solution. If we find that basic information is already taught and that instruction to support learning is indicated, then we might choose a drill or instructional simulation to provide an opportunity for the application of knowledge. If students require motivating instruction, perhaps an instructional game will be developed. The logic is straightforward: Make the solution match the problem.

References

ALESSI, S. M., and S. R. TROLLIP (1985). *Computer-Based Instruction: Methods and Development*. Englewood Cliffs, NJ: Prentice-Hall.

BRAMBLE, W. J., and E. J. MASON (1985). *Computers in Schools*. New York: McGraw-Hill.

CLARK, R. E. (1985). Evidence for confounding in computer-based instruction studies: Analyzing the meta-analyses. *Educational Communication and Technology Journal*, **33**, 249–262.

CRAWFORD, C. (1984). *The Art of Computer Game Design*. Berkeley, CA: McGraw-Hill.

DALTON, D. D., and M. J. HANNAFIN (1985). Examining the effects of varied computer-based reinforcement on self-esteem and achievement: An exploratory study. *Association for Educational Data Systems Journal*, **18**, 172–182.

ELLINGER, R. S., and B. R. BROWN (1979). The whens and hows of computer-based instructional simulations. *AEDS Journal*, **12**, 51–62.

MALONE, T. W. (1983). Toward a theory of intrinsically motivating instruction. *Cognitive Science*, **4**, 333–369.

——— (1980). *What makes things fun to learn? A study intrinsically motivating computer games*. Cognitive and Instructional Science Series CIS-7. Palo Alto, CA: Palo Alto Research Center.

ROWE, N. C. (1981). Some rules for good simulations. *Educational Computer*, **1**(4), 37–41.

SIEGEL, M. A., and L. V. DiBELLO (April 1980). Optimization of computer drills: An instructional approach. Presented at the annual meeting of the American Educational Research Association, Boston.

Related Reading

CONKRIGHT, T. D. (1984). Linear, branching, and complex: A taxonomy of simulations. *Training News*, **6**(3), 6–7, 19.

ELLINGTON, H., E. ADINALL, and F. PERCIVAL (1982). *A Handbook of Game Design*. London: Kogan Page.

GODFREY, D., and S. STERLING (1982). *The Elements of CAL*. Reston, VA: Reston Publishing Co.

LATHROP, A., and B. GOODSON (1983). *Courseware in the Classroom*. Reading, MA: Addison-Wesley.

LIAO, T. T. (1983). Using computer simulations to integrate learning. *Simulation and Games*, **14**(1), 21–28.

SULLIVAN, D. R., T. G. LEWIS, and C. R. COOK (1985). *Computing Today: Microcomputer Concepts and Applications*. Boston: Houghton Mifflin.

Chapter Review Exercises

COMPREHENSION

1. List and describe the four most common CAI lesson designs. (See pages 139–158.)

2. Describe the assumptions typically made in the development of each CAI lesson design. (See pages 139, 144, 149–150, 154.)

3. List and describe the major advantages and limitations of each of the CAI lesson designs. (See pages 142–144, 148–149, 153–154, 155–158.)

4. List and describe the features of effective lessons for each of the CAI lesson designs. (See pages 139–142, 145–148, 150–153, 154–155.)

5. Describe the implications of each of the CAI lesson designs with regard to the following:
   a. Program complexity.
   b. Hardware considerations.
   c. Learner characteristics.
   d. Related instructional support needs.
   (See pages 139–161.)

APPLICATION

1. Identify an instructional need appropriate for computer-based instruction. Evaluate the appropriateness of each of the CAI lesson modes in meeting the defined need.

2. For the instructional need identified, select the most appropriate CAI lesson mode for the required learning.

3. Select the CAI lesson mode that most effectively meets the requirements of the need, given the practical limitations of available computer hardware.

4. Design the necessary activities required to support the CAI design selected for the need.

CHAPTER 11

Designing CAI Frames

People are affected by the visual aspects of their environment. Some visual events are viewed as pleasant, while others are not. Some are easily understood, while others are difficult to interpret. Commercial advertisers have made a science of how people respond to visual stimuli and have been particularly successful in applying this information toward improving the familiarity and recognizability of their products. If visual advertising is effectively organized, products will be easily remembered; if not, the public will not remember the product information and the advertising will be ineffective.

The same is true for organizing instruction. If instructional materials are not readily interpreted by learners, then the instruction will likely be ineffective. If important information is not emphasized and presented clearly, if appropriate support is not provided for assisting learning, and if learners are confused as to the method of presentation, effective learning will rarely follow.

This is especially true for instructional technologies such as the computer. The computer has no inherent sense of the cues to student confusion available in live instruction, such as blank facial expressions, student indifference during a lesson, or general inattentiveness. Some of these can be captured to a degree in the lesson design, but not in the same sense as through live instruction.

Instead, computer-based instruction must use presentation formats that are unequivocally clear and readily interpreted by the student. Like the advertising field, the CAI design profession must treat lesson presentation as a combination of art and science. CAI lessons must be visually appealing but easily interpreted, must not be confusing to the student, and must clearly support the instructional objective. The purposes of this chapter are to examine the different kinds of frames used in CAI lessons and to describe the methods used for presenting frames of instruction.

OBJECTIVES

Comprehension

After completing this chapter you will be able to

1. List and describe the major types of frames used in CAI.
2. Define *frame protocol* and describe the importance of protocol in CAI.

3. Describe which portions of a frame are typically designated for particular functions.

4. Describe the importance of *procedural protocol* in CAI lessons.

Application

After completing the chapter you will be able to

1. Incorporate transitional, instructional, and question frames appropriately into CAI lesson flowcharts.

2. Design unique frame protocol for each type of frame in the lesson.

3. Design frame protocol that is easily interpreted and aesthetically appealing.

4. Design consistent procedural protocol for each frame type used in CAI lessons.

Types of Frames

In CAI, a frame is usually defined as the contents of any single screen of information (Bunson, 1985). As a student proceeds through a lesson, a series of screens is displayed, each of which presents information, instructions, questions, or feedback, or serves any of a variety of purposes. Each of the screens constitutes a single frame.

Basically, there are three major types of frames: transitional frames, instructional frames, and question frames. Each frame type has numerous possible variations.

TRANSITIONAL FRAMES

Transitional frames are used to tie together the different aspects of a CAI lesson. For example, students are often given help options, asked to enter their names, or given instructions or directions on how to use the lesson. The nature of such frames is neither to teach information nor to evaluate learning. The purpose of transitional frames is to support lesson flow, to provide assistance in lesson procedures, or to advance smoothly from one part of a lesson to another. Transitional frames provide *contextual* or *procedural* support for learning during CAI, but not substantive support.

Consider the number of ways transitional frames are used in a CAI lesson. CAI lessons often contain activities designed to support the instruction and questions of the lesson. This is accomplished by providing information that eases the transition from one topic or activity to another or, in some cases, aids the student in organizing the information presented during a lesson.

There are several kinds of transitional frames. Those most commonly used in CAI are described here.

Orientation Orientation frames prepare the student for information to be presented during a lesson. In some cases, these frames will simply state the lesson objectives. This simple orientation frame is illustrated in Figure 11.1. In other cases, however, the orientation frames provide advance organizers, techniques for remembering the information presented, or other information designed to prepare the student effectively for lesson information.

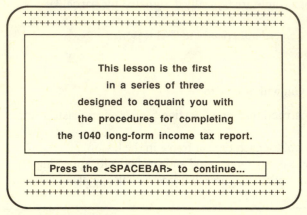

Figure 11.1
An orientation transitional frame.

```
++++++++++++++++++++++++++++++++++++++++++++++++++
++++++++++++++++++++++++++++++++++++++++++++++++++

        You have done very well
           to this point, Barry.
        Now that you have completed
        the section on tax rules,
      we will see if you can apply the rules
       WITHOUT my help.



   Press the <SPACEBAR> to continue...
++++++++++++++++++++++++++++++++++++++++++++++++++
++++++++++++++++++++++++++++++++++++++++++++++++++
```

Figure 11.2
A bridge transitional frame.

Bridge   In certain cases, the focus of the lesson changes substantially, such as moving from presentation to practice. This change can appear very abrupt if information designed to bridge one section to another is not provided. The bridge frame shown in Figure 11.2, for example, alerts the student to a shift from the heavy prompting used up to this point to the minimal prompting used in the following lesson section.

Feedback   In some cases, response feedback is included on the same frame as the question. In others, it is necessary to provide feedback on a separate frame. Feedback frames are used to inform students of the correctness, incorrectness, or quality of their responses. Progress toward the learning of already presented information is usually the focus of the feedback. New information is not typically presented at this time. Feedback frames, such as the one shown in Figure 11.3, provide necessary information regarding student responses consistent with the theme of the lesson, thereby easing the transition among instruction and student responses.

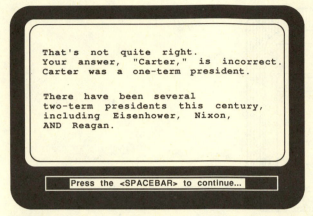

Figure 11.3
A feedback transitional frame.

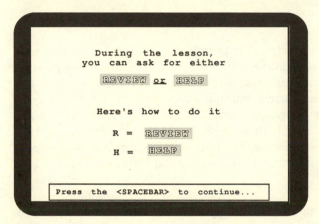

Figure 11.4
A transitional frame that provides directions.

Directions and Instructions One of the most common uses of transitional frames is to present directions or instructions to the student regarding the options, features, and formats of the lesson. It may be important, for example, to inform the student how to obtain assistance during a lesson, as illustrated in Figure 11.4. Or perhaps instructions for lesson control must be presented to alert the student to important procedural features of the lesson. Transitional frames provide this kind of information.

Performance Report Frequently lessons include frames that inform students of their performance. Unlike feedback frames, reporting frames are not response-specific. Instead, they usually contain performance summaries related to lesson objectives and required performance standards. In some cases, reporting frames are provided at various intervals throughout the lesson. In others, as shown in Figure 11.5, they are used only at the end of the lesson. In all cases, however, they offer information that can be useful to students in evaluating their performance relative to individually or lesson-prescribed expectations.

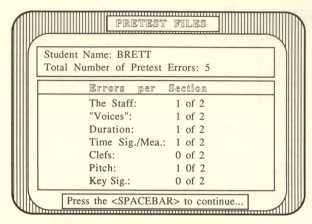

Figure 11.5
A transitional frame used to report to the student.

INSTRUCTIONAL FRAMES

Instructional frames, sometimes referred to as presentation frames, present basic lesson information to the student (Burke, 1982). As noted, there are many possible applications of instructional frames. Typically, instructional frames introduce the relationship between prior and current learning topics, present new instruction, support new instruction by providing examples and other forms of learner guidance, or demonstrate the application of instructed information in different contexts. In each case, *information* designed to support learning is provided. The most frequently used instructional frames are illustrated in Figures 11.6 through 11.9.

Prerequisite   Substantive instructional support, such as the information or skills required for effective learning, can be presented very clearly. Figure 11.6 illustrates an instructional frame designed to alert students to the need for certain skills prior to beginning the lesson. These frames do more than simply raise a flag

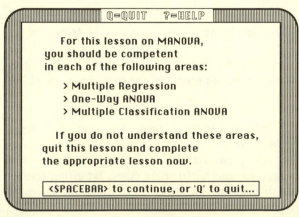

Figure 11.6
An instructional frame presenting prerequisites.

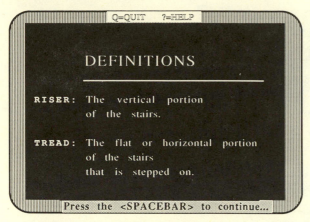

Figure 11.7
An instructional frame that presents definitions.

to students concerning these skills. Prerequisite frames help to identify explicitly the relationships among past and current learning and aid in the integration of current lesson information with existing knowledge.

Definition Definitions are used often in CAI lessons. These frames help to equalize students' understanding of key terms developed throughout a lesson. Figure 11.7 illustrates how directly and emphatically the computer focuses learner attention to definitions by isolating the information from potentially distracting information and by emphasizing different aspects of the definition. Key terms, phrases, important figures, and other lesson information are often presented in this manner.

Example Examples provide important support for teaching and learning, often by clarifying abstract concepts. Figure 11.8, for example, provides a concrete instance to strengthen and clarify the concept of justice. Example frames are also commonly used to illustrate applications, such as the completion of income tax

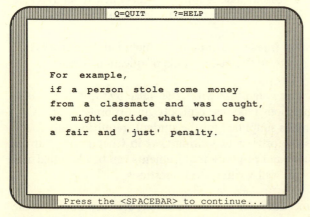

Figure 11.8
An instructional frame that presents an example.

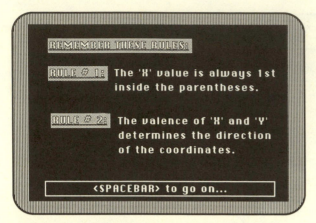

Figure 11.9
A rule instructional frame.

forms. Most lessons, especially those that are technologically based, incorporate examples extensively to support lesson content.

Rule   Much of what students learn is rule-governed. Computational formulas, trouble-shooting strategies, and procedures for changing flat tires are all, to a degree, rule-based learning tasks. CAI lessons will often isolate important rules initially to focus student attention. Figure 11.9, for example, illustrates a rule frame used to read two-dimensional graph coordinates. Without the clearly presented rule, the remainder of the lesson might have confused learners. Instead, the rule frame emphasized the information clearly and permitted students to continue the lesson under a uniform and unequivocal set of assumptions.

QUESTION FRAMES

Question frames, or criterion frames, are used to solicit input that permits individualized instruction based upon individual student responses (cf. Burke, 1982). Usually question frames require the student to respond to a question based on information presented in the lesson. The computer subsequently analyzes or judges the response, and internal decisions are made to determine an appropriate consequence.

A number of different question frames are commonly included in CAI lessons. Figures 11.10 through 11.14 illustrate the major kinds of question frames.

True–False   Virtually everyone is familiar with true–false test questions. Figure 11.10 illustrates this question type as typically incorporated into CAI lessons. Notice how the response is simplified for the student, requiring only that a *T* or *F* be typed. We address the process of writing CAI in Chapter 15, but for now, note how easily the question and response requirements can be identified and read. This is the trademark of all well-written CAI questions.

Yes–No   The format and procedures for yes–no questions are very similar to the conventions used for true–false questions. Again, only two options are available, and both are indicated clearly. Figure 11.11 illustrates a typical yes–no question.

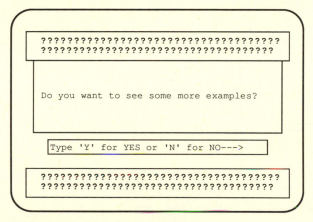

```
??????????????????????????????????????
??????????????????????????????????

Try this one:

Albany is the capital of New York.



Type 'T' for True or 'F' for False->

??????????????????????????????????????
??????????????????????????????????
```

Figure 11.10
A true–false question frame.

```
??????????????????????????????????????
??????????????????????????????????????

Do you want to see some more examples?


Type 'Y' for YES or 'N' for NO--->

??????????????????????????????????????
??????????????????????????????????????
```

Figure 11.11
A yes–no question frame.

In this case, the question was posed in order to execute the lesson based on the student's desire to receive additional examples.

Multiple Choice   Multiple-choice questions require careful allocation of screen space in order to make important aspects of the question easy to locate and to make the question itself easy to read. The multiple-choice frame shown in Figure 11.12 uses line spacing between the question stem and the choices, indentation of the choices for ease of reading, and clear directions to guide student responding. Care must be exercised to assure that the display of questions provides the clearest, easiest method for student viewing.

Completion/Short Answer   Completion questions, such as the one shown in Figure 11.13, typically require one- to three-word responses. The question must be organized completely to permit the response, but must not be cued so extensively that students detect clues to the answer from the structure or wording of the question itself. The question "There are __ __ months in a year" inadvertently

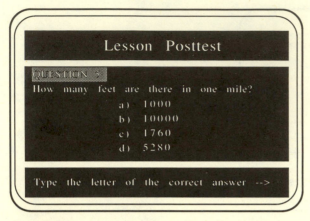

Figure 11.12
A multiple-choice question frame.

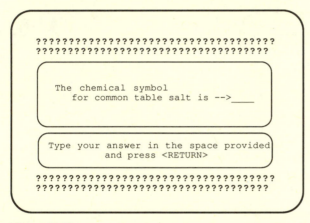

Figure 11.13
A short-answer question frame.

clues the student to provide an answer with two digits by embedding the insert prompts. The use of completion questions poses additional challenges to lesson designers, in that decisions regarding such concerns as spelling errors, capitalization, and punctuation must be made.

Constructed Response/Open-Ended   Constructed-response items, requiring input ranging from a simple phrase to several paragraphs, are among the most complicated of questions for CAI lessons. As shown in Figure 11.14, the question must provide sufficient guidance to the student in order to focus and organize the response. As is true of completion questions, the simplicity of the question belies the complex planning required for effective incorporation into CAI lessons.

FRAME VARIATIONS

It is often desirable to combine the features of transitional, instructional, and question frames. It is fairly common, for example, for lessons to consist of frames

```
                    Diseases:  Unit  4

    PART  I.    Describe  the  three  most  common
    symptoms  of  Parkinson's  Disease.
    Limit  your  answer  to  the  space  provided.

      >_____

      _____

      _____

      _____

      _____

      _____

    Type  your  answer  in  the  space  provided
```

Figure 11.14
An open-ended question frame.

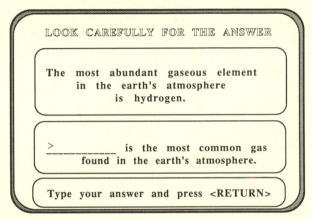

Figure 11.15
A copy frame.

with both instructional and question components or both transitional and instructional information. Figures 11.15 through 11.18 illustrate several frequently used hybrid frames.

Copy Frame Copy frames provide basic instructional information and the associated question on the same frame. The student's task is to locate and identify the necessary information and type the answer accordingly. As illustrated in Figure 11.15, copy frames are often used to focus attention on specific information. To many, copy frames appear too elementary for use in most lessons. However, they can be very useful in systematically directing student attention, obtaining student responses with a high probability of success, and emphasizing important lesson concepts.

Prompt Frames All well-designed frames are organized to aid the student in interpreting information. Some frames, however, provide explicit prompting, using either the frame features or thematic content to aid responding. The frame

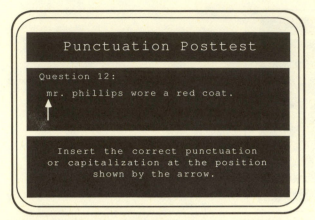

Figure 11.16
A prompt frame.

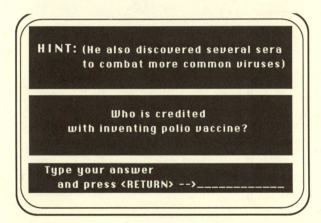

Figure 11.17
A hint frame.

shown in Figure 11.16, for example, illustrates the use of both the frame features and the thematic content to aid responding. Prompt frames are often designed for questions, although prompts also can be used effectively within instructional frames.

Hint Frames Figure 11.17 is an example of a hint frame, given after the student has failed to enter a response to a question. The hint is designed as an intermediate step to aid the student in producing a correct response, before assuming that the student does not know the answer. The hint provides information that might elicit correct responses but does not provide the correct response itself.

Interlaced Frames Often lesson frames consist of bits and pieces of several types of frames. Although such frames are often discouraged, there are circumstances where interlacing is useful. Figure 11.18 illustrates an interlaced frame, incorporating both question and feedback information on the same frame. This is

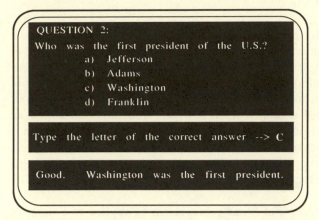

Figure 11.18
An interlaced frame.

particularly useful in this case because the student can examine the response and the feedback together, check for obvious errors, and otherwise use the information effectively.

Protocol in Frame Design

CAI lessons that vary the location of information within frames, procedures used for frame advance, and other features can be frustrating (Mackey and Slesnick, 1982). Confusion is possible in any teaching system, but it may be compounded in CAI because many features of other teaching systems that would aid students to interpret the lesson, such as the opportunity to raise their hands for assistance, turn back pages to review, or ask the teacher to repeat directions, are often unavailable in CAI. The computer provides a more self-contained teaching and learning environment than other systems. During CAI lessons, students do not have the benefit of teacher gestures or vocal inflection to cue them to important points.

How then can the instruction be oriented to ease the task of interpretation by the student? How will the student know how to obtain needed assistance? How can all of this be done given the somewhat limited frame and screen size potentials of most computers?

To provide the needed support, the adoption of consistent, more or less standardized conventions for frame design is often necessary (Heines, 1984; Lentz, 1985; Simpson, 1984). In certain cases, user preferences for frame characteristics have been identified (Grabinger, 1984). If students are provided with consistency in the procedures for obtaining assistance, the location of information on the frame, and the methods for obtaining other important information, then the learning task can be simplified significantly.

Frame protocol refers to the consistent designation of various zones of a frame for specific uses. The protocol adopted is characteristically different among different frame types, but it is consistent for most cases of that particular application. We will see how frame protocol can simplify the process of learning as we proceed through the remainder of this chapter. First, consider how the concept of protocol is applied in the design of CAI frames.

FUNCTIONAL ZONES

Imagine the screen, or CAI frame, as a collection of zones. Each zone has a particular function. The locations of the zones are consistent whenever that type of frame is displayed. For example, directions for proceeding are *always* located at the bottom of the frame. The information component always appears in the center of the frame, while lesson information is centered at the top of the frame. Without even seeing the instructional contents of each frame, you have developed an expectancy for where to find information and how to proceed through a lesson.

In CAI, the consistency provided through frame protocol simplifies the process of reading and comprehending. The student has a recognizable way to "raise his hand" to the computer, ask for repeated instructions, and review lesson information.

Let's examine how the concepts of frame protocol can be applied to a series of instructional frames in a typical CAI tutorial (see also Heines, 1984). The functional zones to be used include the following components: lesson orientation information, directions, options, and new information. As illustrated in Figures 11.19 through 11.22, the lesson orientation information is centered at the top of the frame; directions for proceeding are provided at the bottom; the options for Q (quitting), R (reviewing), or ? (help) are below the orientation information; and new information is centered on the frame. In addition, the frame incorporates borders to further differentiate the zones of the screen. Each zone is used consistently for all instructional frames in the lesson.

The protocol for question frames, though quite different from instructional frames, should also be consistent throughout the lesson. Note that the sample question frame shown in Figure 11.23 also uses four functional zones and a standard border, but the visual appearance of the frame is quite different from that of the instructional frame. The question frame provides different orientation information at the top of the frame, provides no help options, provides student performance updates, retains the directions function at the bottom of the frame, and integrates both the test question and the response prompt in the information zone of the frame. The borders used are also unique to question frames, creating a distinct visual difference between two very different kinds of frames.

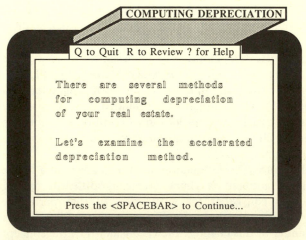

Figure 11.19
Lesson-orientation zone on an instructional frame.

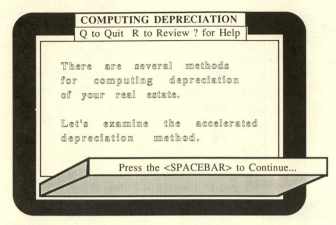

Figure 11.20
Lesson-directions zone on an instructional frame.

Figure 11.21
Lesson-options zone on an instructional frame.

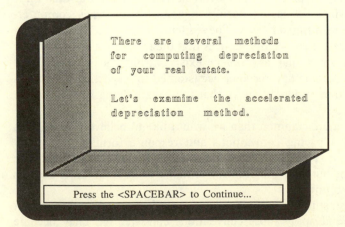

Figure 11.22
New-information zone on an instructional frame.

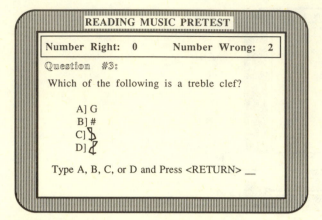

Figure 11.23
A question frame illustrating the locations of functional zones.

Within each frame type, the locations are consistent, but the method of utilization is markedly different. Students develop an anticipatory mental set to the different frame protocols. The task of providing easy-to-use procedures that offer many of the same kinds of options available in other teaching systems is simplified, in terms of both programming needs and student encoding. The key to effective frame protocol is *consistency*.

Procedural Protocol

Procedural protocol refers to the consistent use of conventions for lesson procedures, obtaining student responses, indicating the availability of lesson options, and prescribing other features that affect lesson use. As with frame protocol, it is important that students identify consistent procedures for lesson pacing and consistent conventions for responding to question frames.

Consider the following instance of failed procedural protocol. A student begins a lesson, and the procedure for advancing through the lesson is learner-controlled— "Press Space Bar to Continue." This procedure is followed for the first three instructional frames, when the lesson pacing inexplicably becomes computer-controlled through the use of timed pauses. The student, accustomed to the learner control, presses the space bar repeatedly, notices that the frames are not advancing as anticipated, and assumes that a problem exists within the lesson or the computer. Or perhaps students have become accustomed to inspecting the frames at their own pace, and they suddenly notice that frames are flying by. Surely the computer has run amok!

These conditions are more common than we would like to believe. For reasons that are not at all clear, pacing conventions and response formats often vary without so much as a hint as to the change or any compelling reason for changing the procedures. It seems not only unnecessary to make procedural shifts such as those described, but also unwise.

Given the opportunity, students will routinize the procedures of a lesson, adopt the conventions used, and apply those conventions consistently. They become accustomed to a pacing pattern that simplifies the task of learning. When changes are not made, students need not be taught new procedures and need not invest mental effort to learn the different procedural nuances of the lesson. If frame advancement is accomplished via pressing the space bar for instructional frames, then this procedure should be implemented consistently.

Changes in the procedures of a lesson should be announced beforehand via transitional frames and should be made for important, compelling reasons. There are few instances where the arbitrary shifting of procedural protocol is desirable and even fewer where such a shift is truly necessary. Consistent procedural protocol is generally more straightforward and easier to program from a design perspective, while also being easier to routinize from the student's perspective.

EXAMPLES OF PROCEDURAL PROTOCOL

Let's consider some examples of effective procedural protocol. Notice that the procedures used for advancing instructional frames, shown in Figures 11.24(a) and 11.24(b), are identical. The procedures used for questions, shown in Figure 11.25, are different from those used for instructional frames, but they are consistent for all questions.

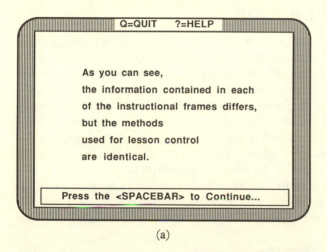

(a)

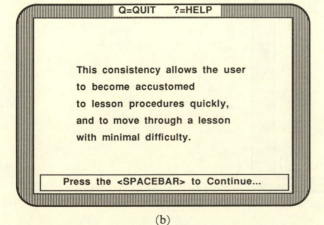

(b)

Figure 11.24
Procedural protocol for instructional frames.

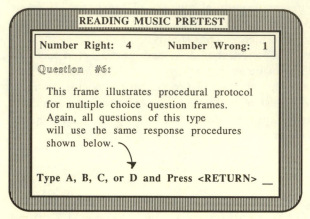

Figure 11.25
Procedural protocol for a question frame.

Programming Implications

Frame protocol can be programmed with relative ease once initial decisions have been made. In fact, the task of programming is often simplified substantially by the adoption of consistent frame protocol conventions. Generally, the process consists of planning and designing frame protocols, programming procedures or subroutines to create the desired frame protocols, and simply inserting lesson information into the frames. Some additional features might be included as well, but most of the information contained in the different zones of the frame will be used consistently throughout the lesson. The task of programming has been simplified significantly as a result of the conventions adopted.

Consider the protocol adopted for question frames shown in Figures 11.26 (a) through 11.26(c). Several questions will be asked during the lesson, but the protocol will be the same throughout. Notice that the only information that

```
╔══════════════════════════════════════╗
║         READING MUSIC POSTTEST         ║
║  ┌──────────────────────────────────┐  ║
║  │ Number Right:  1    Number Wrong:  1 │  ║
║  ├──────────────────────────────────┤  ║
║  │ Question #3:                        │  ║
║  │ A musical staff has ___ lines.      │  ║
║  │       A] three                      │  ║
║  │       B] five                       │  ║
║  │       C] two                        │  ║
║  │       D] seven                      │  ║
║  │                                     │  ║
║  │  ┌────────────────────────────────┐ │  ║
║  │  │ Type A, B, C, or D and Press <RETURN> __ │ │  ║
║  │  └────────────────────────────────┘ │  ║
║  └──────────────────────────────────┘  ║
╚══════════════════════════════════════╝
```

(a)

Figure 11.26
Examples of procedural protocol for successive questions.

```
┌─────────────────────────────────────────────┐
│  ▐▌ READING MUSIC POSTTEST ▐▌                 │
│  ┌──────────────────────────────────────┐   │
│  │ Number Right:  2      Number Wrong:  1 │   │
│  │                                        │   │
│  │ Question  #4:                          │   │
│  │ In  a  piece  of  music,  staffs  come  in │
│  │ groups  of  ___.                       │   │
│  │           A]  2                        │   │
│  │           B]  3                        │   │
│  │           C]  4                        │   │
│  │           D] all  of  the  above       │   │
│  │                                        │   │
│  │  ┌──────────────────────────────────┐ │   │
│  │  │ Type A, B, C, or D and Press <RETURN> __ │ │
│  │  └──────────────────────────────────┘ │   │
│  └──────────────────────────────────────┘   │
└─────────────────────────────────────────────┘
```

(b)

```
┌─────────────────────────────────────────────┐
│  ▐▌ READING MUSIC POSTTEST ▐▌                 │
│  ┌──────────────────────────────────────┐   │
│  │ Number Right:  2      Number Wrong:  2 │   │
│  │                                        │   │
│  │ Question  #5:                          │   │
│  │ In  sheet  music,  the  term  'allegro' │   │
│  │ means  _____.                         │   │
│  │    A]  slower  and  softer             │   │
│  │    B]  faster  with  gusto             │   │
│  │    C]  pause  momentarily              │   │
│  │    D]  shift  to  the  next  highest  octave │
│  │                                        │   │
│  │  ┌──────────────────────────────────┐ │   │
│  │  │ Type A, B, C, or D and Press <RETURN> __ │ │
│  │  └──────────────────────────────────┘ │   │
│  └──────────────────────────────────────┘   │
└─────────────────────────────────────────────┘
```

(c)

Figure 11.26 (*Continued*)

changes from frame to frame is the question number and the question itself. All other information, including the directions for responding, the location of the various functional zones, the borders used, and the options provided, are identical. The identical elements need to be programmed only once; then they can be used repeatedly throughout the lesson.

Chapter Summary

The systematic use of distinctive frame features and protocol provides a method for supporting student learning that is tied neither to instructional sequence nor to the application of learning strategies. Effectively designed frames support learning by easing the task of locating and interpreting lesson information, thereby minimizing possible confusion and interference in comprehending lesson information. Since students must rely solely on the comprehensibility of the computer-based lesson itself, the use of easily interpreted frame design conventions is important.

The keys to effective frame design are related to two major factors: consistency and clarity. When information is organized haphazardly or crammed unsystematically in lesson frames, the task of learning will only be complicated. Presentation formats are best when clutter is minimized, locations are defined and consistently used, and information is ordered and displayed in easily recognized patterns.

Frames are the visible vehicle through which lesson planning is represented. The best of ideas, plans, and designs will be lost if the method of presentation is improper or ineffective. Like the debater who plans and organizes compelling arguments in support of a position, the final test of the arguments rests with the presentation. The best planning efforts can only fail miserably if the presentation of the arguments is disorganized. Lesson frames represent visually the quality of instructional planning. This is not necessarily an accurate representation, but it is the indicator most apparent to users. If the product is easily understood, the information will be well received; if not, the best of plans will simply fail.

References

BUNSON, S. (1985). CAI frame by frame. *Tech Trends*, **30** (4), 24–25.

BURKE, R. L. (1982). *CAI Sourcebook*. Englewood Cliffs, NJ: Prentice-Hall.

GRABINGER, R. S. (1984). CRT text design: Psychological attributes underlying the evaluation of models of CRT text displays. *Journal of Visual and Verbal Languaging*, 4(1), 17–39.

HEINES, J. M. (1984). *Screen Design Strategies for Computer-Assisted Instruction*. Bedford, MA: Digital Press.

LENTZ, R. (1985). Designing computer screen displays. *Performance and Instruction*, **24** (1), 16–17.

MACKEY, K., and T. SLESNICK (1982). A style manual for authors of software. *Creative Computing*, **8,** 110–111.

SIMPSON, H. (1984). A human-factors style guide for program display. In D. F. Walker and R. D. Hess (eds.) (1984). *Instructional software: Principles and Perspectives for Design and Use*. Belmont, CA: Wadsworth.

Related Readings

DEAN, C., and Q. WHITLOCK (1983). *A Handbook of Computer-Based Training*. London: Kogan Page.

GODFREY, D., and S. STERLING (1982). *The Elements of CAL*. Reston, VA: Reston Publishing.

HUNTINGTON, J. F. (1979). *Computer-Assisted Instruction Using BASIC*. Englewood Cliffs, NJ: Educational Technology Publications.

MEREDITH, J. C. (1971). *The CAI Author/Instructor*. Englewood Cliffs, NJ: Educational Technology Publications.

RICHARDSON, J. J. (1980). The limits of frame-based CAI. Paper presented at the annual conference of the Association for the Development of Computer-Based Instructional Systems, Atlanta.

Chapter Review Exercises

COMPREHENSION

1. List and describe the major frame types used in CAI. (See pages 165–175 and Figures 11.1 through 11.18.)
2. Define *frame protocol*. Describe the importance of protocol in CAI. (See page 175.)
3. Describe which portions of a frame are usually designated as serving particular protocol purposes. (See pages 176–178 and Figures 11.19 through 11.24.)
4. Define *procedural protocol*. Describe the importance of procedural protocol in CAI lessons. (See pages 178–179.)

APPLICATION

1. Design a CAI lesson flow chart that incorporates transitional, instructional, and question frames.
2. Design unique frame protocol for the transitional, instructional, and question frames to be included in the CAI lesson. (See Figures 11.1 through 11.8 and 11.12 through 11.14.)
3. Design protocol for each frame type that is easily interpreted and aesthetically appealing.
4. Design procedural protocol affecting the execution of each frame type throughout the lesson. (See Figures 11.24 through 11.26.)

CHAPTER 12

Distributing Emphasis During a Lesson

The capacity to systematically direct student attention is one of the hallmarks of well-designed CAI. Well-designed frames make it easier to locate the kinds of information and options available. The protocol adopted permits the consistent location of different zones and allows the student to readily use the information presented within the frame.

Student attention can be focused still more through the use of techniques that make information within each portion of the screen more obvious. Perhaps there are certain key words, important warnings, or other lesson features that must stand out to the student. In this chapter, a variety of attention-directing techniques, some using features of the computer itself and others focusing the lesson information, will be presented.

OBJECTIVES

Comprehension

After completing this chapter you will be able to

1. Define the concept of *distribution of emphasis* as applied to CAI.
2. Describe how amplification techniques aid in distributing lesson emphasis appropriately.
3. Describe the differences between cosmetic and information-based amplification techniques.
4. List and describe methods used for both cosmetic and information-based amplification techniques.
5. Describe the effects of hardware limitations on amplification and protocol decisions.

Application

After completing this chapter you will be able to

1. Design lessons using effective cosmetic amplification techniques for a selected instructional need.
2. Design lessons using effective information-based amplification techniques for a selected instructional need.

3. Design lessons that incorporate both cosmetic and information-based techniques to distribute lesson emphasis appropriately.
4. Design lessons that incorporate amplification techniques that are consistent with computer and output display limitations.

Directing Student Attention

Perhaps the most important task for the designer is to develop methods of computer use that systematically direct attention to the important features of the lesson. This is an extremely important task in CAI lesson design, due to the absence of the kinds of support to which learners have become accustomed. Students do not highlight a computer lesson with a yellow marker. They do not typically reread CAI lesson pages. They cannot raise their hands to request an alternative explanation, or make notes in the margin, or use most of the learning techniques developed for traditional teaching systems. When students receive instruction via computer, they depend more on the foresight of the lesson designer than for virtually any other teaching system.

The task, then, is to develop methods and techniques that permit the student to attend systematically to those aspects of the lesson that are most relevant and important (Hathaway, 1984). *Distribution of emphasis* describes the extent to which the important aspects of a lesson are emphazied over less important aspects.

There are several techniques of directing student attention to important lesson information. Some of these techniques employ the capabilities of the computer to highlight information. Others rely on manipulations of the instructional content. In this section, several techniques for amplifying important lesson content will be presented.

COSMETIC AMPLIFICATION

Effective lessons use the capabilities of the computer to amplify information, by varying the use of features such as color, print size, text display rate, and others. Note how the information amplified in Figures 12.1 through 12.4 is easier to locate, standing apart from the remainder of the frame.

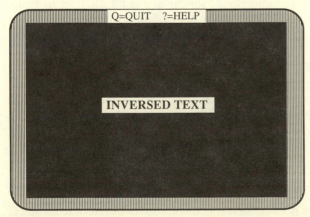

Figure 12.1
Inversing text on a frame.

Figure 12.2
Varying type size for effect.

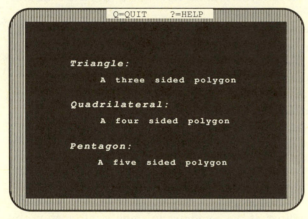

Figure 12.3
Changing type style for effect.

Inversing Inversing simply exchanges the current background color with the foreground color, and vice versa. The effect, shown in Figure 12.1, is to make information stand out more clearly. Inversing is commonly used to emphasize important vocabulary terms, key lesson information, and lesson control information (Schloss, Schloss, and Cartwright, 1985).

Flashing Flashing is accomplished by alternating the background and foreground colors continuously to create the illusion of a flash. This is often applied to warnings and cautions, where a message must be seen but the information itself is not to be learned. Flashing is extremely effective in gaining student attention, but it can be very distracting. As a consequence, flashing is sometimes encouraged for directing attention to the procedural aspects of a lesson, but it is generally discouraged for emphasizing lesson *information*.

Type Size Some computers permit the simultaneous use of different letter sizes, allowing information to be enlarged. Figure 12.2 illustrates the use of different type

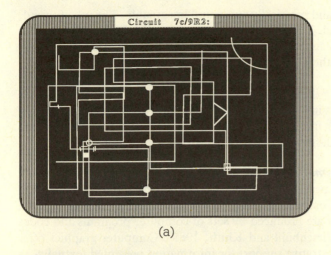

(a)

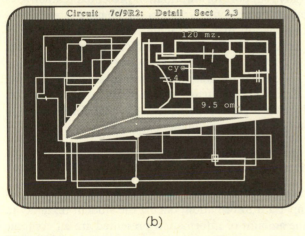

(b)

Figure 12.4
Zooming in on frame information for effect.

sizes to direct student attention to impending disaster. It is unlikely that this warning will go unnoticed.

Font In some cases, it is useful to vary the type style, or font. In Figure 12.3, the font has been altered, creating an effect that is easily recognized. Instead of the standard characters provided by the computer, the important vocabulary terms are presented in italics.

Color Many computers permit the use of different color combinations. For example, it might be useful to present new vocabulary in red letters. The remainder of the text could be presented in standard background and text colors, creating the desired effect only where desired.

Sound Sound is used in many lessons to reinforce correct answers, to prompt the student to illegal responses, to entertain the student, and even to teach musical note identification. Sound may take the form of musical compositions, brief melodies, whirring sirens, and practically any sound imaginable. The use of sound, however, must be tempered. Young students may enjoy a brief melody, but older students may not. While sound can be effective in directing attention, it can also distract the learner and others in the immediate vicinity.

Zooming and Panning   Television production techniques that are applicable to the design of CAI lessons involve zooming in (enlarging) and panning (gradually moving across) important frame detail. Figures 12.4(a) and 12.4(b) illustrate zooming techniques to enlarge the detail of an electronic circuit.

Other Methods of Cosmetic Amplification   Two techniques commonly found in CAI that are in part cosmetic but are often substantive are computer graphics and animation. Computer graphics are visual images, such as objects, histograms, and maps, that are produced by sets of computer programs and codes (Cf. Alessandrini, 1984; Hirschbuhl and Kluth, 1985). Computer graphics offer the potential to provide illustrative support for information presented textually, as well as providing numerous other applications. Graphics can be used as attention-gaining devices, to present information that is difficult or impossible to convey verbally, or simply to help provide additional organization to lesson content. Likewise, computer animation may be employed as a motivational or prompting device or it may be used to depict motion. Both graphics and animation applications have increased dramatically during recent years, and both offer considerable promise for CAI lesson designers. It is incorrect, therefore, simply to characterize the uses of either graphics or animation as cosmetic.

INFORMATION-BASED AMPLIFICATION

Amplification can also take the form of manipulation of the content or procedures of the lesson. Repetition of important information, cueing the student textually to key concepts, and reducing the amount of information presented are all content-based methods for amplifying instruction. The principal advantages of information-based amplification techniques are that they rely on strategic manipulations of the lesson content itself and not on the capabilities of the computer used to deliver the CAI. They integrate important instructional content *directly* rather than depending on a visual or aural cue to attend to the necessary information. Figures 12.5 through 12.9 illustrate several information-based amplification techniques.

Orienting Strategies   Orienting strategies are organizing devices that prepare students for lesson concepts and information prior to starting the lesson (Hannafin and Hughes, 1986; Sweeters, 1985). Usually such strategies provide a mental framework into which the student can integrate lesson information. Figure 12.5, for example, prescribes the purpose and expectations of the lesson. Orienting strategies prepare students to understand the relationships among the information and concepts in the lesson and, in some cases, aid in the integration of current with existing information (Mayer, 1977).

Repetition   Students tend to gauge the importance of CAI lesson information by the same kinds of verbal cues normally employed. Repetition of important

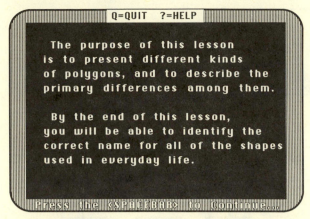

Figure 12.5
An orienting strategy for a geometry lesson.

Figure 12.6
Repetition designed to support learning.

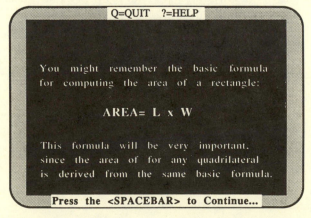

Figure 12.7
A recollection of important information into the current lesson.

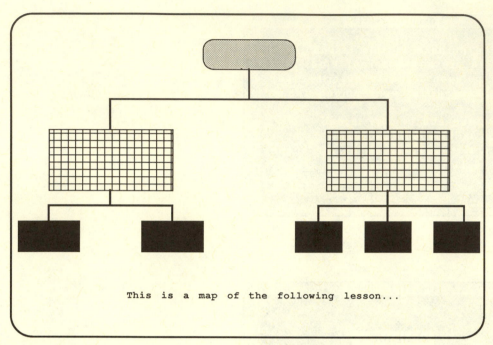

Figure 12.8
A learning taxonomy diagram.

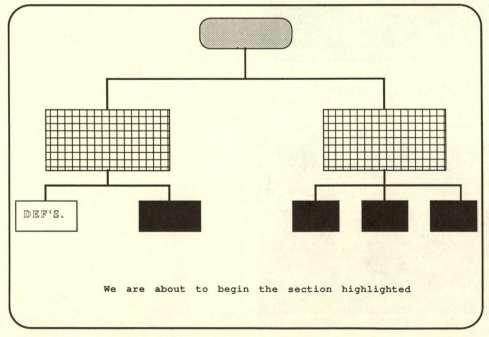

Figure 12.9
Clarifying the position of current instruction in the learning taxonomy.

information in a systematic way, whether in live lecture or in a CAI lesson, will help students to remember. In Figure 12.6, for example, the "Remember..." message is repeated every four frames during this section to reaffirm the importance of the rule. Other lesson information, such as definitions, important names and dates, and basic facts, is often repeated.

Recollection In some lessons, it is helpful to recall information from either the current lesson or previous lessons. Figure 12.7, for example, integrates a previously taught concept into the current lesson, due to the importance and relevance of the information. This technique accentuates the importance of the new instruction and better prepares the student for learning.

Identifying Relationships Some computer-based teaching systems offer devices that aid learning by specifying the relationships among the parts of a concept. In Figure 12.8 is a diagram illustrating the taxonomic relationships among lesson sections and content, similar to the one used by Merrill and Stolurow (1972). The diagram serves as a mental map that can be used to understand the pieces of a lesson more completely. Figure 12.9 illustrates where the content of the current lesson relates to the overall unit, allowing the student to better associate what has already been learned with the current lesson.

Hardware Considerations in Frame Design and Amplification Techniques

The capability of different computers to support frame designs and amplification techniques varies. The use of color, for example, which is often very useful in defining different screen zones, may be unavailable. In some cases, the computer may be capable of utilizing color, but the output device may not. Monochrome displays, such as the black and white, amber, and green screen monitors, do not support the use of color. Similarly, CAI delivered interactively via hard-copy terminals either precludes the use of certain protocol features, such as borders, or makes their use somewhat more complicated. (Hard-copy terminals essentially act as electronic typewriters under computer control, printing from left to right and from top to bottom.) Consider some of the problems in frame protocol and amplification commonly associated with computer and output capabilities and some of the options available to designers to overcome the problems.

COMPUTER DIFFERENCES

Depending upon the specific system used and its capabilities, certain features commonly used in frame protocol and amplification may not be available. Narrow borders of different colors are used effectively to define the functional zones of the frame. Computer systems that do not offer color, or in which color is restricted to graphics-only applications, can render this design technique difficult or impossible. Similarly, some systems are limited in their ability to amplify information through inversing background and foreground colors.

Where limitations of the computer restrict protocol or amplification options, it is useful to consider less flashy but perhaps equally effective techniques. Whereas a

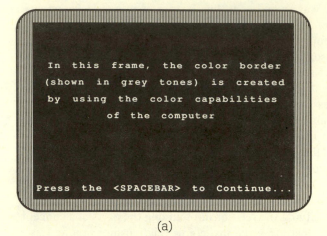

(a)

(b)

Figure 12.10
Graphics and text techniques for frame protocol.

given computer may not permit the use of color within text frames, the use of text characters in lieu of the color can serve the identical purpose. Figures 12.10(a) and 12.10(b) illustrate the use of colored borders (shown as different tones of grey in the black and white illustration) and the identical information and frame protocol portrayed by text characters to help define the functional zones of the frame. Notice that the net effect is basically the same. Each frame is easily read and interpreted, the frame zones are defined identically, and the zones are used consistently throughout the lesson. The principal difference is that an apparent limitation of the computer to support frame protocol has been overcome through the use of universally available text characters.

OUTPUT DISPLAY DIFFERENCES

Typewriter-like terminals provide, in typed format, information that is otherwise displayed to a computer monitor. Such terminals operate much like a typewriter, printing one character at a time, from left to right, line after line, from top to bottom. Generally, they are unable to move about the frame in the random manner possible with computer monitors. Consequently, all information to be displayed—lines, borders, directions, and so on—must be programmed left to right, top to bottom, and one line at a time to be displayed in the proper position. This makes the design and use of effective frame protocol very complicated and often unfeasible.

During recent years, however, the typewriter terminal has become all but extinct for CAI purposes. Instead, computer monitors are used to display program output, where any location on the monitor screen can be accessed readily from any other location on the screen almost instantaneously. The emergence of the computer monitor has opened a tremendous range of possibilities for creating frame protocol, since the various zones can be defined, created, and presented very rapidly and in virtually any order or position desired.

Still, differences in the capabilities of the monitors themselves will influence the protocol conventions adopted. In some cases, standard television sets that incorporate a radio frequency (RF) modulator will be used. Dedicated computer monitors possess widely varied capabilities, ranging from composite video, to RGB signal reception and conversion, to standard color display, to black and white display, to amber and green screen monitors. Some, such as RGB monitors, permit the separation of computer colors (Red, Green, Blue) as well as the high-fidelity display of various colors and color combinations. Others require conversion of the computer signal via an RF modulator, as with standard television sets used as computer monitors. Still others, such as green screen monitors, represent color as different monochromatic patterns for color contrast. In short, all monitors allow the screen locations to be used in any manner deemed appropriate, but the extent to which protocol decisions are supported varies with the capabilities of the different monitors.

Consider a simple, but very common, example of the influence of computer monitor differences on frame protocol. As a designer, you determine that blue borders will be used to accentuate the new information portion of the frame, key letters in the option section will be colored red, and new information will be displayed on white background and blue text lettering. As you test this format on your color monitor, you are satisfied with the protocol and amplification techniques adopted.

However, when students use the lesson, they display the output on green screen monochrome monitors, where none of the amplification techniques visibly support the instruction. In fact, as represented in Figure 12.11, the color patterns displayed on the green screen are almost undecipherable, actually distracting rather than supporting key information. The difference in monitor capabilities has rendered many of the protocol techniques useless and, in some cases, counterproductive.

Certainly the most effective way to avoid problems such as these is by identifying carefully the display capabilities of the systems on which the lessons will actually be implemented and by adopting appropriate protocol conventions, verifying the readability of the instruction on alternate systems, or selecting contrasts that are easily interpreted across different computer monitors. Most potential problems associated with frame protocol and amplification can be circumvented readily *if* they are anticipated in advance. When they are not accounted for, however, problems such as the one described are quite possible.

Figure 12.11
An example of color graphics displayed on a monochrome monitor.

Chapter Summary

The interdependence among the different aspects of lesson design, development, and evaluation should be acknowledged at all stages of the process. We have the capacity to design lessons that can utilize the incredible capabilities of the computer in astounding ways. In systems-based design, the question is not so much "Can we?" but "Should we?"

The systems process provides important information about the learners, the learning task, and the learning setting. Each of these information sources affects, to varying degrees, the use of amplification techniques. Older learners are less likely to be motivated through the use of sound and animation than younger learners. The learning task consists of important terms, relationships, and concepts that must be learned. The learning setting has certain computer and monitor capabilities to support our design decisions. In what ways, then, should the capabilities of the computer be used to support learning?

We have described several methods to manipulate the cosmetic features of the lesson to amplify information contained within the frame. In each case, the techniques work best when used selectively. It is not so much the techniques themselves as the selective difference created through their use that is effective. The use of large letters in vocabulary, for example, aids in amplifying the word presented. Imagine using all large letters. Would the vocabulary word be as well amplified? Or consider the use of color to highlight key terms within a frame. The technique is effective because it is used only under certain conditions. If all text were colored, the technique would be ineffective.

The same should be noted for information-based amplification. Such techniques are very effective in alerting students to, and perhaps even providing strategies for, remembering important information. If such techniques were used for all aspects of the lesson, could we expect them to be successful? It does not seem likely.

The purpose of amplification is to direct attention through the creation of selective differences. Amplification works for fairly simple reasons: novelty, importance of information, and selectivity. If the cueing technique is not noticeable and does not stand apart from the remaining information, attention cannot be focused differentially. If unimportant information is amplified, students will learn to disregard the cues. If amplification techniques are not employed selectively, the presence of amplification cannot be taken as a cue by students. In short, amplification is best when it is used sparingly, systematically, and purposefully.

References

HANNAFIN, M. J., and C. HUGHES (1986). A framework for integrating orienting strategies in computer-based interactive video. *Instructional Science*, 15, 239–255.

HATHAWAY, M. (1984). Variables of computer screen display and how they affect learning. *Educational Technology*, 24(1), 7–10.

HIRSCHBUHL, J, and J. KLUTH (1985). In the mind, not in the hardware: Using graphics in CBT. *Data Training*, 4(4), 20–22.

MAYER, R. E. (1977). The sequencing of instruction and the concept of assimilation to schema. *Instructional Science*, 6, 369–388.

MERRILL, M. D., and L. M. STOLUROW (1966). Hierarchical preview vs. problem oriented review in learning an imaginary science. *American Educational Research Journal*, 3, 251–261.

SCHLOSS, C. N., P. J. SCHLOSS, and G. P. CARTWRIGHT (1985). Placement of questions and highlights as a variable influencing the effectiveness of computer-assisted instruction. *Journal of Computer-Based Instruction*, 12, 97–100.

SWEETERS, W. (1985). Screen design guidelines. *Proceedings of the 26th International ADCIS Conference*, 42–45.

Related Reading

ALESSANDRINI, K. L. (1984). *Graphics in CBT*. (Cassette tape recordings with booklets). Santa Monica, CA: MicroConnect.

ALESSANDRINI, K. L. (1983). Instructional design for CAI tutorials. *Collegiate Microcomputer*, 1, 207–214.

BURKE, R. L. (1982). *CAI Sourcebook*. Englewood Cliffs, NJ: Prentice-Hall.

BURY, K. F., J. M. BOYLE, R. J. EVEY, and A. S. NEAL (1982). Windowing versus scrolling on a visual display terminal. *Human Factors*, 24, 385–394.

DEAN, C., and Q. WHITLOCK (1983). *A Handbook of Computer-Based Training*. London: Kogan Page.

DWYER, F. M. (1978). *Strategies for Improving Visual Learning*. State College, PA: Learning Services.

ENGLAND, E. (1984). Colour and layout considerations in CAL materials. *Computers and Education*, 8, 317–321.

GODFREY, D., and S. STERLING (1982). *The Elements of CAL*. Reston, VA: Reston Publishing Co.

GRABINGER, R. S. (1984). CRT text design: Psychological attributes underlying the evaluation of models of CRT text displays. *Journal of Visual and Verbal Languaging*, 4(1), 17–39.

——— (January 1985). *CRT text design: Prominent layout variables based on a factor analysis of models of computer-generated text*. Paper presented at the annual meeting of the Association for Educational Communication and Technology, Anaheim, CA.

HEINES, J. M. (January 1986). The graphics touch. *Training News*, 8(1), 4–5.

——— (1984). *Screen Design Strategies for Computer-Assisted Instruction*. Bedford, MA: Digital Press.

HOOPER, S., and M. J. HANNAFIN (1986). Factors affecting the legibility of test during computer-based instruction. *Journal of Instructional Development*, **9**(4), 22–29.

JENKINS, J. M. (1982). Some principles of screen design and software for their support. *Computers and Instruction*, **6**, 25–31.

KIDD, M. E., and G. HOLMES (1982). Courseware design: Exploiting the colour micro. *Computers and Education*, **6**, 299–303.

MERRILL, P. F. (1982). Displaying text on microcomputers. In D. Jonassen (ed.). *The Technology of Text*. Englewood Cliffs, NJ: Educational Technology Publications.

PICKOVER, C. (1985). On the educational uses of computer-generated cartoon faces. *Journal of Educational Technology Systems*, **13**, 185–198.

REED, S. (1985). Effect of computer graphics on improving estimates to algebra word problems. *Journal of Educational Psychology*, **77**, 285–296.

REILLY, S., and J. ROACH (1986). Designing human/computer interfaces: A comparison of human factors and graphic arts principles. *Educational Technology*, **26**(1), 36–40.

RIDING, R., and H. TITE (1985). The use of computer graphics to facilitate story telling in young children. *Educational Studies*, **11**, 203–210.

SNOWBERRY, K., S. R. PARKINSON, and N. SISSON (1983). Computer display menus. *Ergonomics*, **26**, 699–712.

Chapter Review Exercises

COMPREHENSION

1. Define *distribution of emphasis* as it is applied to CAI. (See page 185.)

2. Describe how amplification techniques aid in distributing lesson emphasis appropriately. (See pages 185–191.)

3. Describe the differences between cosmetic and information-based amplification techniques. (See pages 185, 188.)

4. List and describe the methods used for cosmetic amplification. List and describe the methods used for information-based amplification. (See pages 185–188, 188–191.)

5. Describe the effects of hardware limitations on protocol and amplification decisions. (See pages 191–194.)

APPLICATION

1. Identify an instructional need appropriate for CAI. Design CAI frames that use cosmetic amplification techniques effectively. (See pages 185–188 and Figures 12.1 through 12.4.)

2. Design effective information-based amplification techniques for the selected lesson. (See pages 188–191 and Figures 12.5 through 12.9.)

3. Design cosmetic and information-based amplification techniques that distribute the lesson emphasis appropriately. (See pages 185–191.)

4. Design lesson amplification techniques that are compatible with the hardware constraints established for the identified instructional need. (See pages 191–194.)

Making CAI Lessons Meaningful and Interactive

An important concern for effective teaching is the need to encourage active responses during instruction. Active responses are those that require a physical action, as opposed to either a covert mental response or no response at all. For most teaching systems, the absence of meaningful active responding by the student can be a serious limitation. Some systems permit active responding but have difficulty establishing relevance and meaning. Others provide relevant instruction but do not permit meaningful interaction between the student and lesson.

The instructional design profession has long valued the importance of active responding and relevant instruction. However, it is often difficult with many teaching systems to make instruction individually relevant. In many instances, the teaching system neither permits nor encourages interaction between lesson and student, settling instead for lesser involvement. The instructional content, procedures, examples, and other features are fixed for most teaching systems. All students view the same videotape or slide-tape, read the same textbooks, and listen to the same lectures. For some, the information may be relevant and meaningful; for others, it is not.

In CAI, however, certain options are available that are not possible with other systems of instruction. Lessons can be individualized through student interaction during the lesson. In this chapter, the concept of interaction in CAI will be explored, and several techniques for making lessons interactive will be described.

OBJECTIVES

Comprehension

After completing this chapter you will be able to

1. Describe the importance of interaction in CAI lessons.
2. Describe the differences between meaningful and procedural interaction in CAI lessons.
3. List and describe several ways in which CAI lessons can be made more interactive.
4. Define the term *pacing* as it applies to CAI.

5. Describe the differences between learner and computer-controlled lesson pacing.
6. Describe what is meant by *personalizing* CAI lessons.
7. Describe the importance of personalizing instruction in CAI lessons.
8. List and describe several ways in which CAI lessons can be made more personally relevant and appropriate for learners.

Application

After completing this chapter you will be able to

1. Design techniques and procedures that increase interaction in selected lessons.
2. Design techniques and procedures that appropriately vary pacing procedures in selected lessons.
3. Design lessons, techniques, and procedures that appropriately personalize selected lessons.

Encouraging Student Participation

Interaction pertains to both the frequency and the nature of student participation during a CAI lesson. In the simplest case, merely pressing the space bar to control the pacing of a lesson might be considered low-level interaction. In more sophisticated instances, interaction might involve pressing the pedals to control the ailerons of a computer-based flight simulator. In both instances, the student became involved with the lesson by producing a response to a prompt issued within a CAI lesson, but the level of interaction is very different.

As demonstrated, there is an impressive range of possibilities for eliciting interaction during a CAI lesson. Each level offers certain opportunities for the student to participate actively with the information presented. Each offers the potential for different learning or control possibilities not readily available with most other teaching systems. Correspondingly, there are several ways in which information can be made more relevant for the range of students who might use a particular lesson, thereby increasing the mental effort expended by students to learn. This chapter will examine methods to improve the relevance and meaningfulness of lessons, to present the various levels of interaction available for the design of CAI lessons, and to apply such techniques during a lesson.

MAKING INSTRUCTION MEANINGFUL

Lessons can be made more meaningful by embedding methods for personalizing instruction. This can be done in several ways without altering the basic flow or logic of the lesson. In effect, personalizing instruction strengthens lessons by focusing on the *context* rather than the *content or sequence* of instruction. Let's consider several methods for making CAI lessons more meaningful for students.

Using a Name for the Computer   In many lessons, particularly those for young students, the incorporation of the computer's name into the dialogue of the computer will appeal to the student. Typically, this is done to approximate the kind of conversation a young child might have with another child or adult. The computer is usually nonthreatening, often humorous, and frequently responds to

Figure 13.1
Incorporating the computer name into a lesson.

the child's interaction at a readily understandable level. Figure 13.1 illustrates this kind of personalization.

Notice how the computer assumes almost human traits. Often young children understand the kind of interaction, coaching, and advice offered by the computer more clearly when it is couched in more familiar, human terms. In other cases, children appreciate the one-to-one dialogue with the "person in the computer." Regardless of the reasons for the phenomenon, increases in the personalization of a lesson may often be accomplished by simply assigning human attributes to the computer.

Using the Student's Name   Perhaps the most common method for personalizing instruction is to simply incorporate the user's name into the lesson. This is typically done to personalize the dialogue between the student and the computer. For older students, as well as for sophisticated younger students, the incorporation of a name into a lesson will not be as intrinsically satisfying as it is for many young students. However, there are other advantages. The use of the name serves as a reminder that the student's individual performance is reflected during the lesson. The student's name also improves the perception of lesson individualization not found in most teaching systems.

Figure 13.2 illustrates the incorporation of a student name into a CAI lesson. Notice how the name is embedded in much the same position and context that is present during a live discussion or dialogue. In this conversational context, the computer merely uses the student's name as an indication of familiarity. In Figure 13.3, however, the nature of the context is much more formal; it is designed to remind the student that he or she has attained specific performance standards.

Obtaining and Using Background Information   One of the most effective techniques available for personalizing instruction, and for improving perceptions of the relevance of the instruction to individual students, is to integrate information periodically from the background of each student into the lesson (Ross, 1984; Ross, McCormick, Krisak, and Anand, 1985). Essentially, this involves the identification of relevant information ranging from the names of siblings or family pets to the career goals of the student to any other bit of information that can be subsequently integrated within a lesson.

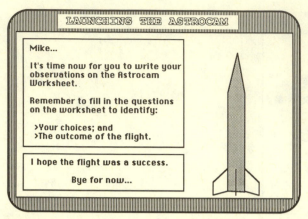

Figure 13.2
Incorporating the student's name into a computer
conversation.

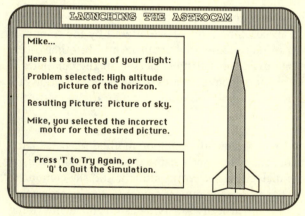

Figure 13.3
Incorporating the student's name for formal
performance feedback.

The information may be obtained by asking the users to complete a computer questionnaire, or by obtaining background data from other sources. Imagine the surprise of students when the name of a favorite uncle or candy bar appears during a lesson days, weeks, or months after the information was initially obtained. Clearly, the potential for personalizing a lesson with this type of information is great.

Figure 13.4 illustrates how a CAI lesson incorporates a unique piece of information—career goal—into each individual student lesson. The basic lesson has not been altered by the integration of the background information, but it should be perceived as more personally meaningful.

Integrating Previous Responses   Often it is useful to remind a student of responses made previously to certain questions. For instance, perhaps a student has experienced difficulty with a particular question or lesson unit, has reviewed a

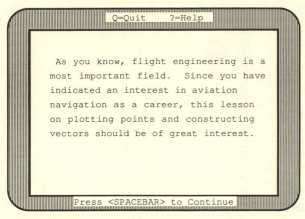

```
┌─────────────────────────────────────┐
│        Q=Quit        ?=Help          │
│                                      │
│   As you know, flight engineering is a
│   most important field.  Since you have
│   indicated an interest in aviation
│   navigation as a career, this lesson
│   on plotting points and constructing
│   vectors should be of great interest.
│                                      │
│                                      │
│      Press <SPACEBAR> to Continue    │
└─────────────────────────────────────┘
```

Figure 13.4
Integrating background information into a lesson.

former section of the lesson, and must answer the question again. Prior to presenting the question, it might be useful to remind the student of the previous response, in order to illustrate the incorrectness of the answer and to prompt the student to a more accurate response. This can be accomplished quite readily by simply keeping track of initial response, then introducing the response at desired points in a lesson.

Examine an example of this procedure in Figure 13.5(a) and 13.5(b). The initial incorrect response, including the incorrect spelling of the name *Jefferson*, has been stored within the computer. Several frames later, the response shown in Figure 13.5(b) is displayed as a prompt to guide the student to a more correct answer. Students can examine their individual responses and identify how they have influenced the way the lesson is controlled.

Use of Relevant Examples   One of the simplest, but perhaps most important, techniques for personalizing CAI and improving lesson relevance is through meaningful and relevant examples. An example describing a simple subtraction application, using apples as the concrete object referent for the student, might be very appropriate for a young student. The objects are readily manipulated and are a common base of experience for virtually all students.

The apple example, however, might be less appropriate for older basic education students who are deficient in the same subtraction skill, because it could be perceived as demeaning. More importantly, there might be a more appropriate example to illustrate the same concept. For example, a supermarket purchase example, illustrating the same simple subtraction skills, would be more relevant to the needs of an older, consumer-oriented student.

Figure 13.6(a) illustrates an application of a nonmeaningful example in the teaching of the concept of competition to college-level economics students. While the example is accurate, it does little to illustrate the concept in the context in which it will be applied. Figure 13.6(b), on the other hand, provides a relevant example of the concept of competition by incorporating a meaningful context within the example.

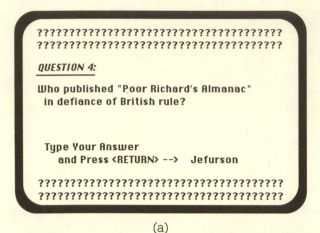

(a)

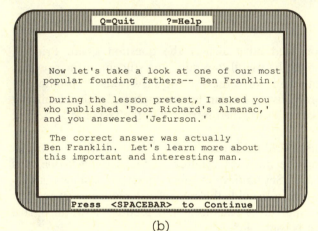

(b)

Figure 13.5
Integrating a previous response into a lesson.

Learner Control of Instructional Options   In many cases, students can make decisions on which instructional activity is appropriate for them. Some students, for example, might feel that only a few practice items are needed to learn particular concepts; or perhaps no examples will be needed for certain concepts, but several will be needed for others. In effect, the unique needs of students may be more efficiently met by providing individuals with control of the activities that comprise the instruction.

Whereas this point has a great deal of intuitive appeal, and an enormous amount of CAI design and programming energy has been consumed in deference to this point, much of the current research contraindicates unrestricted learner control (Hannafin, 1984; Steinberg, 1977). For the most part, students seem to terminate practice activities prematurely and are simply not effective judges of their ongoing learning status or needs (Garhart and Hannafin, 1986).

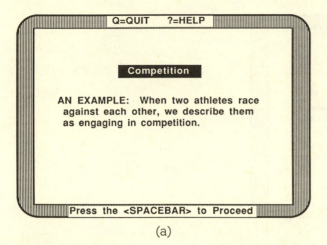

(a)

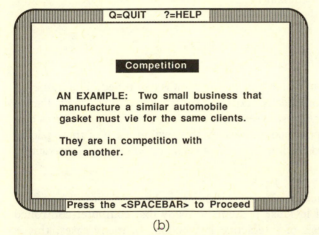

(b)

Figure 13.6
A nonmeaningful versus a meaningful example for
college-level economics students.

There is, however, a technique whereby students are permitted to make instructional decisions but are provided with important coaching and guidance upon which to base their decision. Tennyson (1984) has termed this technique an *advisement strategy*, where students are continually advised as to the effectiveness of their performance and their past decisions and, in some cases, are prompted to make a particular decision. In each case, the student retains the ultimate control but does so after considering relevant performance information. Figure 13.7 illustrates a learner-control strategy comparable to the type developed by Tennyson and his associates.

Learner control transfers the responsibility for learning from the designer or the computer to the student. Instead of being the object of a CAI lesson, the student is placed in a position of importance and control. This may be one of the most important outcomes of learner control, since students should assume as much personal responsibility for successes and failures as is reasonable.

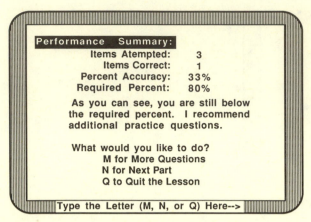

Figure 13.7
An advisement strategy to aid students in making
lesson-control decisions.

PACING CONSIDERATIONS

Pacing refers to the manner in which lesson execution is controlled. The frames of a lesson can be advanced automatically under some form of computer timer. Pacing procedures that require learner responses are also common, as are procedures that employ both timers and response conditions. In this section, each of these pacing options will be reviewed, and the implications of each option on lesson interaction will be discussed.

Computer-Controlled Pacing When could imposed pacing control be of use in designing interactive CAI lessons? It seems to many that computer-controlled CAI lessons are the antithesis of interactive instruction. In many cases, this is certainly true. The student may do little more than sit before the computer monitor and watch the lesson fly by. Lessons are often mistakenly designed to preclude meaningful interaction between the student and the computer, thereby rendering useless the enormous potential of the computer to promote learning through heightened interaction.

However, there are also circumstances where timing the display of frames may be the preferred method of control. Imagine using the computer to teach a complex series of steps and procedures to be followed in the event of a medical emergency. The information must be learned by volunteers who have very limited medical background. Each of the steps has a series of conditions that will affect whether, or how, to do the prescribed steps. The volunteers attend training at their leisure and can spend as much time as they need to learn the procedures. The CAI lesson will provide all of the basic information prior to two days of supervised on-job training. What kind of lesson pacing should be used?

First consider a computer-paced version of the instruction. The designer determines that a maximum of ten seconds is required to read each frame, so the standard is adopted for ten-second computer-controlled pacing. Each frame will be presented for ten seconds, and the next frame will be displayed immediately. This process will continue until completion of the lesson.

Given the amount of information to be learned; the relative lack of familiarity of the students with the information; and the self-study, volunteer nature of the instruction, the decision for computer pacing might be ill advised. It seems likely that the volunteers will want to take notes during the lesson, will want to study some of the information more carefully, and will want a greater degree of assurance of their learning than computer pacing alone will provide. The rapid-fire display of frames at ten-second intervals might be an effective way to encourage fluency with trained personnel, but it will probably be perceived as threatening, difficult, and overwhelming by the novices for whom the lesson was intended.

Yet, this disaster is more a function of thoughtless design than of the inherent inability of computer-controlled lessons to promote interaction. In some cases, it is desirable for a lesson frame to be displayed for only a specified period of time. For example, CAI lessons designed to increase reading speed often control the length of time that frames are displayed. As the lesson progresses, the amount of time allotted for each frame may be gradually shortened, forcing students to read the information more rapidly. In order to participate effectively, students must direct their attention to the frame, attend purposefully for concentrated periods of time, and perform prescribed tasks rapidly and accurately. Under such conditions, it is essential that the control of lesson pacing be embedded in the lesson, and not simply transferred to the student. Clearly, there are circumstances where computer-paced frames are not only a good way, but the best way, to encourage student interaction with lesson information.

Learner-Controlled Pacing Learner-controlled pacing is probably most frequently identified as an individualizing component in CAI. In learner-paced lessons, the student dictates how slowly or rapidly lesson frames will be exchanged—usually by pressing a designated key when he or she is ready to proceed. The popularity of learner-controlled pacing is understandable, since the amount of time needed to learn the information can vary widely from student to student.

However, there are many instances where the unlimited time allotted for viewing frames is unnecessary, undesirable, and even counterproductive. Often learner-controlled pacing does little more than permit the student to "turn the page" in a lesson and does almost nothing to encourage interaction with lesson content. The capability to permit learner-controlled lesson pacing has often been mistaken for substantive interaction with lesson content. Let's consider examples of effective and ineffective learner control.

A CAI lesson to focus on the recall of basic addition facts is to be developed. Recall of the target skills is to become automatic, requiring rapid responses to rapidly displayed problems. This is a very common application of drill and practice designs in mathematics.

The designer decides to employ learner-controlled pacing, where individual arithmetic problems are displayed, with concrete objects representing the addition problem, until the student produces the correct response. The student may look at the problem for as long as desired (forever if the student chooses!). When each question is answered, feedback is provided, and a new mathematics problem is presented.

The problem with this design is that response automaticity is in no way encouraged. The student can simply count the objects displayed or wait indefinitely prior to responding. Such pacing might be an effective technique for introducing the facts initially, but it is incompatible with present performance expectations. The method of pacing did not permit the kind of skill development required. As a result, learning might have been demonstrated, but not necessarily with the rapidity needed.

On the other hand, perhaps the computer will be used to teach troubleshooting skills to electricians, using computer-simulated circuits. The goal is to minimize mistaken diagnosis, due to the high cost of replacement and service time. In other words, accuracy is valued over response speed. Since the student will be required to evaluate a series of symptoms and to study a fairly complex diagram of a circuit prior to making a decision, learner control would be most satisfactory. The learner-control option allows the user to freeze the action depicted on a frame for careful inspection and study. Learner control, under similar circumstances, promotes intelligent interaction with lesson content.

Combined Pacing   In many cases, the correct alternative is unclear. Perhaps the learning task requires some flexibility to study frames at individual rates but also requires that excessive time be eliminated. In effect, the individual control provided by learner pacing needs to be balanced with the time required for lesson completion.

It is important to consider what actually is, or is not, accomplished during the inspection or viewing of a lesson frame. If all time spent viewing a frame were productive, then we would probably concede the value of such pacing. This, however, appears to be a basic misunderstanding of what actually occurs during learning. Tennyson and his associates have studied viewing time as an instructional variable in CAI and have concluded that extended viewing time *does not* by itself improve learning of information contained within the frame. Tennyson has noted that there is a period of time during which the information presented on a frame will be studied carefully. After this period, the increased exposure does little more than slow the lesson, place greater time between responses, and make needed help further removed from the point of observed difficulty.

There is strong intuitive appeal and empirical evidence for combined pacing: Learners control the pacing of a lesson unless unreasonably long viewing periods are observed. We assume that if the user has not executed the learner-controlled pacing option within a prescribed period of time, additional inspection of a particular frame will not prove beneficial. Instead, an alternative option, the time-default procedure, is executed once the allotted time has lapsed.

Consider the following example of combined pacing. A CAI lesson has been designed to teach rather complex principles of genetic probability. The students will vary widely in mathematics aptitude and in prior familiarity with probability. Some students will simply apply the already known computational concepts of probability theory to genetic forecasting; others will learn both probability and genetics for the first time.

In order to accommodate both groups and to have the assurance that all students learn well from the lesson, a combined pacing technique is employed. Upon the presentation of a question, the student is given a maximum of 90 seconds to respond. If the student responds within the 90-second time limit, the response is evaluated for accuracy and the lesson proceeds. If no response is provided within the time limit, however, the student is prompted to the delay, and branched to the portion of the lesson where the particular probability concepts were taught. The benefits of learner control—to provide substantive interaction with the lesson concepts—are balanced against the possibility of sustained, useless viewing of the different frames of the lesson.

THE ROLE OF PRACTICE

Providing the opportunity to practice different aspects of the lesson content increases interaction in several important ways. Students not only produce active responses, but the responses are integrated completely with lesson content (Hannafin, 1987). Students not only remain active in their interaction with instruction; they also develop informational and conceptual bridges among lesson information to aid ongoing learning efforts.

Figures 13.8(a) through 13.8(e) illustrate an example of embedded CAI practice that consists of the presentation of small bits of lesson information. The total collection of lesson bits might enable the student to perform some desired

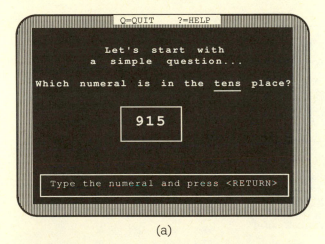

(a)

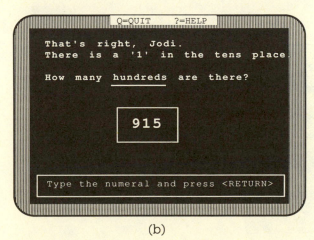

(b)

Figure 13.8
Progressive guidance and practice embedded in a
CAI tutorial.

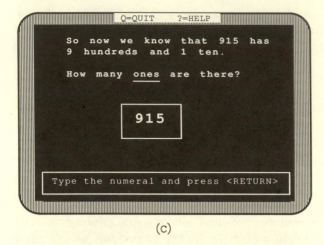

```
                 Q=QUIT      ?=HELP
      So   now   we   know   that   915   has
      9  hundreds   and   1  ten.

      How  many  ones  are  there?


                  ┌──────────────┐
                  │     915      │
                  └──────────────┘


      ┌─────────────────────────────────────────┐
      │ Type the numeral and press <RETURN>      │
      └─────────────────────────────────────────┘
```

(c)

```
                 Q=QUIT      ?=HELP

   Fantastic...

   We have a number with the following
   place values: 9  hundreds
                  1  tens
                  5  ones

      How many tens is this number
      equal or equivalent to?

      ┌─────────────────────────────────────────┐
      │ Type the number and press <RETURN>       │
      └─────────────────────────────────────────┘
```

(d)

```
                 Q=QUIT      ?=HELP
   Here's how to do it...



   9  hundreds  =   9 x (100/10)  =    9 0.0
      1  ten    =   1 x (10/10)   =    1.0
      5  ones   =   5 x (1/10)    =    0.5
                                     ────────
                                      91.5

      ┌─────────────────────────────────────────┐
      │ Press the <SPACEBAR> to Continue...      │
      └─────────────────────────────────────────┘
```

(e)

Figure 13.8 (*Continued*)

skill, but by themselves the skills seem little more than isolated bits of information. Notice that the practice provided from frame to frame builds upon already presented information. Students respond continuously throughout the lesson, which results in highly interactive instruction. In addition, the specific bits of information that the lesson builds upon are presented, practiced, and expanded throughout the lesson.

When CAI lessons provide opportunities for practice, users are able to become more involved, both physically and cognitively, with instruction. It is virtually impossible to remain passive or detached from the lesson, since the interaction between computer and student is continuous. Well-designed practice exercises, however, do more than simply encourage interaction. Well-designed practice fosters skill development while reinforcing correct learning or remediating deficient responses (Salisbury, Richards, and Klein, 1985).

Streibel (1984) has described an interesting method for designing dialogue between the student and the computer. Essentially, the computer engages in a conversation with the student, requiring the formation of conclusions, hypotheses, and other higher-level forms of processing. These methods present interesting alternatives to the simple question-and-answer forms of interaction that can quickly become boring to students.

THE ROLE OF CRITERION QUESTIONS

Unlike practice, where the focus of interaction is typically on shaping or guiding correct responses, criterion questions are those that test the student's capacity to perform the skills, procedures, or tasks specified in the instructional objective. Criterion questions are prescribed by the level and type of objective used, but they also serve as a technique for encouraging learner interaction with the CAI lesson (Hannafin, 1987).

A great deal of research has been reported in the design and location of embedded questions [see, for example, Hamaker's (1986) review and summary of extensive research findings]. Wager and Wager (1985) offered several prescriptions for incorporating questions into CAI. Questions should relate clearly to preceding lesson content, should have clearly defined directions for responding, and should use the allotted screen space intelligently. Research almost unanimously supports the distribution of questions throughout the CAI lesson, although integrative types of questions—questions that require learners to connect various kinds of information presented during the lesson—should also be used upon completion of the lesson.

Perhaps the most prevalent response format requires the student to enter a response, comprised of one or several keyboard characters, and complete the response by pressing the ⟨Return⟩ key. Usually the response is not examined in any way until the ⟨Return⟩ key has been pressed. This kind of interaction is useful for simple response formats, such as true–false or multiple-choice questions, as well as for more complex constructed-response formats.

Figures 13.9(a) and 13.9(b) illustrate typical question frames requiring the ⟨Return⟩ key to signal completion of the answer. The student has an opportunity to examine the response before pressing ⟨Return⟩ in order to check the contents of the

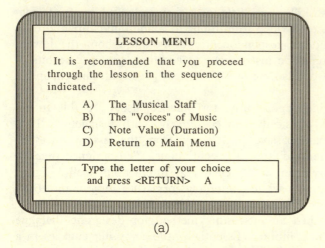

(a)

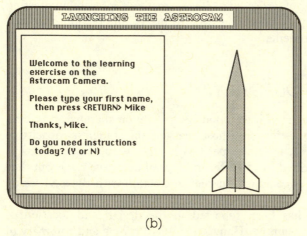

(b)

Figure 13.9
Typical response formats requiring the ⟨Return⟩ key.

answer. Since the response is not examined until the ⟨Return⟩ key is pressed, the answer can be edited, changed, or altered by the student prior to completing the response. In addition, since the same procedures can be used regardless of response length, the format for encouraging student interaction can be consistent throughout the lesson.

Single-keystroke responses, those that require only the pressing of a valid keyboard character, are perhaps the simplest form of interaction. Under guidance provided through the lesson directions, the student simply identifies an appropriate choice and types only the selected key. The ⟨Return⟩ key need not be pressed, and no other interaction is needed to enter a student response. Single-keystroke responses are commonly used for true–false and multiple-choice questions. Figures 13.10(a) and 13.10(b) illustrate single-keystroke criterion questions.

Single-keystroke interaction is very useful, in that it offers simple response procedures that permit more questioning and learner–lesson interaction. Students

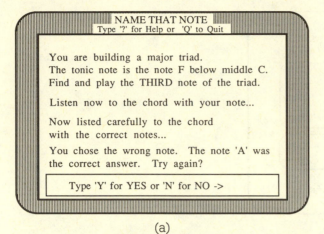

(a)

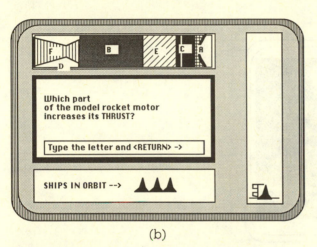

(b)

Figure 13.10
Typical single-keystroke response formats.

can interact meaningfully with lesson information and procedures with minimal response complexity.

However, this type of interaction is susceptible to typing errors that might normally be identified by the user prior to pressing the ⟨Return⟩ key. Unless precautions are taken, lesson execution resumes at the moment a correct *or* incorrect key is typed. These potential drawbacks in encouraging interaction are easily overcome, however, and fairly simple precautions are sufficient to make single-keystroke interaction a useful and versatile technique.

There are other no-return question formats that prompt students to enter responses of a specified length, instead of a single-keystroke, but still not to press ⟨Return⟩ upon completion. Again, as with single-keystroke responses, this is done automatically as a feature of the lesson and program design. Figure 13.11 illustrates this response format for a simple mathematics problem. The student is prompted to enter a response, one character at a time, in the designated frame

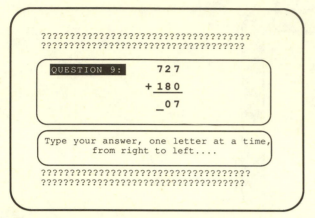

Figure 13.11
Single-keystroke format that allows right-to-left responses.

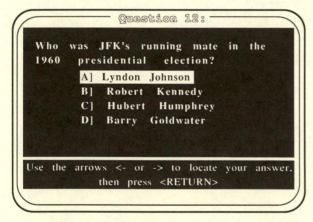

Figure 13.12
Cursor-based response selection format.

position. This is useful in accommodating the right-to-left procedures in most mathematics applications despite the left-to-right orientation of the computer. The format allows input in the units place, then the tens place, then the hundreds place, rather than imposing the inappropriate left-to-right orientation of the computer. Upon receiving a valid character in the third position, the lesson proceeds. Like single-keystroke input, this format can be used readily with naive users or very young children due to its simplicity.

A method gaining in popularity is the use of cursor-control techniques to locate choices. Usually a frame will contain directions for controlling cursor movement and directions for accepting or designating the desired responses. The frame shown in Figure 13.12 is typical of this format. The choice options are displayed in apparent and easily identified locations, and the current location of the cursor is prompted through highlighting. With minimal training, users can adapt very readily to this format, and virtually any forced-choice question can be presented in this manner.

A number of additional options are also available, including the integration of voice recognition, light pens, joysticks, and touch screens. These options will be discussed in depth in a later chapter, but suffice it to say that methods for encouraging learner–lesson interaction are becoming increasingly friendly. Future lessons will undoubtedly require less computer sophistication to interact with, and learn from, computer-based instruction.

Chapter Summary

CAI lessons can be as personal or impersonal, and as interactive or noninteractive, as determined to be necessary. However, it is difficult to imagine many lessons where it would be appropriate to design impersonal instruction. Certainly the support, cooperation, and enthusiasm of the learner must be enlisted. Lessons that are unnecessarily impersonal are not likely to engage the learner effectively.

Yet a surprising number of CAI lessons make little or no attempt to engage the learner at a personal level. Apart from the almost obligatory "Enter your name and press ⟨Return⟩," many lessons do virtually nothing to assure that the instruction is personalized. Personalization implies that the instructional content and the process used to learn the content are perceived as meaningful by individual learners. Without meaning, most learning occurs in isolation from the student's vast memory network. Without meaning, instruction is not readily assimilated and integrated with already learned information and concepts (Mayer, 1984). Providing personalized instruction, instruction perceived as meaningful by individual students, helps to make the integration of newly learned information more effective.

Similarly, it is difficult to imagine where meaningful interaction between the student and the lesson content would not be desired. Yet many lessons offer superficial interaction, such as simple learner pacing, or they maintain low-level interaction due to the simplicity of lesson design. Many designers settle for far less than is possible, resulting in instruction in which the student is more an observer than a participant. This must be avoided.

References

Garhart, C., and M. J. Hannafin (1986). The accuracy of comprehension monitoring during computer-based instruction. *Journal of Computer-Based Instruction*, **13**, 88–93.

Hamaker, C. (1986). The effects of adjunct questions on prose learning. *Review of Educational Research*, **56**, 212–242.

Hannafin, M. J. (1984). Guidelines for using locus of instructional control in the design of computer-assisted instruction. *Journal of Instructional Development*, **7**(3), 9–14.

Hannafin, M. J. (1987). The effects of orienting activities, cueing, and practice on learning from computer-based instruction. *Journal of Educational Research*, in press.

Mayer, R. E. (1984). Aids to text comprehension. *Educational Psychologist*, **19**, 30–42.

Ross, S. M. (1984). Matching the lesson to the student: Alternative adaptive designs for individualized learning systems. *Journal of Computer-Based Instruction*, **11**, 42–48.

Ross, S. M., D. McCormick, N. Krisak, and P. Anand (1985). Personalizing context in teaching mathematical concepts: Teacher-managed and computer-assisted models. *Educational Communication and Technology Journal*, **33**, 169–178.

Salisbury, D., B. Richards, and J. Klein (1985). Prescriptions for the design of practice activities for learning: An integration from instructional design theories. *Journal of Instructional Development*, 8(4), 9–19.

STEINBERG, E. (1977). Review of student control in computer-assisted instruction. *Journal of Computer-Based Instruction*, 3, 84–90.

STREIBEL, M. (1984). Dialog design and instructional systems for an intelligent videodisc system. *Videodisc and Optical Disc*, 4, 216–229.

TENNYSON, R. (1984). Application of artificial intelligence methods to computer-based instructional design: The Minnesota Adaptive Instructional System. *Journal of Instructional Development*, 7, 17–22.

WAGER, W., and S. Wager (1985). Presenting questions, processing responses, and providing feedback in CAI. *Journal of Instructional Development*, 8(4), 2–8.

Related Reading

BLANK, D., P. A., MURPHY, and B. SCHNEIDERMAN (1986). A comparison of children's reading comprehension and reading rates at three text presentation speeds on a CRT. *Journal of Computer-Based Instruction*, 13, 84–87.

BALMAN, T. (1981). Implementation techniques for interactive CAL programs. *Computers and Education*, 5, 19–29.

BURKE, R. L. (1982). *CAI sourcebook*. Englewood Cliffs, NJ: Prentice-hall.

FRIEND, J., and J. D. MILOJKOVIC (1984). Designing interactions between students and computers. In D. F. WALKER and R. D. HESS (eds.). *Instructional Software: Principles and Perspectives for Design and Use*. Belmont, CA: Wadsworth.

GAGNÉ, R. M., W. W. WAGER, and A. ROJAS (1981). Planning and authoring computer-assisted instruction lessons. *Educational Technology*, 21, 17–26.

GAINES, B. R. (1981). The technology of interaction—dialog programming rules. *International Journal of Man–Machine Studies*, 14, 133–150.

GODFREY, D., and S. STERLING (1982). *The Elements of CAL*. Reston, VA: Reston Publishing Co.

HEINES, J. M. (1985). Interactive means active: Learner involvement in CBT. *Data Training*, 4(4), 48–53.

HEINES, J. M. (1984). *Screen Design Strategies for Computer-Assisted Instruction*. Bedford, MA: Digital Press.

Chapter Review Exercises

COMPREHENSION

1. Describe the importance of interaction in CAI lessons. (See page 198.)
2. Describe the differences between meaningful interaction and procedural interaction in CAI lessons. (See page 198.)
3. List and describe several ways to make CAI lessons more interactive. (See pages 198–203.)
4. Define *pacing* as applied to CAI. (See page 204.)
5. Describe the differences between learner-controlled and computer-controlled pacing. (See pages 204–206.)
6. Describe what is meant by *personalizing* CAI lessons. (See page 198.)

7. Describe the importance of personalizing CAI lessons. (See pages 198–204.)

8. List and describe several ways that CAI lessons can be made more personally relevant to students. [See pages 198–204 and Figures 13.1 through 13.5(b).]

APPLICATION

1. Select an instructional need appropriate for CAI. Design procedures and features that increase the interaction of the lesson.

2. Design lesson-pacing techniques and procedures appropriate for the selected need.

3. Design techniques and procedures for personalizing the selected lesson effectively.

CHAPTER 14

Obtaining and Managing Student Responses

In Chapter 13, we stressed the value of meaningful interaction in CAI lessons, where students are required to process the instruction, demonstrate comprehension, and form conclusions. In effect, we have advocated that CAI lessons foster a kind of dialogue between the learner and the computer as a way to strengthen the value of the lesson.

The nature of the interaction or dialogue, however, can place unique demands on the lesson designer. Single-keystroke responses are much simpler to anticipate, interpret, and manage than responses that are more complex. However, simple response formats will not meet all lesson requirements. In some cases, for instance, student responses must not be evaluated simply as correct or incorrect, but as exhibiting different degrees of correctness. At times we may require that a response include a specific component before credit can be assigned for the remainder of the response. Clearly, then, the methods chosen for promoting lesson interaction have a direct bearing on the simplicity or complexity of the procedures used to evaluate student input and to manage resulting lesson execution decisions.

The purposes of this chapter are to describe the importance of sustained computer–learner dialogue in CAI lessons, to examine the implications of different response formats for the planning requirements of a lesson, and to present several methods for managing student input in CAI lessons.

OBJECTIVES

Comprehension

After completing this chapter you will be able to

1. Describe the importance of communication in sustaining meaningful computer–learner dialogue.
2. Define *legal* and *illegal* responses during CAI.
3. Describe appropriate methods for managing legal and illegal responses.
4. Define *anticipated* and *unanticipated* responses during CAI.
5. Describe appropriate methods for managing anticipated and unanticipated responses.

6. List and describe the major types of input that require response management planning.
7. Describe the importance of questioning in controlling student input.
8. Describe the response management implications of different questioning techniques from both lesson-design and programming perspectives.
9. List and describe several techniques used to evaluate or compare user input and describe the advantages and limitations of each.

Application

After completing this chapter you will be able to

1. Design techniques and procedures that maintain meaningful dialogue between the computer and the student.
2. Design techniques and procedures that account for both legal and illegal student responses.
3. Design techniques and procedures that manage both anticipated and unanticipated student input.

Communicating with Computers

In everyday human conversation, dialogue is shaped by ongoing understanding. We speak, listen to the responses or comments of the other participants, formulate mentally what we will say next, speak again, and so forth until conversation is completed. We are able to sustain meaningful dialogue because we not only *present* information but also *understand* the communication of others. We can then continue and modify the conversation based upon other inputs during the dialogue.

This is probably one of the principal reasons why live discussions have always been popular. Participants learn through an on-going dialogue, one that develops ideas and issues dynamically as a function of participation and comprehension. The dialogue is continually modified by an individual's responses, comprehension, and modification of subsequent dialogue. The instruction is dynamic, does not follow a fixed sequence, and develops comprehension based upon the uniquely individual interpretations and contributions of participants.

If there were no comprehension upon which to maintain the dialogue, however, the conversation would necessarily diminish. We could neither offer insights meaningful to other participants nor understand the conversation sufficiently to profit from the interaction. Conversation alone is insufficient to promote a meaningful dialogue; participants must be able to comprehend one another and decide what to do or say next.

Unlike live discussions, students cannot engage in active dialogue with most traditional teaching systems. Students encode information more or less passively and are dependent upon either the quality of text organization or their individual mental strategies for deepening comprehension. It is difficult, for example, to solicit explanations beyond available text, to ask for clarification past what is provided on audiotape, or otherwise engage in the kind of instructional dialogue possible through interactive discussions. If such a dialogue is desired, students must usually turn elsewhere.

Computers offer a possible middle ground between the unlimited and dynamic dialogue of live conversation and the static monologue of the conventional written or recorded word. Depending on several important design factors, the computer can become more like either a basic textbook or a live discussion. The extent to which the computer approximates a dynamic interactive dialogue depends on the same conditions likely to make live dialogue meaningful: The computer and the student must "speak" to each other, both must have the capacity to comprehend the dialogue, and both must adapt dynamically to ensure meaningful interaction. When these conditions are met, the lesson can come quite close to approximating live dialogue; when either or both conditions are not met, the dialogue becomes confusing.

Managing Student Responses

Despite the amazing attributes of the computer, it has little or no inherent capability to understand human dialogue. The capability to understand is provided by the programming commands used to control program execution. Response management, then, refers to the manner in which the computer receives and evaluates input obtained during a lesson. The focus of this chapter is on making communication from the student comprehensible to the computer.

When the capacity to manage and evaluate student input is provided, the computer understands communication from the student. Then the computer might use the information to make decisions ranging from lesson termination to lesson branching sequences to simplify determining the correctness or incorrectness of an answer. As lesson designers, we specify the kinds of dialogue that the computer must understand; as the electronic partner in the dialogue the computer dutifully performs the prescribed tasks.

Without the capability to manage and evaluate student input, however, there is no possibility for meaningful, sustained interaction. If the computer has not been provided the kinds of information needed to understand student input, then no opportunity exists for making decisions of what to do next or how to respond meaningfully.

Imagine receiving the following communication from the computer:

$$>>{}^{\star}7 + + \ \#@ \ J53!)) \ ASC\hat{}(@)$$

The communication is meaningless without some information as to what the computer is communicating to us. We have no basis whatsoever either to understand the communication or to attempt a response. The same is true of information presented to the computer, except that the computer's capacity to comprehend is even further limited only to what has been programmed. Whereas humans might, through trial and error, decode the computer message, the computer is at the mercy of the designer to provide the information needed to understand input.

The task of the designer is to identify completely the domain of possible student input that must be understood by the computer, to identify any conditions that might affect the interpretation of student input, and to prescribe computer responses to student input.

CLASSIFYING RESPONSES

Input can be broadly classified as either legal or illegal, and as either anticipated or unanticipated. This matrix is shown in Figure 14.1.

Legal Input   Legal responses include input that falls within the domain of prescribed response options. The responses need not be correct, but they must be defined as appropriate for the task at hand. For example, multiple-choice tests provide the student with a prescribed domain of response possibilities. All of these options are considered legal, in that the student has provided valid input, given the prescribed set of response options. Several options are incorrect, but all are legal responses.

The question frame shown in Figure 14.2 illustrates how students can be prompted to the legal response options available for a multiple-choice item. Notice that the directions for responding specify the legal responses for the question. This aids the student in understanding the response options and in simplifying the task of managing subsequent input.

Legal responses can be identified for virtually any kind of input. For example, an arithmetic question requiring the typing of a correct sum for simple addition problems can define legal input as any numeric character.

Legal responses are also identifiable through the use of common conventions. Legal phone numbers, for example, can be defined as either seven or ten digits; social security numbers require nine digits to be considered legal. Virtually any accepted convention for the use of numbers or letters can be applied to determine whether legal responses have been provided.

Determining which responses are considered legal is important for several reasons. First, legal responses usually are used to determine what types of

	Anticipated	**Unanticipated**
Legal		
Illegal		

Figure 14.1
Response classification matrix.

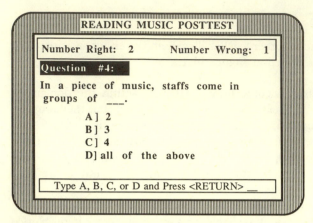

Figure 14.2.
Legal response prompting for multiple-choice
question.

branching or lesson execution will follow. Correct legal responses may branch to a subsequent lesson activity, while incorrect legal responses may repeat the current lesson segment. Legal responses are also used to tally the frequency of correct and incorrect responses.

Before lesson execution proceeds, all responses should be verified as legal input. Several factors might affect the production of a response that is not legal, many of which are related to mistyping or carelessness and are not substantively related to the lesson. Requiring legal responses for lesson execution provides a measure of certainty that the computer's response is appropriate.

Illegal Input   Why is it necessary to account for illegal student responses to a lesson? Can we assume that any noncorrect response is simply incorrect and treat the response as an error in learning? This is certainly one common approach. It simplifies the programming task substantially. Illegal answers, after all, are technically in error. For many, this is reason enough to simply reject the notion of illegal responses as a design and planning concern.

This may be a very shortsighted decision. Illegal responses are those that, by their nature, could not possibly be considered valid. Suppose you were asked for the last name of the first president of the United States. Simply typing *Washington* would be correct, but typing *Adams* would not. Both are legal, but only the former response is correct.

Suppose, however, that in typing the response, a student accidentally typed the number 2 instead of the *W*, yielding *2ashington*. The answer is not correct, but is it a legal response? Should we assume that the student did not know the answer? Or is it reasonable to consider the response illegal since a number was included, and numbers cannot be included in the name of any president? The ability to use the computer to make reasonable decisions rests in the manner in which responses are managed. If we do not provide the element of reason in computer-based lessons, then the lessons will perform unreasonably. If we choose to design lessons that manage input sensibly, we might expect more sensible lesson execution.

Any input that does not fall within the domain specified as legal is considered illegal input. Illegal input usually results from carelessness in typing the response or

(a)

(b)

Figure 14.3
Illegal response input and appropriate consequences
for illegal response.

inattentiveness to the directions for responding. Illegal responses are important to identify because they do not necessarily indicate a lack of effective learning, only a lack of careful responding.

Examine the example of appropriate consequences for illegal input shown in Figures 14.3(a) and 14.3(b). Notice that the first frame prescribes the nature of a legal response. The student response, shown in the frame, has violated the directions for responding. The violation might be the result of inaccurate learning, but it seems more probable that the error is purely typographical. Should the student response be tallied as incorrect? Should the lesson be repeated? All due to an obvious typographical error?

Probably not. The response is illegal but not necessarily inaccurate. It seems more prudent to require that the input be reentered, as prompted in Figure 14.3(b). Effective lessons do not penalize students with poor typing skills (unless, of course, the lesson teaches typing!). Illegal responses should be detected in the lesson, and the student should be given additional opportunities to produce a legal response. Lessons with provisions for illegal responses generally provide a measure of sophistication not found with more rigid management procedures.

Anticipated Responses   Anticipated responses are those for which lesson functions have been designed. Both correct and incorrect responses can be anticipated and treated in different ways. For example, assume that you have designed a CAI lesson to teach the structure of an atom—protons and neutrons comprising a nucleus and negatively charged electrons orbiting the nucleus. Upon completion of the instruction, students are asked to select the part that is positively charged. If selected, the correct answer, *proton*, will result in positive feedback, and another question will be presented. If either of the other alternatives is selected, the lesson will branch to an appropriate segment, depending upon whether the incorrect response was *neutron* or *electron*. In this example, each of the responses was anticipated and resulted in different lesson consequences.

It is also possible to anticipate illegal responses. In fact, illegal responses are often as important to anticipate as legal responses, since a different lesson execution is usually desirable for each one. Consider the example of the lesson on the structure of the atom. Suppose a student responded to the same question with *ion*, a response that is related and plausible but not accurate in the present lesson. The response was illegal but sufficiently common among students that it would have been wise to anticipate it and provide an appropriate message.

Response anticipation gives the designer a basis for specifying lesson execution. How could any lesson branching occur if student responses, correct or incorrect, legal or illegal, have not been anticipated?

Now consider a variation of a previous example to see how response anticipation might be applied. Figure 14.4(a) illustrates a history question pertaining to the discovery of America. The correct answer, according to the preceding lesson, is *Columbus*. This answer is easily anticipated, since the information was emphasized clearly in the lesson. In most other cases, alternative responses would probably be considered incorrect.

However, it is clear that different and valid opinions exist as well. The opportunity for including important lesson features that are worthwhile and necessary depends on whether alternative responses are anticipated. Should answers indicating Eskimoes or Scandanavian explorers be considered? What if a student provides one of these answers? How should the responses be treated?

Once again, the only way to manage input meaningfully is to anticipate the responses initially. We might wish to acknowledge any of these illegal but valid alternatives by prompting the student as shown in Figure 14.4(b). If responses are not anticipated, then options for managing input are seriously restricted, usually resulting in a decision to judge the answer incorrect. Only responses that are anticipated can be used meaningfully to affect lesson execution.

Unanticipated Responses   Perhaps the most fatal of flaws for CAI lessons is the failure to anticipate input, whether legal or illegal. Assume that the question shown in Figure 14.5(a) is presented to a student. The student responds by typing the word *three* instead of the number 3. The response is correct, but the lesson has been designed to deal with numeric input. The designer did not anticipate the other correct response to the question and has no provision for identifying the

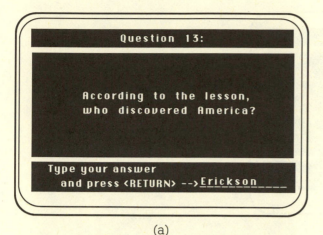

(a)

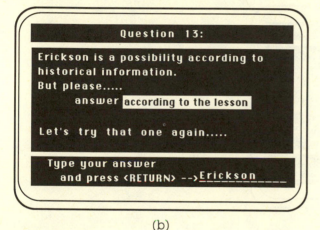

(b)

Figure 14.4
Anticipating illegal but plausible alternative responses.

response as illegal. Imagine the reaction of the student who, after studying the lesson carefully and practicing extensively, is repeatedly presented with the response shown in Figure 14.5(b), indicating that the answer is incorrect.

Unanticipated responses also become troublesome when students enter information that is not accounted for in lesson or program logic. The frame shown in Figure 14.6 solicits input specifying whether the student wishes to continue (C), stop (S), or repeat (R) the lesson—options fairly common in CAI lessons. However, the student, accustomed to pressing the space bar to continue a lesson, presses the space bar instead of using one of the specified options. Unfortunately, the designer made no provisions for options other than those specified and has not embedded a command requiring the selection of an anticipated choice. What will happen next in the lesson?

Few oversights create the kind of havoc that a failure to anticipate responses tends to create. The exact consequences for this example are impossible to predict,

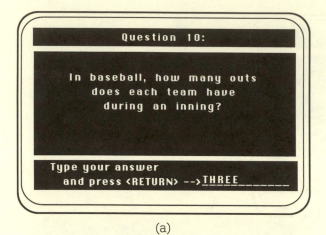

(a)

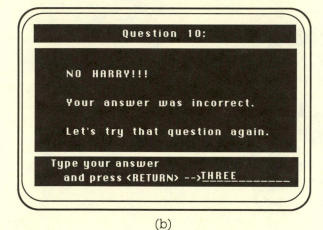

(b)

Figure 14.5
Consequences of a failure to anticipate a plausible response.

What would you like to do next?

C= Continue

S= Stop

R= Repeat

Type C, S, or R...

Figure 14.6
Prompting the student to anticipated responses.

since the lesson will "fall through," that is continue to whatever follows this program segment rather than branch as it should. Since unanticipated responses were not accounted for, the lesson essentially will run unpredictably, executing program statements indiscriminately along the way. However, it is usually fairly simple to create a net to anticipate illegal responses. Improved lesson execution is attained through little more than a common-sense examination of the consequences of student failure to respond as was planned.

TYPES OF INPUT TO BE MANAGED

Information is provided by learners for a variety of reasons and purposes. At times, student background information is collected during the lesson. At other times, information is used to control lesson execution, while in still others, responses are evaluated for accuracy. In this section, we will examine the most commonly used kinds of student input obtained during CAI lessons.

Information Queries   CAI lessons often require the student to input information such as name, age, or date. Usually, the purpose of the query is to obtain information that can be used to verify student status for lesson access, to collect data needed to update records or files, or to gather information that can be integrated into the lesson at a later time. The information is not specific to particular lesson content and does not require that lesson content be learned in order to respond.

Depending on the purpose of the query, the responses may be accepted literally as entered, analyzed further for specified attributes, or compared to other data. In the case of a student entering his or her name during the lesson, the name may be accepted literally as entered and embedded throughout to improve the personalization of the lesson. This requires virtually no response-management precautions, except to assign some variable to the inputted name for further use.

The use of the student name can also be considerably more complex. Students may be asked to input their names and perhaps a password in order to verify status as valid lesson users. In this case, features such as spelling are critical, since further comparisions to class rosters must be made. The use of accurate dates to aid in record keeping is also incorporated with some regularity, again necessitating that the response be inputted precisely.

Lesson-Control Responses   Input is often provided to guide the execution of the lesson. Directions such as "Press any key to continue" require that the student merely type any key, and the lesson will proceed. Little management of student responses of this type is required.

Other lesson-control options can require somewhat greater sophistication. Often lessons offer options that require that the response be evaluated. In the example shown in Figure 14.7(a), input must be evaluated to examine which key was used to control lesson execution. The lesson execution decisions illustrated in Figure 14.7(b) are based upon the specific key pressed. If the *Q* were typed, the lesson execution would terminate; if the *?* were typed, the lesson would provide assistance; if the space bar were pressed, the lesson would simply continue. In each case, the response requires a certain degree of management in order to determine appropriate lesson execution.

(a)

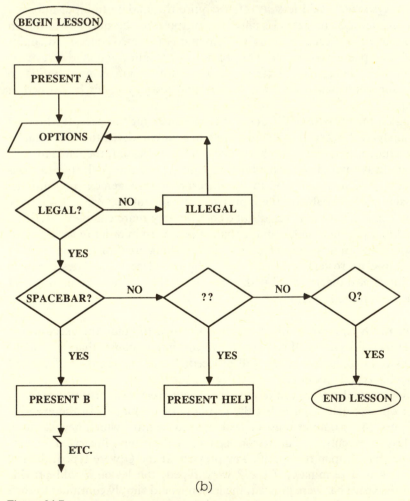

(b)

Figure 14.7
Lesson control options and associated flowchart.

Still, the requirements for response management are comparatively small. For the most part, student responses are simply collected, and fairly straightforward comparisons are made. The task of managing student input for different questions, however, can be considerably more complex. Let's examine some of the common applications of response management in the use of embedded questions.

Answers to Lesson Questions Certain questions, such as true–false or yes–no questions, are very straightforward to manage. The input is brief, exact, and requires little interpretation to determine accuracy. Similarly, answers to multiple-choice questions are usually straightforward and require little or no management of the input.

Short-answer response formats, however, can be especially challenging. Examine the constructed-response question shown in Figure 14.8(a). The question is relatively straightforward, but the possibilities for student responses are wide-ranging. Will the student answer in complete-sentence form? Or in a single word? Must all words be spelled correctly? If not, which words can vary, and by how

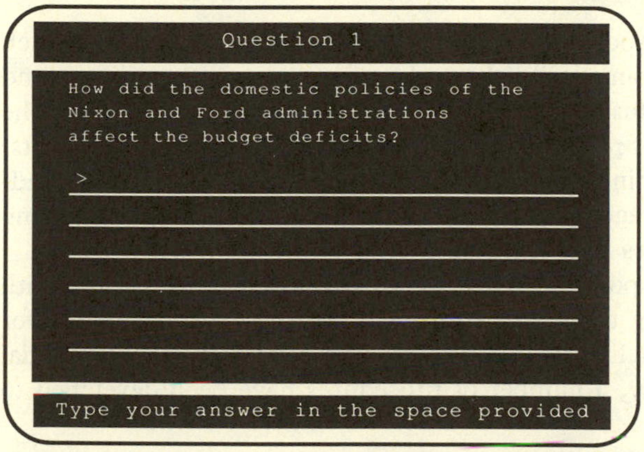

```
            Question 1

How did the domestic policies of the
Nixon and Ford administrations
affect the budget deficits?

  > _____

  _____

  _____

  _____

  _____

  _____

Type your answer in the space provided
```

(a)

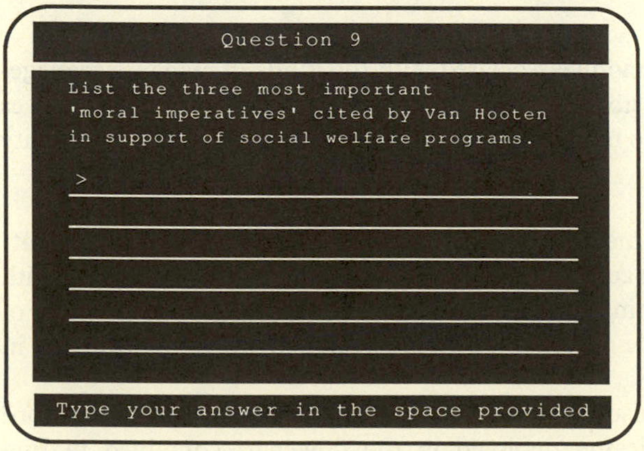

```
            Question 9

List the three most important
'moral imperatives' cited by Van Hooten
in support of social welfare programs.

  > _____

  _____

  _____

  _____

  _____

  _____

Type your answer in the space provided
```

(b)

Figure 14.8
Some broadly stated contructed response questions.

much? Remember, the answers to questions such as these will have a profound effect on the instructional decisions entrusted to the computer: If sensible guidelines are provided, sensible decisions will be made. If not, the decisions may be either unnecessarily harsh or excessively liberal.

Constructed-response questions require a good deal of response-management planning. The question shown in Figure 14.8(b) permits a wide variety of response possibilities for students, but it requires careful consideration for response management. What are the elements of a correct response? Are all elements equally weighted, or are some parts of the answer to be more important than others? Must the answer components be given in a prescribed order, or can the points be given in any order? The task of anticipating responses that are appropriate, as well as those that are inappropriate, is difficult but necessary. The job of analyzing the responses to determine the existence of anticipated response features, to enable the computer to comprehend the response, and to determine the most appropriate action in the lesson dialogue is formidable indeed.

CONTROLLING INPUT THROUGH SPECIFICITY

The use of multiple-choice response formats in CAI lessons has proliferated. Such response formats simplify dramatically the tasks of response management and evaluation. Unfortunately, this has been done much to the exclusion of the development of other forms of responding, such as constructed-response formats. The planning and programming required for the more involved question-and-answer formats have discouraged their use to the point that lessons requiring students to generate responses have become a rarity.

The use of constructed-response formats requires techniques for coping with spelling errors, for permitting the use of equivalent responses or synonyms, for permitting or requiring capitalization in answers, and a host of other potential response features. Fortunately, a number of procedures have been developed to assist in this task.

TECHNIQUES FOR MANAGING COMPLEX RESPONSE FORMATS

Several techniques are commonly associated with the kinds of response management used in CAI. The possibilities range from simple matching of responses against prescribed standards to more complex procedures used to judge the quality of student responses.

Matching   Matching is the most literal and straightforward method for evaluating learner responses. In essence, the student's response is compared literally with a model response and determined to either match or not match. An example of matching applied to multiple-choice responses is shown in the flowchart in Figure 14.9.

Matching techniques are also used for evaluating simple one- and two-word answers. For example, the lesson depicted in the flowchart contained in Figure 14.10 illustrates how simple responses are often evaluated effectively through matching. In this case, however, the response is matched against a series of model responses to allow for some variability in spelling. If any of the matches are successful, then the response will be considered effective.

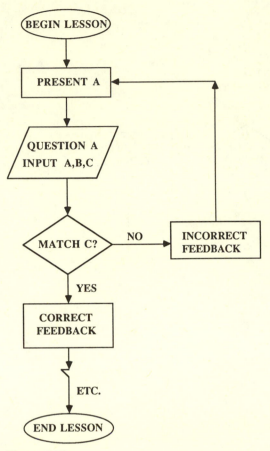

Figure 14.9
Literal matching for one-letter answers.

Since matching is such a literal process, it is often too inflexible for more complex response formats. Imagine the complicated number and types of literal matching statements required to evaluate a typed response for three key features, embedded in variable order within each student's sentence, with several spelling options available for each feature. The planning and programming tasks would be monumental if matching alone were to be employed throughout a lesson. Instead, more flexible procedures have been developed for coping with the response variability characteristic of constructed responses.

Answer Judging   Answer judging is applied when the nature of the student response, or the standards to which it is compared, is sufficiently complex to render matching techniques unfeasible. Answer judging is commonly used to search across student input for key words or letters, to vary the tolerance for spelling or typographical errors, and to otherwise judge input in a nonliteral manner. It permits the designer to use more open-ended constructed-response formats by analyzing input in much the same way that an effective teacher might.

There are several methods for judging the quality of student input. One of the most common is called the *key word* method, where student input is examined for the presence of a particular word or sequence of letters. The keyword method is

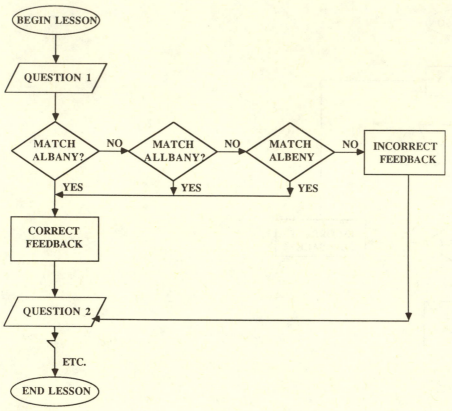

Figure 14.10.
Literal matching for a one-word answer.

illustrated in the flowchart shown in Figure 14.11. In response to a short-answer question, the student types an answer in the form of a sentence. The sentence is then examined for the presence of the key word *aorta*. If the key word is present, then the match is successful; if it is not present, the response is presumed to have been inaccurate.

Another common application of answer judging is to permit a range of spelling variations. For example, a lesson focusing on *mnemonics*, the use of structured memory strategies, might be presented. In the context of the lesson, perhaps a decision has beeen made that it is of little consequence that the student spell the word *mnemonic* correctly. Instead, the *meaning* of the concept itself has been deemed important. The question, shown in Figure 14.12, requires the student to type a word meaning "a structured memory or learning strategy."

Since the first *M* in the word *mnemonic* is inaudible, the designer may choose to accept responses that include N, M, N, and C, the audible letters, in a specific order. Therefore "*NUMONAC*" would be considered a correct response.

Answer judging techniques open a wide range of possibilities for lesson designers. It is possible to require that students recall the gist of a lesson without having to recall answers verbatim. Students can recall answers rather than simply identifying the best choice among alternatives. Perhaps most importantly, answer

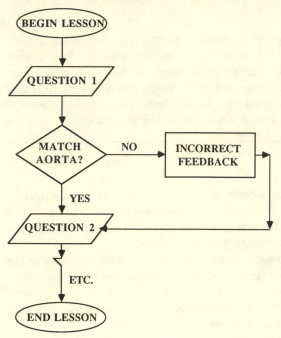

Figure 14.11
Key word method for judging answers.

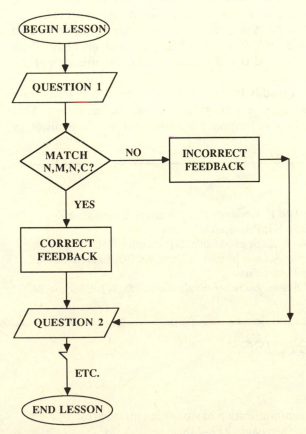

Figure 14.12
Key-letter method for judging answers.

231

judging enables the lesson designer to produce instruction that more closely approximates a normal dialogue, where students interact with the lesson on a conversational level rather than by selecting single letters or short words. In effect, answer judging can make the learning process more consistent with other learning opportunities, rather than simplifying the lesson design to accommodate the limitations of the computer, the lesson designer, or the programmer.

Chapter Summary

Effective planning for lesson input is essential if meaningful instructional options are to be provided. It can also be among the most tedious of planning steps. As a consequence, designers often do not attend to response management planning to the degree that other planning activities are emphasized.

Designers often spend proportionately greater amounts of time attending to the visible features of the lesson. It is easier to identify the products of effort when they are visible and concrete. We can, for example, identify the value of time spent on frame design or graphics. The fruits of such planning may be easier to identify than those of response management, but they are in no way more important.

Decisions affecting lesson execution, based on response-management specifications, are important in a very fundamental sense. The internal execution decisions of a lesson, based on a systematic analysis of student input, ensures the appropriateness of all lesson activities. Information can always be presented in an attractive instructional *form*, but the systematic control of lesson execution based upon student responses accounts for the quality of instructional *substance*. Both form and substance are important in CAI and require the careful attention of the lesson designer.

Since the effort required is not readily identified in the outward appearance of a lesson, there is a tendency to apply less effort than might be necessary. This tendency must be resisted. Effective response management is prerequisite to effective lesson execution.

Related Reading

ALESSI, S. M., and S. R. TROLLIP (1984). *Computer-Based Instruction: Methods and Development*. Englewood Cliffs, NJ: Prentice-Hall.

BURKE, R. L. (1982). *CAI Sourcebook*. Englewood Cliffs, NJ: Prentice-Hall.

HUNTINGTON, J. F. (1979). *Computer-Assisted Instruction Using BASIC*. Englewood Cliffs, NJ: Educational Technology Publications.

MEREDITH, J. C. (1971). *The CAI Author/Instructor*. Englewood Cliffs, NJ: Educational Technology Publications.

Chapter Review Exercises

COMPREHENSION

1. Describe the importance of communication in sustaining meaningful computer—learner dialogue. (See pages 217–218.)
2. Define *legal* and *illegal* responses in CAI. (See pages 219–222.)

   3. Describe methods for managing both legal and illegal responses. (See pages 219–222.)

   4. Define *anticipated* and *unanticipated* responses in CAI. (See pages 222–225.)

   5. Describe methods for managing anticipated and unanticipated responses. (See pages 222–225.)

   6. List and describe the types of input requiring response management planning. (See pages 225–228.)

   7. Describe the importance of questioning techniques in controlling student input. (See pages 228–232.)

   8. Describe the implications of the different questioning techniques for lesson planning and lesson programming. (See pages 228–232.)

   9. List and describe techniques used to evaluate student responses. Describe the advantages and limitations of each technique. (See pages 228–232.)

APPLICATION

   1. Select an instructional need appropriate for CAI. Design techniques that maintain meaningful dialogue between the computer and the student for the selected need. [Figures 13.1 through 13.6(b).]

   2. Design techniques for managing legal and illegal student responses. [See Figures 14.5(a) through 14.6.]

   3. Design techniques for managing anticipated and unanticipated student responses. (See Figure 14.6.)

Producing and Implementing CAI

To this point, we have emphasized the planning considerations appropriate for CAI lessons. As designers, we develop instructional objectives, determine the most appropriate lesson design, design frames that will support the learning of the intended information, and perform a variety of other planning steps. All are essential in order to perform the tasks required in this section: to produce, program, and implement a CAI lesson.

All lessons have features that are uniquely suited to particular applications. However, there are also several features and techniques that are useful and appropriate across CAI applications. The ability to write effectively for CAI purposes, for instance, affects all CAI applications. The ability to identify, locate, and use information gathered during CAI is also an important general skill. The purposes of this section are to present and describe the options available for creating CAI lessons, to provide information useful in writing effective lessons, and to describe and illustrate computer-managed instruction (CMI) applications for CAI lessons.

SECTION GOALS

After completing this section you will

1. Comprehend the implications of the different programming and lesson-authoring options and be able to select the best option for a particular problem or setting.

235

2. Understand and apply the kinds of lesson organization and writing skills appropriate for CAI lesson modes and designs.
3. Understand the different levels and methods of computer management possible in CAI and be able to select the levels and methods most appropriate for given problems.

CHAPTER 15

Authoring and Programming CAI Lessons

Careful planning is the key to effective lesson development. Planning reduces or eliminates the number of blind alleys a designer follows; clarifies the design strategies to be implemented; and otherwise prescribes the techniques, content, and sequence of the lesson. In CAI lesson development, as in the use of virtually any systems-based application, there is no substitute for effective planning.

An important factor to consider during both the planning and production phases is the method used for lesson development. Different development options offer varied capabilities, which influence basic design specifications. Lesson production time can be affected dramatically by the method used for translating the lesson design to a program understood by the computer. The purposes of this chapter are to describe the basic options available for lesson creation, to evaluate each option for strengths and limitations, and to examine the features of each option that are likely to influence lesson design decisions.

OBJECTIVES

Comprehension

After completing this chapter you will be able to

1. Describe the similarities and differences among general-purpose programming languages, CAI authoring languages, and CAI authoring systems.
2. List and describe the advantages and limitations of general-purpose programming languages, CAI authoring languages, and CAI authoring systems.
3. Describe the resources and constraints of the learning setting that affect the selection of a lesson development option.
4. Describe the resources and constraints of the development setting that affect the selection of a lesson creation option.
5. Describe the learning task variables and demands that affect the selection of a lesson creation option.

Application

After completing this chapter you will be able to

1. Select the lesson development option that best meets the requirements of a selected development setting.
2. Select the option that best meets the needs of the learning setting.
3. Create a CAI lesson using the best option for a given instructional problem.

Programming Versus Authoring CAI

There are a number of options that can be used to create CAI lessons. Each option provides unique benefits, but each also has certain limitations. With some options, little or no computer programming expertise is needed; with others, a good deal of programming knowledge is required. In this chapter we describe several of the considerations applied in selecting an appropriate option for the creation of a lesson. In addition, we examine the primary options available for the creation of CAI, describe the advantages and limitations of each option, and provide examples of each option in the creation of a CAI lesson.

There are basically three options available for CAI lesson development: general-purpose programming languages, CAI authoring languages, and CAI authoring systems. Each option offers unique advantages and limitations, which will influence their selection.

GENERAL-PURPOSE PROGRAMMING LANGUAGES

General-purpose programming languages consist of commands or program statements that serve well-defined functions. In order to program a lesson, the correct sequence and logical progression of separate programming statements must be written. A collection of programming commands with a common purpose is called a *procedure*; the collection of related procedures in a particular lesson is called a *file* or *program*.

Simple but accurate assessments of the methods and procedures of programming are provided in several current publications (see, for example, Rothman and Mosmann, 1985; Sullivan, Lewis, and Cook, 1985). Programming languages vary widely in their complexity and ease of use. High-level languages, for example, are more easily understood due to the descriptive nature of the programming commands. In BASIC (*Beginners All-Purpose Symbolic Instructional Code*), for example, the simple command "PRINT" is used for the display of text. Pascal, named after the seventeenth-century mathematician Blaise Pascal, also uses descriptive, high-level names for programming commands. Several other contemporary high-level programming languages, such as C and Forth, have been developed during the past decade, and numerous other languages are likely to continue to emerge. The principal drawback of high-level languages is the requirement for subsequent interpreting and/or compiling by the computer, that is, the conversion of high-level commands into low-level instructions that can be acted upon by the computer. As a result, high-level languages typically require additional time to execute. In most cases, however, these limitations are barely noticeable.

On the other hand, a considerable amount of professional instructional software is programmed in assembly or machine languages. These languages typically communicate more directly with a particular microprocessor. Assembly language programs, for example, are uniquely suited to particular computer systems and will only transfer directly to computers using identical microprocessors. The command structure of these languages is not nearly as descriptive or self-evident as that of high-level languages, but the commands can be understood more directly by the computer. The result is that programs written in an assembly language will execute quicker and more efficiently than a high-level program.

The scope of application for most general-purpose programming languages is relatively broad-based. That is, programming languages provide a great deal of flexibility in terms of the range of application and in specific control of computer functions. However, they also require fairly sophisticated programming skills for all but the simplest instructional applications. Pascal, for example, is used widely for educational, scientific, and general-purpose programming.

Other programming languages, such as COBOL (*CO*mmon *B*usiness-*O*riented *L*anguage) for business and FORTRAN (*FOR*mula *TRAN*slation) for scientific applications, are better suited for some uses than for others, but they are potentially applicable in many areas. So the selection of a general-purpose programming language commits the designer or developer to a language that provides a good deal of flexibility, but one that requires reasonably well-developed programming expertise and was not developed expressly for CAI purposes.

Consider a CAI lesson written in BASIC, a popular microcomputer programming language. Figure 15.1, a portion of the program, is shown with the resulting output.

Notice that several command statements are needed in order to locate the cursor to a particular portion of the screen, to permit double spacing on the screen, to judge the student response, and to branch to different sections of the lesson under different conditions. Notice also that the programming commands, though easily understood (as are the commands of most high-level programming languages) are words or phrases, which control lesson execution. Virtually every possible aspect of lesson execution must be programmed separately, since the BASIC language has no intrinsic sense for the CAI application illustrated.

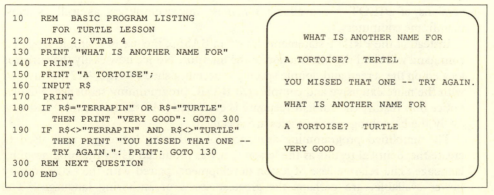

```
10    REM   BASIC PROGRAM LISTING
      FOR TURTLE LESSON
120   HTAB 2: VTAB 4
130   PRINT "WHAT IS ANOTHER NAME FOR"
140   PRINT
150   PRINT "A TORTOISE";
160   INPUT R$
170   PRINT
180   IF R$="TERRAPIN" OR R$="TURTLE"
      THEN PRINT "VERY GOOD": GOTO 300
190   IF R$<>"TERRAPIN" AND R$<>"TURTLE"
      THEN PRINT "YOU MISSED THAT ONE --
      TRY AGAIN.": PRINT: GOTO 130
300   REM NEXT QUESTION
1000  END
```

```
        WHAT IS ANOTHER NAME FOR

A TORTOISE?   TERTEL

YOU MISSED THAT ONE -- TRY AGAIN.

WHAT IS ANOTHER NAME FOR

A TORTOISE?   TURTLE

VERY GOOD
```

Figure 15.1
A sample BASIC program listing.

The decision to select a programming language must be based on several factors. On one hand, high-level programming languages are usually easier to program and more readily understood by humans than are low-level languages. Machine and assembly languages, though more complex to program, are more readily understood by the computer. Both, however, can become quite complex for meeting the specifications of most CAI. Fortunately, these are not the CAI designer's only options.

AUTHORING LANGUAGES

CAI authoring languages are special-purpose computer languages designed specifically for the development of CAI lessons (Hannafin, 1984; Kearsley, 1984). Usually authoring languages are hybrids that assume some of the structural features of programming languages but simplify the programming needed to enable the use of the most common CAI features (Barker and Singh, 1982; Voyce, 1982). The languages typically consist of a limited number of simplified commands, each of which may perform the functions of several more complex programming statements. The emphasis with authoring languages is on the ease of use of a relatively small but powerful number of commands that perform functions frequently applied in CAI.

Imagine, for example, the creation of a lesson featuring extensive use of graphics, music, animation, color, and a host of other features. Since the computer itself is capable of producing each feature, the task of the lesson developer is to select a language or system that will support the lesson specifications. You could select a programming language, but the time and planning required to enable all of the features desired, in all the different contexts, would be substantial. On the other hand, a special-purpose CAI authoring language designed to simplify the use of those features commonly included in CAI lesson helps the development process tremendously. For applications that are very specific, such as the development of CAI lessons, CAI authoring languages may be very desirable.

Examine the PILOT (*P*rogrammed *I*nquiry for *L*earning *O*r *T*eaching) listing shown in Figure 15.2. PILOT is a CAI authoring language designed expressly for instructional applications and offering somewhat more simplified command sequences. The dialect of PILOT in Figure 15.2 is Apple SuperPILOT (1982), but versions of PILOT are available for most microcomputers as well as most mainframe computers.

Instead of the PRINT statements found in BASIC, the use of a simple type (T:) command will send the information to the monitor. Notice how easily the cursor is located on the screen and double spacing is accomplished (TS:g2,4;12), compared with the more extensive and complicated BASIC programming sequence. Finally, notice how readily the student response is evaluated (MS:turtle!terrapin) and how easily the branching contingencies are specified.

The simplified programming sequences of authoring languages were used to create the identical results as the lesson that was produced using the programming language. The relative ease of lesson development, paired with the extraordinary power available, are perhaps the greatest assets of authoring languages. The developer need not become fluent with all aspects of a complicated programming language in order to accomplish what is typically associated with CAI. The

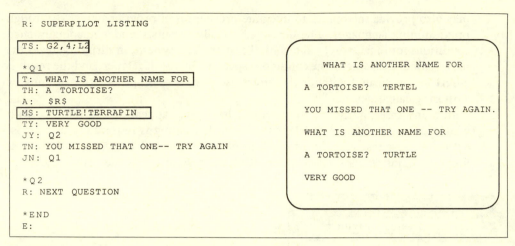

```
R:  SUPERPILOT LISTING

 TS: G2,4;L2

 *Q1
 T:   WHAT IS ANOTHER NAME FOR
 TH: A TORTOISE?
 A:   $R$
 MS: TURTLE!TERRAPIN
 TY: VERY GOOD
 JY: Q2
 TN: YOU MISSED THAT ONE-- TRY AGAIN
 JN: Q1

 *Q2
 R: NEXT QUESTION

 *END
 E:
```

```
          WHAT IS ANOTHER NAME FOR

     A TORTOISE?   TERTEL

     YOU MISSED THAT ONE -- TRY AGAIN.

     WHAT IS ANOTHER NAME FOR

     A TORTOISE?   TURTLE

     VERY GOOD
```

Figure 15.2
A sample SuperPILOT program listing.

developer need only become fluent with the less complex authoring language to create the desired effects.

Several authoring languages are available for various microcomputer as well as mainframe applications. Kearsley (1984) has provided a useful summary of authoring languages and the computer systems for which authoring languages are available. In addition to PILOT, authoring languages such as ADAPT, TenCore, Coursewriter, and Tutor are available for CAI development. In addition, the *Journal of Computer-Based Instruction* devoted the entire Summer 1984 issue to a review of CAI authoring options. Clearly, if an authoring language is desired, one can be identified for CAI development on virtually any computer system.

Authoring languages also possess certain limitations. For microcomputer applications, they tend to execute fairly slowly, due to the additional program compiling required by the computer. In addition, authoring languages often require significant computer memory and disk storage space. This results is either fairly small individual lessons or in the frequent accessing of information from the lesson disk as the computer loads and dumps information during lesson execution. These limitations can be troublesome but, as with most problems, they can usually be minimized or circumvented by a skilled designer.

AUTHORING SYSTEMS

The final option, the authoring system, provides a method for individuals with little or no programming expertise and, in some cases, little or no design experience, to create CAI lessons (Jensen, 1982; Locatis and Carr, 1984; Schleicher, 1982). The options for presenting, questioning, and branching are prescribed within the authoring system. The developer simply responds to computer prompting by selecting the desired option, inserting the necessary information, providing correct responses, listing branching contingencies, and so forth until the lesson is completed.

Authoring systems are prestructured templates, which sometimes provide both embedded CAI logic and programming logic (Merrill, 1985). In certain cases, they may also provide the option to integrate procedures of programs created through programming languages. The developer usually responds under maximally cued conditions into a friendly, nontechnical system. The system, in turn, organizes the information according to the conditions specified by the developer, and the result is a CAI lesson created without the direct use of either computer programming or authoring languages.

In many cases, authoring systems will have great appeal due to the ease with which instruction can be developed. Very little training is required to learn most authoring systems, and the format can often be adapted to account for several different kinds of instructional tasks. Clearly, ease of use is the primary asset of

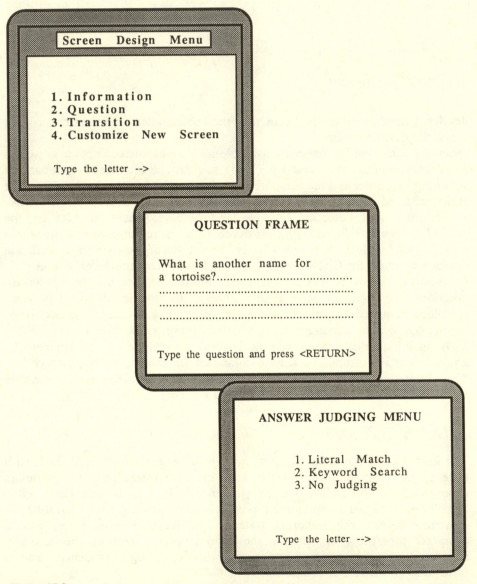

Figure 15.3
Sample authoring system prompts and menus.

authoring systems, since developers need not be programmers in order to design CAI lessons.

The dramatically different structure of a typical authoring system is illustrated in Figure 15.3. Again, the same basic output will be displayed to the screen. The authoring system permits cursor control to various locations, but we have been limited in certain features. For instance, we could not use the exact borders that were specified, since the system provides fixed frame protocol for information and questions. The same answer judging could not be duplicated directly, since the system provides only certain types of answer-judging options.

The menu-driven prompting used in many authoring systems is illustrated in Figures 15.4(a) and 15.4(b). The designer enters teaching, branching, and answer-judging information by responding to the system prompts. Assuming that the basic logic of the instructional design is sound, the authoring system provides an easy-to-use method for lesson creation.

Several authoring systems are available for CAI lesson development. Pauline and Hannafin (1987) describe science teaching applications of the Audio Visual Author

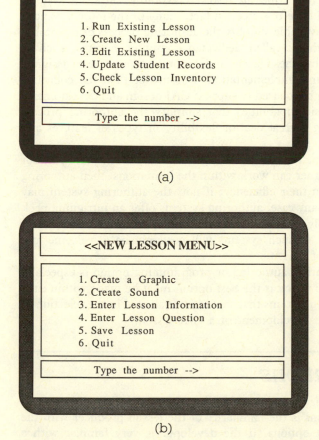

(a)

(b)

Figure 15.4
Prompting features typical of authoring systems.

developed by Bell and Howell, and many of the friendly and powerful features of the system. In addition, The Instructor, The Educator, WISE, E-Z Learner, Microteach, Quizmaster, ADAPT, QUEST, CAS, CAL, and several others are available, depending upon the power and sophistication of the computer system. In most cases, several options exist for the selection of an authoring system.

Authoring systems are not without limitations. The embedded logic of such a system is an asset when it is consistent with desired lesson specifications, but it can be a major problem when the specifications exceed the structural capabilities of the system. Many authoring systems are very rigid in the kinds of options provided. Often the authoring system restricts the activities that can be included, forcing the designer either to adopt the program logic of the system or to seek alternative options. Authoring-system capabilities tend to address fairly basic CAI design issues because of the enormously complicated task of enabling the myriad branching and interaction possibilities of different CAI lessons (Roblyer, 1981). In many cases, CAI designers and developers either outgrow the capabilities of authoring systems or select authoring systems that permit easy linkages to the base language of the system.

It is important to note, however, that authoring systems represent the wave of the future in CAI software and courseware development. Assuming that the important flexibility and creativity issues are resolved favorably, authoring systems will provide an extremely valuable resource. In fact, many of the more advanced authoring systems presently available simplify the authoring process dramatically. This is especially true for the so-called dedicated computer systems, such as Micro-TICCIT, developed by the Hazeltine Corporation, that are designed exclusively for CAI design and implementation. Because of this, the collective potential of the computer can be focused to support CAI design and development. Such systems possess intrinsic capabilities that simplify the authoring process dramatically while permitting a great deal of flexibility in types of features and options.

It should be obvious that the reduction in design flexibility is the price paid for ease of authoring. If the designer can work within the limitations, then authoring systems can be remarkable in their efficiency; if not, the authoring system may pose unwanted problems. In any case, authoring systems offer an intriguing peek into the future of user-friendly computer software development systems. Further development and refinement of such systems will certainly be a welcome and valuable tool in the future of CAI.

The selection of an appropriate authoring or programming option is especially important. The decision as to which is the best option must be made within each setting. Consider some of the questions that should be evaluated in the selection of a language or system for the development of a CAI lesson.

Planning Considerations

1. *With which option is the developer most familiar and facile?* One of the most important initial considerations is the familiarity of the lesson producer with the different lesson development options. If the developer is very familiar with a particular language or option, perhaps it will be unnecessary to consider a different

option. The widespread popularity of BASIC, for instance, has made it a favorite of many noncommercial instructional software and courseware developers. Certainly the greater the initial familiarity of the developer with particular options, the better his or her ability to maximize the capabilities of the computer. Pascal and the various versions of PILOT are also gaining in popularity. Familiarity should be considered an important, but not the only or the dominant, factor affecting the development decision.

2. *Which option(s) provide the greatest development power, and which are the easiest options to implement?* Of potentially greater importance are the power and ease of use of the different options in meeting lesson specifications. Programming languages provide a good deal of flexibility and enable a virtually infinite variety of possibilities, but they can be complex to utilize in the manner desired. Authoring systems are especially easy to use, but they often do not provide sufficient power or flexibility to accommodate the range of specifications likely to be encountered. The best option should, at a minimum, accommodate the lesson requirements in the easiest and most efficient manner possible.

3. *Which option(s) can be used for the least dollar cost?* Cost factors are always an important consideration. In some cases, such as with authoring languages, an option may be available that provides the ideal combination, but at a prohibitive cost. It may be necessary, though not desirable, to select a lesser option due to the high cost of the ideal option.

4. *Which options are already available and usable for lesson creation?* One of the most common factors affecting development is the availability of different alternatives. Microcomputers come equipped with some programming language, typically a dialect of BASIC, and can be programmed directly with no additional expense. The use of a development option other than the resident language of the computer necessarily requires the acquisition of additional hardware or software. It may be desirable, useful, or even necessary to purchase an option not immediately available with given computer hardware. If so, both cost and availability become increasingly important factors when considering the best development option.

5. *With which option can lessons be created fastest and most efficiently?* Another aspect of cost pertains to the amount of time and effort required to produce a lesson. Some options are simply easier to use for CAI purposes than others, generally simplifying the development process and reducing the time required for production. Virtually every CAI application imaginable can be created in several ways, so several options might be capable of producing the prescribed lesson. However, there are likely to be significant differences in the efficiency of each choice. Since development time is a very expensive part of CAI lesson creation, the selection of a time-efficient option is very important.

6. *Which option(s) provide the best alternative for the development of additional related lessons?* When producing a group of related units or lessons, it is important that a certain degree of interlesson consistency, or protocol, be established. The frame layouts, the kinds of alternatives available to the student, and the procedures governing lesson control and execution should be, to the maximum degree possible, available across the lessons. This is usually easier to accomplish using the same creation option across units or lessons, since the protocol and procedures can be transferred directly from lesson to lesson. It may be advantageous to evaluate which option meets the present specifications and which would likely be the best

option for future development efforts at the same time. It will be far easier to maintain consistency and quality in CAI development efforts if this decision is made in consideration of both immediate and long-term needs.

7. *Which option(s) meet the design specifications of the lesson with the least difficulty?* The design requirements prescribed for a particular lesson will also influence the suitability of different options. If, for example, extensive use of sound, graphics, or animation is prescribed, a substantial amount of programming or authoring time and expertise might be needed. Certainly the option that offers the simplest and most powerful capabilities in such areas will receive serious attention. Again, it may be possible through the use of more sophisticated options to develop CAI lessons that include the prescribed design components, but it may be exceedingly complex and time-consuming.

8. *What are the implications of each option on the computer hardware needed to program, and to run, CAI lessons?* Some options frequently require additional, enhanced, or modified computer hardware to implement. For microcomputer applications, the use of an authoring language, programming language, or authoring system other than the native language may require anything from additional memory to additional disk drives.

9. *If training is needed, which option will provide the greatest utility for the amount of time invested?* Assuming training in use of the language or system is needed, the decision of where to apply the necessary effort is critical. Clearly, certain authoring systems can be learned very easily but may not provide the kind of flexibility and potential desired. It is an all-too-common error to simply select the easiest option to learn without regard for the long-term problems associated with the limitations of a primitive system. For individuals contemplating this decision, the immediate needs must be weighed against the long-term ramifications of selecting an option that is either too restrictive or too complex.

Chapter Summary

As are all system components, the planning tasks for lesson design and development are interdependent. On one hand, we are concerned with instructional design features and lesson activities that will support learning most effectively. We strive to embed the most powerful instructional features, to provide methods of interaction that are consistent with the learning task requirements, and to collect, maintain, and use the relevant information obtained during a lesson. The task appears straightforward: Identify the most effective lesson design specifications and program the lesson accordingly.

On the other hand, we cannot develop lesson specifications that simply cannot be executed. The limitations of both machines and people must be weighed in lesson design. The capabilities and limitations of the computer system itself, the availability of different lesson-creation options, the power and flexibility of the available options, and competency in the use of the available options must all be considered. In some cases, these considerations will cause no limitations on lesson design; in others, however, design concessions can be substantial.

The computer's potential range of instructional applications is formidable. Yet the alternatives selected for lesson creation and computer control are critical factors, affecting how fully or incompletely the power of the computer is utilized.

As the availability, sophistication, and power of lesson-creation options continue to improve, the associated power of the CAI lessons will likewise improve.

References

APPLE SUPERPILOT (1982). *Language Reference Manual.* Cupertino, CA: Apple Computer, Inc.

BARKER, P. G., and R. SINGH (1982). Author languages for computer-based learning. *British Journal of Educational Technology*, **13**, 167–196.

HANNAFIN, M. J. (1984). Options for authoring instructional interactive video. *Journal of Computer-Based Instruction*, **11**, 98–100.

JENSEN, J. D. (1982). A taxonomy of microcomputer authoring systems. *Performance and Instruction*, **21**(6), 50–52.

KEARSLEY, G. (1984). Instructional design and authoring software. *Journal of Instructional Development*, **7**(3), 11–16.

LOCATIS, C., and V. CARR (1984). *Systems for Authoring Computer-Based Instruction.* Bethesda, MD: National Library of Medicine/NIH.

MERRILL, M. D. (1985). Where is the authoring in authoring systems? *Journal of Computer-Based Instruction*, **12**, 90–96.

PAULINE, R., and M. J. HANNAFIN (1987). Interactive slide/sound instruction: Incorporate the power of the computer with high-fidelity visual and aural images. *Educational Technology*, in press.

ROBLYER, M. D. (1981). Instructional design versus authoring of courseware: Some crucial differences. *AEDS Journal*, **14**, 173–181.

ROTHMAN, S., and C. MOSMANN (1985). *Computer Uses and Issues.* Chicago: SRA Associates.

SCHLEICHER, G. (1982). Authoring systems can save time in development of CAI. *Electronic Education*, **2**(3), 20–27.

SULLIVAN, D. R., T. G. LEWIS, and C. R. COOK (1985). *Computing Today: Microcomputer Concepts and Applications.* Boston: Houghton Mifflin Co.

VOYCE, S. (1982). A functional analysis of courseware authoring languages. *AEDS Journal*, **15**, 107–125.

Related Reading

BEEBE, T. H., and A. P. MIZELL (1983). Software languages: How to talk to your computer. *Instructional Innovator*, **28**(4), 14–17.

HARTMAN, K. (1982). Authoring considerations in writing instructional computer programs. *The Computing Teacher*, **10**(1), 27–29.

HAZEN, M. (1982). Computer-assisted instruction with PILOT on the Apple computer. *Educational Technology*, **22**(11), 20–22.

MERRILL, M. D., E. W. SCHNEIDER, and K. A. FLETCHER (1980). *TICCIT.* Englewood Cliffs, NJ: Educational Technology Publications.

NORRIS, H. (1983). Lessons take off with SuperPILOT. *Apple-Plus*, **1**(2), 99–107.

POGUE, R. E. (1980). The authoring system: Interface between author and computer. *Journal of Research and Development in Education*, **14**(1), 57–68.

RAHMLOW, H. F., R. C. FRATINI, and J. R. GHESQUIERE (1980). *PLATO.* Englewood Cliffs, NJ: Educational Technology Publications.

Chapter Review Exercises

COMPREHENSION

1. Describe the similarities and differences among programming languages, authoring languages, and authoring systems. (See pages 238–244.)

2. List and describe the advantages and limitations of programming languages, authoring languages, and authoring systems. (See pages 238–244.)

3. Describe how the resources and constraints of the learning setting affect the selection of lesson-development options. (See pages 238–244.)

4. Describe how the resources and constraints of the CAI development setting affect the selection of lesson-development options. (See pages 238–244.)

5. Describe how learning-task variables affect the selection of lesson-development options. (See pages 238–244.)

APPLICATION

1. Identify an instructional need, in a relevant teaching or learning setting, appropriate for CAI. Identify participants to serve as lesson producers in a CAI development setting. Select the lesson-development option that best meets the requirements of the CAI development setting. (See pages 244–246.)

2. Select the lesson-development option that best meets the needs of the learning setting. (See pages 244–246.)

3. Develop a CAI lesson for the identified need and learning setting using the most appropriate lesson creation option.

CHAPTER 16

Organizing and Writing CAI Lessons

When one is approaching the task of creating a lesson, four issues are of concern: (1) What is the instructional content? (2) How is the content best ordered to facilitate learning? (3) What kinds of verbal, pictorial, and other forms of computer support are needed to teach the information? (4) How will the lesson procedures be executed and controlled by the computer? The questions are interrelated, but each is also functionally distinct.

If the question concerns the way to execute a lesson, the issue is what kinds of programming or authoring are needed. The various options used for programming and authoring have been described in Chapter 15. The designer analyzes lesson specifications such as branching needs and contingencies, frame protocol, response handling, and a variety of other specifications that must be converted to program execution statements. Upon completion of the analysis, programming commands and procedures are developed to allow the lesson to be executed in the intended manner. None of these decisions, however, focuses on *what* will be presented— only how and when the presentation will occur.

Organizing, writing, and programming CAI require many of the same types of skills. Each requires the ability to organize information logically, to translate a problem into a usable format, and to anticipate final lesson characteristics and features prior to extensive development. In each case, the creation of effective and efficient teaching CAI lessons is the ultimate goal.

OBJECTIVES

Comprehension

After completing this chapter you will be able to

1. Describe the differences in designing, writing, and programming CAI lessons.
2. Describe the organizational features of drill and practice designs.
3. Describe the organizational features of instructional game designs.
4. Describe the organizational features of instructional simulation designs.
5. List and describe the features of CAI writing that differentiate it from other forms of writing.

6. Describe circumstances affecting whether to recast or repeat lesson information.
7. Describe writing style considerations that are likely to prove effective across lesson designs.

Application

After completing this chapter you will be able to

1. Develop a well designed CAI tutorial for a selected instructional need.
2. Develop a well designed CAI drill for a selected instructional need.
3. Develop a well designed CAI game for a selected instructional need.
4. Develop a well designed CAI simulation for a selected instructional need.
5. Incorporate into lessons the elements of CAI writing required for effective communication.
6. Develop CAI lessons that include appropriate options and embedded support.

What Will Be Presented in the CAI Lesson?

Decisions pertaining to what will be taught, how the information will be sequenced, the types of activities to be included in the lesson, and what style or level of presentation will be used are critical issues in CAI lesson design. The concern at this stage is not so much how the computer will execute the steps desired, but what the steps are. We are concerned with how instruction should be sequenced for presentation, the best possible student-lesson interaction, and the extent to which the interaction between student and computer is effective, appealing, and understood.

In Chapter 10, the generic features of effective tutorials, drills, simulations, and instructional games were described. For the most part, the presence of these features increases the likelihood of effectiveness. However, the inclusion of these features alone does no more to guarantee effective instruction than the use of a T-square guarantees the development of attractive and efficient architectural plans. The T-square will aid in presenting the ideas of the designer, but it cannot assure that the building has been well designed.

Likewise, the design and organization of CAI requires knowledge of how people learn, the learning task at hand (or access to a subject-matter expert), methods for incorporating different instructional activities into a lesson, and methods for relating current instruction to previous or future learning. Good lessons emphasize the features of sound instruction, account for the relevant attributes of the students for whom the lesson is intended, incorporate findings from research on thinking and learning, and use the capabilities of the computer appropriately. The components of effective design are organized collectively to prescribe the sequence, options, and activities of a CAI lesson.

The ability to write CAI involves unique skills. Writing requires awareness and sensitivity to student attributes, to methods for supporting student learning through visual and verbal symbols, and to techniques for using the computer to "converse" effectively with the student. Writing CAI requires absolute clarity, the ability to integrate information from preceding and subsequent frames, the ability to balance the familiar with the unfamiliar, and the ability to organize information, thoughts, and ideas to support rather than complicate learning.

What skills, then, are needed to write CAI effectively? What kinds of activities and devices are likely to improve the information-carrying value of a CAI lesson? What guidelines might be considered in writing CAI, and what pitfalls are to be avoided? Let's examine how the different CAI lesson designs can be organized and written effectively.

Organizing CAI Lessons

During Chapter 10, the different types of CAI lessons were introduced: tutorials, drill and practice, instructional games, and simulations. Each of these designs requires a somewhat unique emphasis on different aspects of the lesson.

TUTORIALS

Perhaps the most useful scheme for designing and organizing CAI tutorials is to adopt a more or less consistent lesson *template*. A template is a sequence of steps or features found consistently across lessons. The template might be used to prescribe the kinds of components and considerations that characterize typical tutorials. All components of the template might not be required for all phases of every CAI tutorial developed, but the template would prescribe the range of factors that should be considered in the design of any tutorial lesson.

A useful organizational template for tutorial lessons has been devised by Gagné, Wager, and Rojas (1981), who applied what they call the *events of instruction* specifically to the creation of CAI tutorials. Essentially, the events consist of nine steps, each of which is thought to elicit cognitive processing that is important for effective learning. Figure 16.1 contains the events of instruction, with the kinds of cognitive processing activity thought to be facilitated by each event.

From an inspection of the events, a pattern or template for tutorial lesson organization can be developed. The tutorial should orient the learner to the instruction at hand, provide both information and an opportunity to apply the skills and information, provide feedback and any necessary additional information to aid in correct and effective learning, and aid the student in generalizing lesson information in order to strengthen learning and promote skill transfer (Alessandrini, 1983). The methods for accomplishing the activities prescribed by the template will vary, but the steps themselves are valuable in virtually any tutorial lesson.

Let's examine how a template can aid in the organization of lesson information and procedures. Figures 16.2 through 16.9 illustrate the events of instruction applied to a tutorial on the composition of the earth's atmosphere. The tutorial template provides a method for structuring lesson content, and for ensuring that the activities typical of effective tutorials are considered and included in the lesson.

1. *Gain attention.* Initially, student attention is directed to the lesson through the use of a relevant and interesting computer graphic. Generally, attention-getting frames should support subsequent lesson information whenever possible, rather than displaying irrelevant or distracting information. The frame used in this example gains student attention but also orients the student toward the lesson theme.

THE EVENTS OF INSTRUCTION	

EXTERNAL INSTRUCTIONAL EVENT	INTERNAL LEARNING PROCESS
1. Gaining Attention	Alertness to Activity to Follow
2. Informing Learner of Lesson Objective(s)	Raise Expectancy, Focus Mental Effort
3. Stimulating Recall of Prior Learning	Call Already Learned Information into Working Memory
4. Presenting Stimuli with Distinctive Features	Attend Selectively to Features of the Lesson
5. Guiding Learning During Instruction	Encode Lesson Information into Memory
6. Eliciting Performance During Lesson	Retrieve Lesson Information from Memory, Respond
7. Providing Rich, Informative Feedback During Lesson	Reinforcement & Confirmation of Intended Learning
8. Assessing Performance During Lesson	Retrieve Lesson Information Per Lesson Objective(s)
9. Enhancing Retention & Transfer of Lesson Information & Concepts	Generalize Lesson Information & Concepts to Existing & Future Related Tasks

Figure 16.1
The events of instruction (Adapted from Gagné, Wager, and Rojas, 1981).

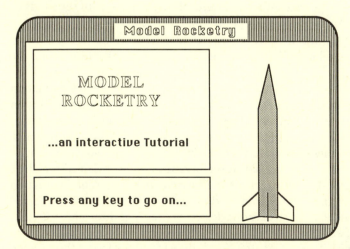

Figure 16.2
Gaining attention.

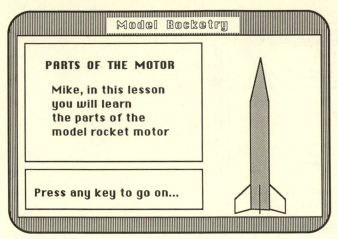

Figure 16.3
Informing student of lesson expectations.

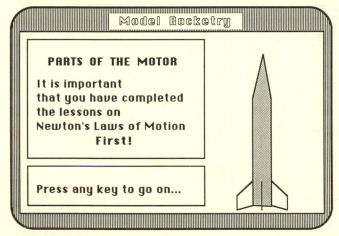

Figure 16.4
Recalling lesson prerequisites.

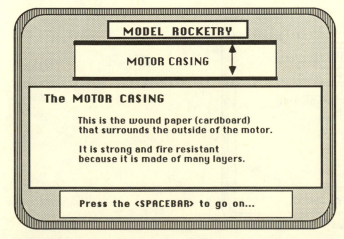

Figure 16.5
Presenting new lesson information.

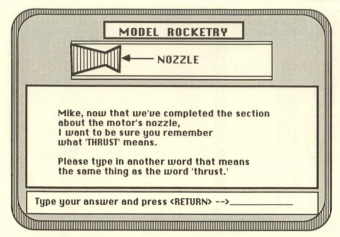

Figure 16.6
Guiding learning and eliciting responses.

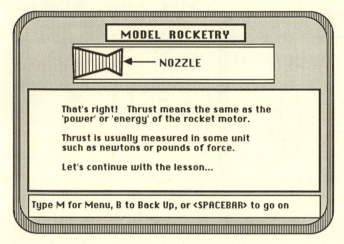

Figure 16.7
Providing feedback.

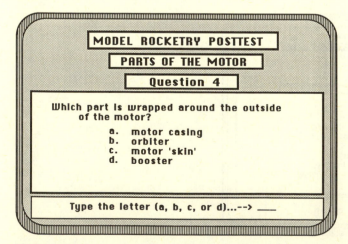

Figure 16.8
Assessing performance.

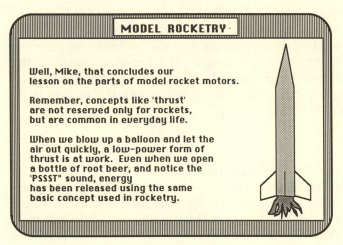

Figure 16.9
Enhancing retention and transfer.

2. *Describe lesson expectations and purposes.* The next lesson frame describes the purposes of the lesson in terms that are readily understood by the student. This is important in preparing the student and in encouraging cognitive activity to support the lesson. It also allows the student to set performance goals and gauge progress during the lesson.

3. *Recall prerequisites.* Next, prerequisite information for the current lesson is described, along with advice if the background information is deficient. This provides a means whereby students can prepare mentally for the lesson by remembering prerequisite information, while alerting the student to alternatives if prerequisite skills are not known. In some cases, the lesson might include a brief pretest at this point and might review, begin, or skip the lesson, depending on pretest performance.

4. *Present new information, provide guidance, elicit response, provide feedback.* The next four frames provide opportunities for the student to strengthen and deepen learning. Whereas previous steps oriented the student to the forthcoming lesson, these steps aid in encoding, comprehending, integrating, and recalling information presented during the lesson. Notice that the learner-guidance function coaches the student to perform in much the same way that an effective tutor might. The practice and feedback provide an opportunity for strengthening learning by confirming correctness and by remediating where it is needed.

5. *Assess performance.* The final frames require that students provide the composite response targeted for learning in the lesson. The assessment phase is usually applied to verify that the criterion skills have been learned. In well-designed, organized, and written lessons, students should be capable of performing the specified skill, since earlier correction and support have been provided throughout the guidance, responding, and feedback cycle of the lesson.

6. *Enhance retention and transfer.* The final frame aids the student in generalizing lesson information and illustrating other applications of the skills. This step is a valuable aid to effective integration of lesson information and is likely to improve student retention of the lesson concepts.

While the template offered by the events of instruction is more or less sequentially arranged, many of the steps are interchangeable. Gagné and associates recognize that it will often be necessary and more appropriate to alter the order in which the events are organized within a lesson. It is also probable that all events will not necessarily be appropriate for all tutorials. It is important, however, that all be considered. If a decision to eliminate given steps is made, make certain that the decision is based upon a better choice and is not simply an oversight in the design and organization of the lesson.

DRILL AND PRACTICE

Drills should provide information to orient the student to the task, to inform the students of performance expectations, and to provide the students with sufficient motivation to perform as well as possible. In addition, there are several aspects of drill and practice that require unique emphasis (Caldwell, 1980; Salisbury, Richards, and Klein 1985). The primary function of CAI drills is to provide as much practice on well-defined skills as possible within a concentrated period. In this section, several techniques for organizing drill and practice will be described, and examples will be presented to illustrate the features of effective drills.

Similar to the structure of tutorials, simple drills can be designed using patterned steps or templates. Drill and practice templates typically orient the student, present questions or items focusing on a well-defined skill or concept, provide a procedure for eliciting student responses, provide feedback regarding the correctness or incorrectness of student response, and offer record-keeping capability.

Figures 16.10 through 16.12 illustrate the application of effective drill features in the teaching of model rocketry concepts. Notice that the first phase of the lesson provides an attention-getting frame, a description of the lesson expectations, a statement concerning the skills needed to complete the drill, and directions for participation in the drill. This information helps to set the stage for student participation by clarifying the nature of the task and the requirements for participation.

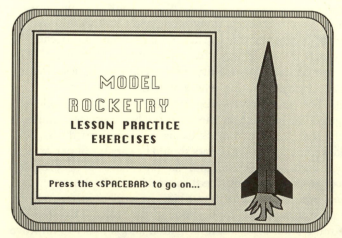

Figure 16.10
Orienting the student during a drill.

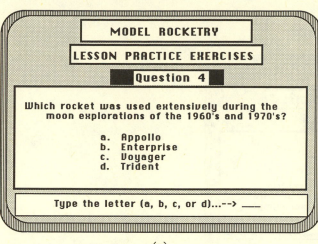

(a)

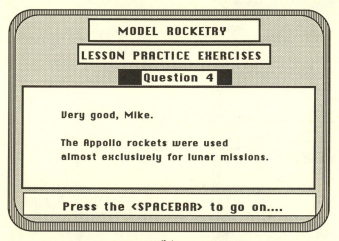

(b)

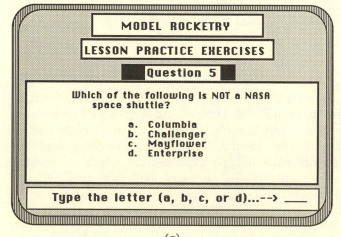

(c)

Figure 16.11
Eliciting student responses and providing feedback.

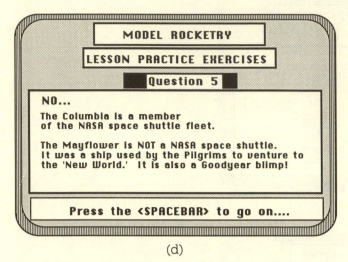

(d)

Figure 16.11 (*Continued*)

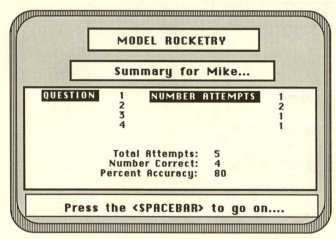

Figure 16.12
Reporting results to student.

1. *Orientation.* The orientation features of drills are similar to those of tutorials, but the purpose is fundamentally different. Tutorials use orientation techniques to prepare students for new information; in drills, the purpose is to orient the student to the application of information that has already been taught. Students should not be immersed in drill activity without a perspective from which to establish performance goals, evaluate whether the necessary skills are available, and understand the basic intent of the drill. The orientation portion of the drill serves this purpose well.

2. *Elicit response and provide feedback.* Once the orientation has been completed, the actual response–feedback cycle usually occurs. The emphasis during this phase is to encourage frequent student response and to provide either response confirmation or corrective feedback for incorrect responses. Notice how the practice items, the directions for responding, and the response requirements are brief and to the point. The practice is not complicated by unnecessary reading or response

requirements that reduce the amount of time for practice and feedback. Instead, brief and focused drills permit more practice than is possible under more elaborate presentation and response formats.

It may not always be possible or desirable, however, to use either very brief participation formats or to focus on very specific drill applications. Some drills will require the application of several skills, such as the those emphasizing correct discrimination and computation in mixed-number mathematics. In such cases, it seems essential that each skill included in the practice be taught and reinforced prior to combining skills in a drill and practice format. Or perhaps the presentation and response formats are necessarily more complex, such as the procedures involved in the computation of cost-of-living indexes. In general, however, drills will be most useful when the formats are as simple as possible, providing more time to practice and receive feedback.

3. *Record keeping and reporting.* The final component of effective drills is management and reporting. These features are illustrated in several ways. First, students may be given a running tally of their performance during a lesson as a sort of ongoing gauge of performance. Next, student performance is summarized upon completion of the lesson, with information that can be used to make further decisions. The lesson also provides a diagnostic feature that helps to isolate the specific sources of error. Finally, the option is available to record student performance to disc and to print a hard copy of the performance summary. The number of ways that the drill could be used to improve instruction for the student, to simplify the record-keeping chores of the teacher, and to otherwise affect the usefulness of the drill should be an important consideration in the design of drill and practice.

INSTRUCTIONAL GAMES

Games tend to vary widely in organization, procedures, and content. However, like tutorials and drills, games can still be characterized as having fairly consistent lesson components. The manner in which the components are put into practice varies tremendously from game to game, but the basic components remain.

In many ways, games are more closely akin to drill and practice than other CAI designs. Usually they are designed to provide a highly motivating context for the practice of already taught skills. As for drills, good instructional games provide extensive practice and feedback for responses in well-defined skill areas. Most games utilize a competitive format, pitting the student against the computer, a different student, or personal performance.

The basic components of instructional games include orientation information, directions for participation, the rules of the game, a game environment or scenario, and some form of conclusion or climax. There are also additional components commonly found in instructional games, such as the element of chance, options for assistance or clarification, and the use of ambiguity designed to heighten student interest and involvement in the game. Examine some examples of game components, and consider the different ways instructional games encourage the development of skills and concepts through the use of motivational lesson formats.

1. *Present orientation information.* As shown in Figures 16.13(a) and 16.13(b), the orientation is similar in nature and function to the information provided during drills. This information is particularly relevant in game formats, since the instructional nature and value of the game often must be reinforced. In many

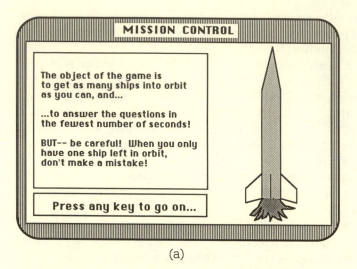

(a)

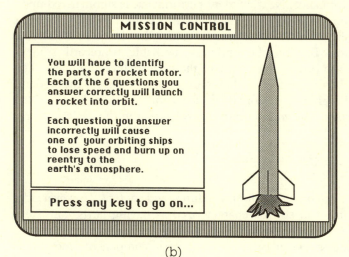

(b)

Figure 16.13
Orienting information for a CAI game.

games, especially those utilizing arcadelike graphics, animation, and sound, the bombardment of stimuli can detract from the instructional value of the game. Effective orientation information clarifies the basic purposes of the game, prescribes the expectations, and informs learners of the skills that are needed to proceed through the lesson.

2. *Present directions for participation.* Directions are a critical feature of instructional games. Some games, as shown in Figure 16.14, become interactive and dynamic during their execution, making ongoing directions virtually impossible. In such cases, directions must often be front-loaded, requiring the student to remember all directions throughout the duration of the game. For fairly simple games, this does not present an unusual hardship. For games that are more complex, however, the heavy concentration of directions at the beginning of the activities can be troublesome.

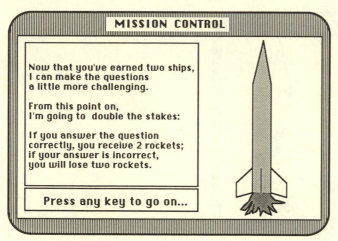

Figure 16.14
Directions embedded during an instructional game.

Other game formats provide directions throughout the lesson, allowing the learner to work with relatively small amounts of information at each point, and minimizing the requirement for remembering complex sets of rules. The sample directions provided in Figure 16.14 exemplify a distributed directions approach, where the directions necessary to proceed are provided only where they are needed in the lesson. This approach is often useful, in that the student need not spend excessive time learning the procedures involved in playing the game. Instead, a minimum amount of time is consumed in learning the procedures, and a maximum amount of time is spent producing responses that control game operation.

3. *Present game rules.* The game rules, shown in Figure 16.15, specify how the game will be won or lost. At this stage, the relationship between skill development and game consequences should be made explicit. If additional points are earned for speed, or if penalties are assessed for errors, such rules should be presented. It is often advisable to include a practice session to familiarize students with game rules

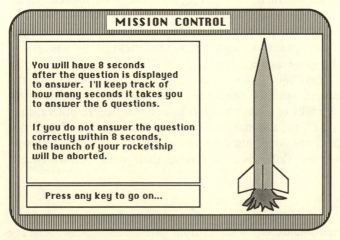

Figure 16.15
Presenting CAI game rules.

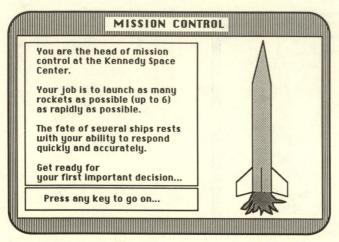

Figure 16.16
An initial game scenario.

and procedures before actually starting a lesson. In many cases, this portion hooks the student into the game by presenting the practice in an entertaining manner. If the rules are unclear, or if the game is simply unappealing to students, problems will surface at this point.

4. *Introduce game scenario.* Figure 16.16 presents the basic set of assumptions pertaining to the game. In addition, the characters or players in the game are usually introduced, the game status assumes an initial jumping off point, and the student is invited to participate. Knowledge of each of the preceding steps is essential if students are to participate in a meaningful way. In many cases, designers will allow the initial scenario to be easily modified by student input to enlist the cooperation of students and to demonstrate the game procedures and features.

5. *Elicit response and alter game scenario.* Throughout the game, students enter information and continuously evaluate the evolving game scenario. In some cases, the game might include a status feature to inform the student of who is winning or losing or otherwise to provide an incentive to perform. The scenario then changes in direct response to the correctness or incorrectness of student performance, and the rules for winning the game are enforced.

6. *Provide summary.* Upon completion of the game, in accordance with the adopted rules and procedures, students should receive a summary. In some cases, this might be as simple as a tally of correct and incorrect responses. In others, such as that shown in Figure 16.17, the summary might include diagnostic and prescriptive information regarding the skills used in the game and perhaps information on how to improve these skills (and, of course, their game performance!).

SIMULATIONS

Simulations pose unique problems. Often simulations have no absolutely correct or incorrect answers. Instead, the function may be to simulate the consequences or outcomes of student responses. Such lessons do not attempt to teach directly, but to demonstrate effects to students. The consequences of a particular action might

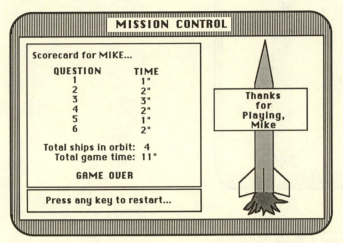

Figure 16.17
Summarizing student performance during a CAI game.

be simulated for the student, but the criterion knowledge required to make necessary judgments will usually be taught prior to the simulation.

The flow, procedures, and rules of simulations also vary considerably from lesson to lesson. In some simulations, the student must plan a series of strategies affecting several variables involved in the simulation, decide upon action for all factors, and proceed with the simulation to examine the collective effects of several concurrent decisions. In others, a single student decision is examined for effect on the conditions of the simulation. This type of simulation is more dynamic, providing sensitivity to each individual decision made by the student and representing the effects of each decision by immediately modifying the scenario.

The organizing and writing possibilities afforded by the various simulations do not lend themselves well to the kind of procedural guidance provided for the design of tutorials. Yet there are some features that typify the kinds of components found in effective simulations. Let's examine these features by looking at the sample CAI simulation shown in Figures 16.18 through 16.21.

Figure 16.18
Orienting information for a CAI simulation.

MISSION CONTROL

Oftentimes, rocketeers like to loft special payloads for experimental or other purposes.

One example of a 'fun' payload is the Astrocam. This is a small camera that can take pictures while in flight.

Press any key to go on...

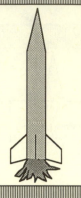

(a)

MISSION CONTROL

The camera takes a picture when the ejection charge is activated.

This is important to remember.

Mike, it is very important that you have completed the tutorial on model rocketmotors before you go any further.

Press any key to go on...

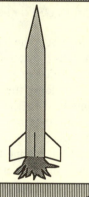

(b)

MISSION CONTROL

After you make the selection, the rocket will be launched and the picture 'taken' by the computer.

You will then see the resulting Astrocam picture.

Finally, you will be asked to write on your worksheet which motor you chose, which flight problem you chose...

Press any key to go on...

(c)

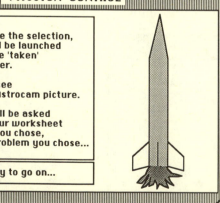

Figure 16.19
Simulation rules, directions, and guidelines for participation.

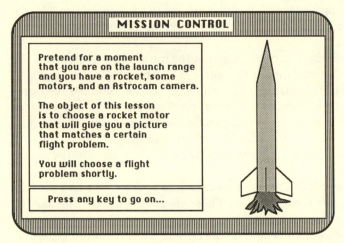

Figure 16.20
The initial scenario of a CAI simulation.

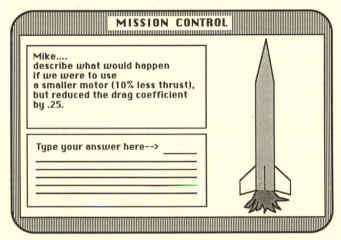

Figure 16.21
A complex, dialogue-based CAI simulation.

1. *Present orientation information.* The need for meaningful orientation information is as critical for simulations as for any other CAI design. The first few frames of the sample simulation are very comparable to the orientation information of a tutorial, drill, or instructional game. The frames prepare the participant for the simulation that follows. The purpose is described, the skills to be applied are often identified, and other information designed to prepare the participant is presented.

2. *Present rules, directions, and guidelines for participation.* Next, the rules governing the simulation, as well as guidelines for student participation, are provided. Since simulations can become extraordinarily complex in the ways information is judged and evaluated, it can be difficult or impossible to fully describe the contingencies of lesson execution in depth. However, the general process of execution can often be summarized effectively.

As a rule, it should be possible to describe the procedures for student participation clearly. Again, the primary function of any CAI lesson is to improve the development and application of skills, concepts, and information. If the simulation directions for participation are unclear, then the instructional effects are likely to diminish.

3. *Introduce initial scenario.* The presentation of the initial scenario provides the circumstances defining the simulation at the outset. The emphasis at this point is to offer the student sufficient information upon which to base an informed response. In some cases, the scenario is intentionally vague, requiring the student to consider alternative responses. The scenario should parallel, to the maximum extent possible, the conditions observed in real life. The function of the initial scenario is to elicit the kind of response that can subsequently be used to modify the conditions of the scenario.

4. *Elicit student responses.* The student response, used to determine how or if the scenario will be modified, is then provided. There are several options for eliciting student responses. Some require a great deal of programming knowledge and can be enormously complex to design. The response options available at this stage may be classified as either open-ended or structured. Each poses unique concerns for writing and organizing simulations.

A format typical in many of the more sophisticated simulations requires the student to type a description of the course of action to be taken. Such formats require extensive response judging and interpretation capabilities, but they permit relatively open-ended student responses. This format is illustrated in Figure 16.21. The student input may be evaluated according to a series of standards, including proper nouns, verbs, and sentence objects. Based upon student input, the lesson will request more information or will modify the simulation based upon its internal logic. Obviously, this format can become extremely complicated and is well beyond the capabilities of all but the most proficient designers and programmers.

The structured option simulation, shown in Figures 16.22(a) through 16.22(c), permits greater control of student response by requiring the selection of a given choice. The student may input information into each option, or the selection of the option itself might constitute the student response. In either case, the range of

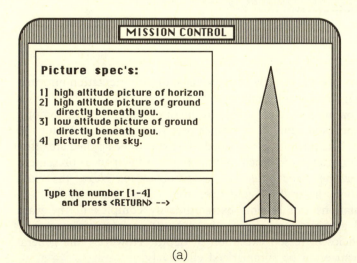

(a)

Figure 16.22
Structured CAI simulation formats.

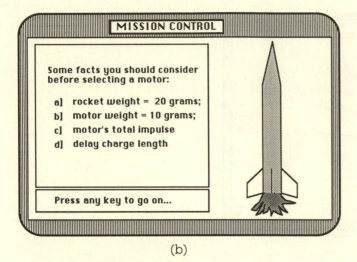

(b)

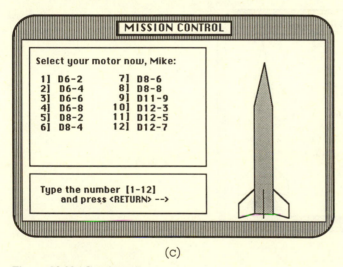

(c)

Figure 16.22 (*Continued*)

response options is prescribed, and not interpreted by analyzing open-ended student responses.

The internal logic of such simulations can still be complex, but it is usually much more straightforward than the open-ended response format. Structured-option formats require that each option be described clearly to the student and that the direction options be prescribed fairly completely within the lesson. This type of simulation is most commonly available for microcomputers.

5. *Present modified scenario.* The modified scenario, an altered version of the initial scenario, is the next major phase of the simulation. The revised scenario generally provides a description or status report for each of the relevant variables of the lesson. In addition, some lessons provide an explicit description of the relationship between the decisions made by the student and the simulation variables. The modified scenario in Figures 16.23(a) and 16.23(b) provides a description of the revised status of the scenario, as well as a description of the overall progress toward a solution.

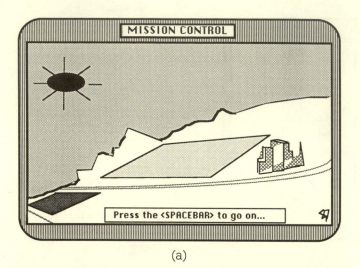

(a)

(b)

Figure 16.23
A modified scenario in a CAI simulation.

6. *Present summary*. Finally, the concluding section should be a part of any simulation. In this section, the final disposition of the scenario should be provided; a description of the final consequences of the student decisions given; and, in some cases, an evaluation of the performance of the student included. In the sample simulation, the student is given overall feedback as to the efficiency of student decisions, with associated consequences, in order to exemplify the importance of the performance in real life. Many simulations are not as evaluative as the sample lesson, but students should be briefed as to their performance, with the consequences of responses simulated as accurately as possible.

OTHER CONSIDERATIONS

Clarity In all cases, lessons must be easily interpreted. Designers control the display and presentation variables of a lesson, but not the unpredictable abilities of learners. Further, a designer cannot control the conceptual difficulty of information to be acquired. Instruction can be organized to facilitate higher-order learning but not to eliminate or reduce the conceptual requirements of required learning. We like to believe that all instructional information can be learned if it is presented clearly. Yet this is often simply not the case. Problems of one type or another will surface despite superhuman efforts to eliminate them. We have but one choice in addressing this problem. If difficulties are encountered during a lesson, they must not be due to the directions, the design, or the lesson control procedures, that is, those variables under designer control. If difficulties are encountered, it must not be the result of insufficient clarity, but the result of learner limitations or the conceptual difficulty of the content itself—variables beyond the control of the designer.

Recasting Versus Reviewing Instruction   The designer must determine how or if to remediate incorrect responses. One choice would simply reroute the student through the same instruction, to study the information more carefully. The lesson might prompt the learner to attend more carefully or might even provide a strategy for viewing the lesson the second time. This decision presumes that students did not attend to the instruction carefully during the initial exposure and that focusing student attention more carefully to the same instruction will improve performance.

In many cases, this is true. Simply repeating a lesson segment will often encourage learners to direct more and better attention to the instruction at hand. In other cases, however, deficient responses are not due to inattentiveness. The incorrect responses reflect a basic lack of comprehension. In such cases, is it wise to reroute the student through the same instruction that has already proven ineffective?

There are other alternatives. If a student did not understand the original explanation of the concept of angle of incidence, it would probably be wise to find a different way to explain the concept a second time. It may be useful to recast the instruction, that is, to present the information in a different way. This provides an alternative description, explanation, or example that can be evaluated in conjunction with the original presentation.

The problem with recasting is that it can be very costly to include such a rarely used feature. Designers attempt to structure lessons to maximize the probability of correct initial learning. If most students learn effectively during initial presentation, is it worthwhile to recast virtually an entire lesson in order to aid the few who might miss some information? Many think it is not. The decision to recast instruction in a lesson must be made with full recognition of the associated costs.

Instructions   Instructions provide the means through which CAI lessons will, or will not, be understood and completed as planned. The best of lesson designs will be useless if the student is unaware of how to proceed. The most sophisticated student support options will be disabled if students are unclear on how and when the options may be used. Instructions direct the student in the ways the lesson information is to be encountered, used, and processed. If the instructions and directions are clear and easily followed, then we should expect that a well-designed lesson will perform favorably. If not clearly written, however, no design exists that can assure effective learning.

Options   The inclusion of different lesson options has become increasingly popular. In some cases, the options are available for student use. Options to obtain help, review a lesson, skip sections of a lesson, and other comparable choices are now fairly common in many CAI lessons. Options for customizing lessons have also gained in popularity. Hidden menus, for example, are sometimes used to allow teachers to access certain lesson features. Teachers are permitted to specify features such as the difficulty, the number of examples or practice items to be presented, the use or disabling of sound in the lesson, and storing to disc or printing of student scores. The popularity of embedded lesson options for both teachers and students appears to be growing and may become a basic expectation of CAI lessons.

Embedded Strategies   There are several techniques available to aid students in remembering lesson information. Advance organizers, mnemonic techniques, and imagery strategies can all be incorporated into CAI lessons to help students to organize, process, and integrate new information. Depending on the memory strategy selected, the techniques may be embedded at the beginning of a lesson to prepare the learner for subsequent instruction, during instruction to organize information as it is presented, or after the instruction to aid in overall comprehension.

Chapter Summary

Recently a particularly enterprising teacher undertook a small but noteworthy experiment. The teacher located an important but poorly organized section of a social studies text. This section was copied and distributed to half of a class of high school students, who read the information. A second version of the section was developed in which the vocabulary was simplified, the readability lowered, and the organization of the lesson altered to improve the flow and sequence. This version was distributed to the remaining students in the class. Upon completing the reading assignment, the students were given a test to assess factual accuracy and inferences derived from the passage.

The findings, though not surprising, accentuate the importance of effective lesson organization and clarity. Students who read the original version varied widely in their recall. Students in the modified version, on the other hand, were consistently high in their recall. In addition, the quality of inference was poor for the original text, while the revised text yielded more accurate and consistent inferences.

The point of the study was to demonstrate the inefficiency of learning from poorly written text and how even simple modifications improve the comprehensibility of lesson information. In CAI, this could not be more relevant. The student is completely dependent on the lesson organization and writing skills of the designer. If the lesson is poorly organized and written, we should expect poor results. Well-organized and written lessons, on the other hand, can simplify the task of learning to a remarkable degree.

The terms *organizing* and *writing* connote far more than the simple production of words. For CAI purposes, writing involves a greater requirement for clarity and precision than virtually any other teaching system. The written word, or displayed word in most cases, must orient, inform, guide, support, and enrich the learner in ways rarely required in most conventional instruction. This poses a challenge, but not an insurmountable problem, for designers of CAI lessons.

References

ALESSANDRINI, K. (1983). Instructional design for CAI tutorials. *Collegiate Microcomputing*, **1**, 207–214.

CALDWELL, R. M. (1980). Guidelines for developing basic skills instructional materials for use with microcomputer technology. *Educational Technology*, **20**(10), 7–12.

GAGNÉ, R. M., W. W. WAGER, and A. ROJAS (1981). Planning and authoring computer-assisted instruction lessons. *Educational Technology*, **21**, 17–26.

SALISBURY, D., B. RICHARDS, and J. KLEIN (1985). Prescriptions for the design of practice activities for learning: An integration from instructional design theories. *Journal of Instructional Development*, **8**(4), 9–19.

Related Reading

ALESSI, S. M., and S. R. TROLLIP (1984). *Computer-Based Instruction: Methods and Development*. Englewood Cliffs, NJ: Prentice-Hall.

BROWN, G. D. (1985). The author as writer: Word processing your CBT. *Data Training*, **4**(4), 24–25.

DIMAS, C. (1978). A strategy for developing CAI. *Educational Technology*, **18**(4), 26–29.

EISELE, J. E. (1978). Lesson design for computer-based instructional systems. *Educational Technology*, **18**(9), 14–21.

FOX, J., and N. RUSHBY (1979). Guidelines for developing educational computer programs. *Computers and Education*, **3**, 35–41.

HANNAFIN, M. J. (1984). Guidelines for determining locus of instructional control in the design of computer-assisted instruction. *Journal of Instructional Development*, **7**(3), 6–10.

HARTMAN, J. (1981). A systematic approach to the design of computer-assisted instruction materials. *Technological Horizons in Education*, **8**(2), 43–45.

HOLMES, G. (1983). Creating CAI courseware: Some possibilities. *System*, **11**(1), 21–32.

HORD, E. (January 1984). Guidelines for designing computer-assisted instruction. *Instructional Innovator*, **29**(1), 19–23.

KEARSLEY, G. (1984). Instructional design and authoring software. *Journal of Instructional Development*, **7**(3), 11–16.

——— (1985). Microcomputer software: Design and development principles. *Journal of Educational Computing Research*, **1**, 209–220.

SPITLER, C. D., and V. E. CORGAN (1979). Rules for authoring computer-assisted instruction programs. *Educational Technology*. **19**(11), 13–20.

Chapter Review Exercises

COMPREHENSION

1. Describe the differences in designing, writing, and programming CAI lessons. (See page 249.)

2. Describe the features of effective tutorial designs. (See pages 251–256.)

3. Describe the features of effective drill and practice designs. (See pages 256–259.)

4. Describe the features of effective instructional game designs. (See pages 259–262.)

5. Describe the features of effective instructional simulation designs. (See pages 262–268.)
6. List and describe the features of CAI writing that differentiate it from other forms of writing. (See pages 250–251.)
7. Describe the circumstances affecting the decision to recast or repeat instruction during a lesson. (See page 269.)
8. Describe the writing style considerations effective across CAI lesson designs. (See pages 251–270.)

APPLICATION

1. Develop a well-designed CAI tutorial for a selected instructional need. (See Figures 16.1–16.9.)
2. Develop a well-designed CAI drill for a selected instructional need. (See Figures 16.10–16.12.)
3. Develop a well-designed CAI simulation for a selected instructional need. (See Figures 16.18–16.23.)
4. Develop a well-designed CAI game for a selected instructional need. (See Figures 16.13(a)–16.17.)
5. Write CAI text incorporating the elements of effective communication.
6. Develop a CAI lesson that includes appropriate user options and support.

CHAPTER 17

Managing Instructional Decisions: Computer-Managed Instruction

The computer has an extraordinary facility for managing information. In data-processing applications, for example, the computer can instantaneously manipulate, with unerring accuracy, millions of bits of information. Data can be sorted, lists compiled, calculations performed, and new data generated based upon existing information, as well as a virtually unlimited range of other useful functions.

For instructional purposes, computer capabilities can be applied to collect and manage information ranging from a single student response to the collective responses of an entire educational system across all curriculum areas. Decisions can be made (or recommended) for a particular student's subsequent instruction or for the instructional activities of an entire school system. Student lesson summaries can be printed, historical performance data for individuals or whole grades can be recalled, and even the frequency with which a particular incorrect answer was given by all students with last names beginning with *H* can be recalled if desired. Essentially, the computer offers the capability to collect and manage virtually all kinds of information that might have some bearing on instructional decisions. The task of CAI designers is to determine how to best use the management capabilities of the computer to improve the kinds of instructional decisions that can be made.

The purposes of this chapter are to examine the types of CMI applications commonly used in educational settings and to demonstate applications of CMI concepts specifically to CAI lessons.

OBJECTIVES

Comprehension

After completing this chapter you will be able to

1. Describe the differences between micro-and macro-level CMI.
2. Describe exmples where micro- and macro-level CMI are appropriate.
3. Describe the differences between direct and indirect CMI.

273

4. Describe examples where direct and indirect CMI are appropriate.
5. List and describe the data sources commonly obtained or used for CMI purposes.
6. Describe how each data source can be applied to make CMI decisions.

Application

After completing this chapter you will be able to

1. Design CAI lessons that collect and use appropriate data sources.
2. Design CAI lessons with micro-direct CMI applications.
3. Design CAI lessons with micro-indirect CMI applications.
4. Design CAI lessons with macro-direct CMI applications.
5. Design CAI lessons with macro-indirect CMI applications.

Computer-Managed Instruction (CMI)

Broadly defined, computer-managed instruction (CMI) may be thought of as any application of the information collection, analysis, or decision-making capabilities of the computer that either aids, or actually enforces, an instructional decision (cf. Baker, 1978; Leiblum, 1982). This definition includes an enormous range of possible CMI applications, some of which have already been suggested. CMI occurs on a continuum ranging from individual responses (micro-level management), through manipulations of collections of related responses (macro-level management). Based in part on the level of management required, designers may identify either individual responses or composite responses averaged across entire classes.

CMI can also affect instructional decisions directly, such as branching to particular lesson segments for given responses, or indirectly, such as the collection of performance information for subsequent use by decision makers. Direct decisions might be made based upon either individual responses or composite averages, but the management tasks of the computer may be confined to the collection of information for decisions not controlled by the computer. In effect, the level and type of management designated for the computer can be characterized by the information base used for management decisions (macro versus micro) and the control function of the computer in enforcing the management decision (direct versus indirect).

DATABASES AND DATA POINTS

to determine what information can be useful for CMI purposes and what is information is worth collecting, it is first necessary to understand the nature of electronic files. Whereas paper filing systems permit as much unnecessary information and untidiness as individuals are willing to tolerate, it is necessary to organize information more logically and systematically for CMI purposes.

A database is a collection of ordered pieces of information that are defined, created, updated, and managed for defined applications. Databases are used to do everything from determining the tax liabilities of individuals to establishing the percentile scores of students on standardized tests.

The contents and structures of databases are defined to include all data required for decision making. The number of variables included in a database is determined based on the nature of the decisions to be made or the related functions to be served. In some cases, a database might include only basic information, such as student name and gender. In such a case, the potential for application of the database would be limited to combinations of name and gender information.

In other cases, the database might be much more comprehensive, including everything from date of birth to favorite color and a vast array of student performance information. The potential for application of this database would be far greater, including all combinations of names, ages, color preferences, specific test scores, averages across given tests, and almost any other combinations imaginable. The potential of the database is determined by the number and nature of relevant variables to be included.

Each individual entry in a database is called a *data point* or *data item*. The date of birth of a particular student, the score obtained on the pretest for Unit 3 in algebra, or any other single entry constitutes a data point. Data points are the smallest unit of measurement available in a database but are typically used in varied combinations to produce required information. For example, although each student has only one data point for gender, it is possible to determine the total number of males and females simply by scanning across all the cases in the database to tally the *F*s and *M*s. Students can also be sorted according to gender in order to print test scores or in response to multiple criteria. Data points can be used by themselves, can be sorted according to specifications, or can be processed mathematically. However, they can only be used if the data exist and the necessary information is accessible in the database.

To be of use, the data included in a database must be structured consistently. The consistency allows us to enter and update the database and to manipulate the information as required. For example, suppose we wanted to add three new students to a database established for a ninth-grade class. The database includes the student name, address, home telephone number, and scores on a series of CAI math and language arts lessons. How would we determine where to enter the information for new students? Can we simply enter the information and hope that the computer will know how to treat it? Not usually. Instead, databases are created with defined, ordered structure that is used to enter and retrieve information contained in the database.

Consider the design of a database to maintain information on student test scores. The database, illustrated graphically in Table 17.1, contains the student's last name, identification number, and the scores obtained on each of five mathematics unit posttests. The database consists of a total of seven fields (name, ID number, and five test scores), which are assigned standard locations in the database. We have designated the first field for recording the name, the next for the student ID number, the third for the first test score, and so forth. Every time we decide to retrieve information from the database, we know that the data will be available in the defined field. If we want to print a list of all students, we know the information will be found in the first field. If we need to determine the average grade for test 1, we average the scores contained in the third field. If a list of all students with grades higher than 80 on test 2 *and* test 5 were required, the information could be easily sorted and retrieved by identifying the appropriate fields and the sorting mechanisms. The structure of the database permits the subsequent access and use of any or all information contained in the database.

Table 17.1
The Structure of a Simple CMI Database

Field 1	Field 2	Field 3	Field 4	Field 5	Field 6	Field 7
Last Name	*ID No.*	*Unit 1*	*Unit 2*	*Unit 3*	*Unit 4*	*Unit 5*
Jones	12345	21	18	25	27	15
Bixby	13579	21	24	22	21	21
Ziegler	24680	23	25	21	23	24
etc.	etc.	etc.	etc.	etc.	etc.	etc.
etc.	etc.	etc.	etc.	etc.	etc.	etc.
etc.	etc.	etc.	etc.	etc.	etc.	etc.

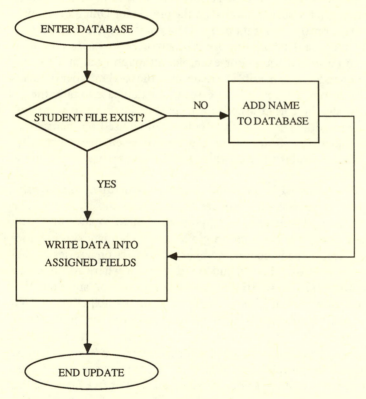

Figure 17.1
Flowchart illustrating how databases can be updated.

The same structure allows updating of the database with additional test information or even with new students. Figure 17.1 illustrates a simplified process for adding a new student to the database created in the previous example. The first step is used to determine whether the student name and identification information exist in the database. If the information does not exist, the name is added and subsequently used with other information contained in the database.

Several alternative methods have also been devised for ensuring the stability of data structures. Some computers use *system delimiters* or *internal flags* as implicit designations for the start and end of individual datapoints. When delimiter conventions are used, the computer simply reads data within individual records until the number of delimiters or flags corresponding to the desired datapoint is located. The precise size of each field is unimportant to the computer, but the consistency of relative location is paramount. Other systems employ methods for flagging variables with unique identifiers, minimizing the need for absolute structure within individual records. The designer might identify each variable within the database with a unique flag, which is then used across individuals. Data can be written to the database, or retrieved from the database, by noting the flag or address of the data within each record. Allowing access to data by noting the position of information within each record is unimportant, but the consistency of the flag is paramount. Most of the databases available for friendly applications employ one of these types of implicit database structure.

The development of meaningful databases is essential for many CMI applications. Applications that include storing permanent records of student scores, incorporating past information into current lessons, and most other long-term CMI applications require the creation of structured databases. However, many CMI applications do not require the long-term storage of information, needing only information generated within the lesson. For such applications, it is unnecessary to create permanent databases.

READ-ONLY, WRITE-ONLY, AND READ–WRITE DATABASES

One additional consideration in the understanding of databases for CAI purposes is the function of the database. Essentially, databases serve the CAI designer's needs by providing necessary record keeping, by assisting in making instructional control decisions, or by providing both record keeping and the capacity to introduce information from the database into the lesson. CAI databases can be loosely described as read-only, write-only, or read–write databases.

Read-only databases are designed primarily to permit the lesson designer to use already generated data. During a lesson, data can be read from a database to verify student status as a legal user, to check on prior achievement, and otherwise to introduce previously obtained information into a current lesson. Read-only databases are also fairly common where personal data must be introduced into a lesson.

Write-only databases, on the other hand, serve as a type of record keeper of student data generated during a lesson. Often lessons are designed to store student scores on posttests or to analyze student comments during instruction. The intent is to retain important information, but not to reintroduce such information into subsequent lessons. Many of the computer-based testing programs used widely in colleges and universities employ write-only databases to protect performance data from unwanted tampering.

Perhaps the most sophisticated of CAI databases are those that permit both the writing of information to, as well as the reading of information from, student databases. Read–write databases provide the flexibility to serve as a recorder of necessary data and to introduce data from previous lessons to current lessons. For the most sophisticated of CAI designs, read–write databases are essential to permit the types of personalization, branching, and adaptivity often required.

Differentiating Levels of Management

CMI options can be as narrowly, or as broadly, defined as is required for a particular application. The designer of a brief tutorial on the parts of the heart will probably require a good number of individual management decisions affecting lesson execution, such as displaying of student performance summaries and other CMI applications of a relatively confined nature. CMI is required only to support the needs of a particular lesson. There are no comprehensive databases to consider, no long-term decisions that require lesson performance data, and basically no management needs beyond the lesson itself that require the collection and use of lesson performance information.

The same could not be said, however, for a comprehensive curriculum consisting of a series of lessons designed to teach surgical procedures to medical students. In this case, individual performance summaries might be maintained for each student across all lessons. Perhaps the relative performance ranking of each student across the lessons must be identified. The CMI needs for this example extend well beyond individual responses within a lesson. Data must be collected and analyzed, and a comprehensive student performance database must be established from which management decisions can be subsequently made.

MICRO- VERSUS MACRO-LEVEL CMI

The foregoing examples illustrate the differences in CMI requirements dictated by the instructional problem or problems at hand. Relatively simple CMI techniques are required if only micro-level management decisions are needed. However, the level of CMI required often includes both the individual lesson micro-level decisions and requirements for collecting, analyzing, and managing information for macro-level decisions.

DIRECT VERSUS INDIRECT CMI APPLICATIONS

One other useful differentiation is based upon the methods used for making management decisions. Most CAI lessons feature at least direct applications of CMI. This occurs at the point where input is evaluated to determine which instructional decision is to be made. Was the response correct? If so, what decision is appropriate? If incorrect, what instructional consequence will follow? The management application is direct, in that individual responses or, in some cases, collections of related responses, have a direct consequence.

This is perhaps the easiest application to understand and the most common for the stand-alone, nonintegrated CAI lessons often developed for microcomputer use. Rarely do such lessons attempt to expand the base of information beyond that which is required for immediate lesson execution. This may be due to the fact that few truly comprehensive, integrated courseware options exist for microcomputer use. Most isolate lessons on one skill or another. Even where the lesson availability is more comprehensive, designers still have tended to focus on only the information required to execute a given lesson.

In many instances, this is understandable. Microcomputers are somewhat limited in their capacity to manipulate concurrently large amounts of performance information in temporary memory while also executing CAI lessons. The integration of external information into a lesson requires referral to external memory storage devices such as floppy discs to store or access necessary information. This process is often quite slow, resulting in lessons that execute unevenly and with noticeable delays. This is generally undesirable and may discourage designers from attempting to use some of the sophisticated indirect CMI procedures available.

While this concern is valid to a degree, there are several CMI techniques that allow the development of databases that permit longer term, indirect instructional decisions to be made. Most involve the front loading from, or the rear loading of information to, external storage. These procedures minimize the problems associated with frequent exchanges between the current lesson and external storage devices by introducing the necessary data prior to the beginning of a lesson or by storing newly obtained information pertinent to the database after lesson procedures have been completed.

SOME CMI APPLICATIONS

Consider the example of a microcomputer lesson designed to teach the identification of musical notes. The lesson integrates relevant information from a database and collects information for subsequent indirect management decisions. The sequence of activities is shown in the lesson flowchart, Figure 17.2. Initially, the computer identifies only information contained in the comprehensive database that is potentially useful in the present lesson. In this case, the relevant data include scores from the three preceding lessons, the number of years the student has taken music lessons, and the instrument with which the student is training.

Each of these pieces of information will be used only in combination with events occurring during the present lesson. Individually, they have no direct effect on the instructional management decisions of the lesson. In combination with the lesson information, however, they will have an indirect effect on the CMI decisions made during the lesson.

Consider the following example. Background information is retrieved prior to the start of the lesson. As the lesson proceeds, several decision points are encountered. At the first point, the student's average score for the past three lessons, paired with the test score on the first section of the lesson, are used to determine the amount of practice and number of examples to be provided. If the student has performed well in the past, and well during the first section, the examples and practice provided will be reduced. If the student has performed poorly in the past, and poorly on the first section, more practice and examples will be provided.

At the next decision point in the lesson, the computer evaluates prior music experience, along with current performance. Depending upon the combination, the performance requirements for that section of the lesson will be modified. Poor performance by a student with no prior experience might be expected, and more liberal standards would be applied. Stricter standards might be required of students with several years of prior experience.

Not all CMI decisions are based upon permanently stored data. In a fundamental sense, the reception and analysis of a single learner response could be considered a CMI application *if* the information is used subsequently to make a meaningful instructional decision. Consider an example of a lesson designed to teach safety

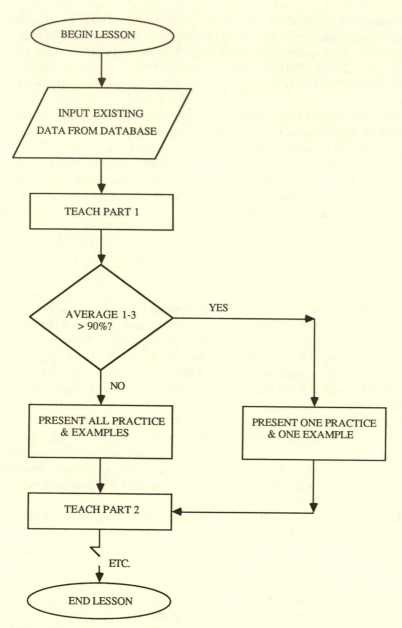

Figure 17.2
Retrieving from, and writing to, a CMI database.

procedures in a woodworking shop. During the lesson, the student must demonstrate, by selecting the correct response option, comprehension of several safety rules. If comprehension of each rule has not been demonstrated, the lesson automatically repeats the relevant segment; if a correct response is given, the lesson proceeds.

Consider now a slightly more complex CMI example. A lesson is designed to adapt the instructional sequence, where students must respond accurately to four successive questions in order to proceed. If the student answers two questions correctly, then misses one, then answers two correctly again, and so forth, the lesson will continue to generate questions until four successive correct responses are provided. This form of computer management requires more complex use of student response information. Response accuracy must be considered for both individual test items and for pools of consecutive responses. Before the lesson proceeds, the computer must be satisfied that the prescribed conditions have been met. While it is still a relatively straightforward CMI decision, the application illustrates a technique focusing on cumulative performance contingencies rather than on single-response contingencies.

Let's take this example a step further. Suppose it is necessary to manage instructional sequence decisions through cumulative response contingencies. In addition, it is necessary to monitor and record the total number of questions attempted, the amount of time taken to produce each response, and the number of times the student requested help during the lesson. There are several individual pieces of information that must be considered, some of which must be stored permanently in a student file. Some of the information, such as response accuracy, will be applied immediately to effect instructional decisions, and some will be collected for later use. Permanent records of each and every student response to a question are required. All information will be used to manage instructional activities and decisions, but the methods for use will vary according to the data source.

We could collect still more useful information to make instructional management decisions. Perhaps we designed the lesson to create, and then use, an integrated database. The database might include a good deal of performance information for each student. The information could be used to check performance in related lessons or to evaluate individual student performance versus both past individual performance and the average performance of the group. The database could be sufficiently comprehensive to permit decisions affecting individual students, groups of students, or entire school systems if desired. The information permits macro-level instructional management decisions, ranging from lesson effectiveness to the need for additional instruction for the overall group of students to virtually any relevant decision affecting instruction on a significant scale.

Clearly, CMI techniques can be applied to manage instructional decisions ranging from the individual branching needs of a given student to the overall effectiveness of a lesson. The principal task at hand, then, is to determine the levels and types of management considered appropriate; the types of information required to make the necessary management decisions; and the methods to collect, analyze, and evaluate the information to support effective instructional management decisions. The computer provides the capacity to simplify and expedite the management process, but only to the extent that appropriate planning decisions have been made.

Information Sources for CMI Applications

Virtually any information could be relevant for the establishment of a CMI database. Usually, though, certain kinds of data are more commonly collected for subsequent use.

INDIVIDUAL ITEM PERFORMANCE

The individual response is the basis for most CMI applications. Student responses may be collected, stored, and used at a later time to either remind the student of a previous response or to compare with subsequent responses. Individual answers may also be used at a macro level to determine the kinds of responses offered by students for given questions. For example, it may be useful to record incorrect responses in order to examine the contents, to evaluate the extent to which the errors are systematic across learners, and to make subsequent system-level changes.

CORRECT VERSUS INCORRECT RESPONSES

It may also be important to maintain a record of correct versus incorrect responses to individual test items. This information may be useful for printing individual student or group performance summaries. Further, the information may be incorporated subsequently to determine mastery of lesson content, the need for review of relevant instruction, or the feasibility of skipping certain sections of later lessons.

COLLECTIONS OF RELATED ITEMS

Often pieces of information are collected related to common concepts. Perhaps five test items are all keyed to a particular performance objective. Or perhaps a series of four objectives may relate to different aspects of simple addition. It may be advantageous to retain each data point in it's most fundamental form, since the data can be later organized for other decisions as well. On the other hand, it may not always be feasible or practical to collect every single data point. It may be useful in such cases to simply maintain a record of the composite information as a single data point.

RESPONSE LATENCY

A variable used often in research, but surprisingly infrequently in application, is the time required to produce responses to individual items, groups of items, or entire tests. In some cases, this information can be used later to make indirect CMI decisions. For example, if response latency increases during a lesson, it may be an indication of fatigue, or perhaps confusion. In such cases, the lesson may query the student about his or her fatigue level and provide options based upon the student's response.

NUMBER OF ATTEMPTS FOR TEST ITEMS

Information on the number of attempts for test items provides an additional measure of lesson effectiveness and efficiency. Students who respond correctly on the first attempt may be considered more successful in acquiring lesson information than those requiring repeated attempts. As with most data sources, information can be applied for either direct or indirect decisions, as well as for micro- or macro-level decisions. For instance, such information can be used to provide correct responses if they are not supplied during either of the first two trials. In addition, the average number of attempts across learners can be applied to gauge lesson clarity.

LEARNER ATTITUDE

It is almost always worth obtaining information concerning attitudes toward the lesson and the use of the computer to teach. Students who are apprehensive, for example, might be provided more lesson orientation information to make the lesson less threatening. On a larger scale, pervasive negative attitudes toward the computer or a particular lesson may be a signal to reconsider how, or if, the computer should be subsequently used.

MAIL BOX

An interesting feature of sophisticated CAI/CMI systems is the inclusion of a mailbox, where users can make comments regarding the lesson, indicate difficulties with lesson content, or ask questions not addressed effectively in the lesson. In most cases, the mail is analyzed by a system operator. In some cases, a reply is provided directly to the original user, usually by inserting a flag the next time the student enters the system. In other cases, however, the comments or questions alert the system operator to important shortcomings, and the reply becomes available to all users, thereby permitting a broader breadth of impact.

IDENTIFICATION INFORMATION

Identification information is required for most off-line CMI databases designed to affect individually based management decisions. This information typically consists of data such as name and student identification number. The information is used to tie the relevant data sources, unique to individual students, to the conditions specified for management decisions. For example, if a particular student has performed poorly in a given lesson, and subsequent management decisions are to be made based upon this performance, then the information must be retrievable on an individual basis. Background data such as the student's name or identification number provide the capacity to effect individual CMI decisions based upon accrued, externally stored data.

A Micro-Direct CMI Application

This is probably the most common CMI application used for microcomputer-based CAI lessons. The information obtained affects management decisions directly, but the applicability is restricted to the current lesson. Information may be saved to some external storage device for record-keeping purposes, but it is not integrated for subsequent management decisions.

The data and procedural requirements, therefore, tend to be relatively modest. Usually individual background information is paired with student responses to test items, or collections of items to lesson objectives. The management decisions are

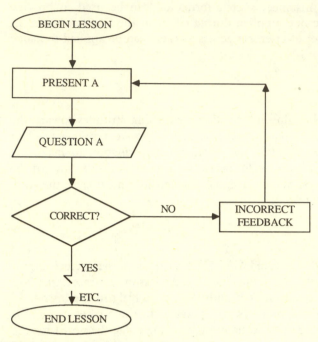

Figure 17.3
Micro-direct CMI procedures.

also straightforward, since they are based entirely on information derived during the lesson. This CMI paradigm, illustrated in Figure 17.3, is quite adequate for many lesson applications.

AN EXAMPLE

A simple micro-direct CMI application is shown in Figure 17.4. The student answers the lesson question. The computer checks the answer and, if it is correct, proceeds to the next question. In the example, however, the answer is incorrect, since the student typed *Jefferson*. Therefore, a different management decision is made. Incorrect responses result in repetition of the initial instruction.

This simple example illustrates computer-based instructional management. If no instructional management were required, all learners would receive instruction in exactly the same manner. In nonlinear lessons, where some form of conditional branching is to occur, a management decision must be made to determine which of the available options is most appropriate. The computer manages the instructional decision in a direct and immediate way.

A Micro-Indirect CMI Application

Often relatively small management decisions are effected through the integration of indirect data sources. The indirect data are usually accumulated and saved external to the lesson itself, although it is possible to collect such information during a lesson as well. The information is retrieved into the lesson and used to prescribe conditions under which direct management decisions will be made.

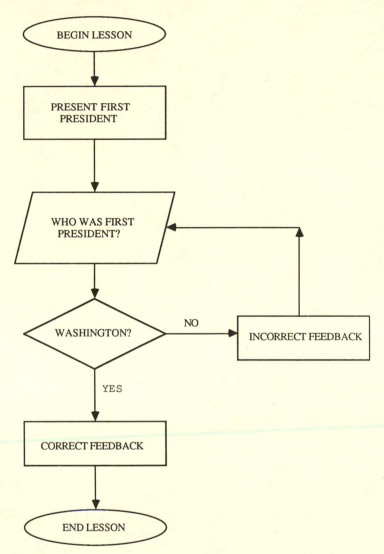

Figure 17.4
A micro-direct CMI application.

Usually the indirect information sources are in the form of previous lesson performance data, such as accuracy, response latency, or number of attempts per item. The data are used in combination with current lesson status to make management decisions based in part upon information beyond the immediate lesson. Figure 17.5 illustrates the manner in which the indirect information sources affect individual lesson execution decisions.

AN EXAMPLE

A micro-indirect extension of the previous history question example is illustrated in Figure 17.6. In this case, the student pretest response is stored initially as incorrect. In a subsequent lesson, the student is again asked to answer the same

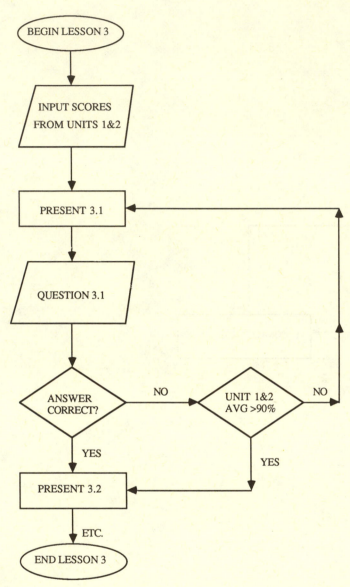

Figure 17.5
Micro-indirect CMI procedures.

question. The new answer is then compared with the pretest response. If the new response is correct, then the computer will congratulate the student while displaying the original incorrect response and noting the improvement.

If the next answer is incorrect but different from the original response, the student will repeat the lesson. Perhaps the designer considers unrelated incorrect responses as random and attributable to inattentiveness. The original response has no direct effect on the single instructional management decisions. In combination with a current response, however, a different decision is made.

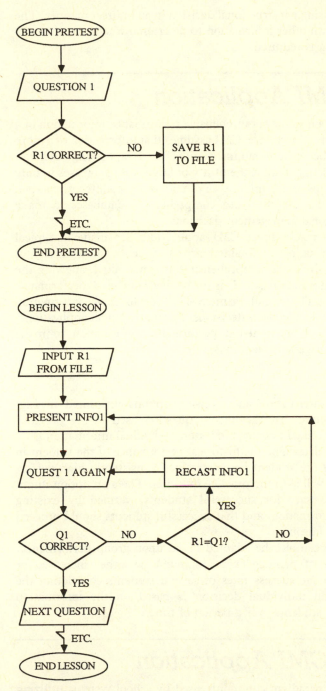

Figure 17.6
A micro-indirect CMI application.

If the response is incorrect and identical to the pretest response, then the student will receive an entirely different explanation. Perhaps the designer assumes that the incorrect information was systematically mislearned and that more convincing instruction must be presented. In any case, the pretest response, stored in a CMI database, is used to effect a single instructional decision in an indirect manner. The information is evaluated with other information to determine whether an instructional management decision is required.

A Macro-Direct CMI Application

Macro-level data often pertain to the comprehensive performance information of a school or educational system. Macro-level CMI assumes that information of a more comprehensive nature can be useful to aid instructional decision making. Generally, however, there is a tendency to limit the utility of large-scale databases to only large-scale applications. This is an unnecessary, and often counterproductive, perception. It is often quite useful to use comprehensive databases to make meaningful direct instructional management decisions.

Figure 17.7 shows how macro-direct CMI applications are made in typical lessons. Performance information is obtained across students for a variety of outcomes. A database, usually quite comprehensive, is constructed, allowing the updating of performance information as well as the retrieval of overall performance information across students. The overall, or micro-level, performance information is available for instructional management decisions. For macro-direct applications, the interest is in the use of accumulated performance information to make individual instructional management decisions.

AN EXAMPLE

Consider the transfer of information and decision options illustrated in Figure 17.8. Once again, assume that the history question used in the previous examples is applied. As the student begins the lesson, individual information from the database is retrieved to determine the historical performance of the student in previous related lessons. If the student has maintained consistently high performance, then the computer will skip the practice question. The assumption might be that practice is unnecessary for successful students, verified by existing cumulative performance information, and that successful students should proceed more rapidly through the lesson.

Individual contingencies can also be adapted based upon group performance. For instance, the number of practice exercises might be either increased or decreased depending upon the success rates of several students completing the lesson. In such a case, an individual decision is based on the information accumulated across several students over a period of time.

A Macro-Indirect CMI Application

Finally, consider the CMI paradigm commonly used by school systems utilizing computer-based instructional management systems. A typical macro-indirect CMI system is illustrated in Figure 17.9. Macro-indirect CMI typically refers to broad, system-based instructional management decisions that the computer cannot enforce, but on which it can only exert influence. Typically, data are collected across a range of skills, the performance is then compared to the standards required for mastery, and test results are stored permanently within the

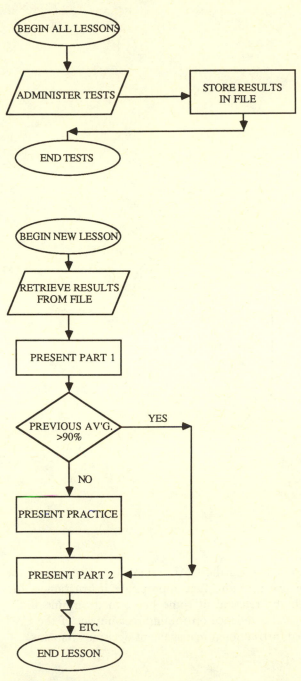

Figure 17.7
Macro-direct CMI procedures.

computer and provided to the student or teacher. Presumably, subsequent instruction will be based on the test results, the recommended prescriptions for remediation, or other information either obtained during the test session or derived from student performance histories.

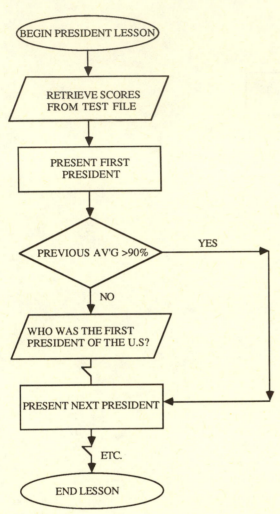

Figure 17.8.
A macro-direct CMI application.

However, this is a presumption. Since the CMI system does not control the instructional decision directly, we presume that appropriate instruction is implemented. The student might be retested at some point to determine if the objectives have been attained, but a reliance on the indirect impact of the CMI system to encourage the needed instructional management decisions remains.

AN EXAMPLE

Students in the Surelearn School District are given biweekly criterion-referenced tests to assess their progress toward meeting prescribed objectives. The CMI paradigm representing this cycle is shown in Figure 17.10. Tests are administered and scored by computer; student skill profiles are updated; target instructional goals are identified; corresponding instructional materials for each target are identified; and reports summarizing the performance information, target goals,

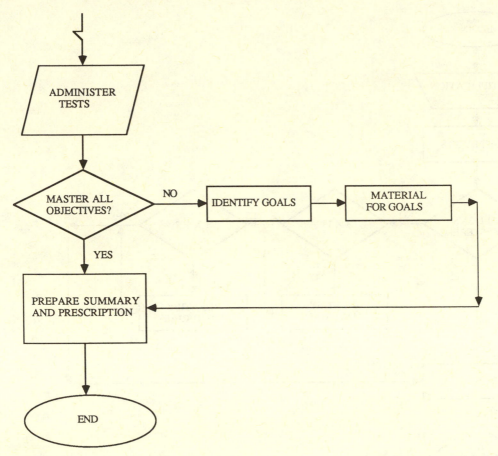

Figure 17.9.
Macro-indirect CMI procedures.

and correlated instructional materials are sent to classroom teachers. The computer has completed the formidable task of managing instructional information, but it can only recommend activities, thereby impacting the system only indirectly. The activities cannot be enforced directly.

Embedding CMI Capabilities in Lessons: Some Considerations

The degree to which CMI capabilities are required for individual lessons depends on several factors. The extent to which historical information should impact current lessons, for example, is a principal factor in establishing the need for an integrated CMI database. It may be of value to store data for reporting purposes, but not to base subsequent CAI decisions on the obtained data. If so, the computer might be effective as a write-only electronic record keeper, but management applications will not be required.

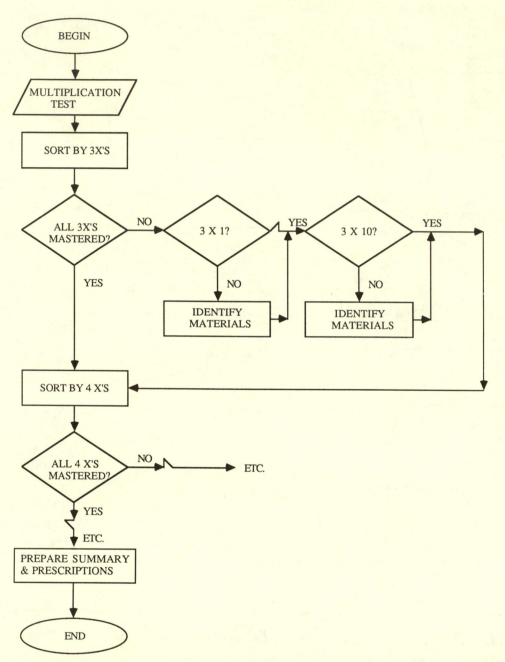

Figure 17.10.
A macro-indirect CMI application.

On the other hand, the cumulative data might be used extensively to adapt lesson difficulty or to retrieve previous responses. In such cases, past performance information must be accessible during lesson execution and must provide the information necessary to make instructional management decisions. From a CMI perspective, the establishment of a database that can be integrated within later lessons poses a somewhat different challenge from the simple collection of lesson information alone.

What of lessons that require on off-line storage, but depend heavily on performance information generated during a lesson? In some ways, the elimination of off-line storage and retrieval simplifies the design process. No permanent databases need be established, and the programming complexity of the lesson is lessened. However, the conceptual steps involved in defining, retrieving, and manipulating performance and other information are basically the same. Variables must still be defined, retrieved from temporary storage, and manipulated in accordance with the requirements of the lesson. The net CMI effect is basically the same: Instructional decisions will be made based upon performance information. The method for obtaining the needed information varied, but the conceptual process itself was identical.

Chapter Summary

The question of how much and what type of computer management should be employed can only be answered within the context of individual instructional settings. Of primary concern in any systems-based approach is the degree to which the solutions meet the adopted unit, lesson, or curriculum specifications. The appropriateness of CMI options must be determined based on the goals of the lesson, the needs for which the instruction is developed, and the capabilities of the setting to support the different CMI options. It is fruitless to consider how, when, or if CMI options are to be applied if basic questions pertaining to the needs and requirements of the solution have not been considered.

The varied CMI applications available to designers of computer-based instruction provide a great deal of utility, but they also pose potential complications. The CMI techniques employed in a lesson may be as simple as making a single instructional management decision or as complex as development and integration of perpetually generated, cumulative performance indexes for each individual student. The power of the computer to permit this range of application is associated with an increase in the technical knowledge and sophistication required to plan, develop, and implement increasingly complex CMI systems.

CMI applications in education will undoubtedly grow and expand. The power and potential of the computer to actually manage instruction are perhaps nowhere more apparent than in well-designed CMI systems. In education, we are faced with the introduction of an alternative technology whose capabilities and utilities are often misunderstood, unknown, or simply not considered. Some applications might be desired eventually but might be perceived as impractical or unnecessary in an immediate sense. Lesson designers will influence future CMI growth by educating others to the potential, and demonstrating the power, of the computer for instructional management applications.

References

Baker, F. B. (1978). *Computer-Managed Instruction: Theory and Practice*. Englewood Cliffs, NJ: Educational Technology Publications.

Leiblum, M. D. (1982). Computer-managed instruction: An explanation and overview. *AEDS Journal*, **15**, 126–142.

Related Reading

ALLEN, M. (1980). Computer-managed instruction. *Journal of Research and Development in Education*, **14**, 33–40.

BAKER, F. B. (1981). Computer-managed instruction: A context for computer-based instruction. In H. F. O'Neil (ed). *Computer-Based Instruction: A State-of-the-Art Assessment*. New York: Academic Press.

DEAN, C., and Q. WHITLOCK (1983). *A Handbook of Computer-Based Training*. London: Kogan Page.

McISAAC, D. N., and F. B. BAKER (1978). *Microcomputer CMI: Performance Specifications*. Madison, WI: University of Wisconsin.

Chapter Review Exercises

COMPREHENSION

1. Describe the differences between micro- and macro-level CMI applications. (See page 278.)
2. Describe examples where micro- and macro-level CMI are appropriate. (See pages 284–291.)
3. Describe the differences between direct and indirect CMI applications. (See pages 278–279.)
4. Describe examples where direct and indirect CMI are appropriate. (See pages 279–281.)
5. List and describe the data sources commonly obtained or used for CMI purposes. (See pages 281–283.)
6. Describe how each data source can be applied to make CMI decisions (See pages 281–283.)

APPLICATION

1. Design a CAI lesson that collects and uses appropriate data sources. (See Figures 17.1 and 17.2.)
2. Design a CAI lesson with micro-direct CMI applications. (See pages 283–284 and Figures 17.3 and 17.4.)
3. Design a CAI lesson with micro-indirect CMI applications. (See pages 284–288 and Figures 17.5 and 17.6.)
4. Design a CAI lesson with macro-direct CMI applications. (See page 288 and Figures 17.7 and 17.8.)
5. Design a CAI lesson with macro-indirect CMI applications. (See pages 288–291 and Figures 17.9 and 17.10.)

VI

Evaluating and Revising CAI Lessons

Thus far, CAI lesson planning, organizing, and producing have been emphasized. Many mistakenly believe that the process ends at this point. This is most unfortunate, since the most important questions and issues have yet to be addressed: Is the lesson effective? Does the lesson teach the skills specified to the prescribed levels? Are revisions needed? What revisions are appropriate? The design and creation of a lesson may meet the conditions specified in the objective, but without some form of evaluation, can we be certain?

The evaluation–revision cycle used in systems models is essential to the development of effective CAI lessons. It is also the most overlooked phase in most development efforts. In some cases, evaluation can be an exceedingly time-consuming and arduous process. However, the evaluation–revision cycle need not be viewed in this light.

The purpose of this section is to describe several considerations and procedures in the evaluation and revision of CAI lessons. The focus is primarily on the informal techniques that can be used to determine lesson effectiveness—procedures that can be easily employed by CAI lesson designers or developers. In addition, the evaluation of externally developed or commercially developed CAI software will be emphasized.

SECTION GOALS

After completing this section you will

1. Understand the different methods in which CAI lesson evaluation can be conducted.
2. Identify the major dimensions along which lesson evaluation should be conducted.
3. Develop a framework for making revision decisions that incorporates the systems process as well as other practical concerns.

CHAPTER 18

Evaluating CAI Lessons

During the first three sections of this text, a good deal of attention was focused on systems approaches. The importance of instructional objectives in systems approaches to CAI lesson design is integral to the design, development, and evaluation processes. Attainment of the specified objectives, however, depends upon the extent to which the methods used in the lesson direct the necessary attention to learn facts, concepts, and procedures.

Evaluation, of course, encompasses more than simply comparing obtained with expected student learning outcomes. Evaluation requires that factors related to attitudes, learning environment, curriculum priorities, and several other concerns be considered carefully before effectiveness can be concluded. As all phases of the systems approach, evaluation is a *process* that occurs continuously, drawing on a variety of information sources and techniques.

The purposes of this chapter are to present a variety of methods used to evaluate the effectiveness of CAI lessons. We focus both on CAI lessons that have been developed commercially and on those that you might develop yourself. Most of the methods are informal. In all cases, however, the techniques and methods will help to differentiate those features of a lesson that are useful and productive from those that are useless and counterproductive.

OBJECTIVES

Comprehension

After completing this chapter you will be able to

1. Describe the differences between formal and informal evaluative techniques and the circumstances where each is appropriate.
2. List and describe the major levels of evaluation appropriate for CAI.
3. List and describe the types of questions addressed during each level of evaluation.
4. Describe the general classes of evaluation activity and the associated kinds of information yielded from each.
5. Describe situations where each class of evaluation is appropriate.
6. Describe relevant hardware and software considerations in the evaluation of CAI lessons.

Application

After completing this chapter you will be able to

1. Develop a plan, incorporating both formal and informal techniques, to evaluate personally developed CAI lessons.
2. Develop and implement formative evaluation of the instructional adequacy of a personally developed CAI lesson.
3. Develop and implement formative evaluation of the cosmetic adequacy of a personally developed CAI lesson.
4. Develop and implement formative evaluation of the program adequacy of a personally developed CAI lesson.
5. Develop and implement formative evaluation of the curriculum adequacy of a personally developed CAI lesson.
6. Develop and implement one-to-one evaluation procedures for a personally developed lesson.
7. Develop and implement small-group evaluation procedures for a personally developed lesson.
8. Develop and implement field-test evaluation procedures for a personally developed lesson.
9. Design and implement procedures to evaluate existing, commercially developed lessons for instructional, cosmetic, program, and curriculum adequacy.

The Role of Evaluation in the Design of CAI Lessons

Objectives prescribe in clear and absolute terms the expected outcomes, the performance standards, and the conditions under which the outcomes should be expected. Objectives guide the lesson design and development accordingly and permit an unusually high degree of precision in specifying the instruction necessary to support desired learning. Well-designed CAI is based largely upon the particular objectives established for the lesson.

A primary function of evaluation in systems approaches to lesson design, therefore, is to determine the extent to which the expected outcomes have been realized (King and Roblyer, 1984). The objectives are treated as precise statements of performance expectancy. They identify the kinds of changes expected in learning, attitude, or motor skills as a result of a given CAI lesson. They are the basis upon which design decisions are made, distribution of emphasis is determined, and practice is provided. They are, in effect, a primary focal point of the evaluation, since they prescribe the desired lesson effects.

In part, then, evaluation can be defined as a systematic procedure used to determine the extent to which lesson objectives have been attained. A lesson might focus on several cognitive objectives as well as on certain affective objectives. Each of the objectives must be inextricably woven into the CAI lesson. Both the information to be learned and the desire to improve student attitudes through the instruction are critical to the organization and design of the lesson. The designer consciously directs the lesson activities to address each of the relevant lesson objectives. It seems only reasonable, then, that the lesson be evaluated systematically to determine the degree to which the lesson has accomplished the prescribed objectives.

It is inadequate, however, to only identify whether objectives have or have not been met. This is especially important when desired outcomes have not been attained, but it is also important even when desired effects have been obtained. Why have the outcomes occurred? What occurred during the lesson that affected the outcome positively, and what affected the outcome adversely? Upon what do we base our decisions to revise the lesson? What features should be revised? How should they be revised?

Clearly, a second important concern for evaluation is the prescriptive value of the process. It does little to determine deficiencies if information is not provided to isolate the probable causes of deficiencies. In some cases, instructional sequences may be well designed, but students may become fatigued during a lesson. Students may perform poorly during a lesson, but the cause may be related to extraneous factors that have virtually nothing to do with lesson design, sequence, or organization.

Evaluation is a particularly important, and exceptionally worthwhile, aspect of systems-based approaches (Dick and Carey, 1985). We gain the capacity to confirm decisions as valid, to improve efforts if needed, or to adjust thinking if appropriate. Yet, despite this promise, evaluation is probably the most overlooked component of systems models. This is a most unfortunate state of affairs, since the potential for improvement is so great and the price so modest.

For our purposes, we will define evaluation as an ongoing process used to determine whether lesson objectives have been met, to identify the reasons for the observed performance, and to identify those portions of a lesson where modifications are required. This definition permits sufficient latitude to address both the outcomes of the instruction and the processes leading to the observed performance.

FORMAL VERSUS INFORMAL EVALUATION TECHNIQUES

Evaluation is often presented as a complicated process that is bigger than life, beyond the capabilities of all but the most able of statisticians, and generally impossible for the mere mortals who design CAI lessons. This could not be further from the truth. In fact, there is a range of evaluation possibilities, including techniques and procedures that are largely informal and intuitive as well as those that require extensive training in formal evaluation design and statistical methodologies. Even in large-scale CAI development settings, the evaluation techniques that tend to have the greatest impact on the quality of CAI lessons are usually those of a less regimented nature.

Consider some examples where informal, or at least simplified, evaluation methods can be successfully applied. During the initial formulation of a lesson designed to teach rocketry concepts via computer simulation, designers often consult with other experts to gauge the probability of success of their plan. They may receive advice, cautions, and other ideas that will later influence different parts of the basic lesson design—all without having actually produced a single frame of computer-based instruction. Is this not a form of evaluation?

Consider a different situation. Perhaps an instructional game designed to strengthen mathematics computation skills and to improve student attention span has been developed. The evaluator decides to observe a few students to determine eye contact with the computer monitor during the lesson. The students become bored quickly and end the activity prematurely. Students might be asked why they terminated the activity so quickly, leading to the conclusion that the game was too easy and not challenging. From these informal observations and interviews, a decision is made to reevaluate the lesson and to increase its difficulty.

In both instances, evaluation activities have occurred. The processes were very simple and, for the most part, very informal. Yet important information pertaining to lesson effectiveness has been obtained. The evaluation techniques may not have been elegant, but they accomplished what all good evaluations should accomplish. The procedures permitted individuals to determine whether the lesson did (or was likely to do) what was expected and provided important information as to why the effects occurred.

Formal evaluation techniques, on the other hand, typically incorporate a planned evaluation paradigm and apply more formal analysis to the data obtained. Such techniques often include the design and use of attitude questionnaires, the collection and collation of student performance data for lesson objectives, and the formal tabulation of student or class performance-by-objective summaries. Formal evaluation techniques allow for the collection of *empirical evidence* rather than the more or less anecdotal data gathered during informal evaluation.

Now consider a scenario where formal evaluation techniques are applied during lesson evaluation. The lesson objective requires that a minimum of 80 percent of the students master at least 80 percent of the lesson content. In addition, the lesson must improve student attitude toward the subject taught. The nature of the evaluation requires that more formal techniques be applied. Student test scores must be collected and organized by objective. Class summaries by objective must also be developed in order to determine whether or not the 80–80 performance criteria have been met. Student attitude scales must also be constructed, perhaps for pre–post administration, in order to measure attitude improvement. The evaluation must include a formal design, as well as data collection and analysis techniques, if lesson effectiveness is to be determined.

Clearly, both formal and informal techniques can be valuable sources of information regarding lesson effectiveness. Each provides unique information that can be applied during lesson evaluation and revision. However, formal techniques often require technical and procedural sophistication not generally available among lesson designers. Such skills are well beyond the scope of this text. Instead, informal techniques for evaluating CAI lessons will be emphasized. The reader is urged to refer to any of the references or recommended readings contained at the end of this chapter for more information on formal evaluation techniques.

Levels of Evaluation: Formative and Summative

Whereas both formative and summative evaluation phases address the issues of lesson effectiveness, there are some very substantial differences in practice. The major distinctions between formative and summative evaluation are related to the uses of evaluative information. Formative evaluation procedures are generally associated with the identification of lesson features that require modification. The formative evaluation process is more or less ongoing, with the goal being lesson improvement based upon the findings of the evaluation. Features are identified, modifications made, and the lesson reevaluated to determine whether additional changes are needed (Golas, 1983).

Summative evaluation, on the other hand, is typically conducted for *signature* purposes. This means that some final decision is generally to be made regarding the lesson, such as whether the lesson will be adopted or purchased. The evaluation is not conducted to identify features for modification or revision. It is typically an end in itself and does not usually result in subsequent modification of the lesson content or procedures.

Both formative and summative evaluations are commonly applied in different phases of CAI lesson design, development, and acquisition. Formative evaluation procedures are applied extensively at varying levels throughout lesson design and development. Summative evaluation procedures are used widely by individuals contemplating the purchase of commercially available software. In this chapter, we will present guidelines and procedures for conducting formative evaluations of lessons that you personally design, as well as summative evaluation procedures and guidelines for the evaluation of CAI lessons that are designed and marketed by others.

PLANNING AND CONDUCTING A FORMATIVE EVALUATION

Formative evaluation in systems approaches is continuous. Issues ranging from basic design logic to the selection of vocabulary words, from the clarity of graphics to branching execution, and from the judging of student input to the clarity of the lesson text, must all be considered. This task may appear monumental, but it is typically so interwoven with the design and development process that formal techniques are either unnecessary or are used simply to document what has already been established through ongoing informal methods.

Dick and Carey (1985) have differentiated formative evaluation along three dimensions, based largely on the developmental stage of the process. These dimensions are useful for considering the kinds of evaluative activities that might be conducted at the various stages of lesson development. The three stages are one-to-one evaluation, small-group evaluation, and field testing.

One-to-One Evaluation One-to-one evaluations are conducted extensively during initial lesson design and development. Usually the procedures are informal and are used to identify potential major problems associated with the planned lesson design. In some cases, early prototypes of a lesson are evaluated; in others, general notions about the planned lesson design are considered.

For example, a designer might consider the use of a particular strategy for a lesson. Prior to investing too much energy in the design, however, the designer might want other authorities to consider the plan. Perhaps a different instructional designer might be asked to comment on the design, to recommend possible improvements, or to project the probability of success for the design. The lesson plan might also be presented to subject-matter experts, such as teachers, to gain insight into the completeness, basic assumptions, and acceptability of the design.

Although the lesson is still only at the planning stage, the evaluative input can have a dramatic effect on the eventual lesson design.

Another application of one-to-one evaluation is found where individual students are presented tentative, preliminary versions of a CAI lesson. Usually the designer observes the individual student closely to identify apparent confusion and other potential lesson flaws. In most cases, the student and designer interact directly as well to offer comments and other useful diagnostic information.

The greatest asset of one-to-one evaluations for CAI design and development purposes is the capacity to obtain valuable information concerning a lesson before unnecessarily expending energy to develop the lesson. Often major problems can be identified, and the lesson design and procedures can be redirected to avoid the potential problems. In other cases, the features of the lesson can be expanded or restricted based upon expert opinions, saving time, effort, and money that would have been expended fruitlessly.

Small-Group Evaluation   Small-group evaluations are usually conducted when the CAI lesson is nearly finished. The purposes are to determine lesson effectiveness, acceptability of the lesson, the appropriateness of the materials and strategies employed, and the extent to which the lesson complied with the constraints identified during needs assessment. Typically, small-group evaluations incorporate somewhat more formal evaluation techniques, such as the collection and interpretation of student performance summaries. However, informal techniques such as interviews, observations, and records of anecdotal information are also used.

Assume you have designed a lesson based upon the information obtained during needs assessment and a one-to-one evaluation. As a result, you have developed the lesson and wish to determine whether the lesson was effective. You are concerned with student attainment of instructional objectives, student attitude toward the lesson, the amount of time required to complete the lesson, and other relevant information identified during needs assessment. The best way to obtain the necessary information is to administer the lesson under roughly the same circumstances in which it will eventually be implemented. However, it is not necessary that the actual students participate, nor is it necessary for entire classes to receive the instruction. Instead, a small number of representative students will receive the instruction, and you will base your conclusions on the performance of the students in the small-group evaluation.

It is important to reaffirm that the purpose of evaluation at this point is to identify where, or if, lesson improvements are needed. The data gathered must address those features considered important to the lesson. The application of both formal and informal techniques provides the flexibility required to obtain the range of information that is useful in the evaluation of CAI lessons.

Field Test Evaluation   The field test is conducted in the actual setting, or one that closely resembles the actual setting, in which the CAI lesson will be implemented. Field tests are conducted when lessons are believed to be of final draft quality. If problems are identified, additional changes may be made. However, the informal evaluations conducted to this point should ensure that the lesson is virtually finished or that only minimal changes will be required.

Field testing usually relies heavily on formal evaluation techniques. Since the evaluation is conducted to confirm the effectiveness of the lesson in real-life settings, little opportunity exists for designer–student interaction. Instead, data related to the specific objectives and other desired outcomes of the lesson are gathered. These data are collated, organized according to the evaluation questions to be answered, and analyzed relative to expected versus obtained outcomes. To the extent that informal techniques are used, they are largely unobtrusive.

COMPONENTS OF CAI EVALUATION

There are several aspects of the lesson to consider during formative evaluation. These fall into four basic categories: Instructional adequacy, cosmetic adequacy, program adequacy, and curriculum adequacy. These concerns are summarized in Table 18.1 and presented in a detailed evaluation form in Figure 18.1.

Instructional Adequacy Instructional adequacy is the extent to which the CAI lesson provides the necessary kinds of support and features to accomplish the objective at hand. Whereas the instructional objective itself is certainly an important focus of the evaluation of instructional adequacy, the features and design of the lesson are examined to attribute cause to the observed effects. The principal components of instructional adequacy are described in detail here.

Are the directions for lesson control clearly stated? Perhaps no aspect of a CAI lesson is more important than the clarity of directions to students. Without effective direction, students can flounder aimlessly during a lesson and become discouraged or frustrated. Lessons must provide clear guidance to users, both in terms of the ongoing directions and the methods for exercising lesson options.

Is the lesson consistent with the outcomes specified in the objective? It is distressing to observe how often the stated objectives, instructional activities, and test questions for the same lessons are inconsistent. It appears as though well-stated objectives are treated as ends in themselves and not as systematic guides that direct lesson activities. Objectives, lesson activities, and assessment questions must be aligned if we are to consider a lesson to be instructionally valid.

Is the instructional sequence easy to follow and empirically based? Lesson flow is critical to the ease with which learning will occur. Lessons that move logically and smoothly from frame to frame and from section to section will likely maintain learner attention effectively. Lessons where progressions are abrupt, not well coordinated, or simply out of order make effective learning more difficult and in some cases impossible. At the very least, students are forced to expend considerable effort to make sense of the lesson, resulting in unnecessary distractions from

Table 18.1
Categories of Formative Evaluation

| Type of Adequacy | Focus of Activity | | | | |
	Design	Procedures	Appearance	Efficiency	Clarity
Instructional	Yes	Yes	No	Yes	Yes
Cosmetic	No	No	Yes	No	Yes
Program	Yes	Yes	No	Yes	No
Curriculum	Yes	Yes	No	No	No

```
┌─────────────────────────────────────────────────────────────────┐
│                                                                   │
│              Courseware    Evaluation    Forms                    │
│                                                                   │
└─────────────────────────────────────────────────────────────────┘
```

Name of Software: Name that Note   Name of Reviewer: Foley
Name of Vendor: Bixler   Date of Review: 9/1/87
Cost of Software: $50   School/District: Bernard
Age/Grade Level: 3-12th grade   Address: RR#1, Bernard, NY
Subject/Content: Music Reading &   Telephone: (212) 999-9999
                 Note Identification

Description of Software: A 2 disc package that focuses on reading sheet
music, identifying notes and selecting the correct key for given notes

Type of Design: Tutorial X   Drill__   Game__   Simulation__   Other__

Hardware Requirements:
Computer: Apple X IBM__   Commodore__   Radio Shack___   Other__
Storage System: Disc X Tape__   Network__   Other__
Monitor Requirements: Color Computer X RGB__   Composite__
            Monochrome__   Standard TV__   Other__
Drive Requirements (if applicable): 1_ 2 X Other__
Memory Requirements: 48K
Other Relevant Information: Can be used with one drive only,
                                but need two for record keeping

---

Evaluation Summary: (Average Rating in Each Category)
Instructional Adequacy: Above Avg- Very Good
Cosmetic Adequacy: Same
Program Adequacy: Very Good
Curriculum Adequacy: Very Good

RECOMMENDATION: Adopt X   Do Not Adopt___   Other___

Figure 18.1
Forms for evaluating the instructional, cosmetic, program, and curriculum adequacy of instructional software.

the task at hand. Lessons should be easy to follow, devoid of gaps, and make the task of comprehending lesson content as straightforward as possible.

Is the lesson readily understood and free from vague and ambiguous text? Often CAI lessons include excessive and unnecessary jargon, text that is vague or ambiguous, or terms that can be interpreted in many ways. This only detracts from the clarity of the lesson in conveying intended information to students, since the student must focus attention on ascertaining what the lesson really means. If more directly

Instructional Adequacy

FOCUS	Very Poor	Below Average	Average	Above Average	Very Good
Design:					
Factual Accuracy					O
Relationship to Objectives					O
Acceptability					O
User Response				O	
Orientation			O		
Consistent with Objectives					O
Examples Provided					O
Sequence of Lesson				O	
Practice Provided					O
Feedback Provided					O
Lesson Logic					O
Distribution of Emphasis					O
Relevance					O
Meaningfulness			O		
Step Size					O
Guidance				O	

COMMENTS:

Lesson activities very easy to follow and understand. Lots of practice opportunities and excellent guidance during the lesson.

Figure 18.1 *(Continued)*

and readily understood techniques exist for conveying information, they should be used.

Is the basic design logic of the lesson sensible, including the components and features of well-designed lessons? On occasion, a designer may make erroneous assumptions about the best way to teach. Perhaps key vocabulary was presented too late in a lesson, or the inclusion of a difficult lesson pretest frustrated students, or insufficient prerequisite and enabling information has been provided. The logic of lesson activities requires careful consideration. The hierarchical relationships among concepts and the determination of which lesson activities are needed are dominant influences on the comprehensibility of the lesson.

Instructional Adequacy (Cont.)

FOCUS	Very Poor	Below Average	Average	Above Average	Very Good

Procedures:

	Very Poor	Below Average	Average	Above Average	Very Good
Directions				◐	
Interaction During Lesson					◐
Personalization			◐		
Pacing					◐
Control Options					◐
Motivational Aspects					◐

Efficiency:

	Very Poor	Below Average	Average	Above Average	Very Good
Leanness				◐	
Record-Keeping					◐
Adaptivity				◐	
Amount of Practice					◐
Individualization of Lesson				◐	

COMMENTS:

Animation very effective (especially for young students).

"HELP" and "REVIEW" options are provided, but "QUIT" option could be a problem for some students (quit too soon?)

Figure 18.1 (*Continued*)

Are lesson procedures and activities efficient? Lessons sometimes teach desired skills but provide excessive information and practice. For example, students might be very proficient at reading and interpreting the entries on an airline schedule and might acquire the skill in relatively few trials. However, the lesson may require practice and give examples well beyond the point of necessity. It is often possible to reduce the dead wood in a lesson by restricting the focus to the lesson objectives or by allowing for variable acquisition rates that result in lesson termination as soon as the required skills have been demonstrated.

Have important terms, concepts, and information been amplified effectively? Effective CAI lessons aid in directing the student's attention through the use of amplification techniques. These techniques cue the learner to those aspects of the lesson that are considered important by the designer, thereby making the learning task easier for

Instructional Adequacy (Cont.)

FOCUS	Very Poor	Below Average	Average	Above Average	Very Good
Clarity:					
Readability				①	
Ease of Comprehension				①	
Text Clarity			①		
Graphics Fidelity				①	
Sound Fidelity					①
Ease of Location of Information					①

> **COMMENTS:**
>
> Some frames are too busy, but overall the information and explanations
> are pretty clear. Watch out for some text displayed in color/shadows--
> difficult to read at times.

Figure 18.1 (*Continued*)

the student. Good lessons amplify important information very systematically but sparingly, ensuring that the cueing function of the amplification remains strong during the lesson.

Does the lesson distribute emphasis according to the importance of the different parts and sections? Perhaps the most challenging task for a CAI lesson designer is that of assigning emphasis within a lesson. Lessons sometimes do not provide enough emphasis on the most important aspects, complicating the task of sorting through the lesson. Important aspects of the lesson, defined perhaps by the instructional objective, must be emphasized more than less important aspects.

Does the lesson provide opportunities for meaningful interaction between the student and the lesson content? In chapter 13, the importance of interaction in CAI lessons was emphasized. Interactive lessons encourage responses to instructional content,

Cosmetic Adequacy

FOCUS	Very Poor	Below Average	Average	Above Average	Very Good

Appearance:

Item	Very Poor	Below Average	Average	Above Average	Very Good
Appeal					○
Typographical Accuracy					○
Frame Protocol					○
Visual Appeal				○	
Animation					○
Use of Available Screen Space				○	

Clarity:

Item	Very Poor	Below Average	Average	Above Average	Very Good
Screen Density			○		
Display Clarity				○	
Amplification					○
Interpretability of Display Elements				○	

COMMENTS:

Use of animation and sound is excellent. Some text shown in color is hard to read in parts of the lesson. Also, certain frames are pretty busy and crowded.

Figure 18.1 (*Continued*)

assist the student in assessing his or her own learning, and guide the learner to comprehend lesson content. Lessons that simply require the pressing of a key to continue the lesson do not provide a meaningful level of interaction. Yet this is unfortunately an all-too-common technique. Under the best of circumstances, lessons should encourage and require the learner to process instruction actively; to produce responses to verify comprehension; and to strengthen the learning of lesson information, concepts, and skills.

Does the lesson personalize instruction appropriately? To the extent possible, CAI lessons should be relevant and meaningful. For young learners, the use of the student's name in a lesson may be useful. For others, the incorporation of

Program Adequacy

FOCUS	Very Poor	Below Average	Average	Above Average	Very Good
Design:					
Execution Commands					①
Consistency with Flowchart			NOT GIVEN		
Lesson Execution					①
Programming Loops					①
Efficiency					①
Security					①
Response Anticipation					①
Display Accuracy					①
Procedures:					
Disc Management					①
Documentation					①
Start-Up Procedures					①
Modifiability			NOT GIVEN		
Consistency Within					①
Consistency from Lesson-to-Lesson					①
CMI Features					①
Efficiency:					
Speed of Execution					①
Use of Variables			NOT GIVEN		
Data Storage & Retrieval					①
"Tightness" of Program Code			NOT GIVEN		

COMMENTS:

Slow to execute at times but overall lesson execution was very good.

Very good at detecting illegal responses and has excellent record-keeping (lesson cannot be duplicated or modified, but very good as is)

Figure 18.1 *(Continued)*

meaningful examples into the lesson might be appropriate. For still others, the nature of the computer–learner interaction might be informal or conversational. CAI lessons should not be perceived as impersonal or unduly regimented. Incorporating techniques to personalize the instruction, making the activities appear relevant for each user, can go a long way toward encouraging greater acceptance of the lesson.

Is the step size appropriate for the kind of learners and the learning task? Often CAI lessons teach far too much information before determining if important lesson concepts have been understood. The most common convention in CAI is to limit step size to the information needed to learn new individual concepts. If lessons

Curriculum Adequacy

FOCUS	Very Poor	Below Average	Average	Above Average	Very Good
Design:					
Portability					①
Accommodation of Teacher Styles					①
Accommodation of Student Styles					①
Lesson Options					①
Integration of Subject Matter					①
Cultural & Social Theme		DOES NOT APPLY			
Information Durability					①
Hardware Restrictions			①		
Supporting Materials					①
Tie-In to Curriculum					①
Procedures:					
Flexibility					①
Familiarity					①
Effectiveness					①
Consistency					①
Compatibility					①
Acceptability					①
Expandability					①
Running Time					①

COMMENTS: Version will only run on Apple II family of computers (IBM, Tandy, and Commodore versions scheduled for release around 6/1/88). This lesson will fit nicely into our music program since it can be used by either the music teacher or classroom teacher (or in the home), and in either small groups or independently by students.

Figure 18.1 (*Continued*)

contain excessive numbers of concepts within the same step or contain a good deal of extraneous information, problems will ensue. It is always possible to bridge concepts once they are acquired; to include too much initially, however, can result in ineffective initial instruction.

Are the pacing procedures and display rate appropriate for the learners and learning task? In general, students need to control the pace of frames that present new information. To place such frames under the control of a timer often does not accommodate the individual variability in reading and study habits that is likely to be encountered. If pacing is computer-controlled, lessons should be evaluated to determine reasonable time needed for frame inspection.

Are lesson activities, content, and procedures likely to motivate students to perform? Little will be accomplished if the lesson is neither interesting nor motivating to students. In many cases, CAI lessons are unnecessarily dry and make little attempt to enlist the enthusiasm of the student. Reasonably well-organized and sequenced instruction is undermined by a lack of concern for the affective orientation of the learner. Since the student's attitude is likely to affect the amount and kind of effort expended during the lesson, attempts should be made to ensure that the instruction is perceived favorably.

Are required or desired record-keeping capabilities available in the lesson? Although this is often considered an optional feature, virtually all CAI lessons include at least progress reports and performance summaries. It is important to capture the important performance information available in the lesson and not lose the potential for meaningful performance summaries, prescriptive information, or information that may be useful for record-keeping purposes. Generally, this information is already solicited during the lesson and needs only to be collected, organized, and stored.

Are appropriate lesson-control options provided? Whereas students have been found not to make wise choices in controlling their instructional decisions, the issue of option availability remains an important concern. Generally, lessons should offer such features as "Help" and "Review" options—options that cannot result in lesson termination. CAI should avoid the impression of trapping the student within the lesson. The inclusion of options that offer greater levels of support and assistance, rather than those that simply exit the student from the lesson, can be quite useful.

Cosmetic Adequacy In the past, more attention has been focused on the cosmetic features of CAI than on other, more substantive concerns. We become mesmerized by the impressive use of color, sound, and motion. The technology is almost seductive in its capacity to entrance an audience with its capabilities.

Unfortunately, the cosmetic features of CAI lessons often become the dominant basis for evaluation. True, visual appeal is an important consideration in lesson design, but it is certainly not the dominant concern. Consider the following cosmetic features as part of a comprehensive formative evaluation plan.

Is screen space used effectively? With all instruction, it is important to present neatly organized information. Since the use of a fixed screen presents certain limitations, such as the number of rows or lines and columns available for information, the potential for problems in the organization and use of available screen space is compounded. Caution must be exercised to assure that all information contained on the screen is easily identified, located, and readable.

Is there a consistent and effective protocol for the various frames in the lesson? Most CAI lesson designers adopt relatively standardized conventions for use of the different portions of the screen: The frames should be designed to aid in the location of essential information and to focus user attention to the primary parts of the frame. The use of protocol conventions may vary, but lesson designers should attempt to use the frame space and locations consistently.

Is the information presented free of crowding and cramming? When a frame is crammed with information, it can be very difficult for the student to sort it out. If the lesson contains repeated frames full of information, learning can become extremely tedious. In addition, the computer's capability to guide learning is compromised, resulting in instruction that is more characteristic of print media than well-designed CAI. Each frame should contain only the information required to sustain progress and interest through the lesson and should not attempt to present all relevant information at the same time.

Do color and sound, if used, support student learning? Since the time that color and sound became commonly available with the microcomputer, as many problems as solutions have been developed. Both color and sound provide the capacity to enliven instruction, to more closely approximate real-life objects and sounds, and to otherwise cue learners. The greatest drawback, however, has been the thoughtless, indiscriminate use of these capabilities. The use of sound to produce musical notes in a music lesson may be wholly justified; sound effects distributed randomly throughout a lesson may not. Similarly, color may aid in the amplification of information, but indiscriminate use may only confuse the learner. Both sound and color have the potential to improve the cosmetic aspects and the instructional value of a lesson, but their use needs to be systematic and for defined purposes.

Does animation, if used, support student learning? Cartoon-like animation can be very appealing to learners—especially young students. Animation can also be very useful in creating motion during games and simulations. However, the use of animation must be tempered and applied systematically, and it must support lesson objectives. If these conditions can be satisfied, animation can be a very effective technique in improving the cosmetic appeal of instruction.

Are lesson frames free from scrolling effects? Scrolling refers to the appearance of a jump of the contents of a computer frame and is caused by a failure to control the cursor systematically. In some cases, scrolling only serves to move information upward on the frame. This can be distracting, but frame information is not removed from view. In other cases, however, scrolling causes one or more lines of computer text to disappear from view. The consequences of this problem can be dire indeed. Scrolling is entirely avoidable, however, and should be eliminated from CAI lessons. Scrolling can only distract students, but it is probably more often an annoyance than a deterrent to learning. Nonetheless, scrolling reduces the polish and appeal of a lesson.

Do lesson activities appeal to students? Often the presumptions made by CAI designers on what will be appealing are based upon personal experience; trial and error; or, in some cases, on asking for preferences. In other lessons, however, the features are not appealing to students. Lesson appeal should not be assumed. As part of the formative evaluation process, it is useful and necessary to verify that the lesson is appealing to prospective students.

Is the lesson free from typographical errors? Perhaps no single cosmetic feature can undermine the credibility of a lesson as quickly as a simple typographical error. Students are typically accustomed to commercially distributed instructional materials that are comparatively free of obvious typographical flaws. As a result, the occurrence of a typographical error in lessons in which they are not characteristically found is easily noticed. Errors of this type are avoidable through the kinds of editing precautions to which all designers should be accustomed. Do not permit the most basic of errors to diminish the cosmetic appeal of an otherwise well-organized lesson.

Program Adequacy   Clearly, the lesson must execute as intended. The best of designs are useless if not executed correctly. Program adequacy is often evaluated through a process referred to as *debugging*. Debugging is a process where lessons are executed, with the resulting input, output, and control decisions examined for accuracy. Program commands are then altered as needed until the program executes as planned. This process normally takes care of most of the obvious program flaws in a CAI lesson.

Many of the program problems, however, are more difficult to detect. In some cases, the bugs occur only under certain conditions, which are difficult to anticipate during debugging. In other cases, lesson execution continues despite breakdowns in program logic. This is a particular problem when programming errors do not cause the lesson to crash, but inadvertently route the learners to plausible, but inappropriate, sections of the lesson. The following are some of the primary concerns for evaluating program adequacy.

Does the lesson run as intended? Perhaps the most important aspect of program adequacy is the programming logic of the lesson. Unlike instructional logic, where the emphasis is on the sequence of instructional activities, program logic pertains to the manner in which the program execution is consistent with the kinds of lesson input, output, and control prescribed in the lesson execution flow chart. The computer must unfalteringly produce the intended actions under all prescribed conditions; if not, then some aspect of the program logic requires correction.

Is the lesson free of conceptual and programming loops? Lessons must execute free from unwanted loops. Either conceptual or programming loops may occur when control of the program is inadvertently exchanged between or among sections of the lesson repeatedly, not permitting normal or desired lesson execution to proceed. As is the case with most potential problems, loops can be identified through systematic evaluation and can be eliminated through careful planning and programming.

Does the lesson minimize the disk-management requirements for the learner? Seldom is it desirable to require conceptual understanding of the computer in order to use a CAI lesson. Lessons should be self-starting, require minimal disk handling, and require as little manipulation of the computer itself as possible. Lessons that force a student to understand the processes needed to catalog and run lessons are usually unnecessary and introduce skill requirements not featured in the lesson content. Whenever possible, the lesson operation should be initiated by the student merely turning on power to the computer, or by the designer providing user-friendly menus, from which lesson execution can easily begin.

Does the lesson run efficiently? Designers of CAI lessons should complete desired activities in the most efficient manner possible. Generally, the use of well-defined procedures, subroutines, and variables will simplify programming needs and provide additional flexibility within the lesson. Attempt to speed lesson execution by shortening the program length and by locating program segments strategically within the lesson.

Does the lesson include sufficient security for both the students and the disk itself? The need for at least nominal levels of lesson security has grown in recent years. As users have increased in sophistication, it has become necessary to embed safeguards in lessons to assure that features such as individual student performance summaries are protected and that lessons are not accidentally or intentionally sabotaged. In some cases, the use of individual passwords to gain entry into a lesson may be used. In others, lesson tracers may be included to detect when a user has gained illegal entry into the program code. In some cases, the lesson may be designed to automatically crash if unwanted access to the lesson is obtained. While these kinds of security are not yet required in many cases, they have become increasingly important concerns for lesson designers.

Has the domain of appropriate responses been carefully anticipated? Response anticipation is a particularly important program concern. Often students may simply type an answer incorrectly or may accidentally press the wrong key on the computer. Usually it is more desirable to embed provisions to detect these illegal responses rather than to assume that students have provided incorrect answers. It is also important to anticipate the range of plausible legal responses to given questions, especially when responding to constructed versus multiple-choice questions. CAI lessons should anticipate illegal entries, plausible legal entries, and as no-response, null entries.

Have appropriate procedures for evaluating student input been provided? In simple multiple-choice formats, little answer judging is usually required. The nature of the responses, as well as the information used for comparison, is so straightforward that simply matching an answer literally against the right or wrong options usually suffices. Considerably more answer judging is required when the possibilities of upper- and lower-case letters are considered, spelling errors are allowed, or partial credit can be assigned. Designers must assure that techniques that permit a reasonable and appropriate range of responses be used in CAI lessons.

Does the lesson display information accurately? The accuracy of display is relevant to both cosmetic and program adequacy, but correction is ultimately a programming concern. For example, some languages used to program or author CAI require the programmer to account for features such as text centering, word truncation, and screen dimensions. It is necessary to verify that words are not inadvertently split at the end of the line, that the position of the information presented is consistent with the frame design parameters, and that all information is output to the appropriate location and is presented as intended.

Have lesson components been logically and systematically located? When one is organizing programming statements and procedures, care must be taken to make subsequent identification, interpretation, and debugging as easy as possible. Program procedures should be labeled for easy identification and to assist the programmer or author in locating lesson segments requiring further modification. Generally, it will be easiest if descriptive labels are used and if such labels are adopted uniformly across both the program itself and the lesson flow chart.

Is lesson execution consistent with the conditions specified in the flowchart? Above all, the program *must* be consistent with the contingencies prescribed in the lesson flowchart. The process of examining program adequacy is virtually hopeless if it is not compared to a lesson execution plan. The flowchart must be the principal basis for comparison when considering program adequacy. If the resulting lesson is unsatisfactory, consider modifying the basic lesson plan before making program alterations.

Curriculum Adequacy   One of the most important factors affecting the long-term acceptability of a lesson is the degree to which the lesson procedures, activities, and formats are consistent with accepted standards. To the extent possible, the lesson must be compatible with the styles of the teachers and students, easily incorporated into existing curriculum activities and structures, and compatible with the kinds of lesson activities and procedures already in place (Wholeben, 1982).

Is the lesson consistent with other related lessons? To the extent that other lessons exist and constitute the norm of instructional software available, new entries must systematically account for the expectations that have evolved. This does not suggest that all lessons must mirror earlier ones. Instead, it is advisable to examine the features that have been popular and effective in existing lessons. Those features are likely to be valued and to have become part of the expectations of the users. In addition, this may be an easier and more precise technique for estimating the kinds of skills coverage that are already available related to the current lesson.

Are lesson procedures consistent with the expectations of users? User expectations are shaped over time through exposure to the procedures of various lessons. Generally, lessons should offer fairly consistent procedures for lesson execution, both within and across related lessons. It is often valuable to examine the procedures used in a given lesson both in terms of their apparent effectiveness for the lesson and their compatibility across lessons.

To the extent feasible and advisible, have teacher and user preferences been included? Teachers and users do not always prefer options that are most effective. They do not always learn best from the kind of instruction thought to match their individual styles. Still, lessons that totally disregard preferences are not likely to be acceptable unless compelling evidence can be presented supporting alternative instructional decisions. Where it is possible and appropriate, the designer should attempt to accommodate the preferences of users. Where it is not feasible or is simply inappropriate, the designer should present a convincing case for the alternative decision.

Could the lesson be used as a basis for additional, related lesson development? Lesson designs and procedures should provide the possibility for expansion. The lesson itself might be expanded in some way, or the creation of additional related lessons might be possible. Lesson protocol and conventions should permit the development of additional lessons or material that might also utilize the same basic protocol, response formats, and other lesson features.

Does the lesson contain information likely to become quickly obsolete? Some lesson content, by its nature, is necessarily dated. Lessons that focus on current events, for example, are likely to be timely for only a limited period. Many lessons, however, are unnecessarily dated by the inclusion of information that is likely to become quickly dated. For example, the inclusion of information regarding the current World Series baseball champion or the current national debt in a lesson pertaining to mathematics tends to make the lesson content appear unnecessarily and prematurely obsolete. The World Series champion and the national debt will change at least annually. Examine the lesson to avoid premature obsolescence.

Can the lesson be completed within the allotted time? Prior to beginning the design process, a very clear understanding of any restrictions on the amount of time to be allotted for lesson completion should be in place. It is insufficient to teach desired skills if the time needed is prohibitive. The range of time needed for completion, including the fastest as well as the slowest among the target group, must be considered during the evaluation and compared to the constraints specified for lesson running time.

Does the lesson contain special options that require specific hardware or software considerations? Occasionally lessons are developed that require hardware that is not generally available. For example, the teaching of graph reading and plotting to junior high school students can be done very effectively through the integration of joysticks for plotting points. However, it would place a limitation on the lesson to absolutely require that a joystick be used and, on occasion, to require that the same type of joystick be used every time. Special features can be very useful and popular if their inclusion does not seriously limit the scope of possible applications for the lesson.

Does the lesson offer flexibility in how it can be used? One of the most popular features of CAI lessons is the inclusion of a hidden menu, from which the teacher (or student, in some cases) can vary certain lesson parameters. Rather than simply embedding sound or rigidly specifying the number of practice examples to be used, the menu permits a teacher to control features without compromising the basic design. Options such as sound, the number of attempts allowed per item, the writing of student scores to disc or printer, and other features may be varied to permit flexible use.

Using Structured Evaluation Procedures

The Courseware Evaluation Form shown in Figure 18.1 is typical of the structured methods adopted for formalizing the evaluation process—especially for evaluating CAI software produced by others. Let's examine a method for evaluating CAI lessons using both the considerations already described and the structured guidance provided by the Courseware Evaluation Form.

BACKGROUND INFORMATION

It is always advisable to catalog descriptive information regarding the software to be reviewed as well as basic information related to the evaluation itself. Information such as the presumed appropriate age or grade level for the lesson and, of course, the cost of the lesson or lessons is mandatory.

LESSON DESCRIPTION

It is also valuable to obtain an impartial description of the software from the evaluator. We have already addressed the various CAI designs and the functional differences among them. It should be clear that lessons will reflect differences in design orientation. To be certain of the basic lesson design, these should be identified by a knowledgeable designer. CAI distributors may exaggerate the features and utility of the software, since they are primarily concerned with marketing their product.

HARDWARE REQUIREMENTS

The hardware required to run the CAI software must be identified. As noted throughout this text, features of CAI lessons are often system-dependent, that is, they can only be utilized on computers with particular capabilities, peripheral equipment, or memory capacity. The hardware requirements of a CAI lesson, where possible, should be minimized to promote transportability of lessons across similar computers. Often, however, this is not the case.

EVALUATION SUMMARY

All good evaluation procedures include an easy-to-understand summary of overall impressions. In systems approaches, the same basic categories of adequacy used for evaluation of your software should be applied to the evaluation of CAI lessons produced by others. While it may be impossible to assess accurately all features of CAI lessons, a careful examination of the instructional, cosmetic, program, and curriculum features should provide a sufficiently comprehensive perspective to make sound choices.

DERIVING CONSENSUS RATINGS

Several points must be considered in deriving summaries. First, many have attempted to quantify ratings in an attempt to increase the objectivity of the process. While this may be useful in certain cases, it is often oversimplified and misleading. Most computation-based methods do not weight differentially the value of the different features. If, for example, a lesson contains fundamentally inaccurate information or crashes under particular circumstances, a poor rating might only be recorded for that single flaw. Perhaps the remainder of the lesson is rated favorably. The apparently high evaluation scores, despite the obvious fatal nature of a single feature, misleads the evaluator into making generally positive conclusions. For this reason, we do not advocate simple summing across features and the creation of norms.

Instead, we recommend a combination of assessing rating consensus plus ultimate fatal criteria. When these elements are considered concurrently, evaluators are less likely to become the victims of their evaluation system than they would be through the use of simple numeric scores.

To determine consensus, determine the frequencies with which each of the ratings has been recorded within each level of adequacy. The most frequently selected rating option (the mode) will probably provide the best overall estimate of the global impact for each level. In effect, this method helps to balance the impact of isolated features rated "very good" against the more pervasive aspects of the lesson. However, it is also important to consider the spread of ratings within each level. Ratings that are heavily loaded on one of the categories reflect consistency in performance; uneven ratings indicate variability in quality in the lesson and should be noted carefully.

Next, determine whether any single rating of "very poor" has been made for any lesson feature. This permits the evaluator to apply the exclusionary rule to the process, where a single rating of "very poor" results in automatic rejection, irrespective of all other ratings. Generally, ratings of "very poor" will be sufficient cause to recommend against adoption or purchase, since the criteria for such a rating are fairly extreme. In certain cases, of course, this rule may be waived. For instance, if the courseware is readily modifiable and correction can be readily made, it may be reasonable to disregard this exclusionary rule.

Finally, examine the consistency of performance across the various levels of adequacy. We caution that you weight the levels carefully. Lessons with very uneven ratings across levels are likely to perform inconsistently. This inconsistency becomes greatest as the differences in ratings across levels increases. The system presented in the Courseware Evaluation Form reflects a great deal of emphasis on the instructional adequacy of the lesson, but clearly other factors must be considered as well. The four levels can be evaluated concurrently, but those factors most important to individual settings can be applied to make final differentiations.

JUDGING THE ADEQUACY OF COURSEWARE FEATURES

One of the most common flaws in evaluation procedures is the inability to define consistent and understandable meanings of the evaluation items and criteria. Our system first divides courseware adequacy into the same four areas described earlier: instructional adequacy, cosmetic adequacy, curriculum adequacy, and program adequacy. This helps to isolate more clearly the components of effective courseware by balancing considerations across different areas.

However, we are still left with the task of prescribing criteria for assigning ratings. This depends somewhat on the degree of the evaluative distinction to be made. It is substantially easier for evaluators to distinguish reliably "very good" from "very poor" features due to the extremity of the rating differences. It is substantially more difficult to distinguish lesson features along the marginal range of the scale, from "below average" through "above average." Unfortunately, this is often where the most telling decisions must be made.

In order to provide the needed uniformity, we have defined each of the rating options operationally. While there will always be elements of uncertainty in assigning ratings, these criteria should help to minimize resulting rating inconsistencies. When paired with the four domains of courseware adequacy, the evaluation procedures gain significant power.

Very Poor   Generally, features rated "very poor" are deficient throughout the lesson or are deficient in a single required component. Lessons that present endless frames of text without opportunities for student responses are likely to be rated "very poor" for interaction during the lesson, although the same lesson might be rated as "very good" for factual accuracy. An otherwise accurate lesson, on the other hand, might include a single but critical factual inaccuracy that would cause a rating of "very poor." The key is to interpret "very poor" ratings in the context of not only the pervasiveness of the problem but also the consequences of the problem. It makes little sense to rate a lesson favorably that contains a single flaw judged to be fundamental to the lesson objectives.

Below Average   Typically, features rated as "below average" demonstrate a marginal compliance with the expected ideal. The rating reflects dissatisfaction with the feature, but the possibility that the deficiency could be accepted if other lesson features are especially positive. For example, the lesson may incorporate a student's name but employ virtually no other attempts to personalize instruction. A basic design element is evident, but its implementation is considered marginal. Below average features should be regarded critically in an overall assessment, since a lesson with multiple ratings of this type is likely to perform very unevenly.

Average   This rating is given to features that meet the basic expectations for well-designed software but are not particularly unique or distinguished. Often, for example, lessons will provide a basic lesson performance summary upon completion but offer little in the way of prescription or elaboration of the summary. The feature is present in an acceptable form, but its presence does not assist the learner or teacher in an especially useful way.

Above Average   Lesson features rated "above average" demonstrate unusual methods or capacities to provide the needed focus. Above-average features might also include particularly comprehensive methods of providing basic features, such as the ability for teachers to customize CMI reporting procedures. This rating should be assigned for features that have exceeded basic requirements in their utility or extended the basic features in a useful, constructive manner.

Very Good   Lesson features that are extraordinary in their capacity to provide necessary support, to provide innovative ideas and activities for student involvement, or to provide learning activities that substantively extend the student's capacity to profit from the lesson are rated "very good." These characteristics are manifested largely through the quality of time investment by students and teachers and the availability of learning opportunities not readily available (or perhaps even possible) in noncomputer environments. Such features create opportunities for students to engage in activities at levels not possible or practical in typical instruction, opening educational experiences that are truly unique and for which the computer provides an effective and useful tool.

Evaluators should be especially sensitive to the tendency to overrate the quality of lesson features. Features that are rated "very good" must reflect rare procedural, strategic, or presentation elements that are markedly distinguishable from alternatives. If this rating is not judged accordingly, then the top end of the rating scale will not be sensitive to the detection of truly extraordinary features. Though they are comparatively rare, "very good" ratings should help to distinguish the routine from the extraordinary.

INSTRUCTIONAL ADEQUACY

The emphasis given to instructional adequacy is evident in the proportion of effort assigned to basic lesson effectiveness questions. Perhaps this has become our bias due to the inordinate emphasis on cosmetic features of CAI in the recent past. Instructional adequacy can be considered under four major foci: design, lesson procedures, efficiency, and clarity.

Design   The elements of well-designed CAI are addressed throughout this text, but a few points are important to underscore. Apart from the obvious need for factual accuracy, evaluators should attempt to determine any evidence of lesson effectiveness. This may be provided by the producer or vendor, but it may also be necessary to conduct small-group tryout of the lessons. Lessons must be judged not only effective, but acceptable to both students and teachers. The information presented in this text should enable prospective designers not only to produce effective CAI but also to transfer notions of well-designed lessons to the evaluation of other software. When combined with the structured guidance of the Courseware Evaluation Form, valid and reliable assessments of the quality of CAI lessons are attainable.

Procedures   Lesson activities must be easy to follow. Students should not be forced to invest mental effort attempting to understand lesson directions and options. In addition, lessons should encourage a good deal of meaningful student interaction and personalization, as well as a reasonable amount of control and self-determination. Above all, lessons must enlist the interest of students by providing motivating activities and stimuli. Sound design is insufficient to promote learning if flaws in lesson procedures are evident.

Efficiency   Much of what we believe to constitute well-designed CAI revolves around notions of quality versus quantity of activity and effort. Lessons should avoid unnecessary and distracting information. Well-designed lessons have the capability to adapt to varied learning rates by increasing or decreasing features such as the number of examples, practice items, and so on. Lean lessons reduce overall unnecessary information while allowing individuals to proceed in a customized, adaptive manner. The capacity to generate and use data derived during lessons is also an important feature in settings where the computer is used extensively. There is simply no reason for teachers to duplicate tests and record keeping unless basic record-keeping features have been overlooked.

Clarity   The information presented—text, graphics, animation, and sound— must be readily interpreted. Lessons should provide strategies to ease the manner in which concepts are comprehended. At the very least, the presentation stimuli should not, by themselves, complicate the task unnecessarily.

COSMETIC ADEQUACY

As noted previously, cosmetic factors often dominate selection decisions. Evaluators can be so struck with the colors, sounds, and other physical features of the lesson that insufficient attention is given to other potentially important factors. Still, the need to consider the cosmetic appeal and features of CAI is inescapable. The key to effective evaluation within systems approaches is to understand the role and importance of appearance in relation to other factors and not to permit cosmetic features to dominate evaluation decisions. The focus of cosmetic evaluation revolves around two areas: appearance and clarity.

Appearance   Lessons that are unattractive or sloppy are likely to be rejected despite the potential of the basic design. This is perhaps an unfortunate attribute of human nature, but we have become accustomed to professional-looking, polished materials. Though perhaps less essential to the cognitive effects of CAI lessons, appearance is an important affective concern.

Clarity   In a cosmetic sense, clarity refers to the capacity to display readily interpreted images—text, graphics, sound, and so on. The basic appeal and utility of the frame protocol must also be considered when evaluating clarity. Effective CAI lessons are unambiguous in their display of relevant information, unless, of course, vagueness and ambiguity are an essential part of the lesson task.

PROGRAM ADEQUACY

Though control of the programming aspects of most commercially produced lessons is beyond the sphere of the evaluator, verification of the integrity of the program is essential. The evaluator must be concerned with basic program design, utilization procedures, and lesson efficiency.

Design Many of the evaluation criteria for program design are below the surface, that is, not readily observable. However, lesson design can be easily constructed or reconstructed simply by documenting the sequence of activities followed under repeated trials. Of particular importance is the need to verify the foolproofness of the lesson. Verify the effects of providing unanticipated responses, of not following directions, and of otherwise acting in ways not prescribed in lesson directions. The failure of software designers to truly foolproof the lesson is alarming. Make certain that the basic lesson sequences remain intact under less-than-optimal student responses.

Procedures Generally, increases in disk management are correlated with increases in problems with lesson use. Examine the sophistication required of the student in order to use the software. Also make certain that lesson documentation is prescriptive enough to allow the student (or teacher, in some cases) to start the lesson, to perform simple troubleshooting, to provide assistance in methods for classroom use, and so on. If the software is part of a set of related lessons, examine elements of protocol and procedural consistency across lessons. Finally, verify the accuracy of the CMI features of the lesson—especially when unintended responses are provided. Much of the software presently available performs and tracks only simple reporting and is not sensitive to unplanned variation.

Efficiency The efficiency of externally produced programs is largely undetectable to most evaluators. Some of the telltale signs that might be used to gauge efficiency are excessive overall execution time; delays in screen displays or computer responses to input; unusual, frequent, or distracting disk access during lesson execution; and the requirement to reenter information previously provided.

CURRICULUM ADEQUACY

Perhaps no aspect of software evaluation will have a more telling impact on the widespread installation of computer-based education as curriculum adequacy. More than other levels, evaluation of curriculum adequacy features provides a guage of the likelihood of effective installation of lessons in their intended settings.

Design The alignment of CAI lessons with intact, or planned, curriculum has become an increasing consideration for large-scale software designers. Of particular concern are the thematic consistency with the overriding curriculum; the shelf-life, or useful longevity, of the information presented; the availability of, and alignment with, related and supporting materials; and the capacity to accommodate student and teacher styles. While all may not be available in the short run, these features will almost certainly dominate long-term installation of CAI in schools.

Procedures User-supplied lesson parameters such as selection of examples, number of practice items, difficulty levels, and so on have become major factors influencing curriculum adequacy. In addition, considerations as to the required running time, the potential expandability, the ease of integration of the CAI procedures, and other concerns have surfaced. At the curriculum adequacy level, CAI software must now be judged using much the same criteria as other instructional resources. It will become increasingly important for CAI designers to ensure the acceptability of CAI lessons within the schools and other organizations who will use them.

Commercial CAI Software Evaluation Services

In addition to the evaluation tools developed for our systems-oriented model, there are numerous additional instruments for evaluating commercial software. [See Bradford (1982), Cohen (1983), Dearborn (1982), and Neumann (1982) for individual evaluative standards, instruments, and criteria.]

In addition, software evaluation services are available, where lessons are evaluated systematically by third-party experts (Holznagel, 1982–1985). Several evaluation banks are also available, where commercial software has been previewed by educators and evaluated according to particular criteria. *Software Reports*, for example, is a subscriber service that provides continuously updated capsulized evaluation summaries for a wide range of educational software. Other services that provide comprehensive coverage include *PC Clearinghouse Software Directory*, *EPIE* (Educational Products Information Exchange), and *Swift's Educational Software Directory*. The principal advantage of such services is the scope of coverage provided. It is possible to identify software by need rather than by name alone. This allows a reviewer to identify several potential products that will meet a defined need, to consider an independent evaluation of the products, and to seek further information as needed. However, most evaluation services are more comprehensive in breadth of coverage than in intensity. Such reviews are useful primarily to identify potential resources and to eliminate clearly inadequate options. Greater detail is usually needed to make meaningful selections.

Which Evaluation Procedures Are "Best"?

When identifying the "best" instruments for CAI evaluation, there are no simple answers. To varying degrees, all evaluation tools, including those developed for local use, reflect relevant priorities. Any evaluation tools or procedures that adequately reflect the priorities and concerns of the local agency could be considered the best for that particular setting.

On the other hand, the concerns and priorities of many individuals and agencies are often misguided. Goals are adopted, priorities established, and evaluation procedures developed based on limited information. The results of misguided decisions range from exceedingly narrow views of the potential uses of computers to a blind commitment to computer-based learning as the solution for the ills of education. Neither position is accurate, but both affect the ways CAI lessons are evaluated. There must be a better way.

While we do not presume that our evaluation model is perfect, it includes the kinds of relevant, broad-based concerns that should be considered. Perhaps several additional components can be added to the model. We encourage the broadening of thinking on the number of factors that might be considered. For, while there are no perfect evaluation tools or models that can be prescribed for all learning settings, they all should consider CAI lessons in their broader context and not confine the decision to a single, narrow dimension.

Chapter Summary

It would be infinitely easier to simply describe evaluation as a discrete process conducted at the end of the design, production, and implementation stages of lesson development. The procedures and techniques could be described in exact detail, cause-and-effect relationships could be assigned easily, and the entire task of lesson evaluation could be presented as a ritualized process. This would simplify the process a good deal, but it would be both inefficient and misleading.

In systems approaches, evaluation is *part* of the design and development process. We constantly engage in evaluative procedures to improve lessons. Each planning decision, design decision, and production decision is subject to evaluative scrutiny of varying degrees because the development of CAI lessons is a *process* and not simply a singular event. The techniques employed during ongoing evaluation may be either formal or informal, but their purpose is unmistakably clear: to improve the likelihood that the resulting lesson will perform effectively.

In this chapter, we have directed a good deal of attention to the use of informal evaluation techniques. In part, this has been done due to the complexity of many of the more formal evaluation techniques. It is simply not possible to present these techniques in sufficient detail in a text such as this. Indeed, several notable authorities have written entire books on such procedures (see, for example, Niedermeyer, 1972; Worthen and Sanders, 1973).

The principal rationale for the emphasis on informal evaluation techniques, however, is due to their powerful potential to impact design and production decisions during the development cycle of the lesson. Decisions are made continuously during the CAI design and production. Necessary information is obtained most readily through informal evaluation techniques and with unusually high efficiency.

While we are certainly not advocating the elimination of formal evaluation techniques and procedures, we also do not condone the disregard or elimination of lesson evaluation efforts due to a lack of familiarity with formal techniques. Apply both formal and informal evaluative techniques whenever possible, but at a minimum, be certain to apply at least informal evaluative techniques to CAI lesson efforts.

References

BRADFORD, J. (1982). The software line-up: What reviewers look for when evaluating software. *Electronic Learning*, **2**(2), 45–48.

COHEN, V. B. (1983). Criteria for the evaluation of microcomputer courseware. *Educational Technology*, **23**(1), 9–14.

DEARBORN, D. E. (1982). A process for selecting computer software. *NASSP Bulletin,* **66**(455), 26–30.

DICK, W., and L. CAREY (1985). *The Systematic Design of Instruction* (2nd Ed.). Dallas, TX: Scott, Foresman, & Co.

GOLAS, K. C. (1983). The formative evaluation of computer-assisted instruction. *Educational Technology,* **23**(1), 26–28.

HOLZNAGEL, D. C. (1982–1985). *MicroSIFT Courseware Evaluations.* Portland, OR: Northwest Regional Educational Laboratory.

KING, F. J., and M. D. ROBLYER (1984). Alternative designs for evaluating computer-based instruction. *Journal of Instructional Development,* **7**(3), 23–29.

NEUMANN, R. (1982). How to find good software. *Electronic Learning,* **2**(2), 40–43.

NIEDERMEYER, F. C. (1972). *Prototype Testing in Instructional Development.* Los Alamitos, CA: Southwest Regional Laboratory.

WHOLEBEN, B. E. (1982). *MICROPIK: A Multiple Alternatives, Criterion-Referenced Decisioning Model for Evaluating CAI Software and Microcomputer Hardware Against Selected Curriculum Objectives.* Portland, OR: Northwest Regional Educational Laboratory.

WORTHEN, B. R., and J. R. SANDERS (1973). *Educational Evaluation: Theory and Practice.* Belmont, CA: Wadsworth.

Recommended Reading

BORICH, G. D., and R. P. JEMELKA (1981). Evaluation. In H. F. O'Neil (ed.) *Computer-Based Instruction: A State-of-the-Art Assessment.* New York: Academic Press.

JAY, T. B. (1983). The cognitive approach to computer courseware design and evaluation. *Educational Technology,* **23**(1), 22–25.

McPHERSON–TURNER, C. (1979). CAI readiness checklist: Formative author-evaluation of CAI lessons. *Journal of Computer-Based Instruction,* **6,** 47–49.

REEVES, T. C., and R. M. LENT (1984). Levels of evaluation for computer-based instruction. In D. R. Walker and R. D. Hess (eds.). *Instructional Software: Principles and Perspectives for Design and Use.* Belmont, CA: Wadsworth.

WAGER, W. (1981). Issues in the evaluation of instructional computing programs, *Educational Computer,* **1**(3), 20–22.

WALKER, D. R., and R. D. HESS (1984). Evaluation in courseware development. In D. R. Walker and R. D. Hess (eds.). *Instructional Software: Principles and Perspectives for Design and Use.* Belmont, CA: Wadsworth.

Chapter Review Exercises

COMPREHENSION

1. Describe the differences between formal and informal evaluation techniques. Describe circumstances where formal and informal techniques are appropriate. (See pages 299–300.)

2. List and describe the levels of evaluation appropriate for CAI. (See pages 299–303.)

3. List and describe the principal questions addressed during each stage of formative evaluation. (See pages 300–303.)

4. Describe the general categories of evaluation activity and the kinds of information yielded from each. (See pages 303–316.)

5. Describe situations where each category of evaluation is appropriate. (See pages 303–316.)

6. Describe the relevant hardware and sofeware considerations in the evaluation of CAI lessons. (See pages 316–322.)

APPLICATION

1. Develop a plan, incorporating both formal and informal techniques, to evaluate your CAI lesson.

2. Develop and implement a plan to evaluate the instructional adequacy of your CAI lesson. (See Figure 18.1.)

3. Develop and implement a plan to evaluate the cosmetic adequacy of your CAI lesson. (See Figure 18.1.)

4. Develop and implement a plan to evaluate the program adequacy of your CAI lesson. (See Figure 18.1.)

5. Develop and implement a plan to evaluate the curriculum adequacy of your CAI lesson. (See Figure 18.1.)

6. Develop and implement one-to-one formative evaluation procedures for your lesson. (See pages 301–302.)

7. Develop and implement small-group formative evaluation procedures for your lesson. (See page 302.)

8. Develop and implement field-test formative evaluation procedures for your lesson. (See pages 303–304.)

9. Design and implement procedures to evaluate the instructional, cosmetic, program, and curriculum adequacy of a commercially developed CAI lesson. (See pages 316–322 and Figure 18.1.)

CHAPTER 19

Revising CAI Lessons

To many, the task of revising instruction is very straightforward: Identify what went wrong and correct the flaw. In some cases, this is perfectly appropriate. The nature of the needed revisions is so apparent that changes can be made with a high degree of confidence and certainty.

However, deciding whether to revise, what to revise, how much to change, and whether to evaluate the changes can be very complex. The nature of needed revision may be unclear, the costs associated with the needed changes may be prohibitive, or perhaps the effects of the changes are likely to be inconsequential. Perhaps the lesson itself requires no revision at all, but initial assumptions may have been inaccurate or the performance expectations unrealistic. Is it reasonable to assume that lesson revisions are necessarily indicated based upon student performance deficiencies?

The purposes of this chapter are to examine alternative explanations for lesson failure, to describe the factors that influence whether lesson revision is necessary, and to present a framework for considering the kinds of revisions to be made.

OBJECTIVES

Comprehension

After completing this chapter you will be able to

1. Describe the importance of the revision process in closing the loop of the design, development, and evaluation process.
2. Describe the relationship between the evaluation and revision components of the CAI lesson design process in identifying needed revisions.
3. Describe the four basic ways that revisions might affect CAI lesson effectiveness.
4. Describe techniques for improving the instructional adequacy of a CAI lesson.
5. Describe techniques for improving the cosmetic adequacy of a CAI lesson.
6. Describe techniques for improving the program adequacy of a CAI lesson.
7. Describe techniques for improving the curriculum adequacy of a CAI lesson.
8. Describe the practical factors that influence whether revisions should be made.

Application

After completing this chapter you will be able to

1. Identify the cause of observed performance deficiencies in personally developed lessons.
2. Determine whether material revisions are needed based upon evaluative findings.
3. Revise CAI lessons to improve instructional adequacy.
4. Revise CAI lessons to improve cosmetic adequacy.
5. Revise CAI lessons to improve program adequacy.
6. Revise CAI lessons to improve curriculum adequacy.
7. Revise CAI lessons through the use of strategies that do not modify the basic lesson design.

Lesson Revision in a Systems Cycle

Formative lesson evaluation is a means, not an end. Ongoing evaluation helps to identify the shortcomings of a lesson and, it is hoped, the deficient lesson features or activities as well. Presumably this information will improve the lesson. But how will the information be used? Does the fact that a performance deficiency has been identified necessarily mean that revisions are required? If so, what kinds of revisions will be needed?

Virtually any draft or working version of a CAI lesson will undergo revision of one kind or another. The systems process is very useful in this regard, since revision occurs continuously throughout lesson design and development. Informal lesson evaluation occurs so continuously that major errors are usually detected before extensive effort is expended. The designer conceptualizes the lesson features, obtains input regarding the lesson design, makes revisions as needed, and so on until most significant problems have been identified and remedied *before* an extensive development effort. As a result, lessons will often have a high degree of success during the more formal field test or summative evaluation.

Revision in ISD Approaches: A Typical Case

A CAI lesson designer has been asked to produce a series of lessons pertaining to computation of the area of quadrilaterals. Lessons are sought for the area of a rectangle, square, rhombus, and trapezoid. The client, a curriculum director for a large school district, has specified that the lessons should be compatible with the styles and preferences of the teachers and has made it clear that the teachers must be involved in the design process. The teachers who will use the lessons are high school mathematics teachers with minimal previous experience in the integration of CAI lessons into classroom instruction. In addition, they have no previous experience working with a CAI lesson designer.

The designer could obtain initial input, then develop the materials in their entirety and deliver the lesson to the curriculum director for a formal evaluation.

However, this approach could create several problems. Could the designer be certain that the lesson procedures and protocol would be acceptable? Will the examples and practice be appropriate? Can the lesson be completed within the time constraints? It would be foolhardy indeed to leave such important issues to chance or until a formal tryout was conducted.

Instead, projects such as the one described usually consist of routine checkpoints, where the various components of the lesson are presented, described, and, in some cases, implemented on a small scale. The information gathered from these informal contacts is then used to make necessary modifications in the lesson design while the project is still very much in the development stage. Typically, minimal production effort is expended until the various design procedures have been verified, to establish their appropriateness and acceptability. In this example, the extensive use of informal evaluation techniques certainly reduces the potential for significant problems during formal evaluation.

Considerations for Determining Revisions

To understand the basis for making revision decisions, reconsider the process to the point where revision decisions are determined. The systems approach to lesson design has shaped lesson assumptions, specifications, design, development, and evaluation to this point. It is the systems approach itself that will be examined when considering whether revisions are desired or required.

INITIAL PLANNING ASSUMPTIONS

Throughout the design and development process, information that shapes the lesson is continuously obtained. A variety of data concerning the learners, the learning task, and the instructional setting are collected and used as basic assumptions in making decisions. When information is correct, good design decisions generally follow. When it is not correct, however, much time and effort can be expended doing work that is based upon misleading assumptions.

The accuracy of the information upon which a lesson is based must be considered. Imagine, for example, designing a lesson under the assumption that prospective users are proficient in all prerequisite skills. It would be assumed that no additional instruction in these areas is needed; the lesson would simply begin with new instruction. If students do not perform well during the lesson, is it possible that the information regarding prerequisite skills was mistaken? If so, the types of revisions required might involve the addition of missing components, not the revision of existing procedures.

The range of assumptions is widespread and has a profound effect on lesson design decisions. In the previous example, prerequisite skills were mistakenly estimated. However, consider some of the other assumptions that must be made. Assumptions such as reading abilities, the types of activities thought to be motivating for students, and the performance standard adopted for the objective all influence lesson designs. If they are inaccurate, the focus of the revision activities should be to obtain accurate information and perhaps to revise the instruction.

DESIGN STRATEGIES

Generally, lesson design strategies are most effective when they are based on empirically derived procedures. Such guidelines include the orientation, presentation, assimilation, and integration activities that are likely to aid student learning. The extent to which design strategies are sensible affects the probability that intended outcomes will be realized.

Consider the following instances where lesson design strategies are likely to require revision: one where an important strategy is missing altogether, and one where the strategy is present but is applied ineffectively. Consider the all-too-common example of lessons that teach fairly complex concepts, such as the written construction of sentences, but offer insufficient guidance and practice. The lesson presents the components of well-written sentences, the parts of sentences, and even several examples of well-written sentences. Upon completion of the lesson, the student is asked to write well-constructed sentences, as stated in the objective.

It is unlikely that such a lesson would enable students to write well-constructed sentences (unless, of course, they were already able to do so!). An important lesson design strategy, practice, was not provided during the lesson. The absence of a major design strategy makes the development of the target skills very improbable. Revision, in such cases, should focus on appropriate practice for the skills to be learned.

The mere presence of the strategies, however, in no way assures success. CAI often includes the basic components of effective lessons, but not properly. Assume that practice was provided during the preceding example. Perhaps the lesson included several questions where the student described sentence features such as the subject, verb, and object of the sentence or perhaps even identified the parts in sentences. Upon completion of the lesson, students were required to produce well-written sentences to demonstrate their mastery of lesson concepts.

The lesson provided a good deal of information and even some guidance and practice, but it did not provide practice that was appropriate to the skills required of the learner. The student practiced pieces of the skill but never actually constructed and wrote sentences during the lesson. The components of guidance and practice were present, but were not implemented effectively, given the intent of the lesson. In such cases, the design strategy should be revised to provide *appropriate* practice during the lesson.

Design templates such as the events of instruction (Gagné, Wager, and Rojas, 1981) help to ensure that important design strategies are included, but they do not necessarily ensure the quality of the strategies. Lesson revision may take the form of improving the student orientation to the lesson, modifying the examples to make them more relevant and meaningful, and increasing the amount of guidance and practice provided during a lesson. Templates simplify the process of revision by identifying the functions of the various features of the lesson and by structuring activities for each feature.

PRODUCTION FEATURES

Revisions are sometimes difficult to detect. When we see a problem with a lesson, we have to determine whether the problem is one of production, which can usually be easily remedied, or one of basic assumptions or design. Production errors are usually the most obvious. Revisions patch up the lesson in a cosmetic sense, either to correct display errors or to make the lesson more visually or aesthetically appealing. Production revisions do not alter the basic design strategies or the information of the lesson; they merely present the lesson in the most accurate and appealing manner possible.

Consider a lesson where the evaluation indicated successful attainment of target objectives by students, but several students identified typographical errors. In addition, it was discovered that students experienced difficulty in identifying certain objects represented in computer graphic form, as evidenced by student comments and by the strained viewing observed during that particular lesson segment. The error involves neither substantive information nor design strategies—just the method of lesson display. In such cases, production revisions could improve the appeal of the lesson and eliminate the cosmetic distractions.

EVALUATION PROCEDURES

Does the failure of a CAI lesson to perform well during formative evaluation mean that lesson revisions are needed? Not necessarily. Perhaps the most overlooked source for revision is the evaluation process itself. In some cases, the evaluation can result in *false positives*, where ineffective instruction appears effective, or *false negatives*, where an effective lesson appears ineffective due to the evaluation itself. Evaluation procedures are far from perfect and can yield information that is misleading and inaccurate.

Consider the following contrasting examples, where the evaluation procedures might themselves require revision before findings could be considered valid. A designer has produced a tutorial on the computation skills and vector geometry principles used in space travel. The lesson is complex and is designed for graduate-level students in astrophysics. The lesson requires highly developed math and physics skills, as well as knowledge of planet orbital patterns. Since there are relatively few individuals with this background, the designer must make do with a group of reasonably intelligent undergraduate students in mathematics. During the evaluation, however, students comment frequently that the lesson is confusing, makes little sense, and is otherwise ineffective.

Perhaps the comments should be taken at face value and revisions made to the lesson materials. On the other hand, it seems possible that the evaluation procedures might be contributors to poor performance. Perhaps the complexity of the learning task, the time constraints, and the absence of student motivation or interest during the evaluation influenced the outcomes. In effect, factors apart from the basic lesson design might contribute to poor evaluation findings. Additional study should be done prior to making substantive lesson revisions. If not, we might conclude incorrectly that the lesson required extensive revision based upon a less-than-ideal evaluation.

Suppose, however, that the reverse were the case. A lesson has been designed to teach undergraduate math students certain introductory college algebra concepts. During formative evaluation, advanced students are used. The findings indicate that students performed very well, understood the directions easily, and in general reacted positively toward the lesson. To conclude that the lesson was successful might be premature, since the students used for lesson evaluation were decidedly more advanced than the target students. Again, further evaluation would be required before it could be determined if, and where, revisions were required.

From Evaluation to Revision

The four levels of formative evaluation again provide the framework within which revision decisions will be made. Let's examine the types of revisions commonly made for each.

IMPROVING INSTRUCTIONAL ADEQUACY

Instructional adequacy is improved through revisions that are either substantive or that pertain to basic instructional design decisions. Usually the revisions affect such aspects as the directions, design strategies, or sequence of the lesson. Instructional revisions are made to improve the clarity, order, and ease of processing of the lesson content.

1. *Edit for substantive errors*. Lesson accuracy *must* be assured. In cases where the designer is proficient in the subject matter, major substantive revisions are rarely required. When the CAI designer works with a subject-matter expert in the design of a lesson, however, the possibility of factual inaccuracies increases. Revisions must be made to ensure that the information contained in the lesson is accurate and appropriate.

2. *Strengthen orientation information*. Sometimes major lesson revisions can be avoided by improving the orientation information and activities provided to students. It is far simpler, when possible, to orient the student more effectively to the purpose and expectations of the lesson than to alter the basic lesson design. Motivational techniques designed to heighten student interest, for example, could be added. If the lesson is marginally (as opposed to extremely) ineffective, it may be useful to focus on lesson orientation information and procedures.

3. *Clarify directions*. Lesson failure does not necessarily mean that design strategies were ineffective. It may be the result of inadequate information to the students to guide their interaction. If students are unsure how to interact during a lesson, the lesson will inevitably fail. Revising directions for completeness and clarity can be a very efficient alternative to wholesale lesson changes.

4. *Align objectives, assessment, and instruction*. In some cases, lessons are simply misaligned. The objective states one skill, the instruction focuses on a second, and the assessment is directed toward neither. All must be in accordance before we can gauge student performance accurately. Revisions of this type may affect any combination of objectives, instruction, or test questions.

5. *Eliminate dead wood*. Information that does not serve an identifiable purpose should be eliminated. Dead wood often does more than slow the learning process; it can direct student attention to unimportant information. At times the elimination of such information from lessons, by itself, aids in clarifying lesson focus and directing student attention more effectively.

6. *Strengthen interaction and guidance*. Make certain that lessons encourage student participation and that students are provided sufficient guidance during the lesson. Often both can be accomplished simultaneously. The basic sequence of a lesson may be appropriate but may not systematically encourage students to engage the lesson information. Increasing criterion-related questioning should help the students to learn more effectively.

7. *Incorporate learning strategies*. As an alternative to extensive revision of lesson organization, the inclusion of strategies to aid learning should be considered. It is

simpler to help students to identify relationships than to engage in extensive revision of the basic lesson design. Learning strategies will likely be effective if performance deficiencies are not too extensive.

8. *Incorporate information transfer activities*. Techniques that aid students in generalizing knowledge may improve lesson outcomes. Transfer strategies broaden the base of information available for learning lesson information and enable some students to comprehend lesson information using both the current lesson and other knowledge sources.

9. *Modify step size*. In most cases, lesson step size will be reduced if it is changed at all. This allows students to focus attention at each step and avoids the problem of presenting too much information at one time. It is also possible to increase step size, although this occurs infrequently.

10. *Revise pacing techniques*. On occasion it may be useful to modify certain lesson-control features. This may be especially true when timed pacing is used to control lesson execution, if the time selected may be too much or too slow. If pacing revisions are to be made, consider the adoption of combined timing–student control for lesson execution.

11. *Alter basic design strategy*. During the early stages of lesson design, the basic strategy is examined repeatedly for possible revision. This is because revisions are easy to make at this stage, and little effort is lost if revisions are required. During later stages, however, changes in basic design can be extremely difficult and costly. Materials have been developed, programming completed, and a host of other lesson development efforts undertaken. Try to identify needed design revisions early to avoid these problems. If problems result later in the development cycle, consider the incorporation of learning strategies or more powerful orientation activities, if feasible, before revising the lesson design extensively. Wholesale design changes should be rare in systems approaches and should usually be considered a last resort.

IMPROVING COSMETIC ADEQUACY

Revisions of a cosmetic nature focus on the improvement of the appearance of the lesson and not on its substantive or design aspects. Cosmetic revisions are especially important in promoting the acceptability and visual appeal of the lesson. Lessons that are effective but unappealing to learners can be revised by using computer capabilities such as color or by organizing frames more clearly. Cosmetic revisions improve lesson appearance sufficiently to be a dominant source of revision for many lessons.

1. *Reduce frame density*. CAI frames that appear cluttered may detract from student perceptions of the lesson, as well as from their performance during the lesson. Many frames are simply too crowded and do not direct viewer attention systematically. In some cases, information may need to be deleted or shortened. In others, the general organization of the frame may require revision.

2. *Modify frame protocol*. In some lessons, frame protocol can be so complex that it actually distracts learners. The uncontrolled use of color, for example, can inadvertently detract from the substantive information that protocol was designed to support. Perhaps the locations of the different zones of the frame are awkward, thereby causing confusion. The techniques used for organizing the information contained in the frame might require reconsideration.

3. *Improve image clarity.* Some images in CAI lessons may be difficult to identify. Graphic representations of complex visual objects, for example, can be very difficult due to limitations of the computer. Likewise, lessons incorporating synthesized speech, a type of computer-generated speech, can be difficult to understand. Efforts to improve the fidelity of lesson images and features are often required.

4. *Incorporate amplification techniques.* To further direct viewer attention, it is often useful to apply certain other computer capabilities. Highlighting words, incorporating sound, and infusing several of the other machine-based amplification techniques can be used to make the instruction more appealing and effective.

5. *Correct typographical errors.* The easiest revisions to make are those that require simple correction to comply with universally accepted conventions. Spelling errors, for example, *always* require correction. With some exceptions, errors of this type are usually not critical to the concepts taught, but they are cosmetically distracting and unnecessary. The credibility of lessons can be hindered if fundamental revisions of this type are not made.

IMPROVING PROGRAM ADEQUACY

Program revisions are more or less dictated by the extent to which lesson execution matches the prescribed specifications. If a lesson does not execute as intended, program revisions are inevitable. This aspect of lesson development has the least to do with the decisions about how best to teach information to students, but the most to do with the actual presentation and operation of the CAI lesson. If lessons are not programmed effectively, we have two choices: Revise our expectations or revise the program itself. In most cases, the latter is done.

1. *Correct programming or authoring errors.* Depending on the sophistication of the design and the complexity of the program, program errors can either be very straightforward or deceptively complicated to detect and revise. Mistyped commands, for example, will usually be rejected by the computer and, as a result, are easy to detect and revise. Branching errors will sometimes be obvious, resulting in lesson activities that are clearly inappropriate. Other errors are more difficult to identify because they are less apparent to the eye. For example, a lesson may branch correctly under all but one prescribed condition, forcing the programmer to trace the lesson logic and program precisely to locate the error. Errors of this type *must* be corrected.

2. *Eliminate infinite loops.* Infinite programming loops are usually easy to detect. Even untrained programmers will sense *déjà vu* as they proceed through a lesson. Conceptual loops, however, can be more troublesome. Usually conceptual loops result from failure to anticipate the conceptual difficulty of lesson content or failure to limit the number of trails for each question. Revisions may affect either form. In some cases, expanding the response management capabilities of the lesson may suffice. For other problems, it may make sense to limit errors by restricting the number of times a student can respond incorrectly to a question.

3. *Reduce disk management requirements.* Lessons can be revised to minimize the physical disk manipulation that is required to use a lesson. The process of making CAI lessons self-starting is very simple and reduces the needs for external management by either teacher or student. In addition, lessons can be revised for access through menus or through manipulating the internal logic of the lesson to

automatically locate and run the next, or most appropriate, lesson. It is usually unnecessary to require both excessive handling of lesson disks and needless searches for follow-up activities or lessons.

4. *Improve lesson security.* Though it is not often a major concern during the initial design phase, the issue of security is increasingly important for more refined lessons. Revisions designed to secure the performance records of students through the use of passwords are occasionally made. In other cases, it may be necessary to secure the lesson code or the disk itself from tampering, causing the programmer to include system-level security.

5. *Modify program to improve display accuracy.* Revisions affecting display accuracy are usually fairly easy to make. Generally, this kind of error requires direct changes to specific program statements and can be made readily.

IMPROVING CURRICULUM ADEQUACY

Because it is important to the successful installation of CAI lessons, revisions designed to improve the curriculum compatibility of a lesson are often essential. Consistent with evaluation findings, revisions of this type focus on the lesson procedures, time constraints, and compatibility with existing and related curricula. The revisions can be sweeping, resulting in basic changes in design strategies, or minor, such as requiring only the production of response summaries consistent with existing record-keeping requirements.

1. *Incorporate similar thematic information.* One of the most important characteristics to consider is the extent to which the themes included in lessons are compatible with those of the local agency. For example, many school districts attempt to incorporate science concepts in mathematics and language arts lessons. The nature of the examples selected, and the general orientation of the lesson, might be slanted toward the thematic biases of the agency. These are best identified beforehand to minimize subsequent revisions, but they must often be made later as well.

2. *Modify procedures and features for consistency.* If software exists that is popular with users, it may be preferable to employ procedures similar to those already proven popular or successful. In some cases, the client may specify the kinds of procedures or control options desired; in others, nothing might be said. However, it is often useful to examine those lessons that are popular and unpopular. Since revisions can constitute major changes later in the development process, try to identify such preferences as early as possible.

3. *Assure expandability to other lessons.* Try to avoid making instructional decisions, or designing instructional software, that cannot be built upon. Lessons perceived as too different procedurally will be difficult to integrate into other instructional activities and, as a result, they may not be used. Consider the probability of developing related lessons to precede and follow single CAI lessons, and make sure that the procedures, methods, and protocol that are used will transfer readily.

4. *Eliminate unnecessary obsolescence.* Eliminate information from the lesson that is likely to become obsolete quickly. This problem is often found in the examples selected, the thematic context of the lesson, and the vocabulary used. Words like

groovy might have been timely for students of the 1960s, but they would be considered corny (if understood at all!) today.

5. *Revise to meet running-time requirements.* Make certain that the lesson can be completed within the time constraints specified during needs assessment. In some cases, the identification of dead wood and excessive instruction will help to limit running time. Lessons that cannot be integrated into the time frames available cannot be implemented.

6. *Improve the flexibility of the lesson.* When possible, design or revise lessons to permit some degree of user-prescribed control. For example, depending on the nature of the option, allow the teacher or student to specify features such as the number of attempts permitted for embedded questions, the number of examples to be provided, the use of computer sound effects, and other options likely to broaden acceptance of the lesson.

7. *Account for hardware differences.* Be prepared to alter features such as color depending on the availability and capability of different computer monitors. In addition, while the printing of student performance summaries may be a good idea, printers may not be available under all circumstances of lesson use. Again, the use of flexible options within lessons may allow the user to specify those features available in each setting. If not, lessons may need to be revised to ensure that the basic lesson will execute appropriately using the different hardware combinations.

8. *Provide necessary user support.* One of the most important features of current CAI software is the extent to which user support and documentation are provided. The documentation may include recommendations for implementation, troubleshooting guides, additional activities to support the lesson, and other information that will improve the use of the lesson.

9. *Account for social and cultural mores.* The social and cultural consciousness of prospective users has increased a great deal. Sex-role stereotyping, for example, should be avoided. The examples employed should reflect a wide range of ethnic and cultural values, with groups represented equitably and without bias. Gender-specific pronouns such as *he* and *she* should be used in all employment contexts, not simply in those with which gender has been traditionally associated. Review the lesson for possible social and cultural bias and plan to revise in order to create an appropriate balance.

Chapter Summary

Often revision is mistakenly viewed as a final step in the design, development, and evaluation cycle. Lessons are seen as planned, designed, developed, and then evaluated in a sequential, linear fashion. Revision is thought to occur after all other steps have been completed; it is thought to be an end unto itself.

Unfortunately, this misperception is quite common. From a systems perspective, nothing could be further from the truth. No part of a system exists in isolation from other parts. All parts are mutually interdependent, causing the decisions made during one phase to affect the decisions of all other phases. Systems are continuous, with no rigidly defined end point. Regardless of the stage of development, changes can be made if required. This is the essence of a system and the basis for the efficiency of systems-based approaches to CAI lesson development.

It is appropriate to consider revision as a potential part of every aspect of the systems model. Revision in systems-based approaches is ongoing, occurring at every level of the systems process. When we examine the needs of a particular setting, we must also consider the possibility of altering the way those needs are defined. When designing instruction, we must continually reconsider decisions, making revisions as necessary. Each component of the system and all of the corresponding decisions can be altered.

The decision to revise a lesson must include all aspects of the process. We cannot always conclude that the end product will require change, but we must consider the process as a whole to determine the necessity for revision. This may not always simplify the process of revision, but it is certain to improve the resulting decisions.

References

GAGNÉ, R., W. WAGER, and A. ROJAS (1981). Planning and authoring computer-assisted instruction lessons. *Educational Technology*, **21**, 17–26.

Related Reading

DICK, W., and L. CAREY (1985). *The Systematic Design of Instruction* (2nd ed.). Dallas, TX: Scott, Foresman, & Co.

GROPPER, G. L. (1975). *Diagnosis and Revision in the Development of Instructional Materials*. Englewood Cliffs, NJ: Educational Technology Publications.

Chapter Review Exercises

COMPREHENSION

1. Describe the importance of revision in closing the loop of the design, development, and evaluation process. (See page 327.)
2. Describe the relationship between the evaluation and revision components of the CAI design process in identifying needed revisions. (See pages 327–328.)
3. Describe the four basic ways that revisions might improve CAI lesson adequacy. (See pages 328–330.)
4. Describe techniques for improving the instructional adequacy of a lesson. (See pages 331–332.)
5. Describe techniques for improving the cosmetic adequacy of a lesson. (See pages 332–333.)
6. Describe techniques for improving the program adequacy of a lesson. (See pages 333–334.)
7. Describe techniques for improving the curriculum adequacy of a lesson. (See pages 334–335.)
8. Describe the practical factors that influence whether revisions are made. (See page 326.)

APPLICATION

1. For a personally developed CAI lesson, identify the cause(s) of performance deficiencies. (See pages 328–330.)
2. Determine whether material revisions are needed, based on evaluative findings. (See pages 329–330.)
3. Revise the lesson to improve instructional adequacy. (See pages 331–332.)
4. Revise the lesson to improve cosmetic adequacy. (See pages 332–333.)
5. Revise the lesson to improve program adequacy. (See pages 333–334.)
6. Revise the lesson to improve curriculum adequacy. (See pages 334–335.)
7. Revise the lesson by employing adaptive techniques that do not alter the basic lesson design. (See page 329.)

SECTION VII

The Status and Future of CAI

In Sections I through VI, you learned to design effective CAI programs, making use of the standard microcomputer systems available today. In this section, we will examine capabilities available when one moves beyond what is currently standard. We will look at options available now and those that will become available as technology progresses.

Chapter 20 examines devices that may be added to microcomputer systems to provide increased functionality or to make the machine more appropriate for specific learner or task characteristics. Chapter 21 discusses technologies that combine the computer's ability to individualize and involve the student with video, slides, and audio segments to produce a combination that is more powerful than these media separately. A discussion of major opportunities for CAI in the near future, including the emergence of larger CAI networks and intelligent CAI (ICAI) is included as Chapter 22.

SECTION GOALS

After completing this section you will

1. Understand alternatives to conventional input and output devices and understand the advantages and disadvantages of using these alternatives.
2. Understand significant trends in microcomputer hardware and software and understand the impact these trends are likely to have on CAI.

3. Understand interactive video and other combinations in which computers control other media to meet instructional objectives.
4. Understand microcomputer networking and its implications.
5. Understand how artificial intelligence is likely to influence CAI in the near future.
6. Understand the impact that the quality of the courseware written in the next few years will have on the acceptance of computers in education and training.

CHAPTER 20

Hardware, Software, and CAI

As design decisions are made based on student, task, and environmental considerations, the conventional means for accepting student input or presenting information may not be appropriate. Fortunately, there are several options available, and the number of such alternatives is increasing steadily.

In this chapter, we examine alternative methods for accepting input *from* the student as well as alternative means of presenting information *to* the student. After the options currently available are examined, trends in hardware and software technology and the impact that these trends will have on the CAI systems of the near future will be explored.

OBJECTIVES

Comprehension

After completing this chapter you will be able to

1. Define the term *peripheral device*.
2. List and describe at least three alternatives to the keyboard as an input device during CAI.
3. List and describe at least three alternatives to displaying computer output that may be used to interactively present information during CAI.
4. Discuss the advantages and disadvantages associated with alternative input and output devices.
5. Discuss trends in microcomputer hardware and software and the impact these are likely to have on CAI.

Definition of Peripheral Devices

The typical CAI station employs a keyboard to accept student input and a video monitor to present computer output to the student. A keyboard is a very flexible device, capable of producing words, sentences, paragraphs, numbers, cursor movements, and keystrokes that have special meanings in CAI lessons. However, the keyboard is not always the optimal way to accept input from the student. Likewise, although the standard video monitor included with most CAI stations is

341

capable of displaying both text and graphics, it may not be the best way of relaying information to the student. Fortunately, several additional options are available.

In the context of computers and CAI, a *peripheral device*, or simply a *peripheral*, is one that exists outside the strict limits of the computer system itself. Examples of peripherals include printers, graphics tablets, joysticks, and even videotape and videodisk players. The purpose of these devices is to expand the capabilities of the computer to which they are attached. Although computer manufacturers produce rather generic products, the owners of more popular models have many options, some developed by the computer manufacturer and some by companies specializing in peripheral products. These options allow computer users to adapt machines to meet specific needs or wishes.

Most computer systems have *expansion slots* inside the computer, into which circuit boards may be inserted, or *ports*, to which cables from peripheral devices may be attached. Note that peripherals designed specifically to work with one computer system may not work on another. On the other hand, many peripherals, such as printers, are designed to be compatible with several computers.

This discussion of peripheral devices is divided into input devices, used to send student responses to the computer, and output devices, used to send information from the computer to the student.

Input Devices

KEYBOARDS

The standard input device used in CAI is the keyboard, illustrated in Figure 20.1. Microcomputer keyboards generally look and act like typewriter keyboards with a few additional keys. When the student presses a key, a signal is sent from the keyboard to the computer, where it is interpreted. Through a series of keystrokes, it becomes possible for the computer to accept words, sentences, and paragraphs as well as single letters, characters, or numbers.

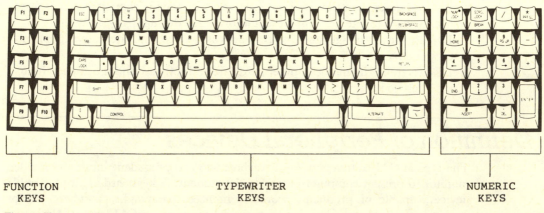

FUNCTION KEYS   TYPEWRITER KEYS   NUMERIC KEYS

Figure 20.1
Typical microcomputer keyboard.

Microcomputer keyboards are generally composed of three or more sections. The central section on most microcomputer keyboards resembles the typing area on a standard typewriter. It is used to enter upper-case and lower-case letters and numbers. One or two specialized *control* keys are generally added to this area as well. Control keys are used in combination with other keys to send special signals to the computer or printer. For example, control keys are commonly employed to interrupt the execution of the CAI program. Although most computer systems are equipped with the *QWERTY* layout found on standard typewriters, a new type of keyboard is gaining popularity. This keyboard arranges the letters differently, to maximize typing speed, thereby increasing the productivity of operators whose main function is to enter large amounts of text. Since typing speed should have little to do with most CAI lessons, it is unlikely that this new keyboard will have much impact on CAI during the next several years.

A second area generally found on microcomputer keyboards contains *programmable function keys*. The programmer of CAI lessons may assign meanings to these keys. For example, one of the programmable, or *soft*, function keys may be used as a *review key*, through which the students may indicate the desire to repeat a concept already presented. Or a programmable function key may be used to indicate that a student is ready to jump to the posttest rather than continuing the lesson.

A third area on most microcomputer keyboards is the *numeric keypad*. Keys in this area are similar in layout and function to the keys found on calculators and adding machines. The numeric keypad is generally used for entering large amounts of numeric data. Another function commonly assigned to the numeric keypad is cursor control. Certain keys in this area are used to move the cursor up, down, and to the right and the left.

The major advantage of using the keyboard as an input device during CAI is flexibility. By using the keyboard, a student may enter single letters, numbers, words, paragraphs, or even pages of information. By pressing one of the programmable function keys, a student may execute any of a series of options designed into the lesson. Another major advantage of the keyboard as input device is low cost. Virtually all microcomputer systems are equipped with a keyboard as part of the base price of the system.

The major disadvantage of keyboards as input devices in CAI is the danger of confusing the inability to type with inadequate knowledge of a correct answer. Younger students, handicapped students, and students who do not type well may experience difficulty in responding, although they actually know tested information. Another disadvantage is that the keyboard seems to encourage the use of multiple-choice or true–false questions in order to minimize typing requirements and to simplify answer judging. A third disadvantage of keyboards is that they make it difficult for students to point to things on the screen. Objectives with action verbs such as *identify, locate, choose,* or *select* imply that the student will discriminate from among several options. Ideally the student would point to the correct answer and the computer would understand the student's response directly. Using the keyboard as an input device for pointing requires that the student either press cursor movement keys repeatedly to move from place to place on the keyboard or select items by label, a task requiring an additional level of abstraction that may interfere with evaluation of the attainment of learning objectives and may diminish the efficiency of the lesson.

TOUCH SCREENS

Touch screens allow the student to respond by pointing to sections of the screen. Usually touch screens employ a transparent membrane placed over the front of the computer's monitor. By using what is referred to as resistive membrane technology pressure on the front of the screen is translated into signals that may be processed by the computer system. The most sensitive touch screens are capable of identifying the location touched to within one millimeter.

Common uses of touch screens include responses to true–false, multiple-choice, and matching questions; selection from menus; and the ability to select from and interact with graphic images on the screen. A simple touch screen is illustrated in Figure 20.2.

Advantages of touch screens include the ability to evaluate student knowledge without relying heavily on typing skills, to allow young children and handicapped students to use CAI, and to eliminate the use of symbolic or abstract response formats that complicate the evaluation of learning.

Some significant disadvantages are associated with the use of touch screens as well. Touch screens are often too expensive to be widely used in CAI applications; the addition of a touch screen may add several hundred dollars to the cost of each CAI station. Because programming for touch screens requires special commands not provided in most authoring systems and languages, their use often requires a special programming language and specialized knowledge on the part of the programmer. Lessons written for touch-screen computers will not run on machines without them. Portability from location to location and marketability of lessons are jeopardized by using touch screens.

The availability of the touch screen tends to promote use even when instructional objectives indicate that this is inappropriate. For example, when given a touch screen, many designers are tempted to write true–false or multiple-choice assessment items. Although these questions are appropriate for some objectives, the use of verbs like *write, list, define, state,* or *discuss* are not evaluated adequately through the use of touch screens. A common solution to this problem is to use

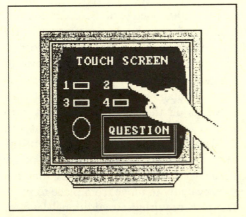

Figure 20.2
Touch screen.

both the touch screen and the keyboard as indicated by the response specified in each instructional objective.

LIGHT PENS

Light pens, often used by the developers of CAI lessons to produce graphic images for display to the student during the lesson, may also be employed to accept student responses during CAI. Illustrated in Figure 20.3, a light pen is similar to a touch screen. The student touches the screen with a pointer connected by wires to the computer. The advantages associated with the use of light pens are virtually the same as those described for touch screens. In addition to the disadvantages identified for touch screens, light pens often present other nuisances. The wire connecting the pen to the computer can be awkward. The need to pick up and put down the pen each time the mode of response changes between the pen and the keyboard can also be inconvenient.

Light pens preceded touch screens. Because of advances in touch-screen technology, light pens are becoming less prominent as lesson input devices, but they maintain popularity in the development of graphics for display during CAI.

MICE

A mouse, in computer terminology, is a small pointing device connected by wire to the computer. Mice were developed to select or move items on the screen. As the mouse is moved across a desk, its movements are translated into movements on the screen. If it moves to the left, the cursor or any other item under the control of the mouse moves to the left. If it is moved diagonally, the diagonal movement is replicated on the screen. As illustrated in Figure 20.4, a mouse is equipped with one or more buttons, one of which is similar in function to the ⟨Return⟩ key. By moving the mouse to indicate the appropriate position and then pressing a button, the user may select from items on the screen.

Advantages and disadvantages of the mouse as an input device in CAI include those identified for light pens and touch screens. An additional disadvantage is that the use of a mouse adds a level of abstraction not present in devices used to

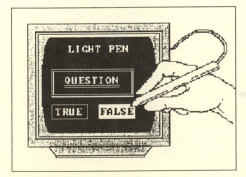

Figure 20.3
Light pen.

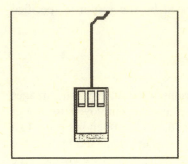

Figure 20.4
Mouse.

point directly at objects on the screen. The student actually moves the mouse on a desktop, which in turn moves another object on the screen. Although adult learners generally adapt quickly, younger learners may experience trouble.

GRAPHICS TABLETS

Although used primarily for the creation of computerized images and artwork, the graphics tablet may also be used as an input device during CAI. A sample graphics tablet is illustrated in Figure 20.5. Equipment generally consists of a drawing surface placed beside the computer and a pen with which drawing is done. Graphics tablets function in a manner similar to light pens and touch screens, with two notable exceptions. The pen may or may not be wired directly to the tablet and, like a mouse, drawings are made on the pad itself rather than on the computer monitor.

The applications, advantages, and disadvantages of touch screens, mice, and light pens are present in graphics tablets as well. An advantage over touch screens is the increase in accuracy afforded by graphics tablets. An intricate grid of wires lies below the surface of the tablet. Since the tablet need not be transparent, these wires may be placed extremely close together. The intricacy of the grid combined with a fine-tipped pointing instrument improves the accuracy immensely.

Graphics tablets, like mice, require that the student identify a position on the tablet that corresponds to the desired position on the screen. This complexity makes

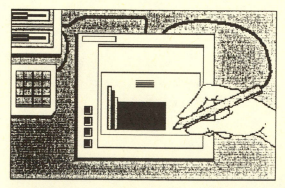

Figure 20.5
Graphics tablet.

graphics tablets less desirable than touch screens or light pens for younger students but still preferable to a keyboard in many instances. Unlike the mouse, however, this limitation may be minimized by placing a template over the tablet. For example, a sheet of paper containing areas labeled *true, false, A, B, C, D, yes, no,* and other recurring answers may be placed on the surface of the tablet before the lesson begins. By looking at the tablet, the student can identify where to touch to indicate anticipated answers.

JOYSTICKS

Joysticks, illustrated in Figure 20.6, are controls similar in function and appearance to the controls used in popular video games. By pushing the control stick to the left, to the right, forward, backward, or diagonally, the student drives the position of the cursor or another object on the computer screen. The joystick generally contains a button which is used to indicate a selection once the cursor or object has been placed over the desired location on the screen.

Because they do not interfere with the student's view of the screen, as do touch screens and light pens, and because they do not require abstract motion across a remote surface, as a mouse and graphics tablet do, joysticks are frequently used in educational games. They are often superior to other input devices for this purpose. Although joysticks may be used to select items visible on the computer screen, they are generally more cumbersome for this task than the other means of selection just described above.

VOICE RECOGNITION

At times it is very useful to eliminate the need for keyboards, mice, light pens, graphics tablets, and touch screens and simply permit students to talk directly to the computer. Voice-recognition devices accept verbal student input through a microphone and translate this information into voice-print patterns recognizable by the computer. The computer then compares this pattern to a set of anticipated patterns and responds based on this comparison. Like other student responses, the input may be classified as correct, incorrect, or unanticipated, and the computer responses may vary accordingly.

The potential of voice recognition exceeds its present capability. The current state of voice-recognition technology often imposes significant restrictions that

Figure 20.6
Joystick.

limit its usefulness. In other words, although voice recognition is available in a limited form today, the technology required to make this process viable on a significant scale has not yet been developed. For example, because the voice prints for different students vary, each student must prerecord anticipated responses to be used in the lesson. The computer files these responses for recall at the appropriate times to determine if the response pattern matches the one recorded earlier. Because current microcomputer systems work with relatively small amounts of memory and storage, it becomes necessary to severely limit the responses the student will be asked to supply. Before a typical lesson using voice recognition begins, the student may be asked to speak several words as they appear on the computer screen. Common inputs recorded include *true, false, yes, no, up, down, left, right, stop, go*, the letters from *A* to *Z*, and the numbers from one to ten.

As long as these limitations exist, voice recognition will be applied on a limited scale. At this point, it is not yet feasible to evaluate free-form natural-language verbal responses as an effective teacher would. Developmental laboratories are making progress in this area. In their efforts to produce a device that converts dictated input into typed output without human intervention, researchers are making progress that will eventually be applied to CAI to solve the current problems with voice recognition. Voice recognition will, in the not-too-distant future, become a viable means of accepting input in CAI. For now, the keyboard remains the most practical option for complex answers.

Advantages of voice recognition in its current state include the ability to eliminate the use of other input devices and the ability to make computers available to younger and handicapped students. Disadvantages include the limited nature of the responses allowed, relatively high costs currently associated with voice-recognition hardware, the requirement for commands not present in authoring systems or languages, and the restricted portability of lessons developed to accept voice input.

Output Devices

VIDEO DISPLAYS

Most computer systems include video display monitors. All video displays can present text to the user, most can present graphics as well, and many can present text and graphics at the same time.

Video images are produced by illuminating concentrated sets of minute dots, or *pixels*, beneath the surface of the screen. Under close inspection, even text characters may be seen as patterns of dots that collectively are perceived as a character. *Resolution* is a term that describes the number of dots available on the screen. The higher the resolution, the more tiny dots come together to form the letters and images displayed. With higher resolution, text becomes easier to read, drawings have smoother curves, and more detail may be represented. High-resolution monitors may be purchased to upgrade most standard computer systems.

The two major advantages of video displays as output devices for CAI are flexibility and cost. Nearly any display imaginable can be represented to some degree as a video display. Unlike printers, which work sequentially from the top of the page to the bottom and are unable to retrace their steps and modify outputs, the video monitor provides a dynamic surface that may change as the designer prescribes. For example, the screen may be filled with a display illustrating how a plant appears at sunrise. The image may then be changed repeatedly by erasing and adding to small sections of the drawing and by changing labels to reflect the changes the plant goes through during the day. Color may be used to focus student attention on the aspects of the drawing that have changed most recently. Such sequences allow the designer to convey concepts such as motion and change that are difficult to convey with other media.

Disadvantages of video displays as output devices for CAI include the inability to produce realistic images. Although there are times when a line drawing is effective in meeting an instructional objective, there are also times when a realistic image is critical. No matter how true a computer-generated graphic may be, it cannot compete with an actual photograph or motion picture when teaching topics such as surgery or the use of color in impressionistic art.

It is possible to convert photographs or drawings to computer graphics. The process generally involves the use of a camera that converts an image into dots corresponding to the screen and determines the color of each dot. Although this digitizing process results in images of impressive quality on large computer systems, microcomputer technology often yields inferior images that consume inordinate amounts of memory and storage resource.

Another weakness relates to the quality of text display. The resolution of even the best video displays does not compete favorably with the resolution available on a printed page. Characters on the monitor are not as easily read as letters on paper, and the 80-character column width on many computer monitors, as well as over-sized characters used in some programs, require extraordinary eye movements, thereby reducing reading speed and comfort.

PRINTERS

Microcomputer output may be sent to a printer as well as to a video display. The many different types of printers available fall into two major categories: dot matrix printers and character, or letter-quality, printers.

Dot matrix printers form letters much as they are formed on the computer screen, by printing patterns of tightly spaced dots to represent letters, numbers, and special characters. Resolution is a factor in dot matrix printing, in much the same manner as in video display monitors. The more dots the printer can place per inch, the better the image. Most dot matrix printers can produce graphics as well as text and numeric output.

There are three principal varieties of dot matrix printers: impact printers, ink jet printers, and laser printers. In impact dot matrix printers, tiny wires push an inked ribbon against paper to form the dot patterns. Ink jet printers shoot tiny droplets of ink at the paper to produce each dot. Some ink jet printers use colored inks and are capable of mixing these inks to produce many colors from four basic colored inks. Ink jet printers are rapidly gaining in popularity because they are fast, quiet, and inexpensive and produce high-quality output.

Laser printers work in a manner that resembles photocopier technology. In a photocopier, a bright light is reflected off the original and onto a drum that has been coated with a photosensitive layer. After the image has been reflected onto the drum, it is transferred to the paper. In laser printers, there is no original from which light may be reflected to the drum. Instead, a microprocessor controls the movements of mechanisms that reflect a laser beam's light onto the surface of the drum, exposing the photosensitive layer. This image is then transferred to the paper. Laser printers are very fast and produce output of impressive quality, but they are too expensive for locations where the requirements for high-quality print, or hard copy, output are not substantial.

Character, or letter-quality, printers are similar to a typewriter, in that a metal or plastic impression of the letter or character to be printed presses an inked ribbon against the paper to produce each character. This process produces higher quality output than is currently available from dot matrix printers, but it is generally slower and more expensive; and it requires more maintenance than the dot matrix options. Character printers generally do not print graphics. Although it is possible to combine characters to produce simple diagrams and charts, applications that include graphics usually require dot matrix printing capability.

Printers are not typically used as the only output device during CAI. This is because printing is slower than displaying information on the screen and because printouts of much of what happens during a CAI lesson are not necessary after the lesson is complete. In addition, CAI lessons often move the cursor over existing information and use animation and overlays, which printers are incapable of handling appropriately.

Printers offer several significant benefits as output devices in CAI. One of the common problems with many CAI programs is that the student has nothing tangible when the lesson ends. Unlike text-based learning, there is generally no easy way for the student to review, study, or regain access to the information presented during CAI after the lesson has ended. By combining printers with video displays, this limitation may be overcome. For example, at the end of each instructional unit, you might want to print summaries or posttests showing the questions, student answers, and the correct answers. Use printers in conjunction with video displays to gain the benefits associated with each.

VOICE SYNTHESIS

Just as it is possible to accept auditory input from the student, it is also possible to generate auditory output to the student. One process that accomplishes this is called voice synthesis because it involves the assembly of sound units. Instead of sending words, phrases, or sentences to the computer screen, voice-synthesis units decode words into *phonemes*, or sound units. The digital representations of these phonemes are sent to a voice-synthesis unit, where they are decoded to produce recognizable, though relatively mechanical, speech through headphones or a small speaker. As is the case with voice recognition, this technology is not yet fully appropriate for use in CAI. The auditory output produced by voice synthesis sounds mechanical and requires equipment often costing as much as or more than the original microcomputer itself.

As the technology evolves, the quality of the speech produced will improve, the costs will decline, and synthesizing voice output will become appropriate for more CAI applications. For now, however, other alternatives that combine computer control with audio playback rather than synthesis produce better quality. These options are described briefly here and in more detail in Chapter 21.

DIGITIZED AUDIO

Digitized audio is another means of adding random access to voice and other audio information to CAI presentations. This technique records input from a microphone onto floppy diskettes or one or more hard discs. The CAI program may branch and call audio segments in any order, much as screens are used in conventional CAI. Because of the minimal surface area on which to record and the massive amount of information carried in patterns of sound waves, digitized audio must use techniques to conserve storage space. Unlike typical magnetic audio recording, the digitizing process does not create one long, continuous recording. The process is more like a movie, where the illusion of continuity is created by playing many still segments rapidly, back to back. Digitized audio samples the sounds entering the microphone many times per second, recording digital information about the incoming sound. This information will be used at playback to recreate seemingly continuous sound.

Because even samples take up a lot of storage space, most digital audio products allow the developer to record at different sampling rates. Increasing the number of samples per second will result in more accurate reproduction but will consume more storage. Female voices seem to reproduce better than male voices due to the differences in frequency of male and female voices and characteristics of the sampling process.

Digital audio is a viable option for CAI designers, especially in cases where learner characteristics make it important to minimize or eliminate demands on reading skills. However, the cost of the hardware required, usually an expansion board installed inside a personal computer, is approximately equivalent to, if not higher than, attaching a videodisc player and a controller card ($700 to $800). Since the initial hardware price is comparable and disc mastering fees have come down significantly in price, more and more designers faced with an audio need are considering installing video hardware and using only the audio tracks. That way, if a video application arises at a later date, the equipment will have already been purchased. Interactive video equipment and processes are described in more detail in the next chapter.

Interfacing Computers with Other Media

It is possible to use the computer's power to control other media. Videotapes, videodiscs, audiotapes, audiodiscs, and 35-millimeter slide projectors have all been interfaced with microcomputers to produce powerful instructional systems. By creating such combinations, the designer gains the advantages of both media and produces a hybrid medium more powerful than the separate media. Interactive combinations of media are discussed in greater detail in Chapter 21.

Implications of Alternative Input and Output Devices

The options just discussed are all presently available and will either improve during the coming years or be replaced by better alternatives. What does that mean to the designer of CAI? By using alternative devices in CAI, the designer is able to adapt the standard computer configuration to meet the needs of specific groups of learners and the needs imposed by extraordinary instructional objectives. For example, enhanced CAI may be used to teach handicapped students when typing is impossible. Or CAI may be used to teach very young children who do not yet know how to read or write how to recognize colors, numbers, or the letters of the alphabet. It also means that designers can use text appropriately, rather than by default as the only available option, and that more learners can be accommodated, making learning more resilient by involving multiple senses in the learning process.

A common criticism of CAI is that the computer is used as an electronic page turner. In many cases, this criticism is valid. However, a closer look at the designer's intent and constraints sheds additional light on the issue. The designer's dilemma may be characterized as follows: "How can I involve the learner and adapt the instruction to the needs of individual students while achieving instructional objectives that require formidable use of language to convey the concepts?" Although the use of screen after screen of text is to be avoided, the option of using print-based training does not account for the designer's desire to adapt instruction to student needs and to actively involve the learner.

By using alternative input and output devices, information can be presented in several ways. For example, the designer might use interactive video, voice synthesis, and/or high-resolution graphics to carry parts of the instructional message. By combining media and using alternative means of input and output, it becomes possible to produce CAI that does not rely extensively on reading or typing skills. When constrained to provide instruction using only keyboards as input devices and monitors as output devices, text-based CAI may be inevitable.

During phase two of CAI development, consider learner characteristics, task characteristics, financial constraints, and the need for the instruction to be portable to other computer systems when determining the appropriateness of alternative means of input and output. The use of alternative input and output devices generally increases the price of the hardware required to run the lesson and limits portability to other computers, reducing the number of potential users of the product.

Trends in Microcomputer Hardware

Computer technology has changed dramatically and will continue to do so. Mainframes, minicomputers, and microcomputers are all becoming more powerful, faster, smaller, and less expensive. In 1979, Evans described the rate of change in the computer industry by comparing it to the automobile industry. According to Evans (p. 76), if the automobile industry had followed a similar rate of change over the same period,

> you would be able to buy a Rolls-Royce for $2.75, it would do three million miles to the gallon, and it would deliver enough power to drive the Queen Elizabeth II. And, if you were interested in miniaturization, you could place half a dozen of them on a pinhead.

These trends have continued and perhaps even accelerated since 1979, and will continue to do so for the next decade. Microcomputer systems will become faster and more powerful, will contain more memory and storage capacity, will be smaller and less expensive, will be more reliable, and will have more peripheral devices available as options.

What effect will this have on CAI? All of these trends can be good news for the producers of CAI. With the advent of more powerful machines, and with costs decreasing to the point where availability becomes less of a problem, the designer will be able to produce instruction relatively unconstrained by functionality or availability. Again, however, the primary issue is how these enhancements are used to improve CAI. Improvement in technology alone does little to improve the effectiveness of instructional software.

Trends in Microcomputer Software

The advancements in hardware technology imply a bright future for CAI. Three trends in software development will contribute as well: the prominence of multi-user, multitasking operating systems; the increasing sophistication and flexibility of CAI authoring software; and the advent of instructional design software.

Microcomputers were originally envisioned and developed as single-user devices. Therefore, the operating system software that controls them was developed to support one single application. On larger computer systems, software was developed to support multiple users concurrently by allowing several users to share computer resources. Developers soon found that multiuser operating systems also allowed a single user to perform multiple operations rather than waiting for the completion of one operation before starting the next. Because the concept has steadily gained popularity, multiuser software architectures are now provided on single-user microcomputers. The UNIX operating system, for example, is written to allow multiple tasks to run concurrently in a single machine and is available in one form or another on many popular micros.

It is when these more sophisticated operating systems are combined with *windowing* capabilities that the potential for CAI improves immensely. Windowing software allows the user to split the computer screen so that two or more programs may be visible at the same time. When this is combined with multitasking, multiple programs may be visible *and* operating at the same time.

How does this capability relate to CAI? More and more jobs involve hands-on contact with computers. More and more training will be aimed at teaching students to use computers and computer programs. Windowing and multitasking operating systems will allow the designers of CAI to write programs utilizing two windows: one in which the actual computer application is running and another in which the CAI is running. By passing information from the CAI window to the application and vice versa, it becomes possible to use CAI to teach students to use computer applications *while they observe the actual application* rather than a simulation of the application. The CAI window can be used to tell the student what to do next and can examine the input for accuracy before passing the response to the next application. Then the application will react to the input, and the cycle can be repeated. The CAI lesson will not only teach but will protect the student from damaging valuable data during the lesson.

For example, imagine a student learning to operate a popular word-processing program via CAI. The screen is divided into two windows. The word-processing program displays in the top two-thirds of the screen, while the bottom of the screen presents instruction to the student. Although the cursor appears in the word-processing section of the screen, the CAI window is really receiving all input from the student. The CAI window says "Press the INSERT key" and waits for a response. If the student presses any other key, the CAI window displays feedback indicating that an error has been made. If the INSERT key is pressed, the CAI window passes the code for that response to the word-processing program, and that window reacts. Although it is currently possible to simulate such things in conventional single-user CAI, the ease with which software training may be developed with such tools, the accuracy of the simulation, and the fact that people learning to use computer programs have access to computers on which to learn provide strong arguments for expanding the role of CAI in computer-related training.

A second trend that will lead to larger numbers of CAI programs available and more use of CAI is the increasing sophistication and flexibility of CAI authoring software. Such programs allow nonprogrammers to produce CAI and allow programmers to produce CAI more quickly. As more authoring products are developed, their quality will improve, price–performance ratios will drop, authoring tools will become more available, and more CAI on a broader range of topics will become available. As a broader range of CAI lessons comes into being, more people will experience CAI, resulting, it is hoped, in more CAI proponents.

A third software development that will impact CAI positively is the advent of software designed to apply principles of instructional design to the development of instruction. Some instructional design software programs are designed specifically for CAI (Merrill and Wood, 1984), and others run on computers but have been designed to assist in the development of instruction in any medium (Seyfer and Russell, 1985). By leading the developer through a series of steps and decisions (much like the checklist provided in this text), these programs provide guidance for developers not trained in instructional design. Although these programs do not produce instruction equivalent to that developed by a trained instructional designer, they suggest that the CAI produced in the near future will be of sufficient quality to meet lesson objectives and increase the number CAI supporters.

Chapter Summary

Several alternative means of input and output are available to the designer of CAI. These alternatives include keyboards, touch screens, light pens, mice, graphics tablets, joysticks, voice recognition, video displays, printers, voice synthesis, and the interactive combination of computers and other instructional media.

These alternatives may be employed to

- Make CAI more appropriate for specific learner groups.
- Make CAI more appropriate for specific instructional tasks.
- Make CAI lessons more interesting.

The use of alternative input and output devices has potential disadvantages that should be considered by the designer. By employing these nonstandard devices, the designer

- Increases the complexity of the development efforts.

- Increases the costs associated with the delivery of the lessons, because the specialized hardware must be added to every machine on which the lesson is to run and because development time is increased.
- Reduces the portability and marketability of the program, since anyone who wants to run the program must also have the optional devices.

Hardware and software technology have improved dramatically and will continue to improve, making the machines that are available to the CAI designer even more capable and available in greater numbers in the near future.

References

Evans, C. R. (1980). *The Micro Millennium*. New York: The Viking Press.

Merrill, M. D., and L. E. Wood (1984). Computer guided instructional design. *Journal of Computer-Based Instruction*, **11**(2), 60–63.

Seyfer, C., and J. D. Russell (June, 1985). Computer managed instructional development. *The Criterion* (newsletter of the National Society of Performance and Instruction's Front Range chapter, 3–5.

Related Reading

Bork, A. (1984). Education and computers: The situation today and some possible futures. *Technological Horizons in Education*, **12**(3), 92–97.

Holcomb, R. K. (1985). Use a speech synthesizer to teach basic vocabulary. *TechTrends*, **30**(4), 18–19.

Malloy, R. (1986). A roundup of optical disk drives. *BYTE*, **11**(5), 215–224.

Chapter Review Exercises

COMPREHENSION

1. Define the term *peripheral device*. (See pages 341–342.)
2. List and describe at least three alternatives to the keyboard as an input device during CAI. (See pages 344–348.)
3. List and describe at least three alternatives to displaying computer output that may be used to interactively present information during CAI. (See pages 348–351.)
4. Discuss the advantages and disadvantages associated with alternative input and output devices. (See pages 344–352.)
5. Discuss trends in microcomputer hardware and software and the impact these trends are likely to have on CAI. (See pages 352–354.)

CHAPTER 21

Interactive Computer-Based Technologies

The ability to involve the learners in the instructional process and to adapt instruction to meet the needs of individual students makes CAI a powerful educational medium. But there are some things that CAI alone does poorly. Chapter 6 noted that CAI is not an especially effective medium for producing realistic visual images, that the production of realistic motion can be quite difficult with CAI, and that CAI places significant demands on student reading ability. While other delivery systems, such as video and slide/tape presentations, may not suffer from these drawbacks, they cannot duplicate the interaction, individualization, and management capabilities of CAI. In many cases, the best solution is to combine media. By placing other instructional media under computer control, the designer creates a new tool. With this new tool, it becomes possible to maximize the strengths of each medium while gaining additional strengths from the combination itself. In this chapter, the potential of such combinations is examined.

OBJECTIVES

Comprehension

After completing this chapter, you will be able to

1. Name at least three media that have been placed under microcomputer control.
2. List the components of an interactive video system.
3. List at least ten advantages and at least four disadvantages of interactive video.
4. Describe interactive slide presentations and list at least three advantages and two disadvantages as compared with interactive video.

Interactive Technologies

Interactive technologies are instructional combinations that place other media under computer control. By adding computer control to audio-, video-, or slide-based instruction, new media capable of solving troublesome educational problems are created.

Interactive technologies have been used to create new instructional experiences as well as to make existing instructional educational media more effective, efficient, and interesting. The remainder of this chapter will focus on alternative interactive technologies, beginning with perhaps the most promising: interactive video.

Interactive Video

Interactive video combines computer control with videotape or videodisc instruction. The components of a typical interactive video system are a standard CAI computer system with optional peripheral devices, a video player, an interface connecting the computer and the video player, a video program (on videotape or videodisc), and computer software consisting of a CAI program with additional instructions controlling the video player (Graham and Hannafin, 1985).

The computer can produce text, graphics, and sound, while the video player can produce video and audio output. These may be presented separately or in combination. For example, in addition to conventional CAI, an interactive video system may present video with or without audio, video still frames with or without computer-generated text and/or graphics overlays, or computer generated text and/or graphics with audio from the video player.

As might be suspected, different hardware products provide different degrees of interactivity. Daynes and Butler (1984) have identified five levels:

Level 0—Provides linear playback only. The student or teacher begins and ends the lesson but does not intervene during the course of the lesson.

Level 1—Adds frame-accurate access, the ability to vary the speed and direction of motion, stereo, freeze frame, chapter search, and scanning features through controls on the video player but is difficult to interface with a computer.

Level 2—Provides everything available in Level 1 machines plus faster access, increased durability, a built-in port for interfacing with microcomputers, an onboard microprocessor, and onboard memory.

Level 3—Is a Level 2 machine connected to a microcomputer.

Level 4—Is theoretical. At this level, anything is possible.

Levels 0 and 1 represent commercially available consumer-level products of little interest to the producer of interactive instruction. Because they can be interfaced with microcomputers, levels 2 and 3 are used in interactive teaching applications. Level 4 refers to future products and more sophisticated uses of interactive video technology. For example, Daynes has discussed the potential for artistic uses of interactive video where interactive images completely surround the user (Innovator Interview, 1984). For our purposes, interactive video instruction occurs at level 3, during which a microcomputer controls the action of the video player.

TAPE AND DISC AS ALTERNATIVES FOR INTERACTIVE VIDEO INSTRUCTION

As mentioned earlier, interactive video comes in two basic formats: interactive videotape and interactive videodisc. Videotapes are similar to audio tapes, in that they consist of a long, thin plastic film covered with a magnetic recording surface, packaged in a cassette. Videodiscs appear more like reflective phonograph records.

From the designer's perspective, the concept of random access is a principal attribute separating videodisc and videotape. Access, in this sense, pertains to the ability to locate the information contained in the lesson. Random access implies that the information may be accessed in any order, rather than in a single linear order. As an example, compare a record and an audiotape cassette. Suppose you wanted to hear a specific song. With a record, you can lift the needle and set the needle down again to quickly gain access to the correct song. With a tape, you are forced to fast-forward or rewind to bypass unwanted songs note by note before gaining access to the correct song, a process requiring considerably more time to complete.

Random access implies quickness and ease in locating specific information. The term *linear* is used to describe media that do not provide random access. Randomness and linearity are relative. There is no definite dividing line between the two, nor is it necessary to stringently classify media into these categories. The appropriate question is really whether a given medium provides adequate speed of access for a given application.

Interactive videodisc technology is an outstanding example of random access, and interactive videotape technology is a good example of using a primarily linear medium in an interactive application. Interactive videodiscs can access any frame on the disc in three seconds or less, while a worst-case search on videotape may require several minutes. Good planning and location of video segments on videotape can reduce the amount of time required to locate segments, but the required time will always be longer than access times for videodisc.

In determining the appropriateness of tape and disc for specific interactive lessons, access time is only one of many factors to be considered. Since videotape players are relatively common in schools and homes, little need be said about them. Videodiscs are relatively new and not as common. The following discussion provides adequate background for comparing videotape and videodisc as interactive instructional media.

Videodisc Technology   There have been two major classifications of videodiscs. *Capacitance discs* involve physical contact between the disc and a *read head* in a manner similar to the way in which the arm of a phonograph comes in contact with a record. This technology has declined in popularity due to significant advantages offered by the second type, *optical laser discs*. Because optical laser discs now dominate, capacitance discs will not be considered in the discussions that follow.

When a master laser disc is recorded, a laser places minute, information-bearing *pits* on the surface of the disc. During playback, another laser reflects light from the surface of the disc in order to read the stored information. Because individual pits are so small, large amounts of information may be stored on a disc. Because the information is stored and read digitally (as a series of zeroes and ones rather than a value somewhere along a scale), the quality of reproduction of both images and sound is excellent.

In *The Videodisc Book: A Guide and Directory*, Daynes and Butler (1984) describe advantages of videodisc technology. These advantages, discussed briefly here, combine to make the videodisc a most capable contributor in instructional settings. Videodiscs provide the ability to produce high-quality pictures in both motion and still frame and the ability to store up to 54,000 images per side, each of which can provide a slidelike still frame or, when played back at the speed of 30 frames per second, can be combined to produce 30 minutes of running video per side.

Like videotape, videodisc provides two audio tracks, which may be played one at a time or together. By playing audio tracks separately, it becomes possible, for example, to produce a single disc that provides instruction in either of two languages. By playing them together, it becomes possible to provide stereo music or combinations of narration and audio.

Videodiscs are extremely durable. Because the player reads the information by reflecting light off of the disc, there is no wear on the disc itself. The image is as crisp and clear the thousandth time the disc is played as the first. Videodiscs provide fast random access. Because the disc spins at 1800 revolutions per minute (Clark, 1984), it is reasonable to expect access times of less than one second.

A major criticism of videodisc technology has been cost. Until very recently, the cost to produce videodiscs was several times the cost of producing videotaped programs. Today, even in moderate quantities, the cost of duplicating videodiscs can be less than the cost of duplicating the same number of videotapes.

Comparing Videodisc and Videotape   Videodiscs offer several advantages over videotape for use in interactive CAI applications. Videodiscs provide superior still-frame images, can locate in two seconds what a videotape might not locate in two minutes, and do not wear out.

However, videotapes have advantages as well. Videotape is more easily modifiable than videodisc. At this time, videodiscs are not modifiable, although progress is being made in this area. In addition, videotape is less expensive to produce than videodisc in small quantities. Although it is possible to have a single videodisc manufactured from videotape for approximately $300, according to Jarvis (1984), one should expect to pay between $2,000 and $3,000 to produce the master videodisc, and $20 per copy in low volumes. These costs do not include the cost of the original videotape production, which should be done on, or transferred to, one-inch videotape, which is usually available only at commercial video studios. Gindele and Gindele (1984) claim a good industrial videodisc player suitable for microcomputer control will cost between $2,500 and $4,500, that it takes about 20 weeks to produce a videodisc, and that total costs may run as much as $100,000 per 30-minute side. The Gindele estimates, although accurate in early 1984, are now more than a bit high. Today it is possible to purchase suitable videodisc players for $600 and to have a master disc pressed for $1,800. The cost of video production may still vary considerably, ranging from next to nothing if in-house equipment and resources are used to the $100,000 figure quoted by Gindele and Gindele if an external video production company is required.

Because more instructional programs are available on videotape than on videodisc, and because videotape players are available in most instructional settings, the cost of transferring these programs to disc and of replacing tape players with disc players is generally prohibitive. Many interactive video programs combine the microcomputer and CAI with the existing tape equipment to improve the effectiveness of previously linear programs. A single tape may be used at times with interactive equipment and at other times in conventional tape players to provide linear instruction.

Videotape may be produced locally, while videodisc production usually involves remote services. Because videodisc technology is capable of producing extremely high quality output, and because the disc's quality will be no better than the input received from the producer, most videodisc production shops prefer one-inch videotape as input. Most schools and educational studios record on 1/2- or 3/4-inch equipment. The image is generally recorded in house and then sent to a production studio, where it is bumped up to one-inch machines and edited before being sent out to be used in the production of the master videodisc, a process known as *mastering*.

Videodisc's 30-minute-per-side limitation can be restrictive in interactive lessons (Innovator Interview, 1984). Videotapes may contain two hours of video in a single cassette. Remember, however, that by using the computer to present instruction and monitor responses, the lesson may take considerably longer than the amount of recorded video.

BENEFITS OF INTERACTIVE VIDEO

Regardless of whether tape or disc is selected, interactive video provides the designer with several important benefits, summarized in Table 21.1. In addition to replicating strengths provided by conventional CAI, interactive video overcomes the primary limitations of CAI by adding realistic images and motion and minimizing the requirement for strong student reading skills.

One of the chief applications for interactive video has been to provide learner control over previously linear media. Although the desirability of learner control has been questioned when students can skip lesson modules or indicate when practice has been adequate (Carrier, 1984; Garhart and Hannafin, 1986), the effect of learner control in granting the student the ability to review and the ability to gain access to the remedial instruction deemed necessary are likely to prove beneficial.

As Grabowski and Aggen (1984) point out, flexibility of interactive video also allows the designer to capitalize on cognitive strategies such as rehearsal, paraphrasing, mnemonics, and imaging to promote encoding of information. Interactive video has been used to provide the variety needed to maintain student interest when issuing the repeated practice needed to make skills and knowledge automatic (Olson, 1984).

Table 21.1
Advantages of Interactive Video

Interactive Video Provides:
- The ability to individualize
- The ability to provide realistic images
- The ability to provide realistic motion
- The ability to provide quality audio
- The ability to provide the same level of interaction present in CAI to video and audio
- The ability to use computer generated highlighting on critical characteristics of video segments
- The ability to more easily modify the program by altering the CAI program rather than the video instruction
- The ability to locate video segments accurately
- The ability to review or supplement video segments
- The ability to access a great deal of information
- The ability to present more readable text in varying fonts and sizes

LIMITATIONS OF INTERACTIVE VIDEO

Interactive video is not the answer to all educational problems. In an attempt to provide a realistic picture of the tradeoffs involved in selecting interactive video as an instructional medium, the following discussion presents some potential problems associated with the production of interactive video.

1. *Interactive video requires additional skill.* The processes of designing and developing interactive video instruction involves the skills required for developing CAI, all that a competent video producer knows about the development of effective video-based instruction, and more. Additional planning is required to minimize the time required to access video segments. Additional knowledge and skill are required of the CAI programmer in order to use the commands that will control the video player, though authoring systems have simplified this process. Additional equipment knowledge is required to identify compatible computers and video players. And additional skill may be required to convince those in control of budgets that interactive video is worth the additional money it will cost.

2. *Interactive video requires additional time and manpower to develop.* By combining media, interactive video increases the number of tasks to be completed and usually the number of people involved. The more tasks, the more time required to complete them. Adding more people helps, but only to a certain point. Once that point is passed, additional people tend to cause delays.

3. *Interactive video may add time to the instructional process.* Although several studies have indicated that interactive video reduced learning time, there are also instances where interactive video has increased the time required to complete the learning task. Schaffer and Hannafin (1986) found that an interactive version of a linear videotape took longer to complete than the linear version. That is easy to understand. Students in the interactive video groups were tested during the lesson, and remediation was provided accordingly, requiring additional time. It is also easy to understand how interactive video can save time. Interactive video has often been compared to more thorough or time-consuming forms of instruction, such as lecture, and students are often able to test out of lesson modules, reducing the amount of training taking place. The Schaffer and Hannafin study showed that although the achievement of the interactive video group was superior, the amount of learning per unit of time was not. Alternatively, linear video students learned more per minute of time spent, but interactive video students learned more overall. This study implies that when completeness of learning is important, consider interactive video. When it is not, question the return on the additional investments in time, money, and energy.

4. *Interactive video is more expensive to produce and to use.* When media are combined, the price increases. Increases in development time mean increased costs. Involvement of additional people also adds to the cost. The cost for each copy of the program changes from the cost of a diskette to the cost of a diskette *and* videotape or videodisc. Cost to package and mail or ship the finished product goes up as well. All of the equipment listed earlier is required for each station on which the lesson is to be played. This drives the cost per student hour up considerably when compared to standard CAI techniques or other instructional media.

5. *Interactive video severely limits portability.* It is difficult to produce even standard CAI that will run on varied microcomputer systems. With the addition of

a video component to the list of required devices, locations that would have otherwise been capable of running the program are eliminated.

To place these limitations in perspective, remember that interactive video can do things that no other medium can do. There are applications for which it is the only logical solution, others for which it is one of several good solutions, and still others where it is simply unnecessary.

APPLICATIONS OF INTERACTIVE VIDEO

Many magazines and professional journals contain recent articles describing the potential of interactive video with what Cambre (1984) calls "alarming redundancy." However, there is little meaningful research on the subject. There are the usual media versus media comparisons which, as might be suspected, generally exhibit findings of "no significant difference" or show interactive video to be superior. But there are few empirical research studies indicating the value of such variables as interactivity itself or the value of superimposing computer-generated output over video segments (Hannafin and Garhart, 1985).

There are, however, many case studies describing instances in which interactive videodisc and videotape technologies have been employed effectively. A university-level biology lesson has been transferred to videodisc, the U.S. army air defense school has used interactive video to train soldiers in the use and maintenance of a missile system, various institutions use interactive video for foreign language training, and Digital Equipment Corporation uses interactive video to train sales representatives. All of the preceding users of interactive video report significant gains over conventional methods of instruction.

Reasons for selecting interactive video have varied. In some cases, the technology has been employed to protect students from hazardous conditions or to prevent damage to expensive equipment. In others, it is used to graphically illustrate the consequences of a particular action or series of actions. In other cases, it was used largely to reduce costs.

Because interactive video can respond to student actions quickly, it is often an ideal medium for simulations. Perhaps the best examples are flight-simulation programs used to train professional pilots. Protected from the actual consequences of mistakes, students see the results of their actions—mistakes as well as successes—and learn in a threat-free environment.

Clark (1984) noted that interactive video is used extensively in the military because of their concern for learner outcomes and for cost effectiveness. As Ebner et al. (1984) point out, even findings citing no significant difference between methods can be considered a positive result if that result was achieved at a lower cost.

Interactive video technology has been used to upgrade existing video-based instruction. Schaffer (1985) describes the process of applying interactive video techniques to existing video-based instruction and has identified several ways in which interaction can contribute to improving the usefulness of such programs. Interactive video has improved existing programs by skipping weak or redundant sections; by testing understanding before, during, and after the lesson; by adding instruction and/or remediation to the lesson, and by granting the learner the ability to review and skip segments of the lesson.

Table 21.2
Questions to Ask Before Selecting Interactive Video

1. Are realistic images required?
2. Is motion required?
3. Is motivation or maintaining attention a problem?
4. Is reading a problem for the target audience?
5. Is teaching to mastery important?
6. Is record keeping important?
7. Is it likely that an objective will require several attempts before successful completion?
8. Are completeness of learning and retention important?
9. How large is the potential audience for this program?
10. Is interactive video equipment already available to this audience?
11. What other instructional alternatives are capable of handling the job?
12. How do the costs of IV training compare to other media?

WHEN IS INTERACTIVE VIDEO UNNECESSARY?

As mentioned earlier, a relatively common mistake is to use an instructional medium despite the fact that there are easier, less expensive ways to achieve the same goals. Because of the cost and complexity involved in interactive video, it is wise to validate the decision to use it. Before committing to interactive video, consider the questions in Table 21.2.

Yes answers to questions 1 through 8 indicate support for interactive video. Question the appropriateness of interactive video if a series of *no* answers emerges. Question 9 requires that the size of the audience be considered. If the audience for the program is potentially very large, interactive video might not be a wise choice because the requirement for unavailable equipment may preclude use of the lesson by a large segment of the potential audience. If the audience is too small, it may be very difficult to justify the cost of interactive video lessons. On the other hand, if the answer to question 10 indicates that appropriate equipment will be available to the target audience, then it may be wise to go with interactive video.

The answers to questions 11 and 12 aid in evaluating the use of interactive video from the perspective of cost effectiveness. If other, less expensive alternatives are capable of handling the instructional task, reconsider the decision to use interactive video.

Other Interactive Alternatives

It is likely that a preference for interactive video is based as much on the need for interactivity as the need for video. The remainder of this chapter focuses on additional alternatives that provide interactivity, good images, or good audio without requiring the skill, time, and budget to produce interactive video.

INTERACTIVE SLIDE PRESENTATIONS

A low-cost alternative to interactive video is the combination of 35-millimeter slides with CAI. In applications that require realistic images but not the motion or audio capabilities provided by CAI, interactive slide presentations provide an attractive alternative (Pauline and Hannafin, 1987).

This medium requires the connection of the microcomputer system to a slide projector. Interface boards and slide projectors designed for random-access applications are available commercially for the most popular microcomputer systems. An alternative to commercial systems exists as well. Peck and Hannafin (1983) described an easy-to-build interface that connects Apple II microcomputers with Kodak Carousel slide projectors. The interface may be built by the novice in less than an hour from parts costing less than $25.

Using a conventional projector, slides may be projected on a nearby wall or a full-sized screen. Or a device such as the Bell and Howell Caramate, which reflects the image onto a rear-projection screen, might be used to make the medium more appropriate for learning carrel environments.

Advantages of interactive slide presentations include high-quality images, low production costs, and the fact that only skills present in most educational settings are required. The presence of two screens allows CAI-based instruction and unobstructed, realistic images to appear simultaneously and allows instruction to appear while slides are changing. Disadvantages of interactive slide presentations include the inability to produce realistic motion, the inability to superimpose images and computer output (since they do not appear on the same screen), and the absence of audio capability. Although interactive slide presentations are often not as glamorous as interactive video, they may be used effectively to attain desired educational results without incurring the costs associated with more expensive options.

INTERACTIVE AUDIO

When sound is important and images are not, consider using interactive audio. In addition to voice synthesis and digitized audio, discussed in Chapter 20, interactive audio may be produced by recalling recorded segments from either tape or disc. Like interactive video, audiodisc provides superior access time, while audiotape is considerably less expensive. Since audiotape does not require the complex threading that videotape does, interactive audiotape machines generally provide faster tape shuttling, both forward and reverse. However, interactive audiotape still cannot compete with interactive audiodisc for quality or speed of access.

Similar to videodisc technologies a few years back, audiodiscs are available in two principal forms: magnetic discs and laser discs. Magnetic discs combine the read/write mechanisms commonly associated with microcomputer diskette drives and the recording mechanisms normally associated with audiotape. Laser audiodiscs are gaining in popularity. Similar to the compact discs sold in record stores, laser discs respond rapidly and produce exceptional sound, but they cost much more than their magnetic counterparts.

Comparisons between audiodisc and audiotape technologies resemble the preceding discussions on videodisc and videotape. The major exception is that magnetic audiodisc technology provides a reasonably priced random-access technology within the reach of the smaller budgets present in most educational environments.

Chapter Summary

Interactive technologies combine instructional media to form new, powerful ways to achieve instructional goals. By combining CAI's ability to involve the learner and to adapt the instruction to the needs of individuals with realistic images and audio, difficult educational problems may be solved.

Although much is written about interactive video, little research has gone beyond the typical medium versus medium comparisons. Little is known about how the specific characteristics of the medium contribute to the learning process or about the applications for which interactive video is best suited.

Interactive instructional combinations offer great promise for educaton and training. However, these new technologies increase the cost, effort, and expertise required and may or may not be more effective than other alternatives. Interactive technologies should not be employed simply because they are new or popular; they should be employed when they provide a superior means for solving instructional problems.

References

CAMBRE, M. A. (1984). Notes on new technologies: Interactive video. *Instructional Innovator*, **29**(6), 24–25.

CARRIER, C. (1984). Do learners make good choices? *Instructional Innovator*, **29**(2), 15–17.

CLARK, D. J. (1984). How do interactive videodiscs rate against other media? *Instructional Innovator*, **29**(6), 12–16.

DAYNES, R., and B. BUTLER (1984). *The Videodisc Book: A Guide and Directory*. New York: John Wiley & Sons.

EBNER, D. G., D. T. MANNING, F. R. BROOKS, J. V. MAHONEY, H. T. LIPPERT, and P. M. BALSON (1984). Videodiscs can improve instructional efficiency. *Instructional Innovator*, **29**(6), 26–28.

GARHART, C., and M. J. HANNAFIN (1986). The accuracy of cognitive monitoring during computer-based instruction. *Journal of Computer-Based Instruction*, **13**(3), 88–93.

GINDELE, J. F., and J. G. GINDELE (1984). Interactive videodisc technology and its implications for education. *Technological Horizons in Education*, **12**(1), 93–97.

GRABOWSKI, B., and W. AGGEN (1984). Computers for interactive learning. *Instructional Innovator*, **29**(2), 27–30.

GRAHAM, J., and M. J. HANNAFIN (1985). Interactive video with Apple SuperPILOT. *Educational Technology*, **25**(3), 30–32.

HANNAFIN, M. J., and C. GARHART (1985). Research methods for the study of interactive video. Paper presented at the annual meeting of the Association for the Development of Computer-Based Instructional Systems, Philadelphia.

Innovator Interview (1984). Rod Daynes, Interactive Technologies Corporation. *Instructional Innovator*, **29**(6), 30–32.

JARVIS, S. (1984). Videodiscs and computers. *Byte*, **9**(7), 187–203.

OLSON, J. S. (1983). Gagné on the uses of new technology. *Instructional Innovator*, **28**(5), 24–25.

PAULINE, R., and M. J. HANNAFIN (1987). Interactive slide-sound instruction: Incorporating the power of the computer with high-fidelity visual and aural images. *Educational Technology*, in press.

PECK, K. L., and M. J. HANNAFIN (1983). How to interface slides and computers. *Instructional Innovator*, **28**(8), 20–23.

SCHAFFER, L. C. (1985). Is interactive video for you? In E. Miller and M. L. Mosley (eds.). *Educational Media and Technology Yearbook*. Littleton: Libraries Unlimited.

————, and M. J. HANNAFIN (1986). The effects of progressive interactivity on learning from interactive video. *Educational Communications and Technology Journal*, **34**, 89–96.

Related Reading

HANNAFIN, M. J. (1984). Options for authoring instructional interactive video. *Journal of Computer-Based Instruction*, **11**, 98–100.

———— (1985). Empirical issues in the study of computer-assisted interactive video. *Educational Communication and Technology Journal*, **33**, 235–247.

HANNAFIN, M. J., C. GARHART, L. RIEBER, and T. PHILLIPS (1985). Keeping interactive video in perspective: Tentative guidelines and cautions in the design of interactive video. In E. Miller and M. L. Mosley (eds.). *Educational Media and Technology Yearbook*. Littleton: Libraries Unlimited.

HANNAFIN, M. J., and C. HUGHES (1986). A framework for incorporating orienting activities in computer-based interactive video. *Instructional Science*, **15**, 239–255.

HANNAFIN, M. J., T. L. PHILLIPS, and S. TRIPP (1986). The effects of orienting, processing, and practicing activities on learning from interactive video. *Journal of Computer-Based Instruction*, **13**, 134–139.

HANNAFIN, M. J., and T. L. PHILLIPS (1987). Perspectives in the design of interactive video: Beyond tape versus disc. *Journal of Research and Development in Education*, in press.

Interactive video on a shoestring. (1984). *Instructional Innovator*, **29**(6), 29, 40.

THORKILDSEN, R., and S. FRIEDMAN (1984). Videodiscs in the classroom. *Technological Horizons in Education*, **11**(7), 90–95.

Chapter Review Exercises

COMPREHENSION

1. Name at least three media that have been placed under microcomputer control. (See pages 357, 363–364.)

2. List the components of an interactive video system. (See page 357.)

3. List at least ten advantages and at least four disadvantages of interactive video. (See pages 360–362 and Table 21.1.)

4. Describe interactive slide presentations and list at least three advantages and two disadvantages as compared to interactive video. (See pages 363–364.)

CHAPTER

22

The Future of CAI

Computers have revolutionized life in the United States and around the world. Most of the jobs available ten years from now will be computer-related and will bear titles that do not exist today. As we move from an industrial economy to an information-driven economy, the need for training and retraining will mushroom. Computers will play a major role in the cost-effective distribution of the required instruction. In addition, students will learn about computers so that they may become able to use them as multifunctional tools.

You have learned when to use, how to plan for, how to design, how to produce, and how to evaluate CAI. You know quite a bit about CAI as it exists today. The type of CAI addressed in this book will undoubtedly continue to grow during the next few years. But what form will CAI take in five years? In ten years? In what other ways can computers contribute to the revitalization and ultimate success of overburdened educational systems?

In this chapter, we examine changes that are likely to take place during the coming years and discuss what the application of computers in novel nonteaching roles may mean for education.

OBJECTIVES

Comprehension

After completing this chapter you will be able to

1. Discuss microcomputer networking and list at least four advantages associated with it.
2. Describe an intelligent CAI system and discuss how intelligent CAI systems may impact education in the future.
3. Discuss the use of the computer as a tool in educational settings.
4. Describe the role of computers when used in tutor, tool, and tutee modes (Taylor, 1980).

The Need for Change in Education

One major educational goal is to prepare people to become productive members of society. Success in the upcoming information age requires a set of skills and

367

knowledge quite different from those required to date. Technological and sociological changes have presented new options to professional educators, yet education has changed very little. Concerned educators have called for self-analysis that could lead to very basic changes in the educational system itself (National Task Force on Educational Technology, 1986). If a comprehensive analysis were conducted to determine what should be taught, where learning should take place, how instruction should be delivered, who should prescribe and deliver instruction, and when instruction should be available, the results would probably not support the curricula and methods that exist today. It is likely that the presence of computers will influence what should be taught as well as how, where, and when learning will take place (Hannafin, Dalton, and Hooper, 1987).

WHAT SHOULD BE TAUGHT?

We are moving from a time during which people were inclined to select and remain in a single career to a time during which it is likely that the average person will change careers several times. Many of these changes will be to careers that do not exist today. Many careers will be computer-related, and information will often become the focus of both the inputs and outputs of these new occupations. As workers change jobs, new skills and knowledge will be required. This is a phenomenon that is all too common to the heavy-industry sector of society. Because of the amount of learning to be done, education must teach students how to learn in addition to dispensing information.

According to Derringer (1983), much of what has been considered basic in today's educational system has become, or may become, trivial during the next few years. For example, the availability of calculators and computers may allow arithmetic skills to be replaced by algebra, problem-solving skills, and estimation skills. Topics such as computer science, computer literacy, and word processing may become standard in the K–12 curriculum.

The amount of information generated each day is staggering. And the rate at which information grows is itself increasing. Storage of information on paper has become impractical in many cases. The almost instant electronic distribution of information has become competitive in cost with delivery of paper-based information. During the coming years, more information will be stored by computer and will be accessible from remote locations. An example of this trend is a series of projects initiated by libraries across the country. A project implemented by the Colorado Alliance of Research Libraries (CARL), for example, provides computerized access to information presently maintained in the card catalogs of the state's major research libraries. From terminals in the libraries or personal computers in remote locations connected to the project's computer by modems and telephone lines, students may conduct computer searches of the holdings of any of the CARL libraries. Students may search by author, title, or subject. Subject searches may include several words and are not restricted to standard listings in subject headings in normal card catalogs.

With each passing day, more information is stored within computerized systems. We must teach students how to use the tools to gain access to this information and how to use the computer to analyze and manipulate this information. Computer literacy must become a standard part of school curricula. Many districts have begun to do just that. For example, the Indianapolis Public School District has expanded the curriculum to include knowledge of major components of computer systems; knowledge of common computer terms; ability to interpret computer user manuals; understanding the uses, advantages, and limitations of computers; skill in simple programming using the BASIC language; knowledge of similarities of alternate computer programming languages; and an understanding of the ethical and legal implications of computer use. Other districts teach the operation of several software packages, most notably word processing, electronic spreadsheet, database management, and graphics programs.

Lenkway (1986) describes "minimum student performance standards for computer literacy" established by the state of Florida for its graduates. Acknowledging the importance of computer skills in a student's preparation for the world of work, the state added these standards to standards already established for reading, writing, mathematics, and science. In order to graduate, students must demonstrate (1) the ability to operate a computer for instructional purposes by loading and running programs, (2) an understanding of the basic parts of a computer, (3) an understanding of the role and function of software and languages in computer technology, (4) knowledge of the impact of computer technology on society and the need for its ethical use, (5) an understanding of the capabilities and applications of various computers and computer systems, and (6) an understanding of the process of programming. More specific skills leading to achievement of the goals stated here have been identified and associated with a grade level at which the skill is to be attained. The state understands that the goals, objectives, and skills required of its graduates will change and has provided for revision of the plan every five years.

Although the need for such programs is difficult to deny, nationwide implementation of innovative programs will not happen overnight. Based largely on the demands of concerned parents and progressive teachers, the process will be more evolutionary than revolutionary. Exemplary programs, some on a large enough scale to have significant impact, are proving the value of such changes.

WHERE SHOULD LEARNING TAKE PLACE?

Many people believe that as the future unfolds, the primary location for education will once again be the home. The consumer market for computer equipment is larger than the educational market, and consumers act more quickly than schools in accepting new technologies. According to Derringer (1983), one study revealed that while 62 percent of 13-year-old students had used computers, only 23 percent had used them in school, implying that student contact with computers is probably greater outside school than in school. Many home computers, thanks largely to advertising campaigns by major distributors of personal computers, were purchased with education as a primary application.

As more computers become available in the home, more CAI software will become available for home use. Libraries will begin to stock CAI programs for public use, and subscription networks will expand their CAI offerings. Topics available for home use will include standard K–12 topics, college- and university-level courses, and even career development programs.

Videotape-based college courses called *telecourses* are currently used to reach students in remote locations and students with circumstances that make travel to a college or university difficult. The student enrolling in these courses receives study materials, completes reading assignments before viewing the lessons on broadcast television, and completes post-viewing assignments, only occasionally coming to the campus. As computers become more common in the home, a similar plan employing CAI instead of video-based instruction seems inevitable. Diskettes would be less expensive to distribute than workbooks. Instead of students coming to campus for testing, tests could be taken at home using CMI techniques that record output files to diskettes, to be mailed or electronically transmitted to the supervisor for evaluation. Computer teleconferences could allow all students enrolled in a course to interact with the professor and to download the content of the discussion to a diskette and/or printer for review.

HOW SHOULD INSTRUCTION BE DELIVERED?

According to Wedman (1983), approximately one million computers were built prior to 1980. By 1985, several manufacturers expected to produce more than one million computers each in that year alone. As these computers and more find their way into homes, offices, and factories, people will need additional training. The demands that an increasingly technological society will place on training and education are significant. Because qualified instructors will be in short supply, because the number of topics that require training will increase, and because of the complexity of these topics, traditional methods of instruction will not meet these needs. Educators must make effective use of the very technologies that are causing the changes in order to provide the educational experiences that will be in demand in the next decade.

CAI will become increasingly important. The extension of current trends will reduce CAI costs, will increase the number of people using CAI, and will create an environment that fosters CAI development (Pressman and Rosenbloom, 1984). Lowered costs and the increased availability of microcomputers will afford CAI the opportunity needed to prove its value.

WHO SHOULD PRESCRIBE AND DELIVER INSTRUCTION?

In traditional educational settings, the teacher's primary charter is to teach. In addition to teaching, however, the teacher must determine what is to be taught, locate or develop instructional materials, determine when students are experiencing difficulty, determine why students are experiencing difficulty, determine how to overcome this difficulty, evaluate student performance, report measures of student performance to teachers and administrators, and model adult behaviors and attitudes. Although teachers have done an admirable job, computers can remove some of this burden.

As educators begin to understand the computer's potential contributions, the teacher's role will be redefined. Computers can be used to analyze student needs, deliver some of the instruction, and analyze and report on student performance. Free to analyze the computer's findings on student performance, to locate additional instructional materials, and to present instruction to individuals and small groups, the teacher will be able to guide the learning process, filling in gaps that are often unnoticed in conventional classrooms.

WHEN SHOULD INSTRUCTION TAKE PLACE?

Course schedules inevitably conflict with work schedules, domestic responsibilities, and with each other. CAI can be used at any time. With minimal supervision, computer labs may be made available around the clock. Once CAI equipment is widely available in the home, it will become possible to minimize travel and the inconvenience associated with attending regularly scheduled lectures.

Factors Influencing the Role of CAI

In addition to the changes already described, the availability of high-quality courseware, CAI consortia, users' groups, and trends in microcomputer networking and artificial intelligence will have a positive effect on the value of computers in education in the near future.

AVAILABILITY OF HIGH-QUALITY COURSEWARE

A major obstacle to the widespread implementation of CAI has been the absence of comprehensive, high-quality courseware. Fortunately, this problem can be solved. Many individuals understand the CAI design process more fully than before. On a larger scale, private industries are spending significant sums of money to produce comprehensive sets of thorough, educationally sound CAI lessons. Recognized leaders in the field are calling for the government to provide funds to help support the development of comprehensive CAI programs (Bork, 1984). These trends are encouraging.

Eventually there will be a comprehensive set of electronic lessons covering more topics than those currently covered by textbooks. It will require both time and money. As with textbook publishing, private industry will be the first to provide adequate resources to produce comprehensive offerings of quality courseware. Competition in an expanding market will result in subsequent efforts that are superior to initial offerings.

MICROCOMPUTER NETWORKING

An emerging trend in the use of computers in the schools is the increasing popularity of microcomputer networks. Networks connect personal computers to each other and to centralized peripheral devices such as mass storage devices and printers. Two examples cited here describe such networks and highlight the advantages, both educational and financial, responsible for their popularity.

West Virginia will soon install a statewide microcomputer network, ultimately incorporating every school in the state (Cook, 1984). Seen initially as part of a long-range solution to the state's unemployment problem, the first phase of the program places $1,350,000 worth of computer equipment in 17 vocational schools, where students will learn to use word processing, electronic spreadsheet, and database management software. A second phase will place similar equipment in the remaining vocational schools and twelve high schools, and the third phase will complete the process by placing equipment in all elementary schools and the remaining secondary schools.

The task force driving the project analyzed many alternatives and identified shortcomings to be avoided. In typical large CAI systems, a mainframe computer is connected to several terminals. The task force noted four major problems with this approach: (1) When the mainframe is inoperative, terminals are also inoperative. The teacher is left without equipment on which to train. (2) Mainframe systems suffer from degradation when several students request information or programs simultaneously, making response times unacceptable. (3) Because the terminals do not have their own processing power or memory, they cannot be taken off site. (4) The equipment is expensive and often requires the use of dedicated phone lines for communication to outlying locations.

The committee recommended the purchase of IBM personal computers, attached via a network to an in-house software library placed on a central storage system. Dial-up modems were recommended to allow schools to use microcomputers and telephone lines to download additional programs residing in the state's central software library.

Adams (1984) described another exemplary program initiated by the Indianapolis Public School District (IPSD). The goals of this program are to train all students (K–12) in computer literacy and "to establish the computer as an instructional tool in all disciplines" (p. 95). The plan calls for classroom labs in all district schools. Each lab is to contain 31 microcomputers and three connected printers, using PCnet local area networks. During phase one, 19 such networks were installed, two in each of the district's nine high schools and another pilot network in one of the district's junior high schools. Additional standalone PCs brought the initial order to 868 IBM PCs and XTs. Several hundred additional microcomputers were purchased as phases two and three were implemented to place microcomputers in twelve junior high and 67 elementary schools. The project cost ten million dollars and was implemented over a three-year period.

The IPSD plan provides more than computer equipment. To guarantee adequate contact to allow students to learn to use the computers as tools, the program provides for six weeks of PC training for each high school student. To foster student interest, the program provides one year of college credit in computer science for students successfully completing the advanced college placement test in that area. To ensure that teachers are adequately prepared to implement the program, release time, substitute teachers, training for staff members wishing to participate, 21 lab managers, a systems manager, an instructional program developer, and CAI programs for English and math classes are provided.

The IPSD staff has encountered and solved speed-related problems with the microcomputer network approach. They discovered that delays occurred as many students attempted to download programs at the beginning of class. This problem was solved by adding additional memory to the teacher's central processors. By serving as a solid-state disk drive, which minimized the need to retrieve files from the disk, this additional memory reduced the time required for all thirty students to gain access to programs from four minutes to one, significantly less time than it takes to distribute papers or workbooks in a conventional classroom.

Additional speed was achieved by using techniques known as *disk caching* and *multisector I/O*. Disk caching allocates computer memory according to the frequency of program use, keeping frequently used programs in memory, thereby eliminating the need for repeated disk access. Multisector I/O allows files to be loaded in multiple-sector blocks rather than one block at a time, again reducing disk access time. Copyright issues are a major concern for IPSD. Formal instruction on copyright law and strict adherence to license agreements keep this from becoming a problem.

Although these two large-scale computer implementations represent bona fide progress in providing computer access for students, the instructional burden assumed by CAI, as measured by the percentage of student education delivered via this medium, is still relatively small. The Waterford School in Provo, Utah, owned and operated by the Wicat Education Institute, provides students more contact with CAI. Used primarily as a proving ground for comprehensive CAI networks and software products, the Waterford School offers a student-to-learning-station ratio of four to one (O'Neil, 1984). Although the school uses CAI extensively, it also provides its nearly 250 students in grades K–9 with appropriate teacher–student contact. This private educational institution has been extremely well received by students, parents, and teachers. The school does not solicit enrollment, receives requests for information on a daily basis, and had over 120 applicants during the first three hours of enrollment for the 20 kindergarten positions open for the 1982–83 school year. Vacancies in higher grades are rare and, like the kindergarten openings, are generally filled by siblings of existing students.

Microcomputer networks are gaining in popularity because they offer several significant advantages. They allow processing to take place in the microcomputer rather than a mainframe, eliminating many of the problems posed by mainframe systems. They eliminate the need for dedicated phone lines, and the micros may be disconnected from the network and used in remote locations. Software may be shared (if allowed by license agreements), as may peripheral devices such as printers and disk drives. The use of floppy diskettes may be minimized or even eliminated. All of these advantages save money. By networking its micros, IPSD calculated that it would save 20 percent on the initial order alone—in this case, two million dollars.

Another advantage to network purchases is that the size of the order gives an incentive for vendors to provide additional benefits. For example, IBM contributed training for eight people and gave significant discounts on additional equipment purchased by students or staff.

The trend for networks seems to be away from mainframe and minicomputer systems for public school CAI purposes. The size of the initial investment, the perception that a mainframe requires a system administrator to attend to the hardware, and the perceived need for computer scientists to develop CAI send many prospective users to microcomputers. Additional factors such as the complexity of installing a mainframe system, the cabling required to connect the terminals to the mainframe, the fact that the terminals may not be disconnected and used as standalones, and the higher price for multiuser software packages serve as additional deterrents.

There are, however, instances in which mainframe systems make sense. For example, costs for mainframe systems may actually be lower than comparable microcomputer systems on a per-workstation basis when a large number of stations are required. When there is a need for extensive record keeping, even networked microcomputers may perform the task unacceptably.

Perhaps the best-known mainframe-based CAI system is Control Data's PLATO system. PLATO offers high-quality graphics and a sophisticated courseware authoring system. One of the first comprehensive CAI systems, PLATO offers an extensive catalog of educational software, covering standard educational topics as well as many career-oriented training programs for adults. Control Data has established training centers across the country, where businesses and individuals can purchase access to computers and CAI software without owning either.

CAI CONSORTIA

Another significant recent development has been the emergence of computing consortia and CAI users' groups. Perhaps the best known of these is the Minnesota Educational Computing Consortium (MECC). When that state found that, like other states, it was spending huge sums of money on incompatible computer systems, that software could have been shared if compatible systems had been purchased, and that software could have been developed by the state for less money than paid for multiple copies, MECC was formed to develop standards for educational computing.

MECC standarized CAI development principally around the Apple II micro-computer and developed an extensive software library for distribution to schools in the state. Requests soon came from out of state, and MECC began to provide software to districts outside Minnesota as well. What began as an attempt to spend the state's money wisely evolved into an organization that has promoted CAI use across the country.

On a smaller scale, users' groups have also contributed to the advancement of CAI. Educators using or designing CAI gather to share successes, problems, and ideas. CAI professionals often exchange original programs and subroutines that may be incorporated into other programs or strategies for acquiring the funds and support required to initiate a new program. Users have even banded together to approach vendors on equipment purchases, finding that the increased order size results in buying power that encourages dealers to reduce prices. Most important-ly, like other good professional organizations, users' groups provide CAI profes-sionals with inspiration and synergy that breed progress. This inertia leads to an increasing role for CAI.

INTELLIGENT CAI SYSTEMS

Several scholars have predicted that technological advances in both hardware and software will result in fifth-generation computers capable of simulating human thought. This thought will include the ability to infer, evaluate, reason, under-stand continuous human speech, and even to learn (Gladwin, 1984). The term *artificial intelligence* is used to describe the capabilities of such computers. The following scenario suggests what an intelligent computer-assisted instruction (ICAI) lesson might produce.

Imagine a student approaching a learning carrel. As the student sits down, a very natural human voice says, "Hi. What's your name?" The student responds verbally. The computer replies, "You haven't been by for a few days. Last time we worked on multiplying mixed numbers. Do you want to start there or work on another topic?" The student responds, indicating that the teacher recommended work in geometry. The computer ascertains that this student has never completed a lesson on geometry and begins with an introductory lesson.

At times the student touches the screen, and at other times the student responds verbally. As the lesson proceeds, the computer notes that analogies work well in teaching this student but that attempts at humor are not appreciated. (They are followed by a brief answer, the tone of which has been identified as negative.) More analogies are incorporated into the lesson; attempts at humor are eliminated.

During a section on triangles, the student asks, "What's a shape called if it has nine sides?" Although the answer to that question was not in the lesson, the computer quickly searches a reference database, using *geometry, shape, sides,* and *nine* as key words. The computer locates the answer, and tells the student, "A nine-sided shape is called a nonagon." The lesson continues. After another few minutes, the student says, "I already know this. Can we move on?" The computer says, "If you can pass this posttest, I'd be happy to move on." A test follows. The student completes the test successfully, and the results are stored for use in a daily report to the teacher.

The student asks, "Now can we work on astronomy?" The computer says, "We haven't worked on astronomy before. Is this a new interest for you?" As the student confirms, the computer stores this interest in astronomy, planning to use it by calling a story dealing with astronomy during the next reading lesson. The computer searches the lesson database and responds with, "Would you like to learn about the planets in our solar system, our moon, quasars, black holes, or is there something else you had in mind?" The student indicates an interest in quasars, so the computer copies that lesson to memory from another computer at the junior college across town. As the lesson begins, the computer rewrites the lesson, selecting words and sentence structures based on the language the student has used in this and other lessons.

Unfortunately, there are no fully functional ICAI systems in existence today. When we talk of artificially intelligent machines, we are implying power and access to large amounts of storage and information. With some exceptions, we are not focusing on microcomputers. We are dealing with networked mainframes. We are not talking about today's technology; we are talking about tomorrow's. This appears futuristic to many. Consider what you would have said in 1960 if people had told you that in the next decade you could have a calculator built into your watch, a computer on your lap in an airplane, or a car that talks to you when your seat belt is not fastened.

Artificially intelligent CAI machines would be extremely flexible. They would accept many types of input, including typed, touch screen, and continuous human speech. They would be capable of producing many types of output, including text, graphics, video, recorded audio, and synthesized human speech. ICAI systems would be able to learn about new topics as required by the student and would be able to reformat the information appropriately for presentation to the student.

ICAI would also be able to learn about the student's needs, language development, background, hobbies, and interests. It would know when to help and how much help to provide. ICAI would also learn from the student, about strategies that work and those that do not work.

As artificially intelligent machines improve their understanding of language, it may become possible for them to actually develop training. Many machines already understand parts of speech and the meanings of thousands of words. Some can actually *derive* the meaning of new words from the context in which they are used. Others understand and coach humans on instructional design. Once machines are able to identify the importance of points in a passage and decipher and restate their meanings, they will not be far from possessing the capabilities required to design and develop their own ICAI.

Computers in Nonteaching Roles

Taylor (1980) categorized educational uses of computers into *tutor, tool,* and *tutee* modes. In tutor mode, the computer is used in the kinds of CAI applications described in this text. In tool mode, students learn to use the computer to acquire and manipulate information. In tutee mode, students benefit by the process of teaching the computer. We have examined the future of computers used to deliver, monitor, and/or evaluate instruction: the tutor mode. The following discussion proposes what the future might hold for the tool and tutee modes.

Computers as the Objects of Instruction

Because computers are powerful tools for gathering and manipulating information, significant numbers of educators propose that the curriculum be expanded to include the computer as the object of instruction in addition to its role as a vehicle for delivering instruction.

Luehrmann (in Taylor, 1980) presents a charming and thought-provoking analogy, comparing CAI to writing-assisted instruction (WAI). In this article, Luehrmann posits reading and writing as skills acquired only by teachers not passed on to students. Two possible endings are proposed: One ending leaves students in the dark; the other teaches students to read and write. Luehrmann concludes by suggesting that replacing WAI with CAI reflects the current status of the use of computers in the vast majority of educational environments today. We currently use this impressive technology to do great things for ourselves but do not choose to teach our students to master this powerful tool. In this enlightening article, Luehrmann responds to the idea of teaching programming and computer use only to a few interested students by asking, "How much longer will a computer illiterate be considered educated? How long will he be employable and for what jobs?" (p. 135) and by suggesting that the school accreditation process evaluate computer access as library facilities are currently evaluated.

We can expect that in the future formal instruction in the use of computers will be incorporated into the public school curriculum and that increased opportunity for students to learn to use computers on their own will be made available.

The Computer as Tutee

According to Taylor (1980), "Neither the tutor nor tool mode confers upon the user much of the general educational benefit associated with using the computer in the third mode, as tutee" (p. 4). Taylor claims that in tutee mode, the computer "can shift the focus of education in the classroom from end product to process, from acquiring facts to manipulating and understanding them" (p. 4).

Seymour Papert (1980), author of *Mindstorms* and a major influence in the development of LOGO—a programming language designed to allow children to program computers—noted that children learn an amazing amount before they come to school. Why not continue to allow unguided educational experiences after children arrive at school, so that this learning may continue? Papert and others believe that computers in tutee mode provide the opportunity to make this possible.

When preschoolers learn, they develop and use many false theories. As these theories are proven false, they are revised or discarded. This process of theory building and revision develops more than correct theories; it develops cognitive processes worth more than individual theories. When students write programs to "teach the computer," they are involved in similar processes of theory building, testing these theories, and modifying them until they achieve the desired result.

Papert also advocated the creation of *microworlds*, in which computers simulate environments where students may discover and test theories they might be otherwise unable to test. While using the graphics programming capabilities of LOGO within microworlds simulating Newtonian physics, students control the actions of dynaturtles, velocity turtles, acceleration turtles, and linked dynaturtles, discovering for themselves concepts difficult for college students to master when formal methods of instruction are employed.

Many educators have shared success stories involving students who learned to program and found the experience stimulating and valuable, not for the product but because of the excitement and pleasure inherent in the theory building, testing, and revising and in the subsequent feeling of success associated with having achieved desired results. The prospect of using computers to provide novel learning experiences and environments, as well as the challenges such experiences pose for educational researchers, are exciting.

Tutee-mode applications seem likely to be slower in evolving than either tutor or tool modes. Society currently values correct theories and information, having for centuries promoted teaching *for* students rather than structuring experiences in which students may discover these theories for themselves. It appears that pockets of support for such experiences will grow, but that these experiences will, at least temporarily, comprise a relatively small portion of the time provided for the student in traditional educational environments.

Will There Be Change?

We discussed changes that should and could happen. Will they? As discussed earlier in this chapter, significant projects are underway. But changes are coming too slowly to please many parents, students, and educators.

Podemski (1984) warned that by denying computers their place in education, "tradition-bound" teachers may be dooming the system they are trying to save, because failure to utilize computer technology will cause parents to question the viability of traditional instruction, which in turn may lead to a rejection of the current educational system. Podemski suggests that CAI could "supplant the traditional educational and instructional system or at the very least become a significant and viable alternative to the public educational delivery system as we currently know it" (p 118).

We know that CAI could make important contributions in education and training. We know that CAI's contributions should have been more noticeable by this time. Suppes (in Taylor, 1980, p. 235) provides a more likely alternative:

> "All teachers everywhere recognize the help that books give them in teaching students. The day is coming when computers will receive the same recognition". Books, like computers, are currently used formally to deliver instruction in teacher-led environments and informally by students without supervision as a means to expose themselves to new words and ideas upon which internally developed theories are based.

How do we cultivate the productive use of computers in schools? Wedman (1983, p. 147) expressed the following opinion:

> Contrary to popular belief, the future is not something that just happens; it is created. Just as teachers write lesson plans which unfold later in the classroom, educators can also write descriptions of possible futures or scenarios which will unfold later in the schools. . . . The future of computers in education can be the product of groups of teachers, administrators, and educational technologists systematically planning for (and eventually creating) the future. The challenge is to stop asking, "What does the future hold for computers in education?" and to start asking, "What type of future do we want to create for education involving computers?"

We have proposed several descriptions of possible futures, and others undoubtedly exist. Computers will make significant contributions only if we determine what their contributions should be and become actively involved in moving our schools and nation in this direction.

Chapter Summary

Current trends in computer use are promising for CAI and other applications of computers in education. Demands for training are increasing, and cost effectiveness is an increasingly important priority. Quality courseware is available. Microcomputer costs are decreasing, their availability is increasing, and technology is providing more powerful machines. Artificial intelligence applied to CAI promises to multiply its current effectiveness. Eloquent authors have described novel environments in which students use computers to learn.

And yet we have a long way to go. Computers have not yet had the impact that might have been expected. Major obstacles are being removed. Now it is time to become involved. Expect computers and CAI to improve educaton, but plan to be a part of that improvement.

References

ADAMS, J. A. (1984). Networked computers promote computer literacy and computer-assisted instruction. *Technological Horizons in Education*, **11**(8), 95–99.

BORK, A. (1984). Education and computers: The situation today and some possible futures. *Technological Horizons in Education*, **12**(3), 92–97.

COOK, J. E. (1984). West Virginia schools to secure a state-wide microcomputer network. *Technological Horizons in Education*, **11**(6), 85–88.

DERRINGER, D. K. (1983). New directions for education in the information society? *Technological Horizons in Education*, **11**(1), 110–111.

GLADWIN, L. A. (1984). Computer-based training in the second computer age. *Performance & Instructional Journal*, **23**(7), 21–23.

HANNAFIN, M. J., D. W. DALTON, and S. HOOPER (1987). Computers in education: Ten myths and ten needs. *Educational Technology*, in press.

LENKWAY, P. (1986). Minimum student performance standards in computer literacy: Florida's new state law. *Technological Horizons in Education*, **13**(9), 74–77.

NATIONAL TASK FORCE ON EDUCATIONAL TECHNOLOGY, (1986). Transforming American education: Reducing the risk to the nation. *TechTrends*, **31**(4), 12–24, 35.

O'NEIL, F. (1984). An alternative model for computer-assisted instruction in an educational environment. *Technological Horizons in Education*, **11**(8), 113–117.

PAPERT, S. (1980). *Mindstorms*. New York: Basic Books, Inc.

PODEMSKI, R. S. (1984). Implications of electronic learning technology: The future is now! *Technological Horizons in Education*, **11**(8), 118–121.

PRESSMAN, I., and B. ROSENBLOOM (1984). CAI system costs: Present and future. *Technological Horizons in Education*, **11**(6), 94–98.

TAYLOR, R. P. (1980). *The Computer in the School: Tutor, Tool, Tutee*. New York: Teacher's College Press.

WEDMAN, J. (1983). The future of computers in education: What are the right questions? *Technological Horizons in Education*, **11**(1), 147–148.

Related Reading

AHLERS, R. H., R. A. EVANS, and H. F. O'NEIL, JR. (1986). Expert systems for department of defense training. *Journal of Computer-Based Instruction*, **13**(2), 29.

GOTT, S. P., W. BENNET, and A. GILLET (1986). Models of technical competence for intelligent tutoring systems. *Journal of Computer-Based Instruction*, **13**(2), 43–46.

HARRIS, S. D., and J. M. OWENS (1986). Some critical factors that limit the effectiveness of machine intelligence technology in military systems applications. *Journal of Computer-Based Instruction*, **13**(2), 30–34.

PIPITONE, F. (1986). An expert system for electronics troubleshooting based on qualitative causal reasoning. *Journal of Computer-Based Instruction*, **13**(2), 39–42.

PLISKE, D. B., and J. PSOTKA (1986). Exploratory programming environments for designing ICAI. *Journal of Computer-Based Instruction*, **13**(2), 52–57.

RICHARDSON, J. J., and T. E. JACKSON (1986). Developing the technology for intelligent maintenance advisors. *Journal of Computer-Based Instruction*, **13**(2), 47–51.

SINGER, M. J., and R. S. PEREZ (1986). A demonstration of an expert system for training device design. *Journal of Computer-Based Instruction*, **13**(2), 58–61.

Chapter Review Exercises

COMPREHENSION

1. Discuss microcomputer networking and list at least four advantages associated with it. (See pages 371–374.)

2. Describe an intelligent CAI system and discuss how intelligent CAI systems may impact education in the future. (See pages 374–376.)

3. Discuss the use of the computer as a tool in educational settings. (See page 376.)

4. Describe the role of computers when used in tutor, tool, and tutee modes (Taylor, 1980). (See pages 376–377.)

Glossary

ACAI. Artificially intelligent computer-assisted instruction.

AI. Artificial intelligence.

amplification. Use of the computer's capability to add emphasis to information on the screen to focus student attention.

animation. The process of repetitively displaying and erasing characters or symbols to provide the illusion of motion on the screen.

ANSI. American National Standards Institute.

answer judging. The process of evaluating student responses, generally into categories of legal, illegal, correct, incorrect, anticipated and unanticipated.

artificial intelligence. The exhibition by computer equipment of traits normally associated with human intelligence. For example, computers can run programs that allow them to gather and use new information, a process similar to learning in humans.

ASCII. American Standard Code for Information Interchange. Often associated with a set of binary representations of common characters and symbols known as the ASCII character set.

assembler. A program used to convert assembly-language programs into machine-language instructions.

assembly language. A lower-level computer programming language. Assembly-language commands are "assembled" into machine language instructions.

authoring language. A set of commands designed specifically to simplify the process of creating computer-assisted instruction. Common examples include PILOT, PASS, and PLATO.

authoring system. A software package designed to lead the user through the process of creating computer-assisted instruction without requiring programming. Authoring systems usually consist of a series of prompts, menus, and utilities that guide the user through the development process. Examples of authoring systems are the McGraw-Hill Authoring System, The Educator, and Teacher's Aide.

BASIC.   An acronym for "Beginner's All-purpose Symbolic Instruction Code," this programming language was designed to be easy to learn as a first programming language. BASIC has its critics, but it has been used to write many effective CAI programs.

baud.   Bits per second. A unit of measurement used to indicate the rate at which information is passed between two electronic devices. 300 baud means 300 bits of information are pased each second.

binary.   Referring to the base-two numbering system, in which the columns represent ones, twos, fours, eights, and so on, rather than ones, tens, hundreds, thousands, and so on. The only digits available are 0 and 1. for example, a binary 1001 equals a decimal 9.

bit.   Condensed from the words *binary digit*, a bit is a single 0 or 1. Just as letters are combined to make words, bits are combined to represent numbers, alphanumeric characters, and special symbols.

bit map.   Characters and graphics placed on the computer's screen are composed of tiny dots, called pixels. For each pixel on the screen, one or more bits of information are stored to indicate whether the pixel is on or off, or what color the pixel is to be. This series of bits controlling the image on the screen is called a bit map, and a screen that uses bit mapping is called a bit-mapping screen.

board.   In computer terminology, a synonym for *circuit board*. A card containing electronic circuitry found inside a computer or other electronic device.

branching.   The execution of an alternative path through the lesson. Without branching, all programs would be linear, following a single path regardless of the learners' responses. Branching allows CAI to adapt to the needs of individual learners.

buffer.   A segment of memory located in a computer or peripheral device, used for temporary storage of information before it is processed. For example, a keystroke buffer may hold input from the keyboard until a program asking for input is encountered.

bug.   An error or flaw in program logic that causes a computer program to malfunction.

byte.   A series of bits that together form a character or symbol. In some machines, seven bits form a byte; others operate on eight-bit bytes, and still others employ different numbers of bits per byte. Eight bits per byte are most commonly used in microcomputers.

CAI.   Computer-assisted instruction.

CAL.   Computer-assisted learning. Used primarily in the United Kingdom, CAL is synonymous with CAI.

cathode ray tube (CRT).   The television-like screen used to display text and graphics on most computer systems today.

CBI.   Computer-based instruction.

CBT.   Computer-based training.

CD–ROM.   Compact disc–read only memory. This technology user laser technology to store and retrieve vast amounts of data for use as input by computer systems. Unlike floppy diskettes or other typical storage media, CD–ROM information is provided by the manufacturer, not the user. (Progress is being made on CD–ROM-like products on which the user may store information, but they are not currently available.)

character.   Any of a series of numerals, letters, and symbols the computer can display as a single entity on the screen.

character set editor.   A program that allows the user to modify an existing set of characters to create new characters. For example, a character set editor may be used to add accents to letters or to create special symbols not available in standard character sets.

chip.   Short for *microchip*, a chip is a collection of electronic components, sometimes numbering in the hundreds of thousands, miniaturized to the point that they may be located on a silicon wafer smaller than a postage stamp.

CMI.   Computer-managed instruction.

COBOL.   General-purpose programming language popular in business applications.

command.   An instruction from the programmer to the computer. A programming language is a set of commands understood by both the programmer and the computer.

compiler.   A program that translates commands from a high-level programming language into machine-executable instructions. The output from some languages must be compiled before running. Other languages, called interpreted languages, may be run without compiling, but compiling often results in programs that run more quickly.

computer-assisted instruction (CAI).   The application of computer technology to solve an instructional problem.

computer-based instruction (CBI).   Instruction delivered primarily via computer.

computer-based training (CBT).   Instruction delivered primarily via computer.

computer-managed instruction (CMI).   Application of computer technology to monitor, track, and report on student and lesson performance.

concurrent CAI.   Computer assisted instruction in which the computer appears to run the CAI program and a software package about which the CAI lesson was written at the same time. This form of CAI allows for significant time savings when creating CAI about software products because the programmer need not simulate the target software program. The student sees instruction from the CAI program and sees the actual application running.

cosmetic adequacy.   Evaluation of the visual appeal of the lesson. Includes such factors as use of screen space, protocol, color, and animation.

cosmetic amplification.   Varying visual characteristics of the screen display to highlight important information. Employs techniques such as flashing, color, inversing, and character fonts and sizes.

courseware.   Educational software. Programs written to achieve instructional objectives.

CPU.   Central processing unit. The brain of the computer system.

crash.   A malfunction of the computer system. The system stops working, sometimes damaging programs or files in the process.

creeping.   Like scrolling, only across the screen rather than up and down.

CRT.   Acronym for "Cathode Ray Tube." The television-like screen used to display text and graphics on most computer systems today.

cue.   A signal to the student that a particular segment of the presented information is of greater importance than the information that surrounds it.

curriculum adequacy.   The degree to which a lesson fits the course of study as well as the characteristics of the students and the instructional environment.

cursor.   A symbol on the screen (often a blinking underscore) indicating the location at which the next character entered will appear.

data point.   An individual data item, such as the response provided by a given student to a particular question. Data points are collected in a database for evaluation.

database.   A collection of data points used to evaluate the performance of individual students or groups of students or the effectiveness of the lesson itself.

debugging.   The process of eliminating bugs from software.

digital.   Information that is represented as a series of bits.

digital audio.   Sound encoded as digital information. Unlike conventional audio recording techniques, the digitizing process stores samples of sound patterns and recalls them at the appropriate time to recreate the illusion of continuous audio segments.

disc (disk).   Any of several types of flat, circular surfaces on which data is stored.

diskette.   A removeable storage medium, usually 5.25 inches in diameter. Some diskettes, known as *floppy diskettes* or *floppies*, consist of a magnetic covering over a flexible plastic surface. Data may be recorded to and retrieved from diskettes by the computer.

DOS.   Disk operating system. The disk operating system is a set of programs that allows interaction between the user and the computer and between the computer and its peripheral devices.

dot matrix.   A method employing clustered dots to represent letters, numerals, or special symbols. Computer monitors (CRTs) work in this manner, as do many inexpensive printers.

drill and practice.   Refers to a type of CAI designed to allow students to practice skills they gain in other lessons.

driver.   A software program that controls peripheral devices. For example, a driver may be developed to allow a specific type of microcomputer to control a four-color ink jet printer.

Events of Instruction.   According to Gagné (1979), nine elements, ranging from motivation through instruction, practice, and evaluation, that should be present in most instructional sequences.

feedback. Information that informs the student about the accuracy of a response. Feedback is not the same as reinforcement.

file. A collection of data stored as a single unit.

firmware. A cross between hardware (equipment) and software (programs). *Firmware* describes electronic components that contain programs. For example, ROMs (read-only memory chips) and EPROMs (erasable programmable read-only memory chips) are considered firmware.

flag. Programmers set flags to indicate whether a certain condition exists. These flags may be values assigned to variables or bits in memory set to 0 or 1. For example, the programmer may set a flag equal to 1 when the student has passed a given point in the program. By checking the value of the flag, the programmer can tell if the student used that part of the lesson.

floppy diskette. A computer data storage device consisting of a magnetic covering over a flexible plastic surface, encased in a protective jacket.

flowchart. A diagram representing the layout of the CAI lesson. A flowchart indicates topics to be covered, questions to be asked, divisions to be made, and the paths to be followed after each possible student response.

font. A style of type resulting in a distinctive set of characters. Common fonts include Roman, Serif, and Sans Serif.

formal evaluation. The scientific collection and evaluation of empirical evidence concerning the performance of students and the lesson itself, as well as student attitudes about the lesson.

formative evaluation. Distinguished from summative evaluation primarily by the way in which information is used, formative evaluation takes place during the development of the product so that changes may be easily implemented.

FORTRAN. A condensed version of "FORmula TRANslator." FORTRAN is a programming language popular in mathematical and scientific applications.

frame. A unit of information on the computer screen. Some authoring systems consider a frame to be all of the information visible on the screen at one time. Others consider each window on the screen to be a separate frame.

frame protocol. The consistent use of various zones on the screen for specific purposes in order to simplify the student's interaction with lesson mechanics. Protocol may vary from frame type to frame type, but it remains consistent within a given frame type.

function keys. Keys present on the computer keyboard designed to serve different functions during the execution of different programs. For example, a function key may be used as a "Help" key during a CAI lesson and as a delete key in a word-processing application program. Because the programmer controls the task assigned to these keys, they are also known as *programmable function keys*.

functional zones. Segments of the computer screen designated for a given purpose. For example, one functional zone often located at the bottom of the screen prompts the user for desire responses.

GIGO. "Garbage In–Garbage Out." This philosophy, popular among computer programmers and users, reminds us that the quality of the computer's contribution is always determined by the quality of the programs and the integrity of the data.

graphics mode.   Most computers have text and graphics modes. In text mode, the computer's screen will display only numerals, letters, and other single-character-sized symbols. When in graphics mode, the points on the screen may be accessed individually to produce illustrations as well as characters.

hard copy.   Computer output on paper.

hard disc.   A magnetic storage device consisting primarily of a rigid platter with magnetic surfaces. Read/write heads in extremely close proximity to the disc read information from and write information to the disc. The head comes so close to the surface of the disc that even small particles of dust would interfere with the process or may even damage the surface of the disc. Because of the need to keep dust out of the way, most hard disc systems are sealed, preventing the user from removing the disc.

hardware.   Computer equipment. As one speaker put it, "If you can kick it, it's hardware." Includes processing units, disc drives, printers, and so on.

help.   A feature offered during many CAI lessons, help functions allow the student to temporarily leave the lesson to review or to gain access to additional information before continuing with the lesson.

hexadecimal numbering system.   Also known as *hex*, the hexadecimal system is based on the number 16. Columns are worth 1, 16, 256, 4096, and so on. Digits are represented by 0 through 9 and the letters A–F.

high-level language.   A computer programming language providing English-like commands to simplify the programming process. Each command is generally translated into several operations performed by the computer.

hint.   In CAI applications, hints provide additional information useful in answering a question or making a decision but do not provide the answer itself.

hybrid designs.   CAI lessons combining characteristics from two or more of the "pure" CAI modes.

IC.   Integrated circuit. Combines many electronic components into a single miniature component. IC technology made the microcomputer possible.

ICAI.   Artificially intelligent computer-assisted instruction.

ID.   Instructional Design. The process of systematically examining and solving an instructional problem.

illegal response.   Any student input that falls outside of the prescribed response options. For example, in a multiple-choice question with three answers (a, b, and c), typing a d would be an illegal response.

impact printer.   A printer that works by compressing an inked ribbon between the paper and metal pins or raised letters, much as a standard typewriter functions.

infinite loop.   A branching condition that continually returns execution to a point that has been executed. Two conditions may result in infinite loops: errors in program logic and conceptual loops, in which there is one or more answer that will end the loop, but the student is unable to provide an acceptable response.

informal evaluation. An attempt to gain information on the effectiveness of a lesson without following extensive scientific procedures.

information-based amplification. Manipulation of the content of the lesson in order to focus student attention. Techniques include repetition, verbal cueing, and reducing the amount of information on the screen.

input. Information coming to the computer from any of a number of sources, including the keyboard, a light pen, a touch screen, a video camera, or another computer.

instructional adequacy. A measure of lesson's ability to meet instructional objectives.

instructional frame. Also known as presentation frames, instructional frames present basic information to the student.

instructional game. CAI mode that employs a game context to teach or to reinforce information, skills, or concepts.

intelligent. Containing *processing power*. In computer devices, intelligence implies that memory and a processor are present in the device. Devices lacking intelligence are called *dumb*, such as a *dumb terminal*.

interaction. Two-way communication between the user and the computer. Interaction involves the learner in the instructional process.

interactive. Providing interaction between the user and the computer.

interface. The hardware and firmware used to connect computers and peripheral devices. For example, an interface may connect a microcomputer and a videodisc player or a computer and a touch screen.

interpreter. A computer programming language that is translated into machine code as it is executed, eliminating the need for compiling prior to execution. BASIC is generally an interpreted language.

inverse video. The process of reversing foreground and background colors, often used to highlight key words in CAI. For example, if the text on the screen is generally white on a black background, inverse video would produce black characters on a white background.

I/O. Input/Output. Often used to describe the function of communications lines or processors.

ISD. Instructional Systems Design. The process of systematically examining and solving an instructional problem.

italics. Letters slanted to produce emphasis.

joystick. An input device most commonly used to position the cursor on the screen or to drive symbols during instructional games.

justification. A process that aligns text on the right as well as the left, producing smooth margins on both sides.

K (kilo). In metric measurement, K represents a multiple of 1,000. For example, a 10K race covers 10,000 meters. In computer applications, K still stands for kilo, but it has come to mean 1024, the closest power of 2 to 1,000. So 256K bytes of memory really means 256 times 1024 bytes, or 262,144 bytes of memory.

kludge.   A program or piece of hardware that is slapped together, usually to meet short-term or testing needs, rather than planned appropriately and developed to provide years of maintenance-free operation.

language.   Used in computer programming contexts, a language is a set of commands producing prescribed outcomes understood by both the programmer and the computer.

learner control.   The degree to which the student is in control of the lesson. For example, the student may be allowed to gain access to help messages or remediation at any time or may be allowed to indicate when to move from unit to unit.

legal response.   Student input that falls within the parameters defined for the response. For example, in a multiple-choice question with three specified answer options (a, b, and c), a response of "b" represents a legal response.

light pen.   An input device employing a penlike tool. The pen is connected to the computer. When the student touches the pen to the surface of the monitor, the computer determines the location of the pen and responds based on the appropriateness of the pen's location.

linear.   Proceeding along a line, without variation. In CAI design, linear programs are those in which all students see the identical lesson; there is no branching. In reference to storage media, *linear* refers to media such as cassette tapes in which information must be located in a specific order, as compared to random access.

LISP.   A programming language used primarily in artificial intelligence applications. Initially running only on mainframes and large minicomputers, microcomputer versions are now emerging.

load.   The process of moving a program from storage on a diskette or other medium into the computer's memory for execution.

LOGO.   A programming language developed at MIT to foster analytical and problem-solving skills in young children.

loop.   A section of a program that is executed repeatedly, or the process of repeatedly executing such sections.

machine language.   Consisting of binary or hexadecimal numbers rather than commands, machine language is executed directly by the computer. Because machine language is difficult for people to use, most programs are written in higher level languages more closely approximating verbal language and are then compiled or interpreted into machine language by the computer before execution.

mainframe.   A large computer system supporting many concurrent users and output devices and costing many thousands of dollars. Mainframes often place requirements on the environment into which they are placed, requiring special attention to such things as electrical power, air temperature, and humidity, and they generally require a dedicated system administrator to keep the machine up and running, to establish procedures for its use, and to help users learn to use it.

mass storage.   Large systems, usually consisting of tape or disc devices, capable of storing and retrieving large amounts of data.

mastery learning.   Philosophy that contends that students should demonstrate proficiency in one area before moving on to other areas. In mastery learning contexts, students often work with concepts, information, or skills until they perform the desired behaviors with 80% to 90% accuracy. Because of its ability to evaluate performance and minimize the need for a human instructor, CAI is often ideal in mastery learning situations.

MECC.   The Minnesota Educational Computing Consortium. An organization established by the state of Minnesota to provide educational computing services to its schools, MECC has been a valuable leader in developing and distributing courseware to other areas as well. Schools and districts can gain access to courseware on a wide variety of topics through subscriptions with MECC.

memory.   Electronic components in a computer that store information for high-speed access while processing takes place. Once in memory, programs and information may be used quickly. Memory is divided into two primary classifications, ROM (read-only memory), in which the computer's manufacturer places information required for the machine's basic operations, and RAM (random-access memory), into which information is temporarily stored as it is needed by the user.

menu.   A list of options presented to the student. By presenting a menu, it is generally possible to simplify the response required to a single keystroke, representing the student's selection.

microcomputer.   A small personal computer system, as contrasted with minicomputers or mainframe computer systems, designed for use by one person at a time, rather than multiple users. Components usually include a keyboard, through which the student communicates to the computer; a central processing unit (CPU), in which processing takes place; a monitor, through which the computer communicates to the student; and one or more diskette drives, used for data storage and retrieval.

microprocessor.   A single chip, or integrated circuit, in which processing of data takes place. More complex computers employ multiple-processor architectures, in which several processors are coordinated to produce powerful, versatile, high-speed machines.

minicomputer.   More powerful than a microcomputer and less powerful than a mainframe, minicomputers generally provide support for multiple users while placing fewer demands on operators and the environment than do mainframes.

mnemonic device.   A technique used to facilitate remembering information, usually employing parts of key words or phrases combined into a meaningful unit. For example, *"Every Good Boy Does Fine"* is used to remember the musical notes represented by the lines on a scale.

modem.   Short for "modulator–demodulator," a modem is an interface that converts the digital signals produced by a computer to analog signals suitable for transmission over telephone lines and converts incoming analog signals into digital signals for interpretation by the computer.

monitor.   The CRT (cathode ray tube) on which computer output is displayed on most microcomputers and terminals. Monitors generally do not have the electronic circuitry associated with a television receiver, and consequently cannot receive or interpret broadcast signals.

monochrome.   As opposed to monitors displaying many colors, monochrome monitors display one color in addition to black. Common combinations are black and white, amber and black, and green and black.

mouse.   A hand-held pointing device used to provide input. As the student moves the mouse along a flat surface near the computer, the cursor moves across the screen accordingly. The mouse generally contains from one to three buttons that the student may use to indicate different actions to the computer.

objective.   An unambiguous description of behaviors the student is to be able to perform as a result of instruction. A well-written objective specifies an observable action the student will perform, the conditions under which that behavior is to be exhibited, and the criteria for evaluating the behavior as acceptable.

operating system.   Software consisting of a set of programs that govern interaction between the user and the computer and between the computer and its peripheral devices.

output.   Information sent from the computer to another device, such as a printer, a monitor, or a file.

pacing.   The manner in which the rate of lesson execution is controlled. Student pacing, computerized pacing, and combinations of student and computerized pacing have all been employed in CAI.

Pascal.   A popular programming language developed to be transportable from computer to computer and to help student programmers develop good programming habits. In Pascal, the programmer writes a series of *procedures* and *functions*, which are combined as building blocks to achieve the desired results.

PASS.   An acronym for "Professional Authoring Software System," PASS was developed by Bell & Howell as one of the first comprehensive feature-rich authoring systems for microcomputers.

peripheral device.   Electronic or mechanical equipment that is connected to a computer as an add-on rather than an integral part of the system. Peripheral devices include printers, additional diskette drives, graphics tablets, video-disc players, and voice synthesis units.

personalizing CAI.   The act of adapting the lesson to fit individual students. Techniques for personalizing instruction have included incorporating the student's name, hobbies, favorite foods and activities, and job to involve the learner in the learning process.

PILOT.   One of the first authoring languages, PILOT provides a relatively small set of commands, usually consisting of a single letter. By combining these commands to form programs, making instruction appear on the screen becomes a relatively simple task.

pixel.   Short for "picture element," a pixel is a tiny dot on the computer's monitor. The resolution of a monitor is determined by the number and size of these dots. The smaller the dots, the more there will be on the screen, and the finer the picture may be. By using software capable of addressing individual pixels, the programmer may produce dazzling and detailed CAI graphics.

PLATO.   An acronym for "Programmed Learning for Automatic Teaching Operations." Developed at the University of Illinois and marketed commercially by Control Data Corporation, PLATO was a CAI authoring and delivery system running on very large Cyber mainframe computers and including advanced graphics capabilities. Because the cost of the computers or computer time was considerable, only large institutions used PLATO initially. CDC recently announced the ability to rent authoring time on their mainframes and to convert the output to run on a number of microcomputer systems.

procedural protocol.   The consistent use of conventions for lesson procedures such as obtaining student responses; lesson pacing; and the availability of review, hints, and other forms of assistance.

processor.   Used synonymously with *CPU* or *microprocessor*.

program.   A list of commands the computer follows, written in any of a number of languages.

program adequacy.   Evaluation of the computer programming to determine that responses are evaluated as anticipated, that all program branches are executed faithfully, and that there are no infinite loops.

programming language.   A set of commands producing prescribed outcomes understood by both the programmer and the computer.

PROM.   An acronym for "Programmable Read-Only Memory." A PROM is a memory chip that is programmed by the computer's manufacturer to contain programs and data critical to the machine's operation. PROMs may be recorded after they are manufactured, as compared to ROMs, which are programmed to do a specific set of tasks at the time of manufacturing. Some PROMs, called "Erasable Programmable Read-Only Memory" (EPROMs), may be erased and reprogrammed.

prompt.   A symbol or brief message appearing to inform the user of the type of action expected next. Examples include "A>," and "Press RETURN to continue."

question frame.   Also known as criterion frames, question frames are used to solicit input from the student. Based on student input, it is possible to determine whether the desired learning has taken place.

RAM.   Random access memory. Chips that temporarily store information for high-speed access while processing takes place.

random access.   The ability to access information in any order, rather than by following a linear path. Diskette drives allow random access to the information stored on diskettes. Cassette tapes, on the other hand, do not provide random access.

random access memory (RAM).   Chips that temporarily store information for high-speed access while processing takes place.

read-only memory (ROM).   A ROM is a memory chip that is produced by the computer's manufacturer to contain programs and data critical to the machine's operation. ROMs may not be altered after they are manufactured, as compared to PROMs, which are programmed after manufacturing.

reinforcement.   A consequence presented after a behavior is exhibited that affects the probability that the behavior will occur again. In CAI, positive reinforcement often takes the form of praise or the ability to play a game or do something fun or interesting. Negative reinforcement usually takes the form of a message informing the user that the response was incorrect, followed by a remedial session to increase correct responses.

resolution.   An indication of the quality of the image a monitor is able to produce. The resolution of a monitor is determined by the number and size of the pixels (dots of which characters and graphics are composed on the screen). The smaller the dots, the more there will be on the screen and the finer the picture may be. High resolution means more dots per inch and a better picture.

response anticipation.   The process of predicting student input and providing contingencies for correct, incorrect, and unanticipated responses.

reverse video.   The process of reversing foreground and background colors often used to highlight key words in CAI. For example, if the text on the screen is generally white on a black background, reverse video would produce black characters on a white background.

ROM.   A memory chip that is produced by the computer's manufacturer to contain programs and data critical to the machine's operation. ROMs may not be altered after they are manufactured, as compared to PROMs, which are programmed after manufacturing.

run.   To execute a program.

scrolling.   Moving all or parts of the screen display as a unit, usually to make room for additional information. The most common example is when the screen fills up and the entire image moves up to allow another line to appear.

simulation.   In CAI, the process of using the computer to model a process or system. Examples include flight simulation in pilot training, simulated chemistry experiments, and simulations modeling the results of business transactions.

software.   The languages, programs, and data that make use of computer hardware. *Hardware* includes the physical devices; *software* encompasses many types of information that apply the hardware to produce results.

speech synthesis.   The combination of electronic sounds to approximate human speech. Sophisticated hardware and software components examine text, break it down to phonemes (sound units), and then assemble representations of these units to produce humanlike speech.

step size.   In CAI, the level of instructional difficulty between screens or teaching units.

storyboard.   A representation (on paper) of what a screenface will contain. A storyboard contains a picture of the screen as well as notes to the programmer conveying the designer's intentions.

string.   A series of letters, numerals, or symbols treated as a single entity. By assigning string values to variables, it becomes possible to capture, display, and record such things as the date, the student's name, and the actual responses the student gives to questions presented in the lesson.

structured programming.   Programming that emphasizes modularity, clarity, and simplicity. Languages like Pascal are designed to result in structured programming.

subroutine.   A program segment set off from the main body of the program to be accessed repeatedly by a specific command. Upon completion of the program segment, execution returns to the point at which the subroutine was accessed.

summative evaluation.   The process of determining the value of the lesson after development is complete. Generally conducted to validate performance rather than to locate areas in need of improvement.

terminal.   Generally consisting of a CRT and a keyboard, a terminal serves as input and output device for a time-sharing computer. For example, terminals may be connected to a mainframe computer to provide access to the computer. Processing takes place on the host computer itself, rather than in the terminal. The terminal serves as a window through which the operator may view what is happening on the host computer and may issue commands to the computer.

TICCIT.   An acronym for "Time-shared Interactive Computer-Controlled Information Television system," TICCIT is a CAI authoring system developed by MITRE Corporation and the National Science Foundation. TICCIT combines video, computer graphics, and minicomputer authoring and delivery systems.

top-down programming.   Programming practice similar to task analysis in that it begins with an understanding of the top-level activities required and breaks them down into subtasks.

transitional frame.   Frames that tie the different aspects of the CAI lesson together. Transitional frames support lesson flow rather than presenting information or assessing student performance.

tutorial.   A type of CAI in which the computer serves as the primary instructor, developing an instructional dialogue between the student and the computer. Student progress is evaluated and remediation is provided as necessary.

user-friendly.   An adjective used to describe systems designed to simplify the interaction between the user and the computer. For example, extensive use of prompts and menus and the presence of a Help key are used to make software user-friendly.

VDU.   Video display unit. (See CRT.)

videodisc.   A recordlike surface containing digital data. Originally developed to store and replay video, this technology has demonstrated great potential for storing other forms of data as well.

window.   A section of the computer's screen that is used independently of the remainder of the screen. For example, the majority of the screen may contain a computer graphic, while a window contains instruction on the information contained in the graphic. The instructional window may be erased and refilled while the graphic remains unaltered.

Bibliography

ADAMS, J. A. (1984). Networked computers promote computer literacy and computer-assisted instruction. *Technological Horizons in Education*, **11**(8), 95–99.

AHLERS, R. H., R. A. EVANS, and H. F. O'NEIL, JR. (1986). Expert systems for department of defense training. *Journal of Computer-Based Instruction.* **13**(2), 29.

ALESSANDRINI, K. L. (1984). *Graphics in CBT* (cassette tape recordings with booklets). Santa Monica, CA: MicroConnect.

—— (1983). Instructional design for CAI tutorials. *Collegiate Microcomputer*, **1**, 207–214.

ALESSI, S. M., and S. R. TROLLIP (1985). *Computer-Based Instruction: Methods and Development*. Englewood Cliffs, NJ: Prentice-Hall, Inc.

ALLEN, M. (1980). Computer-managed instruction. *Journal of Research and Development in Education*, **14**, 33–40.

Apple SuperPILOT (1982). *Language Reference Manual*. Cupertino, CA: Apple Computer, Inc.

APPLEBAUM, W. R. (1985). Course-centered development: A team approach to CBT. *Data Training*, **4**(4), 26–27.

ATKINSON, M. L. (1984). Computer-assisted instruction: Current state of the art. *Computers in the Schools*, **1**(1), 91–99.

BAKER, F. B. (1978). *Computer-Managed Instruction: Theory and Practice*. Englewood Cliffs, NJ: Educational Technology Publications.

—— (1981). Computer-managed instruction: A context for computer-based instruction. In H. F. O'Neil (ed.). *Computer-Based Instruction: A State-of-the-Art Assessment*. New York: Academic Press.

BALMAN, T. (1981). Implementation techniques for interactive CAI programs. *Computers and Education*, **5**, 19–29.

BANGERT-DROWNS, R. L., J. A. KULIK, and C. C. KULIK (1985). Effectiveness of computer-based education in secondary schools. *Journal of Computer-Based Instruction*, **12**(3), 59–68.

BARKER, P. G., and R. SINGH (1982). Author languages for computer-based learning. *British Journal of Educational Technology*, **13**, 167–196.

BARRETT, B. K., and M. J. HANNAFIN (1982). Computers in educational management: Merging accountability with technology. *Educational Technology*, **22**(3), 9–12.

BEEBE, T. H., and A. P. MIZELL (1983). Software languages: How to talk to your computer. *Instructional Innovator*, **28**(4), 14–17.

BLANK, D., P. A. MURPHY, and B. SCHNEIDERMAN (1986). A comparison of children's reading comprehension and reading rates at three text presentation speeds on a CRT. *Journal of Computer-Based Instruction*, **13**(3), 84–87.

BLOOM, B. S. (1956). *Taxonomy of Educational Objectives. Handbook I: Cognitive Domain.* New York: McKay.

BORICH, G. D., and R. P. JEMELKA (1981). Evaluation. In H. F. O'Neil (ed.). *Computer-Based Instruction: A State-of-the-Art Assessment.* New York: Academic Press.

BORK, A. (1981). *Learning with Computers.* Bedford, MA: Digital Equipment Corp.

——— (1984). Producing computer-based learning material at the educational technology center. *Journal of Computer-Based Instruction,* 11(3), 78–81.

——— (1984). Education and computers: The situation today and some possible futures. *Technological Horizons in Education,* 12(3), 92–97.

BRADFORD, J. (1982). The software line-up: What reviewers look for when evaluating software. *Electronic Learning,* 2(2), 45–48.

BRAMBLE, W. J., and E. J. MASON (1985). *Computers in Schools.* New York: McGraw-Hill.

BRIGGS, L. J., and W. W. WAGER (1981). *Handbook of Procedures for the Design of Instruction* (2nd ed.). Englewood Cliffs, NJ: Educational Technology Publications.

BRIGHT, G. W. (1983). Explaining the efficiency of computer assisted instruction. *AEDS Journal,* 16(3), 144–153.

BROPHY, J. (1981). Teacher praise: Functional analysis. *Review of Educational Research,* 51, 5–32.

BROWN, G. D. (1985). The author as writer: Word processing your CBT. *Data Training,* 4(4), 24–25.

BROWN, J. W. (1986). Some motivational issues in computer-based instruction. *Educational Technology,* 26(9), 27–29.

BUNSON, S. (1985). CAI frame by frame. *TechTrends,* 30(4), 24–25.

BURKE, R. L. (1982). *CAI Sourcebook.* Englewood Cliffs, NJ: Prentice-Hall, Inc.

BURY, K. F., J. M. BOYLE, R. J. EVEY, and A. S. NEAL (1982). Windowing versus scrolling on a visual display terminal. *Human Factors,* 24, 385–394.

CALDWELL, R. M. (1980). Guidelines for developing basic skills instructional materials for use with microcomputer technology. *Eductional Technology,* 20(10), 7–12.

CAMBRE, M. A. (1984). Notes on new technologies: Interactive video. *Instructional Innovator,* 29(6), 24–25.

CARRIER, C. (1984). Do learners make good choices? *Instructional Innovator,* 29(2), 15–17.

CHAMBERS, J. A, and J. W. SPRECHER (1983). *Computer-Assisted Instruction: Its Use in the Classroom.* Englewood Cliffs, NJ: Prentice-Hall, Inc.

CLARK, D. J. (1984). How do interactive videodiscs rate against other media? *Instructional Innovator,* 29(6), 12–16.

CLARK, R. E. (1984). Research on student thought processes during computer-based instruction. *Journal of Instructional Development,* 7(3), 2–5.

——— (April 1984). Learning from computers: Theoretical problems. Paper presented at the annual meeting of the American Educational Research Association, New Orleans.

——— (1985). Evidence for confounding in computer-based instruction studies: Analyzing the meta-analyses. *Educational Communication and Technology Journal,* 33, 249–262.

CLEMENT, F. J. (1981). Affective considerations in computer-based education. *Educational Technology,* 21(10), 28–32.

COHEN, V. B. (1983). Criteria for the evaluation of microcomputer courseware. *Educational Technology,* 23(1), 9–14.

——— (1985). A reexamination of feedback in computer-based instruction: Implications for instructional design. *Educational Technology,* 25(1), 33–36.

CONKRIGHT, T. D. (1984). Linear, branching, and complex: A taxonomy of simulations. *Training News,* 6(3), 6–7, 19.

COOK, J. E. (1984). West Virginia schools to secure a state-wide microcomputer network. *Technological Horizons in Education,* 11(6), 85–88.

CRAWFORD, C. (1984). *The Art of Computer Game Design.* New York: McGraw-Hill.

DALTON, D. D., and M. J. HANNAFIN (1985). Examining the effects of varied computer-based reinforcement on self-esteem and achievement: An exploratory study. *Association for Educational Data Systems Journal*, **18**(3), 172–182.

DAVIS, R. H., L. T., ALEXANDER, and S. L. YELON, (1974). *Learning System Design: An Approach to the Improvement of Instruction*. New York: McGraw-Hill.

DAYNES, R., and B. BUTLER (1984). *The Videodisc Book: A Guide and Directory*. New York: John Wiley and Sons.

DEAN, C., and Q. WHITLOCK (1983). *A Handbook of Computer-Based Training*. London: Kogan Page.

DEARBORN, D. E. (1982). A process for selecting computer software. *NASSP Bulletin*, **66**(455), 26–30.

DENCE, M. (1980). Toward defining the role of CAI: A review. *Educational Technology*, **20**(11), 50–54.

DERRINGER, D. K. (1983). New directions for education in the information society? *Technological Horizons in Education*, **11**(1), 110–111.

DICK, W., and L. CAREY (1985). *The Systematic Design of Instruction* (2nd ed.) Glenview, IL: Scott, Foresman and Co.

DIMAS, C. (1978). A strategy for developing CAI. *Educational Technology*, **18**(4), 26–29.

DWYER, F. M. (1978). *Strategies for Improving Visual Learning*. State College, PA: Learning Services.

DYER, C. A. (1972). *Preparing for Computer-Assisted Instruction*. Englewood Cliffs, NJ: Educational Technology Publications.

EBNER, D. G., D. T. MANNING, F. R. BROOKS, J. V. MAHONEY, H. T. LIPPERT, and P. M. BALSON (1984). Videodiscs can improve instructional efficiency. *Instructional Innovator*, **29**(6), 26–28.

EDWARDS, P., and R. BROADWELL (1974). *Flowcharting and BASIC*. New York: Harcourt, Brace Jovanovich, Inc.

EISELE, J. E. (1978). Lesson design for computer-based instructional systems. *Educational Technology*, **18**(9), 14–21.

ELLINGER, R. S., and B. R. BROWN (1979). The whens and hows of computer-based instructional simulations. *AEDS Journal*, **12**, 51–62.

ELLINGTON, H., E. ADINALL, and F. PERCIVAL (1982). *A Handbook of Game Design*. London: Kogan Page.

ENGLAND, E. (1984). Colour and layout considerations in CAL materials. *Computers and Education*, **8**, 317–321.

EVANS, C. R. (1980). *The Micro Millennium*. New York: The Viking Press.

FOSHAY, R. (1985). Good screens and bad: Rules for designing interaction. *Data Training*. **4**(4), 14–15.

——— (1986). CBI: The more things change. . . . *Performance & Instruction Journal*, **25**(5), 29–30.

FOX, J., and N. RUSHBY (1979). Guidelines for developing educational computer programs. *Computers and Education*, **3**, 35–41.

FRIEND, J., and J. D. MILOJKOVIC (1984). Designing interactions between students and computers. In D. F. WALKER and R. D. HESS (eds.). *Instructional Software: Principles and Perspectives for Design and Use*. Belmont, CA: Wadsworth.

FUTRELL, M., and P. GEISERT (1984). The Well-trained Computer: Designing Systematic Instructional Materials for the Classroom Microcomputer. Englewood Cliffs, NJ: Educational Technology Publications.

GAGNÉ, R. M. (1970). *The Conditions of Learning* (2nd ed.). New York: Holt, Rinehart, and Winston, Inc.

GAGNÉ, R. M., and L. J. Briggs (1979). *Principles of Instructional Design* (2nd ed.). New York: Holt, Rinehart and Winston.

GAGNÉ, R. M., W. WAGER, and A. ROJAS (1981). Planning and authoring computer-assisted instruction lessons. *Educational Technology*, **21**(9), 17–26.

GAINES, B. R. (1981). The technology of interaction—dialog programming rules. *International Journal of Man–Machine Studies*, **14**, 133–150.

GARHART, C., and M. J. HANNAFIN (1986). The accuracy of cognitive monitoring during computer-based instruction. *Journal of Computer-Based Instruction*, **13**(3), 88–93.

GINDELE, J. F., and J. G. GINDELE (1984). Interactive videodisc technology and its implications for education. *Technological Horizons in Education*, **12**(1), 93–97.

GLADWIN, L. A. (1984). Computer-based training in the second computer age. *Performance & Instruction Journal*, **23**(7), 21–23.

GLEASON, G. T. (1981). Microcomputers in education: The state of the art. *Educational Technology*, **21**(3), 7–18.

GODFREY, D., and S. STERLING (1982). *The Elements of CAL*. Reston, VA: Reston Publishing Company.

GOETZFRIED, L. L. and M. J. HANNAFIN (1985). The effects of embedded CAI instructional control strategies on the learning and application of mathematics rules. *American Educational Research Journal*. **22**, 273–278.

GOLAS, K. C. (1983). The formative evaluation of computer-assisted instruction. *Educational Technology*, **23**(1), 26–28.

GOTT, S. P., W. BENNET, and A. GILLET (1986). Models of technical competence for intelligent tutoring systems. *Journal of Computer-Based Instruction*. **13**(2), 43–46.

GRABINGER, R. S. (January 1985). CRT text design: Prominent layout variables based on a factor analysis of models of computer-generated text. Paper presented at the annual meeting of the Association for Educational Communication and Technology, Anaheim, CA.

——— (1984). CRT text design: Psychological attributes underlying the evaluation of models of CRT text displays. *Journal of Visual and Verbal Languaging*, **4**(1), 17–39.

GRABOWSKI, B., and W. AGGEN (1984). Computers for interactive learning. *Instructional Innovator*, **29**(2), 27–30.

GRAHAM, J., and M. J. HANNAFIN (1985). Interactive video with Apple SuperPILOT. *Educational Technology*, **25**(3), 30–32.

GRAYSON, L. P. (1984). An overview of computers in U.S. education. *Technological Horizons in Education*, **12**(1), 78–83.

GROPPER, G. L. (1975). *Diagnosis and Revision in the Development of Instructional Materials*. Englewood Cliffs, NJ: Educational Technology Publications.

HAMAKER, C. (1986). The effects of adjunct questions on prose learning. *Review of Educational Research*, **56**, 212–242.

HAMILTON, R. J. (1985). A framework for the evaluation of the effectiveness of adjunct questions and objectives. *Review of Educational Research*, **55**, 47–85.

HANNAFIN, M. J. (1984). Guidelines for determining locus of instructional control in the design of computer-assisted instruction. *Journal of Instructional Development*, **7**(3), 6–10.

——— (1984). Options for authoring instructional interactive video. *Journal of Computer-Based Instruction*, **11**, 98–100.

——— (1985). Empirical issues in the study of computer-assisted interactive video. *Educational Communication and Technology Journal*, **33**, 235–247.

——— (1987). The effects of orienting activities, cueing, and practice on learning from computer-based instruction. *Journal of Educational Research*, in press.

HANNAFIN, M. J., D. DALTON, and S. HOOPER (1987). Computers in education: Barriers and solutions. In E. Miller and M. L. Mosley (eds.) *Educational Media and Technology Yearbook*. Littleton, CO: Libraries Unlimited.

——— (1987). Computers in education: 10 myths and 10 needs. *Educational Technology*.

HANNAFIN, M. J., and C. GARHART (1985). Research methods for the study of interactive video. Paper presented at the annual meeting of the Association for the Development of Computer-Based Instructional Systems, Philadelphia.

HANNAFIN, M. J., C. GARHART, L. RIEBER, and T. PHILLIPS (1985). Keeping interactive video in perspective: Tentative guidelines and cautions in the design of interactive video. In E. Miller and M. L. Mosley (eds.). *Educational Media and Technology Yearbook*. Littleton, CO: Libraries Unlimited.

HANNAFIN, M. J., and C. HUGHES (1986). A framework for incorporating orienting activities in computer-based interactive video. *Instructional Science*, **15**, 239–255.

HANNAFIN, M. J., and T. L. PHILLIPS (in press). Perspectives in the design of interactive video: Beyond tape versus disc. *Journal and Reasearch and Development in Education*.

HANNAFIN, M. J., T. L. PHILIPS, L. P. RIEBER, and C. GARHART (in press). The effects of orienting activities and cognitive processing time on factual and inferential learning. *Educational Communication and Technology Journal*.

HANNAFIN, M. J., T. L. PHILLIPS, and S. TRIPP (1986). The effects of orienting, processing, and practicing activities on learning from interactive video. *Journal of Computer Based Instruction*, **13**, 134–139.

HARRIS, S. D., and J. M. OWENS (1986). Some critical factors that limit the effectiveness of machine intelligence technology in military systems applications. *Journal of Computer-Based Instruction*. **13**(2), 30–34.

HARTMAN, J. (1981). A systematic approach to the design of computer-assisted instruction materials. *Technological Horizons in Education*, **8**(2), 43–45.

HARTMAN, K. (September 1982). Authoring considerations in writing instructional computer programs. *The Computing Teacher*, **10**(1), 27–29.

HATHAWAY, M. (1984). Variables of computer screen display and how they affect learning. *Educational Technology*, **24**(1), 7–10.

HAZEN, M. (1982). Computer-assisted instruction with PILOT on the Apple computer. *Educational Technology*, **22**(11), 20–22.

—— (1985). Instructional software design principles. *Educational Technology*, **25**(11), 18–23.

HEINES, J. M. (1985). Interactive means active: Learner involvement in CBT. *Data Training*, **4**(4), 48–53.

—— (1986). The graphics touch. *Training News*, January, 4–5.

—— (1984). *Screen Design Strategies for Computer-Assisted Instruction*. Bedford, MA: Digital Press.

HILGARD, E. R., and G. H. BOWER (1966). *Theories of Learning* (3rd ed.). New York: Meredith.

HIRSCHBUHL, J., and J. KLUTH (1985). In the mind, not in the hardware: Using graphics in CBT. *Data Training*, **4**(4), 20–22.

HISCOX, M. D., and S. B. HISCOX (1986). The potential of OD-ROM in education. *Tech Trends*, **31**(3), 14–19.

HOLDING, D. H. (1970). Repeated errors in motor learning. *Ergonomics*, **13**, 727–734.

HOLCOMB, R. K. (1985). Use a speech synthesizer to teach basic vocabulary. *TechTrends*, **30**(4), 18–19.

HOLMES, G. (1983). Creating CAL courseware: Some possibilities. *System*, **11**(1), 21–32.

HOLZNAGEL, D. C. (1982–1985). *MicroSIFT Courseware Evaluations*. Portland, OR: Northwest Regional Educational Laboratory.

HOOPER, S., and M. J. HANNAFIN (in press). Factors affecting the legibility of text during computer-based instruction. *Journal of Instructional Development*.

HORD, E. (1984). Guidelines for designing computer-assisted instruction. *Instructional Innovator*, **29**(1), 19–23.

HOUSTON, J. P. (1976). *Fundamentals of Learning*. New York: Academic Press.

HUNTINGTON, J. F. (1979). *Computer-Assisted Instruction Using BASIC*. Englewood Cliffs, NJ: Educational Technology Publications.

INGERSOLL, G. M., and C. B. SMITH (1984). Availability and growth of microcomputers in American schools. *Technological Horizons in Education*, 12(1), 84–87.

Innovator Interview (1984). Rod Daynes, Interactive Technologies Corporation. *Instructional Innovator*, 29(6), 30–32.

Interactive video on a shoestring (1984). *Instructional Innovator*, 29(6), 29,40.

JARVIS, S. (1984). Videodiscs and computers. *Byte*, 9(7), 187–203.

JAY, T. B. (1983). The cognitive approach to computer courseware design and evaluation. *Educational Technology*, 32(1), 22–26.

JENKINS, J. M. (1982). Some principles of screen design and software for their support. *Computers and Instruction*, 6, 25–31.

JENSEN, J. D. (1982). A taxonomy of microcomputer authoring systems. *Performance and Instruction*, 21(6), 50–52.

JURGEMEYER, F. H. (1982). Programmed instruction: Lessons it can teach us. *Educational Technology*, 22(5), 20–21.

KAY, H. (1955). Learning and retaining verbal material. *British Journal of Psychology*, 46, 81–100.

KEARSLEY, G. (1984). Authoring tools: An introduction. *Journal of Computer-Based Instruction*, 11(3), 67.

—— Instructional design and authoring software. *Journal of Instructional Development*, 7(3), 11–16.

—— (1985). Microcomputer software: Design and development principles. *Journal of Educational Computing Research*, 1, 209–220.

KIDD, M. E., and G. HOLMES (1982). Courseware design: Exploiting the colour micro. *Computers and Education*, 6, 299–303.

KING, F. J., and M. D. ROBLYER (1984). Alternative designs for evaluating computer-based instruction. *Journal of Instructional Development*, 7(3), 23–29.

KOLESNIK, W. B. (1976). *Learning: Educational Applications*. Boston: Allyn and Bacon, Inc.

KRAHN, C. G., and M. C. BLANCHAER (1986). Using an advance organizer to improve knowledge application by medical students in computer-based clinical simulations. *Journal of Computer-Based Instruction*, 13(3), 71–74.

KULHAVY, R. W. (1977). Feedback in written instruction. *Review of Eductional Research*, 47, 211–232.

KULHAVY, R. W., F. R. YEKOVICH, and J. W. DYER (1976). Feedback and response confidence. *Journal of Educational Psychology*, 68, 522–528.

KULIK, J. A., C. C. KULIK, and P. A. COHEN (1980). Effectiveness of computer-based college teaching: A meta-analysis of findings. *Review of Educational Research*, 50(4), 525–544.

—— (1980). Instructional technology and college teaching. *Teaching of Psychology*, 7(4), 199–205.

L'ALLIER, J. J., and R. D. TENNYSON (1980). Principles of instructional design applied to an introductory course on educational computing. *Journal of Computer-Based Instruction*, 7(2), 26–32.

LANDA, R. K. (1984). *Creating Courseware: A Beginner's Guide*. New York: Harper & Row.

LATHROP, A., and B. GOODSON (1983). *Courseware in the Classroom*. Reading, MA: Addison-Wesley.

LAUB, L. (1986). The evolution of mass storage. *BYTE*, 11(5), 161–172.

LEIBLUM, M. D. (1980). A media selection model geared toward CAL. *Technological Horizons in Education*, 7(2), 29–33.

—— (1982). Factors sometimes overlooked and underestimated in the selection and success of CAL as an instructional medium. *AEDS Journal*, 15(2), 67–79.

—— (1982). Computer-managed instruction: An explanation and overview. *AEDS Journal*, 15, 126–142.

—— (1984). Some principles of computer-assisted instruction, or how to tame the flashing beast. *Educational Technology*, **24**(3), 16–18.

LENKWAY, P. (1986). Minimum student performance standards in computer literacy: Florida's new state law. *Technological Horizons in Education*, **13**(9), 74–77.

LENTZ, R. (1985). Designing computer screen displays. *Performance and Instruction*, **24**(1), 16–17.

LIAO, T. T. (1983). Using computer simulations to integrate learning. *Simulation and Games*, **14**(1), 21–28.

LOCATIS, C. N., and F. D. ATKINSON (1976). A guide to instructional media selection. *Educational Technology*, **16**(8), 19–21.

LOREE, M. R. (1965). *Psychology of Education*. New York: The Ronald Press Company.

MACK, B., and P. HEATH (1980). *Guide to Good Programming*. New York: Halstead Press.

MACKEY, K., and T. SLESNICK (1982). A style manual for authors of software. *Creative Computing*, **8**, 110–111.

MacLACHLAN, J. (1986). Psychologically based techniques for improving learning within computerized tutorials. *Journal of Computer-Based Instruction*, **13**(3), 65–70.

MAGER, R. F. (1962). *Preparing instructional objectives*. Belmont, CA: Fearon Publishers.

MALLOY, R. (1986). A roundup of optical disk drives. *BYTE*, **11**(5), 215–224.

MALONE, T. W. (1980). *What makes things fun to learn? A study of intrinsically motivating computer games*. Cognitive and Instructional Science Series CIS-7. Palo Alto, CA: Palo Alto Research Center.

—— (1983). Toward a theory of intrinsically motivating instruction. *Cognitive Science*, **4**, 333–369.

MARKET DATA RETRIEVAL (1984). *Microcomputers in the Schools, 1983–84: A Comprehensive Survey and Analysis*. Westport, CT: Author.

—— (1985). *Microcomputers in the Schools, 1984–85: A Comprehensive Survey and Analysis*. Westport, CT: Author.

MAYER, R. E. (1977). The sequencing of instruction and the concept of assimilation to schema. *Instructional Science*, **6**, 369–388.

—— (1984). Aids to text comprehension. *Educational Psychologist*, **19**, 30–42.

McISAAC, D. N., and F. B. BAKER (1978). *Microcomputer CMI: Performance Specifications*. Madison, WI: University of Wisconsin.

McPHERSON-TURNER, C. (1979). CAI readiness checklist: Formative author-evaluation of CAI lessons. *Journal of Computer-Based Instruction*, **6**(2), 47–49.

MEREDITH, J. C. (1971). *The CAI Author/Instructor*. Englewood Cliffs, NJ: Educational Technology Publications.

MERRILL, M. D. (1985). Where is the authoring in authoring systems? *Journal of Computer-Based Instruction*, **12**, 90–96.

MERRILL, M. D., E. W. SCHNEIDER, and K. A. FLETCHER (1980). *TICCIT*. Englewood Cliffs, NJ: Educational Technology Publications.

MERRILL, M. D., and L. M. STOLUROW (1966). Hierarchical preview vs. problem-oriented review in learning an imaginary science. *American Educational Research Journal*, **3**, 251–261.

MERRILL, M. D., and L. E. WOOD (1984). Computer-guided instructional design. *Journal of Computer-Based Instruction*, **11**(2), 60–63.

MERRILL, P. F. (1982). Displaying text on microcomputers. In D. Jonassen (ed.). *The Technology of Text*. Englewood Cliffs, NJ: Educational Technology Publications.

MORRIS, J. M. (1983). Computer-aided instruction: Toward a new direction. *Educational Technology*, **23**(5), 12–15.

National Task Force on Educational Technology (1986). Transforming American education: Reducing the risk to the nation. *Tech Trends*, **31**(4), 12–24, 35.

NEUMANN, R. (1982). How to find good software. *Electronic Learning*, **2**(2), 40–43.

NIEDERMEYER, F. C. (1972). *Prototype Testing in Instructional Development.* Los Alamitos, CA: Southwest Regional Laboratory.

NORRIS, H. (December 1983). Lessons take off with SuperPILOT. *Apple-Plus*, 1(2) 99–107.

NYGREN, B. M. (1983). Let's don't go gaga over computers. *Executive Educator*, 5(5), 40.

OLSON, J. S. (1983). Gagné on the uses of new technology. *Instructional Innovator*, 28(5), 24–25.

O'NEIL, F. (1984). An alternative model for computer-assisted instruction in an educational environment. *Technological Horizons in Education*, 11(8), 113–117.

PAPERT, S. (1980). *Mindstorms.* New York: Basic Books, Inc.

PAULINE, R., and M. J. HANNAFIN (1987). Interactive slide-sound instruction. Incorporating the power of the computer with high-fidelity visual and aural images. *Educational Technology*, in press.

PECK, K. L., and M. J. HANNAFIN (1983). How to interface slides and computers. *Instructional Innovator*, 28(8), 20–23.

PICKOVER, C. (1985). On the educational uses of computer-generated cartoon faces. *Journal of Education Technology Systems*, 13, 185–198.

PIPITONE, F. (1986). An expert system for electronics troubleshooting based on qualitative causal reasoning. *Journal of Computer-Based Instruction*, 13(2), 39–42.

PLISKE, D. B., and J. PSOTKA (1986). Exploratory programming environments for designing ICAI. *Journal of Computer-Based Instruction*, 13(2), 52–57

PODEMSKI, R. S. (1984). Implications of electronic learning technology: The future is now! *Technological Horizons in Education*, 11(8), 118–121.

POGUE, R. E. (1980). The authoring system: Interface between author and computer. *Journal of Research and Development in Education*, 14(1), 57–68.

PRESSMAN, I., and B. ROSENBLOOM (1984). CAI system costs. Present and future. *Technological Horizons in Education*, 11(6), 94–98.

PURCELL, G. A. (1984). Walking it through: Preventive planning for CBT courses. *Training News*, 6(3), 11.

RAHMLOW, H. F., R. C. FRATINI, and J. R. GHESQUIERE (1980). *PLATO.* Englewood Cliffs, NJ: Educational Technology Publications.

REED, S. (1985). Effect of computer graphics on improving estimates to algebra word problems. *Journal of Educational Psychology* 77, 285–296.

REEVES, T. C., and R. M. LENT (1984). Levels of evaluation for computer-based instruction. In D. R. Walker and R. D. Hess (eds.). *Instructional Software: Principles and Perspectives for Design and Use.* Belmont, CA: Wadsworth.

REIGELUTH, C. M. (1979). TICCIT to the future: Advances in instructional theory for CAI. *Journal of Computer-Based Instruction*, 6(2), 40–45.

REILLY, S., and S. J. ROACH (1986). Designing human/computer interfaces: A comparison of human factors and graphics arts principles. *Educational Technology*, 26(1), 36–40.

REISER, R., and R. M. GAGNÉ (1982). Characteristics of media selection models. *Review of Educational Research*, 52, 499–512.

—— (1982). *Selecting Media for Instruction.* Englewood Cliffs, NJ: Educational Technology Publications.

RICHARDSON, J. J. (1980). *The limits of frame-based CAI.* Paper presented at the annual conference of the Association for the Development of Computer-Based Instructional Systems, Atlanta.

RICHARDSON, J. J., and T. E. JACKSON (1986). Developing the technology for intelligent maintenance advisors. *Journal of Computer-Based Instruction*, 13(2), 47–51.

RIDING, R., and H. TITE (1985). The use of computer graphics to facilitate story telling in young children. *Educational Studies*, 11, 203–210.

RIEBER, L. P., and M. J. HANNAFIN (1986). The evolution of computer-based instruction: From behavioral to cognitive. *Proceedings of the 28th international conference of the Association for the Development of Computer-Based Instructional Systems.* Bellingham, WA: ADCIS.

ROBLYER, M. D. (1981). Instructional design versus authoring of courseware: Some crucial differences. *AEDS Journal,* **14**(4), 173–181.

—— (1981). When is it "good courseware"? Problems in developing standards for microcomputer courseware. *Educational Technology,* **21**(10), 47–54.

—— (1983). The case for and against teacher-developed microcomputer courseware. *Educational Technology,* **23**(1), 14–17.

ROSS, S. M. (1984). Matching the lesson to the student. Alternative adaptive designs for individualized learning systems. *Journal of Computer Based Instruction* **11,** 42–48.

ROSS, S. M., D. MCCORMICK, N. KRISAK, and P. ANAND (1985). Personalizing context in teaching mathematical concepts: teacher-managed and computer-assisted models. *Educational Communication and Technology Journal,* **33,** 169–178.

ROTHMAN, S., and C. MOSSMAN (1985). *Computer Use and Issues.* Chicago: SRA Associates.

ROWE, N. C. (1981). Some rules for good simulations. *Educational Computer,* **1**(4), 37–41.

SALISBURY, D., B. RICHARDS, and J. KLEIN (1985). Prescriptions for the design of practice activities for learning: An integration from instructional design theories. *Journal of Instructional Development,* **8**(4), 9–19.

SCHAFFER, L. C. (1985). Is interactive video for you? In E. Miller and M. L. Mosley (eds). *Educational Media and Technology Yearbook.* Littleton, CO: Libraries Unlimited.

SCHAFFER, L. C., and M. J. HANNAFIN (1986). The effects of progressive interactivity on learning from interactive video. *Educational Communications and Technology Journal,* **34,** 89–96.

SCHLEICHER, G. (1982). Authoring systems can save time in development of CAI. *Electronic Education,* **2**(3) 20–27.

SCHLOSS, C. N., P. J. SCHLOSS, and G. P. CARTWRIGHT (1985). Placement of questions and highlights as a variable influencing the effectiveness of computer-assisted instruction. *Journal of Computer-Based Instruction,* **12,** 97–100.

SCHLOSS, P. J., P. T. SINDELAR, G. P. CARTWRIGHT, and C. N. SCHLOSS (1986). Efficacy of higher cognitive and factual questions in computer-assisted instruction modules. *Journal of Computer-Based Instruction,* **13**(3), 75–79.

SEYFER, C., and J. D. RUSSELL (June 1985). Computer-managed instructional development. *The Criterion* (newsletter of the National Society of Performance and Instruction's Front Range chapter), 3–5.

SHAW, M. (1985). Dancing with the disc: The latest step in training technology. *Data Training,* **4**(2), 26–27.

SIEGEL, M. A., and L. V. DIBELLO (April 1980). *Optimization of computer drills: An instructional approach.* Paper presented at the annual meeting of the American Educational Research Association, Boston.

SIMPSON, H. (1984). A human-factors style guide for program display. In D. F. Walker and R. D. Hess (eds.). *Instructional Software: Principles and Perspectives for Design and Use.* Belmont, CA: Wadsworth.

SINGER, M. J., and R. S. PEREZ (1986). A demonstration of an expert system for training device design. *Journal of Computer-Based Instruction,* **13**(2), 58–61.

SKINNER, B. F. (1969). *The Technology of Teaching.* New York: Meredith Corporation.

SMITH, P. L., and B. A. BOYCE (1984). Instructional design considerations in the development of computer-assisted instruction. *Educational Technology,* **24**(7), 5–10.

SNOWBERRY K., S. R. PARKINSON, and N. SISSION (1983). Computer display menus. *Ergonomics,* **26**(7), 699–712.

SOLSO, R. L. (1984). *Cognitive Psychology.* New York: Harcourt Brace Jovanovich, Inc.

SPILLER, R., and J. ROBERTSON (1984). Computer-based training: A major growth opportunity. *Technological Horizons in Education,* **11**(6), 75–76.

SPITLER, C. D., and V. E. CORGAN (1979). Rules for authoring computer-assisted instruction programs. *Educational Technology,* **19**(11), 13–20.

SPLITTGERBER, F. L. (1979). Computer-based instruction: A revolution in the making? *Educational Technology,* **19**(1), 20–26.

STEINBERG, E. (1977). Review of student control in computer-assisted instruction. *Journal of Computer-Based Instruction*, **3**, 84–90.

STERN, N. B. (1975). *Flowcharting: A Tool for Understanding Computer Logic*. New York: John Wiley.

STREIBEL, M. (1984). Dialog design and instructional systems for an intelligent videodisc system. *Videodisc and Optical Disc*, **4**, 216–229.

SULLIVAN, D. R., T. G. LEWIS, and C. R. COOK (1985). *Computing Today: Microcomputer Concepts and Applications*. Boston: Houghton Mifflin.

SWADENER, M., and M. J. HANNAFIN (1987). Gender similarities and differences in sixth graders attitudes towards computers: An exploratory study. *Educational Technology*, **27**(1), 37–42.

SWEETERS, W. (1985). Screen design guidelines. *Proceedings of the 26th International ADCIS Conference*, 42–45.

TAYLOR, R. P. (1980). *The Computer in the School: Tutor, Tool, Tutee*. New York: Teacher's College Press.

TENNYSON, R. (1984). Application of artificial intelligence methods to computer-based instructional design: The Minnesota Adaptive Instructional System. *Journal of Instructional Development*, **7**, 17–22.

TERRACE, H. S. (1963). Errorless transfer of a discrimination across two continua. *Journal of the Experimental Analysis of Behavior*, **6**, 223–232.

THORKILDSEN, R., and S. FRIEDMAN (1984). Videodisks in the classroom. *Technological Horizons in Education*, **11**(7), 90–95.

THORNBURG, H. D. (1984). *Introduction to Educational Psychology*. Saint Paul, MN: West Publishing Company.

VOYCE, S. (1982). A functional analysis of courseware authoring languages. *AEDS Journal*, **15**, 107–125.

WADE, T. E., Jr. (1980). Evaluating computer instructional programs and other teaching units. *Educational Technology*, **20**(11), 32–35.

WAGER, W. (1981). Issues in the evaluation of instructional computing programs. *Educational Computer*, **1**(3), 20–22.

―――― (1982). Design considerations for instructional computing programs. *Journal of Educational Technology Systems*, **10**(3), 261–270.

WAGER, W., and S. WAGER (1985). Presenting questions, processing responses, and providing feedback in CAI. *Journal of Instructional Development*, **8**(4), 2–8.

WALKER, D. F., and R. D. HESS (1984). Evaluation in courseware development. In D. R. Walker and R. D. Hess (eds.). *Instructional Software: Principles and Perspectives for Design and Use*. Belmont, CA: Wadsworth.

―――― (1984). *Instructional Software: Principles and Perspectives for design and Use*. Belmont, CA: Wadsworth Publishing Company.

WEDMAN, J. (1983). The future of computers in education: What are the right questions? *Technological Horizons in Education*, **11**(1), 147–148.

WHOLEBEN, B. E. (1982). *MICROPIK: A Multiple Alternatives, Criterion-Referenced Decisioning Model for Evaluating CAI Software and Microcomputer Hardware Against Selected Curriculum Objectives*. Portland, OR: Northwest Regional Educational Laboratory.

WORTHEN, B. R., and J. R. SANDERS (1973). *Educational Evaluation: Theory and Practice*. Belmont, CA: Wadsworth.

YARUSSO, L. (1984). The decision to use a computer. *Performance and Instruction Journal*, **23**(5), 24–25.

Author Index*

* Page numbers in italics denote bibliographic citations.

Subject Index